Vasudhaiva Kuṭumkam

CULTURAL RECIPROCATION between India and the World

Vasudhaiva Kuṭumkam

CULTURAL RECIPROCATION between India and the World

Sures Chandra Banerji

Sharada Publishing House

Delhi - 110035

1999

First Published 1999

ISBN : 81-85616-59-0

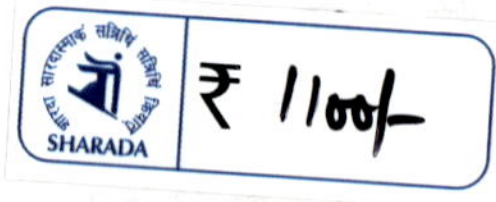

Published by B.L. Bansal for
SHARADA PUBLISHING HOUSE
40, Anand Nagar, Inderlok, Delhi - 110035
Phones: 5117390, 5116763
Typeset by Neographics
1800 Gyani Bazar, Kotlamubarakpur, New Delhi - 110003
and Printed at Santosh Offset, Delhi - 110035

Preface

Thanks to the advancement of science and the invention of quick transport and the media of communication, viz. Television and Radio, the different countries of the world, no matter however great the distance between them may be, have come close to one another. The urge for education has resulted in the seekers of knowledge, general, technical and scientific, going abroad - this is also responsible for intimate contacts among different countries.

Yatra viśvam bhavatyekanīḍam (where the world becomes one nest) - this motto of Rabindranatha's Viśvabhāratī provided the first inspiration to the author for an assessment of the affinities of the Indians with the foreigners in the different spheres of life.

Impelled by a strong desire to study the relation of India with different parts of the globe since prehistoric times, the author took up the present study. In assessing the influence exercised by India and on her, we have tried to be as objective as possible. In selecting the sources and materials, we have taken into account up-to-date research as far as possible.

The plan of the work is briefly this. In the introduction, we have tried to give an outline of Indian literature and culture. This is followed by a general description of the different ways in which contact was established between India and different parts of the world. In the next chapter, the specific modes of India's contact with the particular foreign countries have been dealt with. In the chapter that follows, we have given an account of India's influence abroad in various spheres of intellectual, cultural and religious life. The concluding chapter contains a description of the multifaceted foreign influence on India.

In course of our study, we have referred to a host of places, persons, works, races, dynasties and languages. For ready reference, we have added an appendix each on the above items. For enabling the reader to have a clear historical perspective, we have, at the outset, given a list of the important personages and events mentioned in the work. At the end, we have given as exhaustive a bibliography as possible. It sets forth not only the titles of important books but also the names of noteworthy papers published in various journals, Indian and foreign. In a work like this, the use of the earlier works is indispensable. We have duly acknowledged the help derived from various works.

In conclusion, it is my pleasant duty to acknowledge the unstinted help rendered by my near and dear ones. Of them, my wife, ungrudgingly shouldering the responsibilities of the day-to-day household work, provided the opportunity to devote all my energy to my intellectual pursuits. She helped me with intelligent suggestions. My two daughters, Dr. Chandā Chakrabarti and Sarmilā Chatterji, were at my beck and call for all kinds of work relating to the procurement of books and the supplying of the articles for day-to-day use. In this connexion, my sons-in-law, Dr. Dipak Chakrabarty and Dr. Tushar Chattopadhyay, deserve grateful mention.

So far as odds end ends are concerned, got ready help from my two loving grandchildren, Pampā Chakrabarti and Tuhin Chattopadhyay.

The labours of the author will be amply rewarded if this work goes some way in bringing home, to the denizens of the world, the fact that, though living apart, they belong to a single family sharing many things common in culture, religion and other respects.

M/s Sharada Publishing House deserve thanks for their zeal in publishing expensive books relating to Indology as well as for the cordial relations they have forged with me, and for extending uniform courtesy.

Rathayātrā, 1405 B.S. S.C. Banerji
1998

Contents

CHAPTER - I

Introduction

Before assessing Indian influence abroad, we should have an idea of Indian culture and society through the ages. It is not possible to deal elaborately, in a work like this, with the multifaceted Indian civilisation spanning a period of roughly five thousand years. All that we can do is to touch briefly upon the different aspects.

INDUS VALLEY CIVILISATION[1]

Archaeological explorations have revealed the ruins of an ancient Indian civilisation mainly at Mohenjo-daro in Larkana district of Sind in Pakistan, and at Harappa in south-west Punjab (Pakistan). The highlights of this urban civilisation, believed to be about 5,000 years old, are as follows. It is supposed to have existed nearly 3,000 years before Christ.

The entire area is divided into several sections by roads. Each section comprises several big brick-built mansions each of which contains small rooms. On the highway, below the mansions are shops. There are courtyards in some houses. Occasionally two-storied buildings also are seen.

The public bath, 180' x 108', enclosed by a wall 7-8 ft. thick, contains a swimming pool 39' x 23' and 8' in depth, which is surrounded by a row of polished bricks plastered with bitumen one inch thick.

The granary at Mohenjo-daro is 150' x 75' and 25' high (the one in Harappa is smaller). The fort, meant for defence, is close to the granary and bath.

An examination of the skeletons and skulls reveals that the area was inhabited by the people of the following races—Caucasian, Mediterranean, Alpain and Mongolian. It is, however, not known who the architects of this civilisation were. Some scholars think, not on positive evidence, that some foreigners, who came by sea-route, built up this civilisation. Others are of the opinion that it was indigenous, and was ruined by the onslaught of the Aryans.

Among the foodstuffs of the people were barley, wheat, sesame, peas, oilseeds, etc. and the meat of the sheep, boar, fowl and tortoise, etc., sea-snails and dried fish.

Their garments consisted in cloths and shawls made of cotton. The articles for household work were utensils made of copper, bronze, stone and clay. Among the implements for daily use were knife, stone-axe, ploughshare, ornament-box; colour-containers also appear to have been used. Weights and measures indicating different quantities and soft-stone seals inscribed with letters tend to hint at the practice of reading and writing. The Indus Valley script has not yet been deciphered. It has, however, been surmised that writings have to be read from the right to the left.

Ornaments appear to have been made of gold, silver, conch-shell, precious stones, bones and ivory. Mirror, razor, fishing hook, needle, etc. were made of copper and bronze. Earthen dolls, marbles, etc. were playthings for children and dice-men (like those for playing chess), etc. were for adults. Specimens of sculpture are seen in the bronze figure of a female dancer and stone image of a Yogin.

The people were mainly phallus-worshippers. It seems, the worship of Paśupati Śiva, seated in a Yogic posture and surrounded by deer, elephants, tigers, rhinoceros, buffaloes, etc., and earthen images of Mother-goddess, was in vogue.

The society was divided into several classes and various industrial communities such as potters, and other craftsmen. There is not much evidence of the currency of coins as media of exchange. Barter system was, perhaps, adopted in commercial transactions. It seems that, as in ancient Egypt and Mesopotamia, here also the state granary functioned as the treasury; revenue also was probably realised and the pay of employees disbursed through it.

Explorations have revealed striking similarities between archaeological materials found in the ruins of the Indus Valley civilisation and in Sumeria, Mesopotamia, Bahrein, Persia, etc. Some scholars at one time thought that the above culture was not wholly Indian. So, they variously designated it as Sumero-Indian, Irano-Indian etc. Let us examine the question in the light of the facts known hitherto.

Danish excavations at Bahrein have brought to light seals having affinities with those discovered in North-west India on the one hand, and with seal-engravings on the cylinder seals in south Mesopotamia on the other. Situated in the Persian Gulf, the island of Bahrein is not very far from the Mesopotamian shore, having the cities like Uruk and Eridu within easy reach. This island stands on the shipping route leading up to the Indus. Thus, it is likely that Bahrein was connected by trade with both Mesopotamia and India. Some seals, found in this island as well as in Uruk in Mesopotamia, contain typically Indian motifs, *e.g.* bull with lowered horns.

Seals, discovered in Tell Asmar, east of the river Tigris, dating back to about 2400 B.C., vases and some other minor things, bear great resemblance with their counterparts in the relics of the Indus Civilisation.

The unique figure of a bull, with an elephant's trunk, is found on a Mesopotamian cylinder seal (*c.* early third millennium B.C.), not occurring on other seals, is a common motif on Mohenjo Daro sealings. A group of vases, mostly of cut soft-stone, has similarity with a fragment of this type found at Mohenjo Daro. Some such vases were discovered also in Persia and Baluchistan. While some suggest the origin of this type in Eastern Iran, others think that the provenance was Mesopotamia where the most perfect specimen was unearthed. These similarities suggest direct connexion between India and West Asia roughly between the end of the third millenary B.C. and the end of the second millennium B.C.

Excavations at Lothal, another site containing relics of Harappa culture, reveal the motif of bullock-cart on seals, terracotta sherds, etc. Mesopotamian history records the use of similar carts.

Mother-goddess is another motif common in Indus Valley culture and in that of Sumer, Tell Halaf in north Syria and Crete. The Mohenjo Daro type of Mother-goddess, dressed but with bare breasts, with high head-dress, has its oldest prototype in Syria and Crete. Some pearls of a particular type, found in Crete, have been proved to be exactly of the same material as those discovered in Indus Valley.

Some elements in the Syrio-Cretan type of Mother-goddess are found in its counterpart in the Indus Valley. The goddess is associated with the dove as also with the snake in the former type, especially in Crete. The goddess appears to have been connected with trees. The dove, snake and tree are all found associated with the corresponding finds in Indus Valley. The mother-goddess, surrounded by doves, is typical in statues found on relics discovered in Crete (Mycenae), Tepe Hissar and Mohenjo Daro.

Textile ornamentation is common on Harappan painted pots and in Tell Halaf culture of Syria and in the Cretan art. This type of decoration is found also in small pots discovered in Nal in East Iranian frontier with India (modern Pakistan).

Excavations at Kot Diji in the Indus Valley have revealed pots decorated with intersecting circles in earlier strata. These belong to pre-Harappa culture, and form the common background for Indian and Syrio-Ægean culture.

Figures of some persons, engaged in group-dance, are depicted in some finds of the Indus sites. These have similarity with vase paintings in the ancient rural cultures of the Iranian plateau.

Ornamental forms inlaid in Indian amulets, seals and pots, some of the shape of kidney or heart, have close parallels in Syria. Cross, *Svastika* sign, intricate band-design, etc., used as inlays or stamp-seal designs in India, have their likes in materials discovered in Iran, Syria and Crete.

An animal, with several heads, is a motif common in India, Syria and Crete. A bird, holding a fish, has been found in materials discovered in Mesopotamia and Lothal.

A very similar hunting scene, already struck, with arrows sticking to its body, has been found in India, Susa, Crete, Palestine (Megiddo) and also in later Assyrian art.

The monkey-motif of India has parallels in some monkey-figures of Crete. The famous Babylonian lion and the Khajuraho lion group appear to represent the same subject.

We have noticed similarities between artefacts of ancient India and some foreign countries of Asia. The question is how to explain these affinities. The affinities might be accidental. The objects concerned might be the products of minds thinking alike. Some are inclined to think that, in the countries concerned, there were a common background and a general similarity of social, economic and technical skill. There are evidences of trade between India and other parts of west Asia. So, the possibility of mutual influence cannot be ruled out; but we are not in a position to determine which country was the borrower and to what extent. It can, however, be stated that there is no definite proof of a foreign origin of the early Indian civilisation, at least at the stage of the Harappan urban civilisation. So, as far as our knowledge goes, there is no reasonable ground to label the Indus Valley Civilisation as Sumero-Indian or Irano-Indian, etc.

INDIA—THE LAND AND THE PEOPLES[2]

By India we mean here the India before independence and partition in 1947. It is situated in the southern extremity of Asia, jutting out to the sea. It is bounded on the south by the Indian Ocean, Bay of Bengal and Arabian Sea, on the north by the Himalayas, on the east by Burma, (Myanmar), on the west by Afghanistan and Iran. India was known as *Jambudvīpa* which was one of the seven *dvīpas* into which the world was supposed to be divided according to the Purāṇas. As attested by the records of Aśoka and the Pāli works of

Ceylon, *Jambudvīpa* or ancient India comprised the present India, Pakistan, Bangladesh and a large part of Afghanistan; it was included in the empire of Aśoka. As we shall see, India had commercial and cultural contacts with many foreign lands not only of Asia but also of other continents.

India is, perhaps the only country where people of so many diverse ethnic groups with distinctive physical features, dress and habits, social customs, languages, etc. dwell. The two major races of India are Aryan and Dravidian. The people of Aryan origin live mainly in the whole of India excepting the south (of the Vindhyas) where mainly the people of Dravidian extraction live. Besides these two, there are many tribes some of which immigrated into this country. They live in pockets mostly in the outlying areas in close proximity to forests and mountains. They were, perhaps, pushed to those regions by the more powerful Aryans. Such people can be divided into six major groups most of which have sub-groups.[3] We state their names below in a tabular form.

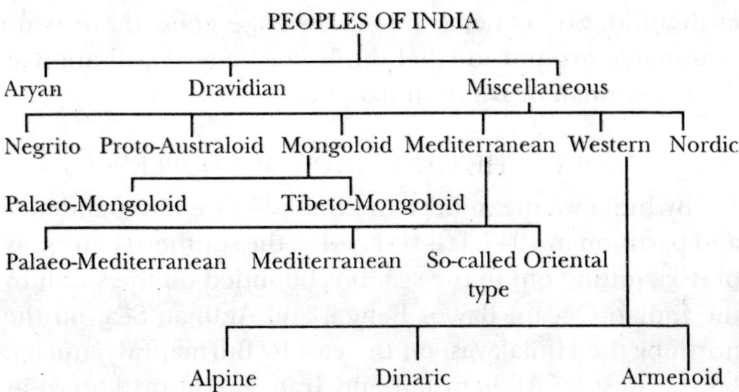

SANSKRIT LANGUAGE AND LITERATURE[4]

Sanskrit is the English rendering of the word *saṃskṛta* which means 'refined'. Thus, it presupposed a language which was crude. Some say that it was the pre-Pāṇiniyan language of India. The earliest specimen of the pre-Pāṇiniyan Indian language is that of the Vedas. In the Vedic literature, the language shows the verve and vigour of a living tongue not yet fettered by a rigorous grammatical discipline. For example, the three past tenses, indicated by *Luṅ*, *Laṅ* and *Liṭ*, are used promiscuously,[5] whereas, in the later language, *Luṅ* has limited forms, in the Vedic it has as many as seven. While the infinitive is indicated in the later language by the affix *tumun* only, it is indicated by as many as fifteen affixes in the earlier language.[6] In view of the erratic character of the Vedic language, Pāṇini had to say *bahulaṃ chandasi* for eleven times[7] in the Vedic portion of his grammar.

It was Pāṇini (*c.* 4th cent. B.C.) who, for the first time, tried, in his grammar, to regulate the language so that it could conform to certain norms. Since then, it came to be called *Laukika* (as distinguished from *Vaidika*) or *Saṃskṛta* (polished, refined).

According to some modern scholars, the Indo-Aryan languages passed through the following principal stages :

Ancient High Indian, the language of the Vedas, Ancient Indian, Sanskrit or Classical Sanskrit (standardised by Pāṇini). The language of the two popular epics is also called Sanskrit, though it (particularly that of the *Mahābhārata*) defies many of Pāṇini's rules, and has some characteristics of its own; Middle Indo-Aryan comprising Pāli, Prākṛta and Apabhraṃśa; New Indo-Aryan- the modern vernaculars, Hindī, Bengali, Oriyā, Nepāli and so on.

SANSKRIT LITERATURE

Sanskrit literature can be broadly divided into the following classes.

A. Pure literature
B. Technical literature.

A. Pure Literature

It can be divided into the following classes :
a. Vedic
b. Epic
c. Purāṇic
d. Classical

a. *Vedic Literature*

The Vedas are the earliest records of not only the Indians, but also of the Indo-Europeans. This literature passed through two periods, viz. *Mantra* and *Saṃhitā.* In the *Mantra* period, the hymns appear to have been orally composed[8] and transmitted till at last these were collected (*saṃhata*), and came to be called *saṃhitā.* The *Saṃhitās* were four in number, viz. *Ṛgveda, Yajurveda, Sāmaveda* and *Atharvaveda.*

The *Ṛgveda,* which at one time existed in several recensions, of which twenty-one[9] are mentioned in Patañjali's (*c.* 2nd cent. B.C.) *Mahābhāṣya,* comprises 1028 hymns divided into ten Books,[10] called *Maṇḍalas* each of which is divided into *Anuvākas,* each *Anuvāka* consisting of several *Sūktas* (hymns). Each Sūkta consists of several stanzas called *Ṛks.* The language is accented. There are three accents, called *Udātta, Anudātta* and *Svarita.* The *Ṛks* are metrical, the Vedic metres being determined by the number of syllables; the short and long vowels, which are considered in metres of classical Sanskrit, are of no consideration.

The hymns are mostly addressed to deities like Indra, Varuṇa, Sūrya, etc. who, supposed to possess anthropomorphic traits, are personifications of natural phenomena. There are some secular hymns too; e.g., Wedding hymn (X.65), Funeral hymns (X.14-18), Gambler's Lament (X.34), etc.

It has been aptly said that the dates, suggested for this Veda, are like nine pins set up to be bowled down again. The proposed dates generally range from 12,500 B.C.[11] to 1,500 B.C.

The *Yajurveda* is the Veda of the *Yajus* or sacrificial formulae. The aforesaid Patañjali refers to 101 recensions of this Saṃhitā, of which two, White (*Śukla*) and Black (*Kṛṣṇa*) are extant. The former exists in two recensions, viz. *Kāṇva* and *Mādhyandina*, while the latter has four, viz. *Kāṭhaka, Kapiṣṭhala, Maitrāyaṇī* and *Taittirīya.*

The *Sāmaveda*, the Veda of the *Sāmans* or songs, which appears to have had numerous recensions, is now available in three recessions, viz. *Kauthuma, Rāṇāyaṇīya* and *Jaiminīya.* The major portion of this Veda has been taken from the *Ṛgveda.*

The *Atharvaveda*, as the title suggests, is the Veda of the *Atharvans* or magic formulae. In ancient times, it was not included in the Vedas which were referred to as *Trayī* (the triad of *Ṛk, Yajus* and *Sāmavedas*). The reason for its exclusion may have been the fact that, unlike the other Vedas, it had no direct application in sacrificial rites.

Vedic literature comprises, besides the *Saṃhitās*, a class of literature called Brāhmaṇa. The Brāhmaṇas are prose works containing the following subjects: *Vidhi*-rules about sacrifices, *Arthavāda* - explanation of *mantras*, etc., *Āraṇyakas* - forest texts, the result of the meditations of the sages, and *Upaniṣads* which are partly included in the *Āraṇyaka* and are partly independent works containing speculations about the Highest Reality (Brahman), the goal of life, etc.

For the study and explication of the Vedas, some accessories, called Vedāṅgas, were written. These can be divided into two broad classes, viz. exegetical and ritualistic. The exegetical Vedāṅgas are five, viz.

Śikṣā (Phonetics), *Vyākaraṇa* (grammar), *Nirukta* (etymology), *Chandas* (Prosody) and *Jyotiṣa* (astronomy).

The ritualistic Vedāṅga, called *Kalpa*, is divided into four classes, viz.

Śrautasūtra - dealing with Vedic rites,
Gṛhyasūtra- dealing with domestic rituals for householders, e.g. *Upanayana, Vivāha* and other *Saṃskāras*, etc.
Dharmasūtra - dealing with religious and secular laws.
Śulvasūtra- geometrical rules designed to help the construction of sacrificial altars in strict conformity with rules.

The different types of Vedic literature may be stated in the following tabular form.

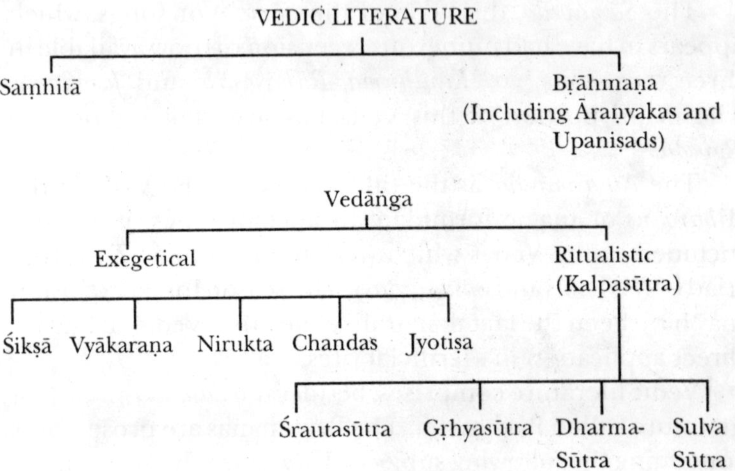

b. *Epic Literature*

The epic literature comprises the two famous works, *Rāṃāyaṇa* and the *Mahābhārata.* It appears that, in their earliest forms, they consisted of ballads (*gāthā*) sung by two classes of singers - the *Sūtas* or bards living in royal courts and *Kuśīlavas* who, like the French troubadours, were travelling singers. After a long time, these ballads came to be written down. The *Rāmāyaṇa*, existing in three recensions, viz. Bengal, West Indian or North-western or Kashmirian and South Indian, comprises seven Books called *Kāṇḍas.* According to some modern scholars, the first and seventh Books are entirely, and the fifth and sixth partly spurious having been dovetailed into the original work by later writers. Winternitz is inclined to think that the epic, in its present form, perhaps arose in the second or third century A.D.

The *Mahābhārata,* called *Śatasāhasrī-saṃhitā* (a collection comprising one lac verses), is available in several recensions which can be broadly divided as North-Indian and South-Indian. The former is threefold, viz. Kashmirian, Central Indian (Nepāli, Devanāgari and Maithili) and Bengal. In the Deccan, it exists in three versions, viz. Tamil, Telugu and Mālayālam. The epic comprises eighteen chapters called *Parvans.* The *Harivaṃśa,* sometimes called *Harivaṃśapurāṇa,* comprises three sections, called Harivaṃśa-, Viṣṇu - and Bhaviṣya-parvans, and is regarded by orthodox scholars as an integral part of the epic; it is regarded by modern scholars as a *Khila* or supplement.

The *Bhagavadgītā,* briefly called *Gītā,* which is the *Bible* of the devout, is a part of the Bhīṣmaparvan (chapters 25-42) of the *Mahābhārata.* Comprising 750 verses, divided into 18 chapters, it is written in the form of a dialogue between Kṛṣṇa, the charioteer, and Arjuna riding the chariot in the battlefield facing the enemies arrayed against him. Arjuna, perplexed to find the near and dear ones in the opposite camp, declines to fight. Kṛṣṇa whips up his drooping spirit by an exhortation in course of which he dilates upon the three ways of life suitable to the three kinds of temperament of people. The three ways are those of *Niṣkāma Karman* (desireless action), *Jñāna* (knowledge) and *Bhakti* (devotion by which the devotee completely surrenders himself to God). As a gospel of the philosophy of life, the *Gītā* is unique in India, and, perhaps, unrivalled in the world. The great German philosopher, Humboldt, characterises it as the only truly philosophical poem in all the literatures known to us.

The *Mahābhārata,* in its present form, is believed by Winternitz to date back to about the fourth century A.D.

c. *Purāṇic Literature*

We have included it under pure literature. But, besides literature in the general sense, it contains diverse topics like philosophy, dharmaśastra, science, etc. In fact, these are mostly compilations based on different sources.

The Purāṇas are traditionally known to deal with five kinds of topics, viz. *Sarga* (creation), *pratisarga* (re-creation after Dissolution), *Vaṃśa* (genealogies of gods and sages), *manvantara* (periods of time supposed to be presided over by Manus), *vaṃśānucarita* (genealogies of kings). The *Bhāgavatapurāṇa* (XII.7. 9-10) mentions the following ten characteristics :

(i) *Sarga* - creation;

(ii) *Visarga* - the world of the moving and non-moving, produced as a result of the creatures' desires in the previous existence;

(iii) *Vṛtti* - means of livelihood;

(iv) *Rakṣā* - the desire of God residing in the beings, for counteracting anti-Vedic tendencies:

(v) *Antara - manvantara* - explained earlier;

(vi) *Vaṃśa* - explained earlier;

(vii) *Vaṃśānucarita* - explained earlier;

(viii) *Saṃsthā* - four kinds of *Laya* (Dissolution), viz. *Naimittika, Prākṛtika, Nitya* and *Ātyantika*;

(ix) *Hetu* - the creatures who, acting through nescience or ignorance, are the cause of creation, etc. of the universe;

(x) *Apāśraya* - Brahman.

The above characteristics are not exhausive, because, as stated above, the Purāṇas compile various matters, *e.g.* philosophy, prosody, poetics, politics, etc. from different treatises.

The Purāṇas are divided into two broad classes, viz. *Mahā* or major Purāṇas and *Upa* or minor Purāṇas. Those of the latter class appear to have been intended for different sects, *e.g.* Śaiva, Śākta, *Saura, Gāṇapatya,* etc.

The Mahāpurāṇas are generally said to be 18 which, according to some Purāṇas, are

Brahma, Padma, Viṣṇu, Śiva (or Vāyu), Bhāgavata, Nārada, Mārkaṇḍeya, Bhaviṣya or Bhaviṣyat, Agni, Brahmavaivarta, Liṅga, Varāha, Skanda, Vāmana, Kūrma, Matsya, Garuḍa and Brahmāṇḍa.

The Upapurāṇas, according to Raghunandana (16th cent.), the famous Smṛti writer of Bengal, are as follows :

Sanatkumāra, Narasiṃha, Vāyu, Śivadharma, Āścarya, Nārada, Nandikeśvara, Uśanas, Kapila, Varuṇa, Sāmba, Kālikā, Maheśvara, Kalki, Devī, Parāśara, Marīci, Bhāskara or Sūrya.

The dates of the Purāṇas present a bewildering problem. Modern research has revealed that, in some particular Purāṇas, different chapters were written at different periods of time. By and large, it can be said that the earlier Purāṇas date back to a period before the seventh century A.D. The lower limit of the period of their composition may be fixed as late as 1400 A.D.

The Purāṇas, though full of exaggerations and hyperboles, are not devoid of value. They are invaluable as a source of the religious history of India. They have some geographical importance as they mention many rivers, mountains, places of pilgrimage, etc. As regards political history, some Purāṇas throw light on some royal dynasties, *e.g.* Nanda, Maurya, Śuṅga, Andhra and Gupta. Though not a pleasing phenomenon as literature, they supply themes for many works, poetical and dramatic, of classical Sanskrit.

d. *Classical Literature*

Usually, the literature in the language, standardised by Pāṇini (*c.* 4th cent. B.C.), is called classical Sanskrit literature, as distinguished from Vedic, Epic and Purāṇic. The Purāṇas, generally using the Classical Sanskrit language, form a class of literature by themselves. So, they are not included by us under Classical literature comprising *belles-lettres* or prose, poetical and dramatic works.

The entire gamut of classical Sanskrit literature, generally designated as *Kāvya,*[12] can be divided into two broad classes, viz. *Śravya* (that which can be heard) and *Dṛśya* (that which can be seen). *Śravyakāvya* may be in prose (*godya*), poetry (*padya*) or *miśra* (mixed prose and poetry). *Dṛśyakāvya* or drama may be of ten major and eighteen minor types, the former being called *Rūpaka* and the latter *Uparūpaka.*

The different types of classical Sanskrit literature may be shown in the following way.

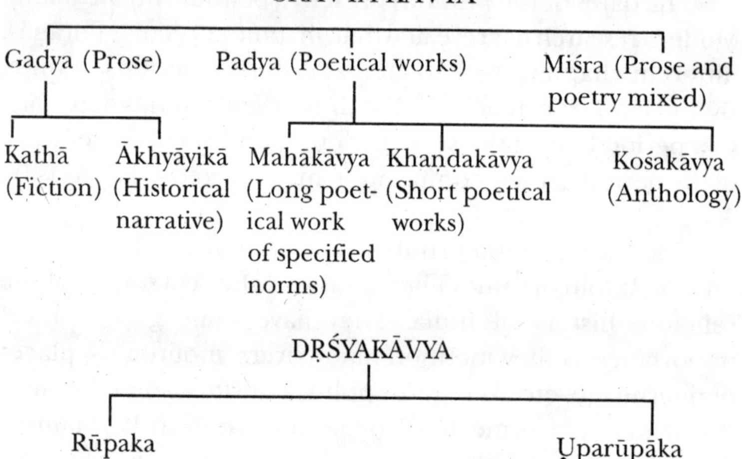

GNOMIC AND DIDACTIC POETRY

A type of Sanskrit poetry can be labelled as gnomic and didactic. It lays down, through the medium of verse, the principles of morality, ethics and worldly wisdom. It may be characterised as sententious poetry. Besides moral and ethical principles in general, political principles also come within the purview of this literature. Some such works are as follows:

Rājanītisamuccaya, Cāṇakyanīti, Cāṇakyarājanīti, Vṛddhacāṇakya, Laghucāṇakya, etc.

The most well-known author of such works is Bhartṛhari who is generally supposed to have flourished in the seventh century A.D. To him are attributed the renowned trilogy comprising *Nītiśataka* (a century of verses on moral principles and worldly wisdom). *Śṛṅgāraśataka* (a century of verses depicting the various stages of love and the ultimate hollowness of it) and *Vairāgyaśataka* (one hundred verses containing instructions about practical life, laying stress on the worthlessness of love and earthly happiness).

To the Sanskrit didactic literature belongs also a kind of fable in prose with verses interspersed; the verses mostly are on morality, ethics and worldly wisdom. The only work, known hitherto, is the *Pañcatantra,* generally attributed to Viṣṇuśarman of uncertain date. The date of the work is also uncertain. It was rendered into Pahlavi in the middle of the sixth century A.D. which, therefore, is the *terminus ad quem* of its date. It consists of five books, viz.

(i) *Mitrabheda* (separation of friends),

(ii) *Mitra-prāpti* (acquisition of friends),

(iii) *Sandhi-vigraha* (peace and war),

(iv) *Labdhanāśa* (loss of what has been acquired),

(v) *Aparīkṣita-kāritva* (rash action).

The original work is lost. It came down in three recensions, viz. North-western, and other two lost. From one of its lost versions were derived the South Indian *Pañcatantra,* the version of Nepal, the *Hitopadeśa* of Bengal (believed to have been written by Nārāyana between 900 and 1373 A.D.). From another lost version were derived the Kashmirian *Tantrākhyāyika* of unknown authorship and date, and the Jaina versions (one abbreviated and the other enlarged). The *Tantrākhyāyika* is the earliest, and regarded as the nearest approach to the original.

Some scholars believe that there was a Prākrit original of the *Pañcatantra.*

HISTORICAL WRITINGS IN SANSKRIT

Some scholars complain that Indians have no historians nor any historical sense. It is not wholly true. The fact is that, in comparison with other kinds of Sanskrit literature, historical writings are meagre.

The Jaina *Paṭṭāvalīs,* containing genealogical lists of pontiffs, record some exact chronological data, but they aim at attractive edification rather than serious history. The Purāṇas, though of considerable value as history of religion and the society, lack serious political history. They, no doubt, contain information about some royal dynasties, but fact is jumbled with fancy and exaggeration so that it is difficult to sift true historical material. The most outstanding historical work is the *Rājataraṅgiṇī* of Kalhaṇa (12th cent.). It purports to be a history of Kashmir. In the earlier part, the author deals with legendary kings, and in the latter part, it gives accounts of the kings of the historical period. The *Rājataraṅgiṇī* has two continuations, one by Jonarāja (14th cent.) called *Dvitīya-rājataraṅgiṇī,* and the other by his pupil, Śrīvara, called *Jaina-rājataraṅgiṇī.* Some other noteworthy historical works are the following:

Vikramāṅkadeva-carita of Bilhaṇa (11th-12th cent.),

Navasāhasāṅkacarita of Padmagupta or Parimala (11th cent.),

Pṛthvirāja-vijaya (fragmentary and unfinished, of unknown date and authorship,

Kumārapālacarita of Hemacandra (1088-1172)

Rāmācarita of Sandhyākaranandin (11th cent.).

Real history is recorded in the numerous inscriptions in Prākrit and Sanskrit. We find inscriptions relating to Land-grants which mention the donor, the donee and the subject of donation with the dates concerned. Some temples contain tablets recording information about the occasions and dates of their establishment and particulars about the founder. Inscriptions of a unique kind were introduced by Aśoka (3rd cent. B.C.). These were edicts inscribed on pillars, rocks or caves, designed to educate people. It is interesting to note that Aśoka used also Greek and Aramaic in his inscriptions at Qāndāhār and Jālālābād Inscriptions both in Brāhmī and Kharoṣṭhī. Numerous inscriptions of various dates, and issued by many kings and other persons, exist.

B. Technical Literature

The technical literature of ancient and medieval India is varied. Broadly speaking, it is divided into the following classes, Scientific, Literary, Legal, Philosophical and Artistic.

The scientific works deal with Agriculture and Horticulture, Alchemy, Architecture, Astronomy and Astrology, Botany, Chemistry, Erotics, Mathematics, Mechanical devices, Mechanics (Kinetic) Medical Science, Metallurgy, Physics.

The technical literary works deal with Grammar, poetics and prosody, Lexicography, politics and statecraft. The legal works comprise religious and secular Laws. The philosophical works fall into two broad classes, Orthodox and Heterodox. The orthodox philosophical works are of six kinds, viz. Nyāya-Vaiśeṣika, Sāṃkhya, Yoga, Mīmāṃsā and Vedānta. The heterodox philosophical systems are three, viz. Buddhist, Jaina and Cārvāka.

The artistic works deal with music and dance, sculpture and painting.

We shall briefly indicate the highlights of those branches of literature only which have a bearing on the culture of the foriegn lands. Let us start with the scientific works. Of the various branches of science, Astronomy (and astrology) and Medical science appear to have produced very great impact abroad.

POETICS AND PROSODY

The earliest extant work on poetics and dramaturgy is the *Nāṭyaśāstra* attributed to Bharata who is believed to have flourished earlier than the fourth or fifth century A.D. Poeticians differ on the soul or essential element of poetry. Generally, four schools are recognised, viz. Alaṃkāra School (headed by Bhāmaha, 7th-8th cent.), Rīti School (propounded by Vāmana, 8th-9th cent.), Dhvani School (greatest exponent Ānandavardhana, 9th cent.) and Rasa School (to which belong all later writers from Dhanañjaya, 10th cent., to Jagannātha, 17th cent.).

As regards figures of speech, these are of two main types, *Śabdālaṃkāra* and *Arthālaṃkāra,* the former belonging to words and the latter to sense. The *Śabdālaṃkāras* are *Anuprāsa,* Yamaka, etc. The *Arthālaṃkāras* are *Upamā, Utprekṣā,* etc.

PROSODY

It is called *Chandas* which was one of the *Vedāṅgas* (accessory works of Vedas). The earliest extant work on prosody is *Chandaḥ sūtra* of Piṅgala who is sometimes identified with Patañjali (*c.* 2nd cent. B.C.), author of the *Mahābhāṣya.* Metres of classical Sanskrit literature are broadly of two classes, viz. those determined by a fixed number of syllables which are short or long and those determined by *Mātrā* (Prosodial or syllabic instant, the time required to pronounce a short vowel). Examples of the first kind are *Anuṣṭup* or *Śloka, Indravajrā, Upendravajrā, Upajāti, Sragdharā, Śārdūlavikrīḍita,* etc.

POLITICS AND STATECRAFT

The *Mahābhārata* contains a portion dealing with these subjects. Chapter VII of the *Manusmṛti* is devoted to *Rājadharma.* The earliest extant work, dealing exclusively with politics and statecraft, is the *Arthaśāstra* attributed to Kauṭilya. While it is generally believed to date back to the 4th cent. B.C., a recent scholar would place it in the 2nd cent. A.D. (see Chronological table).

GRAMMAR

The earliest extant grammar is that of Pāṇini who is believed to have lived in the 4th century B.C. Divided into eight chapters, it is called *Aṣṭādhyāyī.* It deals with both Vedic and classical languages. Its earliest and most renowned commentary is the *Mahābhāṣya* of Patañjali (*c.* 2nd century B.C.).

A well-known grammarian was Candragomin who was probably a Bengali Buddhist scholar of the seventh century A.D. or of an earlier date. He was the author of the celebrated *Cāndravyākaraṇa* the object of which appears to have been to abridge Pānini's grammar. It has omitted Pāṇini's rules regarding Vedic grammar and accents.

LEXICOGRAPHY

Sanskrit literature is rich in lexicons. The earliest attempt at the production of such works is represented by the *Nighaṇṭu* which contains glossaries or lists of rare and obscure words of the Vedic hymns. In the classical period, there was a number of lexicons the most well-known of which is the *Nāmaliṅgānuśāsana,* popularly called *Amarakośa,* attributed to Amarasiṃha (*c.* 4th century A.D.).

LEGAL LITERATURE (RELIGIOUS AND SECULAR)

The literature has its roots in Dharmasūtras, aphoristic works which arose several centuries before Christ. These were followed by metrical Smṛti, generally known as Dharmaśāstra. Though traditionally twenty writers of Dharmaśāstra are known, actually there were many more. The most authoritative and the earliest work is the *Manusmṛti* which appears to have passed through several stages of evolution. The extant *Manusmṛti* is believed, by P.V. Kane, to have been evolved in the period between the 2nd cent. B.C. and the 2nd cent. A.D. The contents of the work may be divided as follows : *Ācāra* (custom), *Prāyaścitta* (expiation),

Vyavahāra (secular law) and *Rājadharma* (politics and statecraft). The other great authority was Yājñavalkya (*c.* 1st, cent. A.D.). The *Yājñavalkya-smṛti* was of high authority in secular law.

PHILOSOPHY[13]

As already stated, Indian philosophy falls into two broad classes, viz. Orthodox and Heterodox. The orthodox schools acknowledge Vedic authority and the existence of God. These are six : Nyāya-Vaiśeṣika, Mīmāṃsā-Vedānta, Sāṃkhya-Yoga. The contents of these systems of philosophy can be broadly divided as Epistemology, Ethics, Eschatology, Metaphysics. We shall give a brief outline of each of the different schools.

ORTHODOX SYSTEMS

NYĀYA PHILOSOPHY

The first work is the *Nyāyasūtra* of Gotama or Gautama who is supposed to have flourished in the 6th cent. B.C. The entire philosophy can be divided into four parts, viz. theory of knowledge, theory of the physical world, theory of individual self and its liberation, theory of God. It is an elaboration of sixteen philosophical topics (*padārthas*) which are : *Pramāṇa* (means of knowledge) *Prameya* (object of knowledge), *ṣaṃśaya* (doubt), *Prayojana* (necessity. object in view), *Dṛṣṭānta* (example), *Siddhānta* (conclusion), *Avayava* (members of the syllogism), *Tarka* (hypothetical argument), *Nirṇaya* (certain knowledge), *Vāda* (logical argument), *Jalpa* (wrangling), *Vitaṇḍā* (argument for refutation only), *Hetvābhāsa* (fallacy), *Chala* (quibble), *Jāti* (evasive and shifty answer) and *Nigrahasthāna* (ground of defeat).

Nyāya recognises four means of valid knowledge, viz. *pratyakṣa* (perception), *Anumāna* (inference), *Upamāna* (comparison) and *Śabda* (verbal testimony).

According to this philosophy, the self (*ātman*) is different from the body, senses, mind and the stream of consciousness.

Liberation (*mukti* or *mokṣa*) means freedom from all pain and suffering. It can be attained by *Śravaṇa* (listening to scriptural instructions about the self), *Manana* (firmly establishing the knowledge of the self by means of reasoning) and *Nididhyāsana* (meditation on the self in conformity with the principles of *Yoga*). Nyāya believes in god who is the eternal infinite self who creates, maintains and destroys the world. He is the moral governor of all living beings including ourselves.

VAIŚEṢIKA

It is so called as *Viśeṣa,* a category of knowledge, has been elaborately discussed in it. The first systematic work of this philosophy, founded by Kaṇāda, who is supposed by some to have been a contemporary of the Buddha (6th-5th cent. B.C.), is the *Vaiśeṣika-sūtra.*

This system recognises seven *padārthas,* and comprehends all reals under them. These are : *Dravya* (substance), *Guṇa* (quality), *Karman* (action), *Sāmānya* (generality), *Viśeṣa* (particularity), *Samavāya* (relation of inherence), *Abhāva* (nonexistence). Vaiśeṣika recognises only two sources of knowledge, viz. perception (*pratyakṣa*) and inference (*anumāna*); the latter includes comparison (*upamāna*) and testimony (*śabda*).

Its theory of creation is characterised by the fact that it reduces all composite objects to the four kinds of atoms of earth, water, fire and air. It is sometimes referred to as the atomic theory of the world. There is fundamental difference between this theory and that of the atomism of the western science and philosophy. The Vaiśeṣika theory is partly materialistic, partly spiritual. But, the western theory is purely materialistic. According to the former, the ultimate source of the actions of atoms is the creative or destructive will of the Supreme Being who guides the operations of atoms in accordance with the unseen deserts (*adṛṣta*) of individual souls and with reference to the end of moral dispensation.

According to the western view, the order and history of the world are the mechanical result of the fortuitous motions of innumerable atoms in infinite space and lime, and in different directions. There is no necessity of postulating mind or a conscious power governing and guiding the operations of the atoms.

MĪMĀṂSĀ

The foundation of this philosophy was laid by the *Sūtra* of Jaimini who is believed by some to have flourished in the fourth century B.C.

The sources of knowledge, according to this school, are the traditional four, referred to above, plus *arthāpatti* (postulation) and *anupalabdhi* (non-perception).

Mīmāṃsā believes in souls as eternal spiritual substances. According to it, the material world comes into being out of atoms according to the moral law of *Karman*. It also believes in what is called *Apūrva* or unperceived potency. As soon as a ritual is performed, it generates in the soul of the performer the *Apūrva* which bears fruit in the next world. The soul is eternal and infinite. According to this school, liberation is an unconscious state free from pleasure and pain.

The early exponents of Mīmāṃsā are silent about God; the later ones reject the proofs of the existence of God.

VEDĀNTA

The Upaniṣads are called Vedānta. As a system of philosophy, it started with the *Brahmasūtra* (variously called *Vedāntasūtra, Śārīrakasūtra, Śārīraka-mīmāṃsā, Uttara-mīmāṃsā*) of Bādarāyaṇa (sometime between 500 and 200 B.C. or between 200 and 450 A.D.)

According to different interpretations, different schools of Vedānta arose. The main schools are those of Śaṃkara, Rāmānuja, Madhva, Vallabha, Nimbārka. The most important point of difference is concerned with the nature of relation between the self (*jīva*) and God (Brahman). The above schools are known respectively as *Advaita* (non-dualism or monism), *Viśiṣṭādvaita* (qualified monism), *Dvaita* (dualism), *Śuddhādvaita* (pure monism), *Dvaitādvaita.* (dualistic nondualism).

Vedānta regards the world as unreal, and only Brahman as real. The attainment of Brahman or Paramātman is the highest goal of life. Rituals are not adequate for leading to the realisation of the self. Knowledge of the self or God is the means of liberation which is not merely the absence of all misery, but a positive state of bliss arising out of self-realisation.

SĀṂKHYA

The name is derived from *Saṃkhyā.* It may mean the highest knowledge; the philosophy that aims at it is called Sāṃkhya. Or, Sṃkhyā means number. The philosophy which aims at right knowledge of reality, by the enumeration of the ultimate objects of knowledge, is called Sāṃkhya.

The traditional foundation of this system is the *Sāṃkhyapravacana-sūtra* attributed to Kapila who is believed to have flourished several generations before the Buddha.

Sāṃkhya is dualistic in the sense that it recognises the two fundamental principles, Puruṣa and Prakṛti, as underlying creation. The ultimate cause of the world of objects is Prakṛti, constituted by the three *guṇas, Sattva, Rajas* and *Tamas,* which is unconscious (*jaḍā*), uncaused, eternal and all-pervading, very fine, always ready to produce the world of objects. Puruṣa or self is pure, eternal and all-pervading consciousness. While Prakṛti is one, Puruṣas are many; one is connected with each body.

The contact of Puruṣa and Prakṛti causes the evolution of the world. The order of creation is as follows :

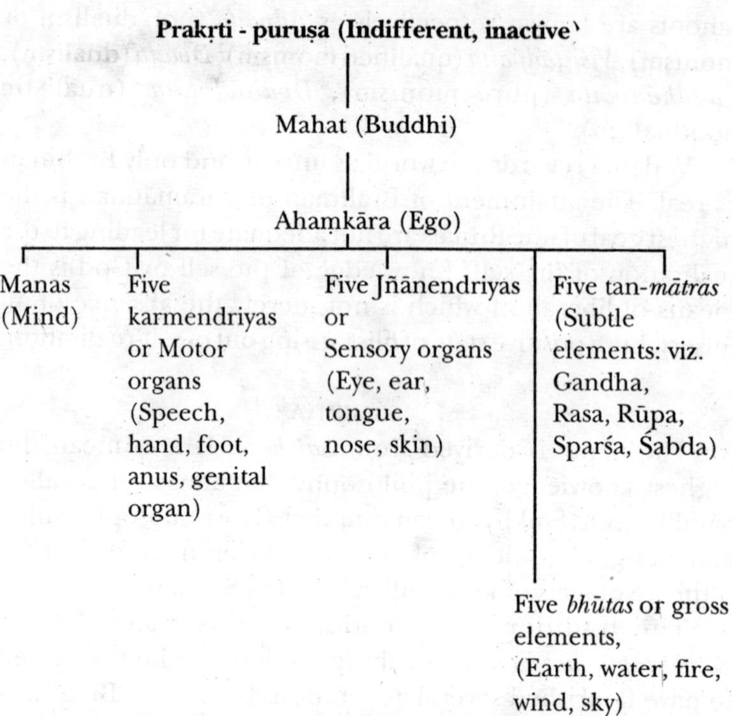

Sāṃkhya recognises three sources of knowledges, viz. *Pratyakṣa, Anumāna* and *Śabda*; *Arthāpatt*, and *Anupalabdhi*, are included under the above three.

According to Sāṃkhya, life on earth is subject to threefold pain, viz. *Ādhyātmika* (intraorganic, *i.e.* bodily ailment and mental suffering), *Ādhibhautika* (produced by extra-organic causes; *e.g.* man, animal, thorn, etc.) and *Ādhidaivika* (produced by extra-organic supernatural causes, *e.g.* ghost, demon, storm, etc.). Liberation means absolute cessation of all kinds of pain. Ignorance is the cause of suffering. Freedom from suffering can be attained through right knowledge. Two kinds of liberation are recognised; viz. *Jīvanmukti* (liberation in life) and *Videhamukti* (liberation after death).

Sāṃkhya declares that the existence of God cannot be established by proofs.

YOGA

The first work of this system is the *Yogasūtra* or *Pātañjalasūtra* attributed to Patañjali who is regarded, by some, as identical with Patañjali (*c.* 2nd cent. B.C.), author of the Great commentary *Mahābhāṣya,* on Pāṇini's grammar. The work consists of four parts, viz. *Samādhipāda* (dealing with *Samādhi* or concentration of mind, meditation), *Sādhanapāda* (dealing with the means of attaining *Samādhi*), *Vibhūtipāda* (on supernormal powers acquired by *Yoga*) and *Kaivalyapāda* (describing the nature and forms of liberation, the reality of the transcendent self and the other world).

According to it, liberation can be attained through the direct knowledge of the self's distinction from the physical world including the body, mind and ego (*vivekajñāna*).

Yoga means the suppression of the functions or modifications of the mind (*cittavṛtti-nirodha*). The eight accessories or means of *Yoga* are as follows : *Yama* (restraint, absention from injury to life, falsehood, theft, incontinence and avarice), *Niyama* (cultivation of good habits), *Āsana* (steady and comfortable postures), *Prāṇāyāma* (threefold regulation of breath, viz. inhalation, retention and exhalation), *Pratyāhāra* (withdrawal of the senses from their objects), *Dhāraṇā* (fixing the mind on the desired object), *Dhyāna* (steady contemplation of the object without any break), *Samādhi* (absorption of the mind in the object of contemplation).

This system recognises God.

HETERODOX SYSTEMS

BUDDHIST PHILOSOPHY

This philosophy is ethical, and does away with metaphysical discussions as having no practical utility.

The Buddha proclaimed four Noble Truths, viz. *Duḥkha* (life is full of misery), *Samudaya* (cause of suffering), *Nirodha* (suppression of suffering) and *Mārga* (path leading to the cessation of suffering).

The above path, which advocates the middle course between the two extremes of a life of unbridled enjoyment and total renunciation, consists in : Right view, right resolve, right speech, right conduct, right livelihood, right effort, right mindfulness, right concentration.

This philosophy denies God and soul.

In course of time, as many as four schools of Buddhist philosophy arose. These are Vaibhāṣika, Mādhyamika, Sautrāntika and Yogācāra. According to the Vaibhāṣika school, the Buddha is only an ordinary man who attained *Nirvāṇa* (cessation of desires) by Buddhahood, and *Mahāparinirvāṇa* by death. The knowledge about Truth that he gained, without the help of others, was his divinity. According to this doctrine, the existence of both solid and external objects is admitted. Knowledge of the phenomenal world is obtained directly by perception, and not by inference.

According to Mādhyamika, the doctrine of *Śūnyatā* does not mean absolute void or nihilism, but only the emptiness of the phenomenal world. By *Śūnyatā* is meant the indescribable nature of the phenomenal world; it is a kind of relativity. The real that lies behind the visible world is intelligible only by *Nirvāṇa.* This reality is not by itself denied; what is denied is its comprehensibility through the senses.

According to the Sautrāntika school, knowledge about the external objects is obtainable by inference. From their forms or from impression about them, knowledge about them arises.

The Yogācāra totally denies the external world, recognises the existence of only the mind. Or, it may be said that it emphasises *Yoga* and *Ācāra.* This doctrine is named *Vijñānavāda.* The restrained mind is able to dispel delusion about the external world and to remove attachment to it.

Here are some common doctrines in Buddhist philosophy.

Pratītyasamutpāda- all that arises has a cause. For example, an earthen vessel has two causes, one *upādāna* or material (the clay) and the other *nimitta* or efficient (potter). It is called the theory of dependent origination.

Śūnyavāda - doctrine of emptiness. Already explained.

Sarvāstivāda - according to it, the existence of both the external and internal objects is recognised.

Kṣaṇikavāda-theory of momentariness; things exist for one partless moment only.

JAINA PHILOSOPHY

It has little or no influence in foreign countries. So, we shall add just a few words on it.

According to it, consciousness is the essence of the soul. It manifests itself and other objects. Knowledge is twofold, immediate and mediate. Some of its prominent doctrines are *Syādvāda* (theory that every judgment is relative), *Saptabhaṅgīnaya* (seven forms of judgment).

Coming to metaphysics, we find that, according to it, every object possesses innumerable characters, positive and negative, it requires new characters with changes in time. Hence, an object has infinite characters. So, only the omniscient can know an object fully.

A substance possesses some unchangeable essential characters (*guṇas*) and changing modes (*paryāyas*). Change and permanence are both real. There are three factors in reality, viz. permanence, origination and decay.

According to this philosophy, the soul or *jīva* is a conscious substance. The soul, possessed of infinite potentiality, is associated, owing to *Karman*, with matter; thus, its bondage occurs. Liberation is purging the matter from the soul. For this, right faith, right knowledge and right conduct are necessary.

CĀRVĀKA OR LOKĀYATA PHILOSOPHY
(Materialistic School)

There is no systematic work of this school. Its views are known from the criticism in different schools.

According to it, perception is the only source of knowledge. It takes matter as the only reality, because it alone is perceived. Matter is composed of five kinds of elements (*Pañcabhūta*), viz. *Kṣiti* (earth), *Ap* (water), *Tejas* (fire), *Marut* (wind) and *Ākāśa* or *Vyoman* (ether). Of these, ether being not perceptible is rejected by this school. It denies the existence of soul apart from the body. It also denies God. According to this school, the supposition of the creator-god is unnecessary; the world comes into existence by the fortuitous combination of the material elements. The followers of this school hold that heaven is a myth; as such, it cannot be the goal of life. Liberation, as freedom from all suffering, is an impossible ideal. Pleasure, though accompanied by pain, is the only possible good, and pleasure, not virtue (*dharma*) nor liberation (*mokṣa*) is the ideal of life. Wealth is to be longed for only as means to enjoyment. Vedic rites are absolutely useless.

In recent times, a work, entitled *Tattvopaplava-siṃha*, attributed to Jayarāśi, has come to light. It is the only Sanskrit work, known hitherto, of the Cārvāka-Lokāyata school.

[Edited and trs. into English (first half of the text) by E. Franco, Delhi, 1994]

MIDDLE INDO-ARYAN LANGUAGES AND LITERATURES[14]

PĀLI LANGUAGE

The oldest language of this group is Pāli.[15] Gradually, *Prākṛta*[16] language evolved. A further stage of development is represented by *Apabhraṃśa* which, according to Namisādhu (commentary on Rudraṭa's *Kāvyālaṃkāra,* i.11-f.), is identical with Prākrit; according to the *Mahābhāṣya* of Patañjali (*c.* 2nd cent. B.C.), denotes un-Pāṇiniyan words constituting a language; according to Daṇḍin (*c.* 8th cent. A.D. - *Kāvyādarśa,* i. 36, 37) it is the language of the Ābhīras (cowherds) and the like.

We do not know exactly when and where Pāli originated. This much can be said that, till the sixth or seventh century A.D., no evidence exists about the use of the word Pāli to indicate a language. According to a Ceylonese tradition, it was the *mūla-bhāṣā*, the basic language, in vogue in Magadha, the region where Buddhism originated. In the *Vinayapiṭaka* (Cullavagga, III.38), the Buddha is stated to have asked his followers to propagate his message in their own language (*sakāya niruttiyā*) which is taken by Buddhaghoṣa as the language of the Master himself, that is Māgadhī or Pāli. Scholars like Rhys Davids and Oldenberg, however, point out fundamental divergences between Māgadhī and Pāli. According to Westergaard, Kuhn, and others, Pāli was a dialect of Ujjayinī. Otto Franke thinks that it was the language of the region adjoining the Vindhya Hills. Differing with scholars like Grierson, Sten Konow holds that Paiśācī Prākrit, to which Pāli is allied, originated not in the north-west of India, but in the regions contiguous to the Vindhyas. In his opinion, Pāli, like Paiśācī, originated probably in Ujjayinī. Oldenberg noticed fundamental agreement between Pāli and the language of the inscriptions on the Khaṇḍagiri hill in Orissa. So, he as also E. Müller thought that Kaliṅga was the homeland of Pāli.

Pāli is a *Kunstsprache.* Various dialects appear to have contributed to its development. The influence of Māgadhī on it is the greatest. This is, perhaps, because the Buddha's activities were mainly carried on in and around Magadha.

PRĀKRIT LANGUAGE

Pāli was the earliest Prākrit. In course of time, different kinds of Prākrit became current in different regions. The regional classification of Prākrits is as follows :

A. Central

Śaurasenī, the dialect of Śūrasena or the region of Mathurā and its neighbouring areas in modern Uttar Pradesh which was Madhyadeśa in early times.

B. Outer

In the east, there was Māgadhī prevalent in and around Mathurā. In the south, was evolved Māhārāṣṭrī, the Prākrit par excellence (*maharāṣṭrāśrayāṃ bhāṣāṃ prakṛṣṭaṃ prākṛtaṃ viduḥ* - *Kāvyādarśa* of Daṇḍin, I.35).

The historical and chronological classification of Prākrits is as follows :

1. Old
   Same as Pāli.
2. Middle
   Including Māhāraṣṭrī, Śaurasenī, Māgadhī, etc.
3. Late Prākrit or Apabhraṃśa.

APABHRAṂŚA LANGUAGE

It represents the stage of the colloquial speech when the literary Prākrits became almost archaic, and were polished and stereotyped by grammarians.

Various types of Apabhraṃśa, *e.g.* Vrācaṭa or Vrācaḍa, Nāgara and Upanāgara, were current in different regions.

A geographical classification of Apabhraṃśas, according to some, is as follows :

Pūrvī (Eastern), *Paiśācī* (language of goblins adjoining the Vindhya Hills) and *Dakṣiṇī* (southern).

In the sense of the natural spoken language, some modern writers divide Prākrits as Primary, Secondary and Tertiary.

The aforesaid Māgadhī has several sub-dialects, called Śākārī, Cāṇḍālī, Śābarī, Ḍhakki or Ṭakki.

A Prākrit dialect is called Ardhamāgadhī which, having been mostly used by the Jains, was called Jaina Prākrit by Jacobi. Some Prākrit dialects, with certain individual characteristics, are also styled Jaina-māhārāṣṭrī and Jaina Śaurasenī.

Considerably different from the above types of Prākrit is Paiśācī, the *Bhūtabhāṣā* or language of goblins and demons.

It appears to have been in vogue round about the Vindhya range. It has a sub-dialect, called Culikā Paiśācī.

PĀLI LITERATURE

This literature can be broadly divided into two categories - Canonical and Non-canonical. The Canonical literature consists of the *Tipiṭaka* (lit. three baskets) comprising the *Vinayapiṭaka* (on discipline), *Suttapiṭaka* (containing learned discourses) and *Abhidhammapiṭaka* (on higher religion, philosophy). The first two *piṭakas* are concerned respectively with *Saṃgha* (Monastic order) and *Dhamma.* The subject of the third one is also *Dhamma,* but it is more learned.

The Jātaka, included in the *Khuddaka-nikāya* of the *Vinayapiṭaka,* contains accounts about the supposed previous births of the Buddha as Bodhisatta. According to a Burmese tradition, the *Milindapañho* is one of the treatises included in the above *Nikāya.*

The Non-canonical Pāli literature may be divided into the following classes :

1. Non-canonical works preceding the famous commentaries.
2. Famous commentaries. The three great commentators were Buddhaghoṣa, Buddhadatta and Dhammapāla.
3. Historical works, e.g. *Dīpavaṃśa* (chronicle of Ceylon), *Mahāvaṃśa* (historical work of Ceylon), *Thupavaṃsa* (historical account of Theras sent by Thera Moggaliputta Tissa to different parts of India for propagating Buddhism and geographical information about important places in India), etc.
4. Compendiums.
5. Poetical Compositions.
6. Grammar.
7. Poetics and Prosody.
8. Lexicography.

To the aforesaid fifth category belongs the *Milindapañho*[17] (questions of Milinda). Probably originating in north-western India, it contains questions asked by Milinda and answers given by Thera Nāgasena, a renowned Buddhist monk. Milinda is the Prākrit name of the Greek King Menandros or Menander who reigned in the Punjab from *c.* 160 to 140 B.C. This anonymous work was probably composed in north-western India in the period between 100 and 200 A.D. It contains questions and answers relating to certain abstruse matters of Buddhism.

PRĀKRIT LITERATURE

The published Prākrit works, like those in Pāli, can be divided into two broad classes, Religious and Secular. The former class comprises the religious works of the Jainas, which are generally called *Siddhānta* or *Āgama*. The *Siddhāntas* include the following :

A. Dvādaśāṅga

B. Dvādaśa Uvaṅga (=Upāṅga)

C. Dasa Painna (=Prakīrṇa)

D. Ṣaṭ Cheyasutta (= Chedasūtra)

E. Four Mūlasūtras

F. Others comprising Nandi or Nandisutta (= Nandisūtra).

G. Anuogadāra (=Aṇuyogadvāra).

The above classes of works belong to the Śvetāmbara sect of the Jainas. To the other sect, the *Digambara*, belong the following classes of religious works :

A. Prathmānuyoga

B. Karaṇānuyoga

C. Drvyānuyoga

D. Caraṇānuyoga

The above classes of works are also designated as *Caturveda*.

The non-canonical Prākrit works can be broadly divided into the following classes :

1. Poetical works
2. Prose and Campū (mixed prose and verse)
3. Drama
4. Philosophy and rules of conduct of the Jainas
5. Grammar and Lexicon.

Besides purely literary works, there is a number of Prākrit inscriptions.

APABHRAṂŚA LITERATURE

This literature, spreading over a period of about six hundred years (400-1000 A.D.), can be broadly divided into two classes, Jaina and Non-Jaina. From the literary point of view, the Apabhraṃśa works can be divided into the following classes :

A. Jaina Prabandha
B. Spiritual or mystic works of Jainas
C. Jaina didactic poetry
D. Bauddha Dohā
E. Lyric
F. Miscellaneous.

INDIAN SCRIPTS[18]

It is not definitely known when and how the Indians learnt to write. The earliest specimens of Indian writing are the Indus Valley script, not yet deciphered. This civilisation is generally believed to be pre-Vedic, having developed some 3,000 years before Christ.

The *Ṛgveda* is the earliest written record of not only the Indians, but also of the Indo-Europeans. This Vedic *Saṃhitā* is generally assigned to a period ranging from 1500 to 1200 B.C. Some scholars are, however, inclined to hold that it came into being as early as 6,000 B.C. A very recent scholar, is inclined to hold that it originated about 12,500 B.C. Whatever the truth may be, it is aptly held by some scholars that centuries elapsed between the *Mantra* period, when the Ṛgvedic hymns originated and were orally transmitted, and the *Saṃhitā* period when they came to be written down. Thus the *Saṃhitā* period, the precise age of which is still uncertain, may be regarded as the time of origin of the alphabet used in it. The script is called *Brāhmī*[19]; it is written from the left to the right. Alberuni (973-1048) appears to have believed that Indian alphabet originated with the beginning of *Kali Age*, in 3102 B.C.

Besides Brāhmī, another major script was *Kharoṣṭhī*[20]; it is written from right to left. The inscriptions of Aśoka, dating back to the third century B.C., and found in a very wide area of the sub-continent, are written in the above two principal characters. The Brāhmī script, generally supposed to have originated about 500 B.C., passed through a long process of evolution before it developed into the later forms in the new Indo-Aryan scripts. Sanskrit works used to be written in the regional scripts. It was as late as the eighteenth century A.D. when Devanāgari script came to be used for writing Sanskrit all over India. The origin of the name Devanāgarī is obscure. Some think that it was the script of the *nāgaras* (from *nagara* meaning city) or people of the city. According to others, the name was derived from the Nāgar Brāhmaṇas of Gujarat.

Brāhmī script evolved differently in north and south India. In north India, the first change occurred in the first and second centuries A.D. in the Kuṣāṇa reign. The second change took place in the fourth and fifth centuries A.D. under the Guptas. Towards the second half of the seventh century, this script assumed three distinct forms in north and east India. These are

1. Śāradā - north-west India, in Kashmir-Punjab region.
2. Nāgara - south-west India *i.e.* Gujarat, Rajputana, (Rajasthan), Mālava and Madhyadeśa.
3. Kuṭila - east India.

From Nāgara, mentioned above, developed Devanāgarī, Gujarāṭī, Kāyathī. From Śāradā evolved Gurumukhī in Punjab, and Kuṭila gave rise to Bengali, Maithilī, Asamiyā, Oḍiyā, Nepālī.

In South India, Brāhmī developed in a different way, and gave rise to Vaṭṭejhu, Ttu and Pallava, and, through them, were evolved Tāmil, Telugu, Kanarese, Mālayālam, Grantha, etc.

The Jaina works, *Pannavanā-sūtra* and *Samavayaṅga-sūtra* contain the names of eighteen scripts including *Brāhmī* and *Kharoṣṭhī.* The Buddhist Sanskrit work, *Lalitavistara,* gives a list of sixty-four scripts of which the first two are *Brāhmī* and *Kharoṣṭhī.*

The scripts, mentioned in the literary works, may be divided into several groups, *e.g.* provincial, tribal, sectarian, etc. Several foreign scripts also were, perhaps, in use in some parts of India. For example, *Yavanāni* (Greek script) has been mentioned by Pāṇini (III.2.21).

LANGUAGES OF INDIA TO-DAY

Language is the commonest means of communication among human beings. As India[21] came into contact with various foreign countries through trade and commerce as well as religion and foreign invasions, it is natural that the Indians had to communicate with foreigners. In doing so, some foreigners may have picked up some Indian languages. Likewise, Indians, in their turn, are likely to have picked up some foreign tongues. What is more important is that some foreign ethnic groups settled in India, and thus gave rise to pockets of linguistic groups confined to the area of their habitation. The two big families of indigenous languages in India are the Indo-European and the Dravidian. Here we shall briefly trace the foreign languages current in this country.

Two families of foreign languages exist in India. These are Austric and Tibeto-Chinese. Besides these, there are two languages.

The languages of the Austric and Tibeto-Chinese families are shown in the following table.[22]

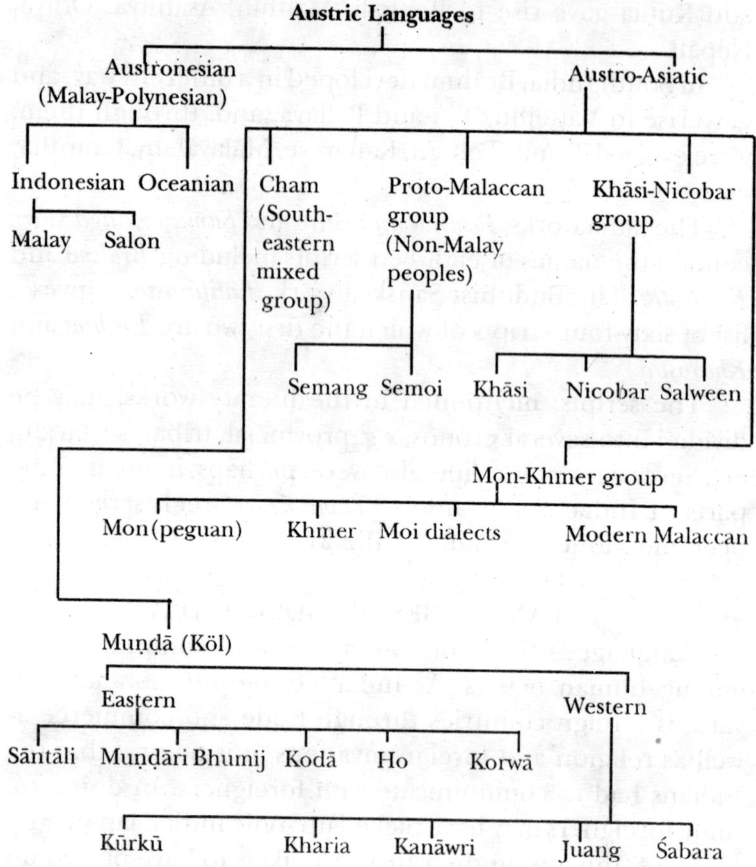
Austric Languages
Austronesian
(Malay-Polynesian)
Austro-Asiatic
Indonesian
Oceanian
Malay
Salon
Cham
(South-
eastern
mixed
group)
Proto-Malaccan
group
(Non-Malay
peoples)
Khāsi-Nicobar
group
Semang
Semoi
Khāsi
Nicobar
Salween
Mon-Khmer group
Mon(peguan)
Khmer
Moi dialects
Modern Malaccan
Muṇḍā (Köl)
Eastern
Western
Sāntāli
Muṇḍāri
Bhumij
Kodā
Ho
Korwā
Kūrkū
Kharia
Kanāwri
Juang
Śabara

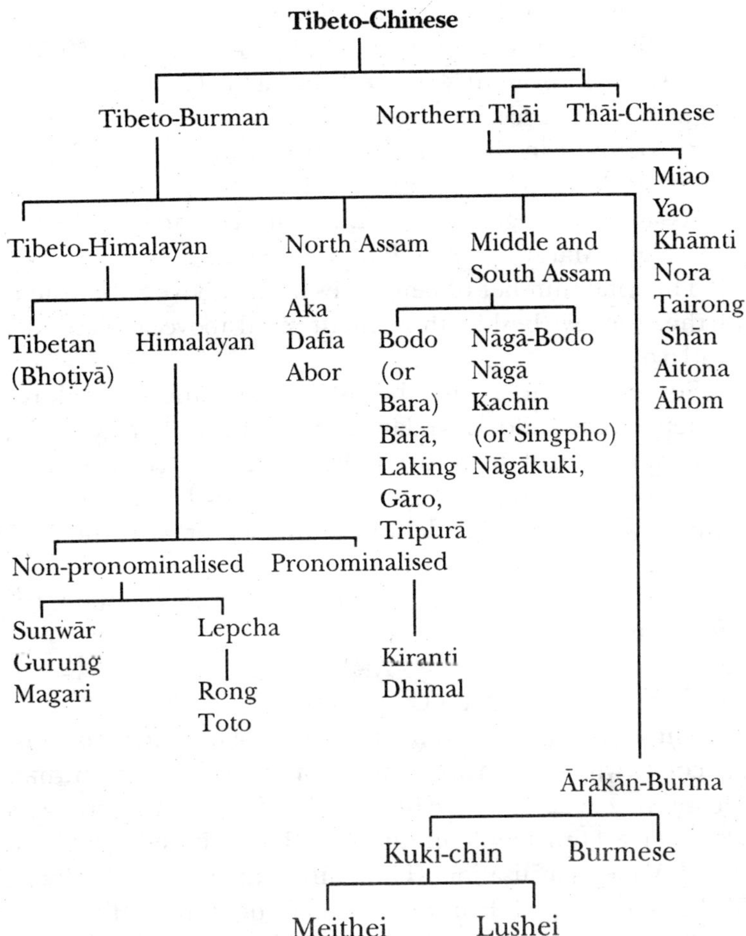
Tibeto-Chinese
Tibeto-Burman
Northern Thāi
Thāi-Chinese
Miao
Yao
Khāmti
Nora
Tairong
Shān
Aitona
Āhom
Tibeto-Himalayan
North Assam
Middle and South Assam
Tibetan (Bhoṭiyā)
Himalayan
Aka
Dafia
Abor
Bodo (or Bara) Bārā, Laking Gāro, Tripurā
Nāgā-Bodo
Nāgā
Kachin (or Singpho)
Nāgākuki,
Non-pronominalised
Pronominalised
Sunwār
Gurung
Magari
Lepcha
Rong
Toto
Kiranti
Dhimal
Ārākān-Burma
Kuki-chin
Burmese
Meithei
Lushei

We have seen that the Indo-Aryan family of languages passed through two stages, viz. Old Indo-Aryan and Middle Indo-Aryan. At present, we have in India the New Indo-Aryan languages. Of the several languages of this family, the following are recognised in the Constitution of India, 1949 [Eighth Schedule, Articles 344 (1) and 351]

Assamese, Bengali, Gujarāṭi, Hindi, Kannada, Kashmiri, Mālayālam, Mārāṭhī, Oriyā, Punjabi, Tamil, Telugu.

The total number of languages in the above Schedule is 14; the other two besides those mentioned above, are Sanskrit and Urdu.

Some Austric and Tibeto-Chinese languages have influenced the Indo-Aryan languages of India. For example, the conjugation of the verb in Behari is indebted to Muṇḍā.[23] *Kuḍi,* denoting 20, used in all Indo-Aryan languages, is a Muṇḍā word. *Burañji,* denoting history or chronicle in Assamese, is an Āhom word.

We note below some foreign loan-words in the Bengali[24] vocabulary.

ARTS

MUSIC[25] AND DANCE[26]

These arts, spontaneous expressions of human emotions, are coeval with human life, civilised or uncivilised, and Indian life was no exception. The history of Indian civilisation dates from at least third millennium B.C., the supposed age of the Indus Valley Civilisation. The ruins, unearthed chiefly at Mohenjodāro and Harappā, reveal the flute with seven apertures, the *Mṛdaṅga* (a kind of drum or tabor), lute, *Karatāla* (perhaps Cymbal), dancing figures. Thus, there is no doubt of prevalence of music and dance in that far-off age.

We are in the dark about these arts in inter regnum between the above civilisation and Vedic age. *Ṛgveda,* earliest traceable work, dating back to at least 1,500 B.C., testifies to musical bent of mind of sages. The language is accented; three accents of *Udātta, Anudātta* and *Svarita* are musical, indicating different degrees of pitch. The eighth Book of this *Saṃhitā* is called *Pragātha* (replete with songs).

Ṛks or stanzas of the above Veda, which used to be sung in sacrificial rites, mainly constitute *Sāmaveda* or Veda of *Sāmans,* i.e. melodies. Its best known recension, that of Kauthumas, comprises two parts, *Ārcika* and *Uttarārcika.* The *Ārcika,* consisting of melodious *Ṛks,* contains *Grāmageyagāna* (book of rural songs) and *Araṇyagāna* (book of forest songs). Connected with them are two books called respectively *Uhagāna* and *Uhyagāna.*

Besides, Vedic Saṃhitās contain references to dance and musical instruments like *Kṣoṇī, Bāṇa* (a kind of large lute), *Dundubhi* (a kind of large kettle drum).

The later Vedic works like Brāhmaṇas, Āraṇyakas and Upaniṣads testify to close familiarity with music.

Of ancillary Vedic works, *Nāradīya Śikṣā* deserves special mention in this connection. It mentions seven notes (*svaras*), three *grāmas* (scales), twenty-one *mūrchanās* (regulated rise and fall of sounds) and 49 *tānas* (protracted tones).

There are many references to music and dance in *Rāmāyaṇa* (present from *c.* 2nd or 3rd cent. A.D.) and *Mahābhārata* (present from *c.* 4th cent. A.D.).

Copious references to above arts are contained in some Purāṇas, notably *Mārkaṇḍeya* and *Vāyu* both of which are supposed to date back to the period between 3rd and 5th centuries A.D.

Tantras also contain some information about musical lore. In this connection, *Vīṇātantra,* included in *Yāmalatantra* is noteworthy.

Classical Sanskrit literature is full of references to various elements of music and dance. In this connection, we may mention Bhāsa's (pre-Kālidāsa) *Svapnavāsavadatta,* Kālidāsa's (*c.* 5th cent. A.D.) *Abhijñānaśakuntala, Meghadūta,* Śūdraka's (*c.* 6th cent. A.D.) *Mṛcchakaṭika,* Bāṇabhaṭṭa's (7th cent.) *Kādambarī,* etc., to name only a few.

Coming to treatises dealing with these arts, we meet with Bharata (*c.* 2nd or 3rd cent. A.D.) to whom the voluminous *Nāṭyaśāstra* is attributed. It is the earliest extant treatise on not only *Nāṭya* or dramaturgy, as the title suggests, but also on music (vocal and instrumental) and dance. Of post-Bharata works on these arts, of whom we have a lot, the most authoritative and systematic work, dealing with all the three branches of *Saṃgīta*, is the *Saṃgītaratnākara* of Śārṅgadeva (13th cent.).

The basic things of vocal music are briefly as follows. The fundamental notes (*svaras*) are seven. These are *Ṣaḍja* (Sa), *Ṛṣabha* (Ri), *Gāndhāra* (Ga), *Madhyama* (Ma), *Pañcama* (Pa), *Dhaivata* (Dha) and *Niṣāda* (Ni). *Svara* are distinguished from *śruti* which is explained in English as a division of octavo, a quarter tone or interval. These are nuances having no resonance unlike the *svaras*, and are supposed by Bharata to be twenty-two in number.

Ancient Indian music is characterised by *Rāgas* or melodies, constituted by *Svaras.* There are differences of opinion about the number and names of *Rāgas.* Generally, principal *Rāgas* are regarded as six in number. In *Saṃgitadarpaṇa* of Dāmodara (17th cent.), the following six *Rāgas* are enumerated : *Śrī, Vasantaka, Bhairava, Pañcama, Megha* and *Naṭṭanārāyaṇa.* Some later writers have conceived not only consorts of each of above *Rāgas,* but also their issues.

Songs were broadly divided into two classes, *Mārga* and *Deśī. Mārga* was classical music based on *Ālāpa* which consists in manifestation of a *Rāga* by means of some utterances carrying no sense. *Deśī* was the designation of a song confined to a particular *deśa* (region), and was sung with some meaningful words.

Tāla plays a prominent part in Indian music and dance. Derived from root *tal,* conveying the sense of foundation or basis, it is so called because, as Śārṅgadeva says, music and dance are based on it. It has been defined as time determined with the help of measures called *Laghu* (short), *Guru* (long) and *Pluta* (prolated). Tāla is broadly twofold - *mārga* (classical) and *deśī* (regional, local).

Musical instruments are divided into four classes, viz. *Ānaddha* or *Avanaddha* (with both ends covered by leather), *Tata* (stringed), *Suṣira* (with holes) and *Ghana* (metallic).

Dance is generally rendered into Sanskrit as *nṛtya*. But, in Sanskrit dramaturgy, *nṛtya* and *nṛtta* are different from each other. Śārṅgadeva defines *nṛtya* as that which manifests emotions or feelings by gestures (*āṅgikābhinaya*). According to him, it is known as *Mārga*. He characterises *nṛtta* as movement of limbs devoid of any imitation of any condition. Dhanañjaya (10th cent.), in his *Dasarūpaka,* says - *anyad bhāvāśrayam nṛtyaṃ, nṛttaṃ tālalayāśrayam.*

It means that, while *nṛtya* is based on *bhāva* (emotion or feeling), *nṛtta* is related to *tāla* and *laya* (tempo, e.g. *druta* or swift, *madhya* or medium, and *vilambita* delayed, slow). From *Nāṭyaśāstra* we learn that the art of dance was highly developed. According to Śārṅgadeva, *Nṛtta* is performed by means of *Karaṇas* and *aṅgabhaṅgī* (gestures and postures). The *aṅgas* are six, *viz.* head, hands, chest, sides, hip and feet. Some include shoulder too. *Pratyaṅgas* (limbs) are neck, arms, back, belly, thighs, shanks. According to some, wrist, knees and ornaments, worn on the limbs, are also included in *pratyaṅgas*. There are twelve *Upāṅgas* (minor limbs) in the head, *viz.* eyes, brows, eyelids, eye-balls, throat, nose, breath, lips, teeth, tongue, chin and face. The other *upāṅgas* are heels, ankles, fingers, toes, soles of feet.

In connection with dance, we should mention *Karaṇas.* The graceful action of hand, foot, etc. together, which is in consonance with the *Rasa* (sentiment) concerned, is called *Karaṇa. Karaṇas* may be innumerable. Śārṅgadeva mentions one hundred and eight as most common and important. Of these *Karaṇas,* some are standard, and prevail everywhere; others are *deśī* being in vogue in particular regions. The latter includes the various *Utplutikaraṇas* or *Karaṇas* performed with jumps.

Cārī, derived from root *car* (to move), means aggregate of various graceful and simultaneous movements of the face, shanks, thighs and hip. *Cārī,* performed with one foot, is of two kinds, *Bhaumī* (terrestrial, *i.e.* performed on ground) and *Ākāśikī* (aerial, *i.e.* performed in air, above ground). Each of

Bhaumī and *Ākāśikī Cārīs* has sixteen varieties. These are called *Mārga,* i.e. classical or standard. There are also *Deśī Cārīs* with regional or local characteristics.

PAINTING[27]

Of paintings of paleolithic age, there is a host of specimens in different regions, *e.g.* Vindhya region in Central India, neighbouring areas of village Singhanpur in Raigarh, Mirzapur district of Uttar Pradesh, western parts of Madhya Pradesh. Hundreds of cave-dewellings with paintings have been discovered. The period of origin of these paintings is supposed to range between *c.* 6,000 B.C. and 400 A.D. Prominent among these paintings are those of various animals, particularly of elephants, tigers and rhinoceroses. In many cases, one or more men are represented as engaged in hunting bison, buffalo, deer, nīlgāi, etc. with weapons like bow and arrow, spear, etc. materials, mostly used, consisting in colour prepared with dust of red stone and thin branches of thorny plants. The pictures are realistic and possessed of verve and vigour.

To copper-bronze age belong paintings on earthwares discovered among the ruins of Indus Valley civilisation (*c.* 3000 B.C.) mainly at Mohenjodāro and Harappā. These paintings are mostly of animals and birds, trees and creepers as well as textile designs. The figures on seals, unearthed here, resemble the above. The banian-leaf design is prominent in both.

The Jogimārā cave-paintings in Rāmgarh hill of Sargujā in Central India, are regarded as the earliest specimens of the historic period. Those of the first phase appear to have originated in 1st century B.C. In painted panels on surface of caves, we find figures of animals and humans. The panels are fringed with decorative designs of fish, shark and other sea-creatures.

The earliest paintings on caves (Nos. 9, 10) of Ajantā are almost contemporaneous with the above. These represent Buddhist themes, and are the earliest specimens of the classical Indian style. Depicting as they do narratives in a series of separate scenes, and close-knit figures of men and women, beasts and birds, trees and creepers, etc., they remind one of the contemporary gate and railing of Bhārhut and Sānchi.

Like Gupta sculpture, Ajantā paintings of Gupta age (*c.* 320-510) testify to the glory of India in this art. In the whole gamut of Buddhist paintings, two stand out prominently. One is the picture of Avalokiteśvara, full of compassion (Cave No. 1). Another shows Rāhula and Yaśodharā (Cave No.17) near a huge-sized Buddha. The pictures exude an atmosphere of serene purity; nowhere is there any sign of vulgarity. Another noteworthy feature is delineation of moods by Śāstric *mudrās* and postures. Compared with earlier paintings, these are more sophisticated and developed.

Coming to Bāgh caves (Nos. 3 and 4), we find paintings here are akin, in style, to Ajantā paintings of the second phase. Though Bāgh paintings also have Buddhist themes, yet these are more secular in character, but lack the delectable charm of their counterparts at Ajantā. The painter's skill has found expression in a superb manner in the picture of a grief-stricken woman (Cave No. 4).

Cave-temple of Badāmi (Cave No. 3) is dedicated (578 A.D.) to Viṣṇu. But, pictures appear to be Śaivite. The most important one is that depicting marriage of Śiva and Pārvatī. Though sharing characteristics of style and form of cave-paintings of Ajantā and Bāgh, yet Badāmi paintings have some individuality. These reveal more clearly the roundness and flexibility, and lines of Badāmi paintings are more graceful than those of Ajantā.

The paintings of Ajantā, Bāgh and Bādāmi belong to the classic style which characterises also post-Gupta paintings in South Indian temples of Kailāsa at Ellora (8th cent.), Viṣṇu Tirumalaypuram (7th cent.) Kaliāsanātha at Kāncipuram (8th cent.), Bṛhadīśvara at Tanjore (11th cent.). The above characteristics are more clearly visible in Buddhist manuscript-paintings of Bengal, Bihar and Nepal, belonging to the period between 10th and 13th century.

A distinct style of painting, known as *Udīcī* or Northern, emerged in the medieval age. It is believed to have been brought from the north by nomadic tribes of Central Asia in different stages. This style is evidenced in the sculpture of Ellora and Cola art of far south. But, it was fully developed in the paintings of Jaina manuscripts of Gujarāṭ, which started generally in the beginning of the 12th century and lasted till the end of the 15th. These at first appeared in palm-leaves, and later in paper. These paintings, as a class, are small-sized; hence this art is designated as miniature painting. Due chiefly to inroads of Muslims, painters of Mālwā, Rājputanā and eastern Gujarāṭ sought asylum under Jaina and Hindu rulers of Ābu, Idar, Acalgarh, Dungarpur, etc. In these places, they started such paintings under the supervision of Jaina religious institutions. The tapering and sharp nature of lines, application of conic shape in showing different parts of the body, particularly knee, elbow, etc. are some of the distinct characteristics of this type of paintings. A notable feature is the presence of both eyes in a profile, *i.e.* to show even the hind eye in a face bent aside. The space, meant for painting, is divided up and down or sideways before painting is done. All around the main picture are painted flowers and foliage, birds and animals and there are geometrical ornaments. Among other colours, the golden colour is most prominent. The paintings, however, lack realism and natural vigour.

In this connection, we should mention also paintings in Buddhist manuscripts of Pāla-Sena periods, found in East India, *e.g.* Bengal, Bihar and Nepal. Revealing characteristics of Indian classic style, they belong to the period between the tenth century and thirteenth, and represent the last phase of models set by paintings of Ajantā and Bāgh.

This style was followed by two almost contemporaneous styles, known as Mughal and Rājput. In between, the emergence of a Sultān or Afghān style has been proved by the discovery of some specimens belonging to the regimes of Khiljis of Mālwā (1436-1531), Sultāns of Gujarāṭ (1396-1572) and Sharkis of Jaunpur (1394-1572). These reveal a style perhaps similar to the contemporary Persian art.

The Mughal style originated under Akbar (1556-1605) who got many manuscripts painted. It was deeply influenced by Persian art, as we have stated in connexion with foreign influence in India. In course of time, it emerged as a distinct style born out of a synthesis of the Persian and the Indian. The Mughal school of painting reached its zenith at the time of Jahāngir (1605-1627), himself a connoisseur. Under him hunting, recreation, picnic, dance and song, etc. were represented in paintings. The emperor was especially interested in painting of various aspects of nature, *e.g.* rare birds and beasts, flowers and foliage, etc. A noteworthy fact about Mughal art of this period is that artists came in touch with European painting. Since then, there was a greater tendency of taking nature as the theme. Painting portraits of aristocratic people and noblemen became another characteristic of Mughal art.

Shāhjāhān (reign 1627-1658) was more interested in architecture than the above arts. In this period, despite a wealth of colour and themes, art of painting became stereotyped, lacked verve, and languished. An added feature in this period was the portrayal of figures of saints and other holy men.

It was Aurangzeb's reign (1658-1707) that sounded the death-knell of Mughal painting. The puritanistic and purist emperor was not only averse to this art, but also abolished (1665) the State department of painting. The helpless artists took shelter in courts of provincial rulers. With patronage of the Nawab of Ayodhyā, a distinct style of Mughal painting developed at Lucknow. Thus, Mughal art eked out a poor survival towards the close of the 18th century. Its decadence continued, and by middle of the 19th cent. it languished and ultimately became extinct due to the impact of the western style of painting. Mughal painting is characterised by realism and distinctive subject style. The main feature was portrayal of luxurious life of rulers and their ministers. Painters of this period were adepts in imparting a dramatic air and bringing out portraits in their proper perspective.

To the patronage, extended by feudal rulers of Rājasthān in medieval age, Rājput art owed its existence, and developed at Chittor, Jaypur, Jodhpur and other places in the province, and spread far and wide. Arising in the last quarter of the 16th cent., this art continued its glorious career up to the end of the 18th cent. and existed even up to the beginning of the 19th cent. The themes were predominantly Vaiṣṇavite devotion (*bhakti*) and love (*preman*). Materials were adopted even from Purāṇas and current ballads.

Some paintings relate also to the Rājpūt rulers, expedition, hunting, battle and love. The *Rāgamālā* paintings in the beginning of the main portraits are a rare phenomenon in the history of painting not only in India, but also abroad. Drawn with a rural bias, the paintings reveal the great skill of the Rājput painters in the use of line (*rekhā*) and colour (*varṇa*). Unlike those of their ilk in other parts of India, they succeeded in producing a lyrical effect. This art, having come into contact with the Mughal art, became more sophisticated, and blossomed fully in the middle of the 17th century. This development made it more suggestive than objective

Parallel to the northern Indian art, a south Indian school began to develop since the beginning of the second half of the 16th cent. The centres were Bijāpur, Ahmadnagar, Golcondā and Hyderābād respectively under the following regimes : Ādilshāhi (1489-1686), Nizāmshāhi (1490-1633), Kutbshāhi (1512-1667) and Nizām-ul-mulk Asafza (1724-1748). The southern school of painting originated and developed under the direct influence of the Persian and Turkish painters. Later on, it was influenced by Mughal art which again appears to have influenced the southern art.

After the plunder and pillage of Delhi (1739) by Nādir Shāh, some Hindu painters, trained in the Mughal art, took shelter under Hindu kings of the inaccessible areas of Punjab-Himalaya. As a result, a Pāhāri Miniature painting style came into being. The three centres of this school were Bāsoli, Guler and Kāngrā, each marked by its own characteristics.

In the last decade of the 19th cent., a novel art of Indian painting was born thanks to the lead given by E.B. Havel and Abanindranāth Tagore. They introduced foreign elements in Indian painting.

SCULPTURE[28]

India is rich in sculpture, religious and secular. There is a host of images, Hindu, Buddhist and Jain, scattered throughout the length and breadth of the country. Besides images of deities, there are statues of great personalities who were distinguished in religious or political life. Besides images, there are various designs, floral and others, on temples and buildings.

We do not know when this art originated in India. The ruins of the Indus Valley are the earliest extant specimens of a civilisation that arose about five thousand years ago. Two small images of sandstone, discovered there, though mutilated, bear witness to the kind of sculpture that prevailed in those far-off times. One of the above two appears to have been made to represent a dancing posture. The bodies of the two figures show a fine sense of proportion on the part of the sculptors. The dancing figure appears to have set a model for such figures in later ages. In the slim fawn-eyed dancing figure of Mohenjodāro, made of mixed metals, we find a precursor of the images of gods and goddesses of later times. A lime-stone figure of the same place, with beard and upper garment, seems to represent an aristocratic man. We find some figures engraved on seals. One such figure is that of a male with horns, hands decked with a number of bangles, seated in a Yogic posture. Above and below there are representations of elephant, rhinoceros, tiger and buffalo, all standing. It is considered by some to be a figure of Śiva-Paśupati.

We do not know what kind of sculpture was current in the Vedic age. In fact, we do not find any image or idol before the Maurya (*c.* 322-185 B.C.) and Śuṅga (*c.* 185-73 B.C.) periods. With Aśoka's name are associated some columns with bright and smooth images of sandstone at the top. Of this time there is a half-finished figure of a rock-cut elephant at Dhauli in Orissa. The columns, fully round and tapering upward, have, at the top, imitations of bells of the shape of louts-petals sliding down. On these are animal-images on a round or rectangular base. On the surface of the base, we find slightly engraved grape-leaves or rows of flying swans or moving elephant, bull, lion and horse; these are separated in the middle by signs of wheel. On such a base is the well-known lion-capital of the column at Sārnāth; the lions are, in all respects, lifelike. Since Aśoka's times, such a pageantry of animals became a feature of Indian sculpture.

In the post-Harappan period, we do not meet with human images before the first-second centuries A.D. Of the sculptural specimens, definitely known to belong to this period, we have the walls of the *stūpas* of Bharhut and Sānchi. Besides, there are, in Pāṭaliputra and Mathurā, a few images of standard-sized men and women or male and female Yakṣas. These images reveal remarkable similarity with ordinary humans. The image of a woman, discovered at Didarganj, presents the likeness of a life-loving youthful damsel in its bodily build and dress and ornaments.

The creative art of the Maurya period left its impressive sculptural designs in the ornamental decorations on the enclosures of *Stūpas,* as in Bharhut, the engravings on the *Stūpa* gates, etc. In this connection, the engraved ornamentation on the walls of artificial caves on the hills, Udaygiri and Khandagiri in Orissa, made by the Jainas, also deserves mention. In the above Buddhist sculpture, we find the representation of various events connected with the later and past lives of the Buddha.

In later times, three distinct schools of Indian sculpture developed. These were the schools of Mathurā, Gandhāra and Amarāvatī. Though Puruṣapura (Peshawar) was the capital of Kaniska (reign *c.* 120-144), yet Mathurā was one of the prominent centres of Kushāna supremacy. At Mathurā, a great centre of art developed under the patronage of the Kushānas. The stone statue of Kaniska, discovered at Mathurā, is a superb piece of sculpture. It vividly represents the appearance, outfit and the domineering personality of the emperor. It was, perhaps, the handiwork of some Śaka sculptor living in India. In the images of other Kushāna kings or their employees, there is the impress of Indian influence. Mathurā represents, for the first time, the Buddha in different postures, standing or seated and absorbed in meditation, etc. The images of Jaina Tīrthaṃkaras were also there. In the Jain area, notable are images of women engraved on stone pillars. The figures are vivid representations of the budding and vivacious youth.

The sculpture of Gandhāra was the result of the inspiration mainly of foreigners settled in the area. In this school also images of Buddha and Bodhisattva were made. But, based on Greek models as they were, they lacked the distinctive and evocative Indian traits of the images.

Amarāvatī in Andhra Pradesh, though far away from Gandhāra, came under the influence of the art of that region. A noteworthy feature of the Amarāvatī sculpture is the representation of a joyful crow centring round the Buddha. Each person is represented as wearing tight-fitting shoes, combining graceful gait and dance-rhythm. The images of women have charming physique and are lively. Besides, birds and beasts, fruits and foliage and rich ornaments are also represented.

Then we come to the Gupta Age (*c.* 320-510 A.D.) which saw not only the efflorescence of manifold Indian culture, but also Brāhmanical revival. In this age, along with Buddhist images, there were the images of Brāhmaṇical deities and sculptural representations of Purāṇic stories. Several standing images of the Buddha, made of red stone, have symmetrical and well-proportioned body of huge size. They reveal a wonderful combination of compassion (*Karuṇā*) and consciousness of the inner self. Like Mathurā, Sārnāth also developed into a great centre of contemporary sculpture. The Buddha images of this place reflect the characteristics of one immersed in meditation. The famous image, seated in *Dharmacakra-mudrā,* has a halo decked with gorgeous ornaments, and reflects matchless detachment. It has proportionate muscular body, locks of curly hair, broad eyes and immaculate ornaments. Though a few in number—all this imparted a distinct stamp to the Gupta sculpture. Parallel to the Buddhist sculpture of Mathurā, Sārnāth, Sānchi, Ajantā, etc., there developed Brāhmaṇical sculpture at Kauśāmbi, Deogarh, Udaygiri, Vidiśā, etc.

A typical specimen of the post-Gupta sculpture is preserved in Birmingham Museum. It is made of eight metals, and stands in *Abhaya-mudrā.* It represents the culmination of the polished build and the tendency of touch in the handfingers, held in *Abhaya-mudrā,* found in the images of later times, particularly of the Pāla (*c.* 750-1155) and Sena (*c.* 1095-1245) periods. The main urge of the unprecedented and incomprehensible pervasiveness of sculpture was supplied by the desire of decorating the walls of the temples. In the images of very hard stone, found in Bengal and Bihar, the following characteristics are prominent : slender and tall body, polished physical beauty, very prominent edge of the body, immaculate ornaments, etc. The main image is either standing or seated sometimes with the Śakti by the side. A peculiar grace is found in the ancillary deities on both sides of the principal image. Besides the numerous images, made of touchstone, mention should be made of a host of images, made of eight metals, of wonderful workmanship, which testify to the sculptural skill of that age.

The spurt in the production of sculptural objects in the eastern region from the end of the Gupta period (*c.* 320-510) was like brisk sculptural activities in the south from the time of the Pallavas (from about the middle of 4th cent. to about the close of 9th cent.). In this region, sculpture, first manifested itself in the walls of temples carved out of rocks as well as in the walls or artificial caves. Specimens of this art are mainly Brāhmaṇical, and preserved in the walls of the chariot temples of Mahāvalipuram and also in other rock-cut things, *e.g.*, representation of Arjuna's penance, Goddess Durgā engaged in fight with the buffalo-demon. These images suggest prowess and are well-built. The influence of this type is noticeable in the walls of the noted rock-hewn Kailāsanātha temple as also in the attached *maṇḍapas* at Ellora. The stout and heroic bodies of Ellora, the pageant of diverse images of Tanjore, the galaxy of graceful eight-metalled images of the Chola period (from about middle of 9th cent. to 1096), particularly the images of the dancing Naṭarāja (Śiva) and those of Umā or Gaurī and the countless dancing figures of the Hoysala regime (*c.* 1110-1326), excessively adorned with ornaments, are mute witnesses to the high degree of excellence of the sculpture of India. The *Gopurams* of the southern temples are veritable exhibitions of sculpture

The temples of Orissa, with towering tops, harking back to the period between the eighth century and the thirteenth, represent a distinct sculptural style. The *sanctum sanctorum,* containing the idol, is dark. The outer side of the surrounding walls depicts a pageantry of the seven regions. Tier upon tier represents animals, humans, Gandharvas, Kinnaras, divine damsels and a host of deities.

The wealth of sculptural designs is visible also in the images of the Khajurāho region in Central India, The Rājasthān temples, where built in the design of stars.

SCIENCES

[For a systematic and detailed treatment of science in ancient and medieval India, see Bose, D.M. and others, *A Concise History of Science in India*]

Of the Indian scientific works, those dealing with medical science as well as those on Astronomy (and astrology) have considerable relation with foreign countries either as borrowers or as lenders. So, we shall give an outline of the Sanskrit literature on the above two branches of the science.

MEDICAL SCIENCE[29]
(Āyurveda)

The evolution of this science in India can be roughly divided into the following stages:

1. *Palaeomedicine* - it probably existed before 100,000 B.C. among the people of the palaeolithic age.
2. *Prehistoric medicine* - *c.* 100,000 and 2500 B.C. when the people successively passed through the palaeolithic, mesolithic and neolithic stages.
3. *Primitive medicine* - roughly between 2500 and 1500 B.C. in the Bronze Age Civilisation in India.
4. *Archaic medicine* - among the Aryans after 1,500 B.C.
5. *Modern medicine* - roughly from 18th cent. A.D.

Some sort of medical knowledge can be presumed to have prevailed ever since people appeared in India. But, nothing definite about it is known.

The history of Indian medicine, in a more or less systematic form, begins with the *Ṛgveda*, and can be divided into the following periods :

1. *Vedic period* - between *c.* 1500 and 800 B.C.
2. *Post-Vedic period and the classical Age*—roughly from 800 B.C. to 636 A.D.
3. *The Medieval Age* - roughly from the advent of the Arabs (637) up to 1700 A.D.
4. *Modern period* -1700 A.D. onwards.

From an examination of the skeletal remains, unearthed in the site of Harappan civilisation, the following facts have come to light.

1. The Harappans practised Cranial Surgery for brain disorders.

2. Medicinal herbs used to be exported to Egypt from ancient India.

3. Some soporific medicines were perhaps used by the Harappans before operation and for cranial surgery.

4. Fumigation and sterilisation by fire seem to have been practised.

5. Metals like copper, silver and gold or cinnabar as also calcined cowries and shells were perhaps, used for medicinal purposes.

6. Decoctions and invigorating drinks were probably used.

7. Horns of Sambar (*Cervidae*), bitumen (*Śilājatu*), stored in pots, antimony preparations in small pots, collection of cattle-bones - all these suggest their use for medicinal purposes.

8. Some sort of acupuncture may have been known.

The beginnings of Āyurveda can be traced in the *Ṛgveda*, the earliest written record of India. There are, however, reasons to believe that elements of this science, existed in the pre-Aryan Indian society among the aborigines, and were, to some extent, absorbed by the Aryans. The practice of curing some diseases, supposed to have been caused by evil spirits, by exorcism, the use of amulets, by the recitation of such *mantras* as were in non-Aryan language,[30] etc., occur in the *Atharvaveda*. These things, perhaps, indicate their origin among the aborigines. Elements of ancient Dravidian medical system are believed to have come down intact in the non-Āyurvedic, rather pre-Āyurvedic, systems of medicine still surviving in some areas of South India, and codified in extant treatises in Tamil and other South Indian languages. The existing fragments of *Agadatantra* (dealing with the use of poison in curing diseases, and the treatment of bites of poisonous creatures and counteracting the effect of other kinds of poison), found in the Vedic lore and in treatises of Āyurveda, appear to indicate the existence of a branch of non (perhaps, pre -) Aryan medical knowledge adopted in *Āyurveda.* The same remark applies to *Bhūtavidyā* or black magic and treatment of psychological diseases and cases of possession. It is significant that Rāvaṇa, a non-Aryan demon-king, has been referred to as a master of several sciences including medical science. It also deserves notice that Lakṣmaṇa, struck down by the lethal missile, *Śaktiśela,* was revived by the rare plant, *Viśalyakaraṇī,* prescribed by a learned ape-doctor; the apes, perhaps, stand for the darkskinned aborigines.

Elements of systematic Āyurveda occur in the Vedas. For example, the *Ṛgveda* is aware of *Tridhātu* (viz. *Vāyu* or wind, *Pitta* or bile, *Kapha* or phlegm) which is the pivot around which later *Āyurveda* revolves and is generally known as *Tridoṣa.* This and the *Atharvaveda* name diseases like *Ajakā* (stated to be caused by a poison - VII. 50.1), *Apacit*[31] (AV. VI. 25.83, VII.74, 76) *Harimāṇa* (Jaundice RV. I.50.11, 12), *Hṛdroga* (heart-disease AV. I. 22.1.V.20, 12 etc.), *Sipada* (elephantiasis - VII.50.4), *Yakṣmā* (consumption RV. I.122.9X.85.31). RV. VII.50.2 attributes the inflammation of the knee and the heels to the effect of a poison. RV. X.39.8 refers to iron legs being given to one who lost his legs. Does it hint at orthopaedic surgery ? There are references to eye-sight being restored. Some diseases are stated to be caused by poison. The word *bheṣaja* (medicine) is mentioned (e.g. RV. I.23.19, VIII.9.15), but there is no reference to specific medicines. Sunshine (RV.I.50.11), water (RV.VII.50.4) and fire (RV. VII.50.2) are stated to cure some diseases, especially those caused by poison. RV. X.162.1.2 refer to female diseases of the uterus. Obstruction to pregnancy and death of the foetus are also mentioned (X.162.3). The *Atharvaveda* mentions about forty maladies, e.g. *Apasmāra* (epilepsy—IV.20.37). *Āsrāva* (diarrhoea - I.2.4) *Jalodara* (dropsy - VI.24.127), *Kilāsa* (white leprosy, leucoderma - I.23,24), *Mūtrarodha* (obstruction of urine - *Kauśika-sūtra,*[32] (25.10.18), *Śūla* (rheumatism, colic pain - Kauśikasūtra, 31.7), *Vidratha* (abscess—VI.127), etc.

Anatomical knowledge is vouched by the *Atharvaveda* (X.2) and the *Śatapatha Brāhmaṇa* (X.5.4.12; xii.3.2.3.f.). We know of Vedic ideas of embryology and hygiene.

Considerable development of the medical science in the Atharvavedic period is borne out by the fact that this Veda classifies diseases into five groups; viz.

(1) Those caused by disorders of any of the three elements; this is like the *Tridoṣa* theory of Āyurveda.

(2) Those supposed to be produced by sorcery.

(3) Those believed to be the result of possession by evil spirits or demons or wrath of gods or resulting from evil deeds.

(4) Those produced by worms (*kṛmi*), infestations in humans and animals.

(5) Those due to hereditary or congenital causes (*Kṣetriya*).

In connection with Vedic medicine, it should be noted that diseases were generally determined by observing the signs and symptoms; precise etiology does not seem to have been known. Various diseases were named in accordance with the parts of the body affected; e.g.

1. Diseases of head and neck - *Śīrṣaṇya* (of the head), *Apacit* (neck-gland), *Karṇaśūla* (ear-pain), etc.
2. Lung-disease *Kāsa* (cough), *Yakṣman* (consumption) etc.
3. Heart-disease (*Hṛdroga*).
4. Diseases of abdomen and liver - *Jalodara* or *Udara* (dropsy), *harimāṇa* (jaundice), *Āsrāva* (diarrhoea), *Kṛmi* (worms).

Several skin-diseases are mentioned; e.g. *Kilāsa* (leucoderma), *Kuṣṭha* (leprosy), *Visarpa* (eruption), *Vidratha* (abscess). The genito-urinary disorder, called *Prameha,* is mentioned. *Unmatta* or insanity has been mentioned. Some Gynaecological and Obstetrical disorders have also been mentioned. The *Ṛgveda* (I.18.9) stresses the use of honey and milk by pregnant women. The *Atharvaveda* mentions obstetrical processes for delivery of the foetus.

Some passages of the *Ṛgveda* and *Atharvaveda,* especially of the *Vājasaneyī, Taittirīya* and *Maitrāyaṇī Saṃhitās* of the *Yajurveda* emphasise the use of medicinal plants and herbs.

Certain modes of treatment were as follows. *Yakṣman* was treated by fumigation of *Guggulu* (*Commiphora mukul* or *Alianthus malabarica*) or by the oral administration of milk, honey, ghee, flour and *khadira* (*Areca catechu*), *Apāmārga* (*Achyranthesaspera*), *Vaṭa* (*Ficus bengalensis*) *Pṛśnīparṇī* (*Uraria lagopoides*), *Śigru* (*Moringa pterygosperma*), *Uśīra* (*Andropogon squarrosus*) *Roniṇīprananda, Pūtika* (*Basella rubra* or *Caesalpinia bonducella*) are some of the medicinal plants used in the treatment of some diseases. *Muñja* and *Dūrvā* grass are also mentioned among curatives.

The therapeutic value of sun-rays and water was recognised. The sun has been invoked as healer of leprosy (RV. II.2.3), sickness of heart and yellow colour (due to jaundice?) on the body (RV. I.9.7,11). Medicinal property of water is mentioned in V.I.5.6.19; I.5.6.2.

In the *Atharvaveda,* while the portion, called *Āyuṣyāṇi,* deals with prophylactic treatment for keeping good health, the *Bhaiṣajyāni* portion deals with curative treatment.

This Veda prescribes treatment by putting leeches on sores (XX.16), and cauterisation for counteracting the effect of snake-bite. It also prescribes enemas for certain diseases.

As regards surgery, the following are mentioned: artificial limb (RV. I.116.15), removal of diseased eyeball (RV.I.116-16), probing nrethra for retention of urine (AV.XXV.15.16).

Later medical science, called Āyurveda or Vaidyakaśāstra, is regarded as an *Upāṅga* or accessory to the *Atharvaveda.* It is characterised as *Aṣṭāṅga* because of the eight topics dealt with in it. These are : *Kāyacikitsā* (healing of diseases), *Śalyacikitsā* (major surgery), *Śālākya-cikitsā* (minor surgery) *Bhūtavidyā* (demonology), *Kaumārabhṛtya* (pediatrics). *Agadacikitsā* (treatment of diseases caused by poison), *Rasāyanacikitsā* (treatment with elixirs), *Vājīkaraṇacikitsā* (treatment with aphrodisiacs). Demonology deals with diseases supposed to be caused by demons.

A section of Āyurveda deals also with veterinary science. *Vṛkṣāyurveda* deals with the treatment of the diseases of plants.

The *Kāyacikitsā* section deals with both physical and mental ailments. Diseases are stated to be threefold, viz.

Svābhāvika- natural, caused by the disorder of any of the bodily elements of *Vāyu* (wind), *Pitta* (bile) and *Kapha* (phlegm), *e.g.* fever, headache, cough, etc.

Saṃkrāmaka - infectious like measless, small or chicken pox, etc.

Āgantuka - accidental; *e.g.* burn, hurt caused by fall, etc.

As regards surgery, it should be stated that Suśruta mentions over one hundred instruments, some of them highly sophisticated, and fourteen kinds of bandage. Release of blood from the vein near the elbow, release of blood by stopping the flow of blood by bandage and pressure, release of water by tapping in diseases like dropsy and hydrocele, etc. were parts of surgical treatment. A sort of plastic surgery was also known. For example, we learn of repairing an ear that has been cut, with skin cut off from the cheek. Operation was done inside the abdomen through incision a little below the navel. After cutting a part of the intestine, the split parts were stitched. There is reference to causing the delivery of the child by caesarian section. We have references to the removal of cataract and restoration of eyesight and also general anaesthesia caused by a particular powder.

In connection with child diseases, there is mention of infusing life into a still-born child by means of artificial respiration.

The *Vājīkaraṇa* section deals with the means of stimulating sexual vigour, and prescribes medicines for augmenting the capacity for retaining semen, etc.

Patañjali (*c.* 2nd cent. B.C.) testifies to the cultivation of Āyurveda in the hoary past. It should be noted that not only

Sanskrit works on medical science were composed. The Buddhist Pāli work, *Vinayapiṭaka* (Mahāvagga, vi, 1-14; Majjhimanikāya, 101, 103) and some other texts reveal a wide range of knowledge of elements of this science, surgical instruments, use of hot bath, etc.

Of the authors whose medical works are extant, the famous three (*Vṛddhatrayī*) are Caraka (1st or 2nd cent. A.D.), Suśruta (later than Caraka) and Vāgbhaṭa (before seventh century A.D.). There was another author, named Vāgbhaṭa, believed to have been a descendant of the aforesaid author of this name. Caraka, author of the *Carakasaṃhitā*, is the earliest and most renowned author on medicine. *Suśruta*, author of the *Suśruta-saṃhitā*, is the greatest authority on surgery.

The *Carakasaṃhitā* consists of eight parts which are as follows :

I. *Sūtrasthāna* - remedies, diet, duties of a physician.
II. *Nidānasthāna* - deals with eight major diseases.
III. *Vimānasthāna*-general pathology and medical studies.
IV. *Śārīrasthāna* - anatomy and embryology.
V. *Indriyasthāna* - diagnosis and prognosis.
VI. Cikitsāsthāna - special therapy.
VII, VIII. *Siddhisthāna* - general therapy.

The *Suśruta-saṃhitā* consists of the following parts :

1. *Sūtrasthāna* - deals with general questions. In it we are informed that Suśruta was a pupil of king Divodāsa of Vārāṇasī.
2. *Nidānasthāna* - pathology,
3. *Śārīrasthāna* - anatomy and embryology,
4. *Cikitsāsthāna* - therapeutics,
5. *Kalpasthāna* - toxicology.

The *Uttaratantra* appears to be a later addition intended to be a supplement.

In this connection, it should be mentioned that some Tantras also prescribe various drugs, mostly herbal, some chemical, and elixirs, for a number of diseases in general, of diseases of males, females and children. Noteworthy among such Tantras are the following :

Ādiyāmala, Ādityayāmala, Arkaprakāśa, Aśvinītantra, Bhāvaprakāśa, Bhogatantra, Bījacintāmaṇi, Ḍāmaratantra, Gāruḍītantra, Gaurīkāñcalikā, Indrajālatantra, Kāmaratna, Kumāratantra, Mahākālatantra, Matsyasūkta, Matsyatantra, Nāgārjunatantra, Nīlatantra, Phetkāratantra, Prayogacintāmaṇi, Rudrayāmala, Śaṣṭhītantra, Tārāpradīpa, Toḍalatantra, Uḍḍīśatantra, Vārāhītantra, Videhatantra, Yāmalatantra, Yoginītantra.

The Buddhist literature also reveals its familiarity with the medical science. Medical information has been mixed with religion by the Buddhists. The *Bhaiṣajyavastu,* a part of volume III of the *Gilgit Manuscripts,* contains instructions on the use and dosage of medicinal drugs, classification of herbal drugs, the useful parts of various plants, etc. The *Cīvaravastu* (part 2, volume 3 of the *Gilgit Manuscripts*) describes the medical training of Jīvaka, a contemporary of the Buddha and physician of king Bimbisāra. If the account is true, then it can be presumed that the following medical matters were known :

Surgery, like *Kapālamocana* (removal of a part of the skull and reaching the brain), optical surgery, curetting of the cervical region, removal of vaginal tumour, treatment of dropsy, internal tumours, varicose vein, eye-diseases, etc.

Ancient India did not think of curing the diseases of humans only. Treatises were composed dealing with the ailments of animals, birds and even of plants. The cow was the most useful animal. No wonder, therefore, that much was written about bovine diseases and their remedies. The encyclopaedia of medical knowledge, entitled *Rājamārtaṇḍa,* by Bhoja (11th cent.), refers to a *Gavāyurveda* by Gotama. It appears to have been exclusively devoted to cow-diseases and their remedies. The *Agnipurāṇa* (*c.* 9th cent. A.D.) deals (ch. 292) with the treatment of diseases of cows. The *Viṣṇudharmottara Purāṇa* (II.43.1-27) also deals with this subject.

In veterinary science, the *Hastyāyurveda* or *Pālakāpya-saṃhitā*, attributed to sage Pālakāpya of unknown date, deals elaborately with elephant diseases and their treatment.

Horses also received the careful attention of several writers. The aforesaid *Agnipurāṇa* quotes excerpts from *Śālihotra-saṃhitā*. Some think that it was redacted by Kalhaṇa (12th cent.) under the title *Śālihotra-samuccaya*. Other noteworthy versions are the *Aśvavaidyaka* of Jayadattasūri and *Aśvaśāstra* of Nakula. Bhoja's medical encyclopaedia quotes passages from *Haya-līlāvatī-nāmasaṃgraha* by Jayadeva, *Vāji-cikitsāsaṃgraha* by Jayadatta and *Sārasaṃgraha*, an anthology by Nakula, based on different works on this subject.

At least one work, called *Śyainikaśāstra*,[33] attributed to Rudradeva or Candradeva or Rudracandradeva, and assigned by Haraprasād Sāstri to a period not later than the 17th cent., deals incidentally with the diseases, and the treatment of the bird called *Śyena* (falcon). Such birds were used by kings in hunting other birds.

That a medical science, relating to plants, developed quite early is attested by the terms *Vṛkṣāyurveda*, *Gulmavṛkṣāyurveda* occurring in such ancient works as the *Arthaśāstra* (4th cent. B.C.; according to a recent scholar, 2nd cent. A.D.) *Agnipurāṇa* (*c.* 9th cent.) and *Bṛhatsaṃhitā* (5 th or 6th cent.). Diseases of plants and their treatment have been discussed mainly in the Vṛkṣāyurveda chapter of the *Bṛhatsaṃhitā*, the *Agnipurāṇa* (ch. 281) and in the *Upavanavinoda* chapter of the *Śārṅgadhara-paddhati*.

In India, the Unāni medical system thrived side by side with the indigenous Āyurvedic system, as we shall see in our observations on foreign influence on Indian medical science.

The allopathic and homoeopathic medical systems were introduced by the westerners.

Besides works on Āyurveda, there were also treatises on Alchemy or Rasaśāstra.[34] It aimed mainly at prevention or deferment of senile decay, rejuvenation and prolongation of life. It gave some recipes also for the treatment of some diseases.

The chief ingredients, according to this system, were mercury (*Rasarāja* or *Pārada*) and base metals like copper transmuted to gold.

In Alchemy, the Buddhist Nāgārjuna (134-194 A.D.) figures most prominently. The *Rasaratnākara* is attributed to him. Several later writers composed works on this science.

There is historical evidence of the use of Alchemy. Hiuen Tsang (stay in India 630-645 A.D.) refers to it. Akbar (1556-1605) is said to have learnt it. The Venetian traveller, Marco Polo attributed (1280 A.D.) the high longevity of the Indians to a drink containing sulphur and quick silver used twice a month.

ASTRONOMY, ASTROLOGY[35]

ASTRONOMY

Elements of astronomy are found in the Vedic Saṃhitās. The *Ṛgveda* mentions *Nakṣatras.* In the *Yajurveda,* we get, for the first time, the mention of the whole series of *Nakṣatras,* 27 or 28 in number, headed by *Kṛttikās.* This Veda also contains details of *Darśa - purṇamāsa* (new and full moon sacrifices), *Cāturmāsya* (the four monthly sacrifices). In connection with *Mahāvrata* rites, the importance of winter solstice is stressed. The *Yajurveda* also deals with *Gavām Ayana* and *Sattras* to be performed in fixed periods. The *Sāmaveda* contains information about the aforesaid *Gavām Ayana* and *Sattras.* The *Atharvaveda* contains stray reference to solar eclipse, *Rāhu* (for the first time), intercalary month and a list of 28 *Nakṣatras* including *Abhijit.* Moreover, this Veda contains cosmogonic hymns, the glorification of the sun, and the personification of time as a primeval power—all related to astronomy.

The Brāhmaṇa literature, which is another constituent of the Veda, also contains astronomical elements. The Brāhmaṇas of the *Sāmaveda,* dealing with *gavām Ayana* and *Sattras,* are interesting from the standpoint of calendrical astronomy. Through *Mahāvrata* rites, they stress the importance of winter solstice. Dealing as they do with the exposition of sacrificial texts, they bring out the embryonic astronomical ideas of the Saṃhitās.

Coming to the *Sūtras*, belonging to the *Kalpa* Vedāṅga, we find astronomical ideas emerging more clearly, particularly in respect of Vedic calendars. The *Sūtras* lay down different modes of year-reckoning and calendar-keeping. In this respect, the *Lāṭyāyana-śrautasūtra* and the *Nidānasūtra* of the *Sāmaveda* deserve special mention.

The earliest work, devoted exclusively to astronomy, is a treatise of Vedāṅga (accessory of the Veda) called *Jyotiṣa Vedāṅga,* preserved in two recensions, one each for the *Yajurveda* and the *Ṛgveda.* It discusses the following matters; a calendar arranged on the basis of a five-year *Yuga,* with year of the duration of 366 days, position of the sun and the moon at the solstices, new and full moon related to the *Nakṣatras.*

Further development of some degree is attested by works like the following :

The fragmentary *Gārgısaṃhitā,* another fragmentary work of Pauṣkarasādin (Weber MS.), the *Nakṣatra* and other supplements of the *Atharvaveda,* the *Paitāmaha-siddhānta* mentioned by Varāhamihira, astronomical hints of the *Vṛddhagarga-saṃhitā.* Some light on ancient Indian astronomy is thrown by some Jaina works the chief of which is the *Sūryaprajñapti,* the epics, Purāṇas, Smṛtis and old writers like Parāśara known from fragments.

The above sources betray ignorance of the mean notions of the sun and moon resulting in the wrong calculation of the duration of years and months. They are devoid of the knowledge of true motion as distinguished from mean motion. They tell us of an equal daily increase or decrease of the length of the day, divide the sphere into 27 or 28 *Nakṣatras.* They, however, appear to have queer ideas about the constitution of the earth and the universe. We are not in a position to determine the precise age of the above sources.

The aforesaid sources reveal two useful ideas; (1) the conception of great *Yugas* during which a complete change of heavenly bodies takes place; (2) conception of the lunar day, called *Tithi*, which is the thirtieth part of a synodical month.

In the post-Vedic period, the first great astronomer was Varāhamihira (d. 587). In his *Bṛhatsaṃhitā*, he has mentioned quite a number of astronomers like Garga, Parāśara, etc., thus indicating the cultivation of this science for a long period preceding him; some may have been his contemporaries. Most of the astronomers, named by Varāha, exist in name only while glimpses of the writings of others are available in references to or quotations from their works.

Traditionally there were eighteen treatises, called *Siddhāntas* (conclusions or final solutions), on this science. Most of them are lost. The *Sūryasiddhānta*, as summarised by Varāha and as improved by writers, exists. The salient features of four other Siddhāntas have been set forth by Varāha. These are *Paitāmaha, Vāśiṣṭha, Pauliśa* and *Romaka*. These, along with the *Sūryasiddhānta*, are included in his *Pañcasiddhāntikā*.

Varāhamihira's *Bṛhatsaṃhitā* is by far the best known among the works on astronomy. It deals also with astrology. Besides Varāhamihira, the prominent astronomers were Āryabhaṭa (b. 476), Bhāskara (*c.* 600 A.D.), Brahmagupta (*c.* 598 A.D.), Āryabhaṭa II (*c.* 950 A.D.), Bhāskara II (b. 1114 A.D.).

There exist several commentaries some of which are anonymous. The most famous commentator was Bhaṭṭotpala (966 A.D.).

The main topics, discussed in the works on mathematical astronomy, are as follows :

The sphere and the coordinates, direction, place and time.

(The sphere and some important Great Circles; Coordinates, Latitude, Zenith, Distance and Declination, As censional difference or *Cara*).

The *Ahargaṃa* and the method of computing the mean longitudes of planets.

Planetary theories

(Eccentric Model, Epicyclic Model, Inequality of the Sun, Planetary schemes).

Size of the sun and moon, their distance from earth, eclipse and parallax.

Astronomical Instruments

(Water-clock or clepsydra, *Śaṅku* or Gnomon, *Cakra* or Circle, *Cāpa, Dhanus, Kartari, Turīya, Golayantra* or ārmillary sphere).

It may be noted that Sawāi Jai singh tried to develop observational astronomy in India towards the end of the 17th cent. and beginning of the 18th. For this purpose, he used two kinds of instruments, viz. metallic ones as were used by Muslim astronomers and masonry instruments which he himself designed and made.

ASTROLOGY

We meet with the following Sanskrit words denoting astrologer : *Sāṃvatsara, Jyautiṣika, Daivajña, Gaṇaka, Mauhūrtika, Mauhūrta, Jñānī, Kārtāntika.* From the Vedic age onward, we meet with astrologers in the Indian society. The Brāhmaṇas and *Sūtras* attest the belief in a lucky star. According to Dharmasūtras, an astrologer is a must among the royal employees. Astrologers are included, in the *Arthaśāstra,* among the royal functionaries of lower rank. The soothsayer is indispensable in war. He will predict the result from the signs, encourage the army, and terrify the enemy.

That astronomy and astrology were quite popular is borne out by the fact that Varāhamihira divides Jyotiṣa into three branches; viz. (1) astronomical and mathematical foundations called *Tantra*. (2) Horoscopes, called *Horā.* (3) Natural astrology, called *Samhitā.*

The early Buddhists, however, denounced astronomy and astrology, particularly the latter. Their literature contains the term *nakṣatra-pāṭhaka* (a reader of stars) denoting both astronomer and astrologer. The Buddha contemptuously referred to astronomy and astrology as *tiracchānavijjā* (low kind of learning), and prohibited the study of these subjects for the monks.[36] This attitude mellowed later on, and the *bhikṣus*, living in the forests, were asked to learn the elements of astronomy.

The most well-known work on astrology is the *Bṛhajjātaka* of Varāhamihira. It deals, in 25 chapters, with the *Horā* section of astrology. That there were other writers preceding him is proved by the fact that he cites, among the authorities, Asita, Devala, Garga, Vṛddha Garga, Nārada and Parāśara. Of the fragments of such earlier works, the most important are those of the *Vṛddha-garga-saṃhitā* or *Gārgī Saṃhitā* supposedly belonging to the first century B.C. The *Bṛhatsaṃhitā*, referred to earlier, is undoubtedly more important in view of the fact that it deals with both astronomy and astrology.

Several astrological works were composed after Varāhamihira. But, these are of no consequence. It is interesting to note that the astrological work *Jyotirvidābharaṇa* is traditionally attributed to Kālidāsa. But, it is actually an apocryphal work.[37] In this connection, we should note also the works of the Tājika class, notably Nīlakaṇṭha's *Tājika* (1587).[38]

ARCHITECTURE[39]

The earliest traceable remains of Indian civilisation have been unearthed in the Indus Valley, mainly at Mohenjodāro and Harappā. Generally believed to date back to the third millennium B.C., it was an urban civilisation. The relics reveal highly developed architecture. There are two-storied buildings with several rooms, bath and a very good system of drainage.

References to architectural work in the Vedic age are not very clear. The terms *Pastya* (*Ṛgveda* X. 96.11) *Chardi* (*Rv.* I.48.15) *Harmya* (*Rv.* VII.55.6) indicate that buildings of different types were constructed in that age. The word *pura*, denoting city, occurs in the *Ṛgveda*. Both bricks and clay were probably used in making houses. In those of the latter type, reeds appear to have been plastered with clay. Stone-walls were also probably in use.

The *Rāmāyaṇa* (present from, *c.* 2nd or 3rd cent. A.D.) testifies to highly developed architecture. The terms *prāsāda, vimāna, harmya* and *saudha* perhaps refer to different types of palaces or mansions. *Prāsādas* are described as *saptabhauma* (seven-storied), *aṣṭabhauma* (eight-storied), *anekabhauma* (multi-storied). Thousand-columned palaces are mentioned (V. 15.16, VI.39.22). There are references to decorated arches (*torana*); one kind of *toraṇa* was named *jālatoraṇa* (latticed arch ?), V. 2.53. Besides living rooms, there is mention of *Yajñaśālā* (sacrificial hall), *agniśālā* (fire-chamber), *devāyatana* (temple of god) and *Caitya.*[40] We have references to brick (*iṣṭaka*) and *sudhā* (whitewash). *Śilāgṛha* (V.41.19) perhaps means a house made of stones. The terms *sthapati, vardhaki* and *takṣaka* appear to denote different types of architects. The Kiṣkindhākāṇḍa (canto 51) narrates the story of how Maya acquired the knowledge of *Śilpaśāstra* (science of architecture). The legend refers also to the treatise of Maya.[41]

The *Mahābhārata* also contains copious references to architecture. Despite exaggerations and poetic hyperboles, an idea of the types of architecture, in vogue in ancient times, can be formed. The Ādiparvan (184) describes the hall in which Draupadī's self-choice of husband (*svayaṃvara*) was held. It is described as surrounded by palaces, decorated with *toraṇas* (arches). Ādi 207/41-48 refer to artificial sporting hills in the city. The assembly-hall of the Pāṇḍavas are stated to have been built in such a way that it could be shifted (Sabhā, I.13, III.28). This epic also refers to the architectural achievement of demon Maya.[42] Besides columns, the skill of building palaces was well-known among the architects (Sabhā, XI.14). In the description of the nether world, there is mention of various kinds of *prāsāda, harmya, valabhī* (turret), etc. (Ādi, III.133). A multiroomed building is referred to in Udyoga (89/11,12).

Coming to the historical period, we find a city built, at the time of Bimbisāra, in the sixth century B.C. The huge rampart, with the palace inside, stands as a monument to the architectural skill of ancient India.

There are specimens of the architecture of the Buddhist age which extended roughly from the sixth century B.C. to about the fourth-fifth cent. A.D. These are columns, *stūpas* (topes), *Caityas* (places of worship) and *Vihāras* (monasteries) found mostly at Sārnāth, Uttar Pradesh, Bihar, Sānchi, Bharhut, Takṣaśilā, etc. and deserve special mention in this connection.

Then we come to the Gupta age. Though this age extended from *c.* 320-510, yet the Gupta style of architecture continued up to about the 13th cent. A.D. Numerous structures are scattered in Orissa, Khajurāho, Rājasthān, Gujarāṭ and Mahārāṣṭra. The temples of Bhuvaneswar, Puri, particularly the famous Sun-temple (13th cent.) of Konārak stand as glorious monuments to artistic architectural style. In course of time, two distinct styles developed in north India and in the south. Generally, the former was called *Nāgara*[43] and the latter *Drāviḍa.*[44] These two styles were differentiated mainly on the basis of temple-architecture. In the south Indian works on architecture, there is mention of another style, called *Vesara.*[45] According to some, *Vesara* is divided into two types, viz. *Āndhra* and *Kāliṅga.* That temple architecture was very highly developed and sophisticated is attested by the fact that some works on *Śilpaśāstra* mention several styles, called *Lāṭa, Vairāṭa, Bhūmija,* etc. In the works, called *Śilparatna* and *Iśānagurudeva-paddhati,* mention is made of twenty types of temples. These are *Brahmacchanda, Viṣṇucchanda, Indracchanda* and *Rudracchanda* etc. In some later works, the names *Brahmakānta, Viṣṇukānta,* etc. also are found.

Some Purāṇas, e.g. *Garuḍa, Bhaviṣya, Skanda, Nārada, Liṅga,* contain some information about architecture. We meet with *harmya* (mansion), *prāsāda* (palace), temples, cities, etc. in the Purāṇas. They deal exhaustively with temples.

At one place, we get the names of five principal or basic kinds (*Prakṛitis*) of temples, called *Vairāja, Puṣpaka, Kailāsa, Mālika, Tripiṣṭapa.* Their *vikṛtis* or variations are stated to be of forty kinds. *Maṇḍapas* are stated to be of three kinds - *Catuṣkoṇa* (rectangular), *Aṣṭakoṇa* (octagonal) and *Ṣoḍaśakoṇa* (16-cornered). Again, these are stated (*Matsya* 270, 12-6) to be threefold, viz. *Jyeṣtha* (large), *Madhya* (medium-sized) and *Kaniṣtha* (small). In all, twenty-seven varieties of *Maṇḍapas* are mentioned. *Prāsādas* or palaces are stated (e.g. *Matsya,* 254/17 ff.) to be of five kinds. Of these, the best one is 108 cubits wide. In connection with military affairs, six kinds of forts are mentioned. With regard to town-planning, the Purāṇas provide that a city, rectangular, square, circular or semi-circular, covering a space of one, half or one-fourth *Yojana* (1 *Yojana* = 4 *Krośas* = 8 or 9 miles), should have enclosing ramparts with doors on all sides. The *Vāyu* (8/122) provides that a city will have a surrounding drain, one step wide.

The origin of Indian temples is veiled in obscurity. There is a view that Buddhist *Stūpas* served as models. Whatever that might be, the temples reveal a good deal of independent characteristics. The temples, with *Śikharas,* were of a definitely later origin. There is difference of opinion as to the date and extent of the influence of north Indian architecture on the south Indian types. The fact, however, remains that, in course of time, the styles of both parts of India mixed with each other. According to some scholars, the Aryan temple-styles of the north were, to some extent, influenced by the architecture of the non-Aryans like Asura and Nāga.[46]

At present, various types of early temples are found all over India. Almost all of them date back to the sixth century A.D. or a later period. No structure of the earlier period is available. But, many scholars are inclined to think that temple architecture started in this country in the second or first cent. B.C.[47]

Dravidian architecture developed a distinct style. It prevailed in the region between the Vindhya hills and

Kanyākumārī (Cape Comorin), and spanned twelve centuries from the sixth century A.D. to the seventeenth. This architecture can be divided into five well-defined types, viz.

(Periods are approximate)

1. *Pallava* - 600 - 900 A.D.
2. *Cola* - 900 - 1150 A.D.
3. *Pāṇḍya* - 1150 - 1355 A.D.
4. *Vijaynagar* - 1350 - 1565 A.D.
5. *Mādurāi* or *Nāyaka* - 1565 - 1700 A.D.

The principal characteristics of the above types are as follows. The *Pallava* type is distinguished by *Ratha, Maṇḍapa* and decorative designs. The *Cola* temples are surrounded by walls the length of which is east-west. The entrance is in the middle of the eastern wall. The *Maṇḍapas* are single-storied. The roof is supported by columns. The importance of a temple depended on the height of the *Śikhara.* The *Pāṇḍya* temples are characterised by surrounding walls and special types of *Gopuram* (ornamental gateway). The straight portion of the *Gopuram* is generally stone-built, and adorned by images of deities. The *Śikhara* is made of brick, lime and sand. The *Vijaynagar* type is distinguished by the excellent workmanship of the columns. Dravidian architecture reached its zenith in the *Mādurā* type of temples. The special features of the *gopuram* in the Mīnākṣī temple deserve mention. The contemporaneous Rāmeśvara temple also reveals similar features. A lion-image, carved out of black granite, inside the temple, is almost common.

The temples, built in the Cālukya regime, in the seventh and eighth centuries, at Aiho, Badāmi, etc. reveal a mixed style. Some bear the characteristics of the Gupta styles, others are built in the *Pallava* style.

BOTANY[48]

The *Ṛgveda* reveals knowledge of the rich plant-kingdom. Ethnobotany seems to have been known in some form. The entire ninth book is addressed to an unidentified plant, called *Soma*, the juice of which has been lauded both as a sacrificial offering and as a stimulating drink. An entire hymn (X. 146) is addressed to Forest. The Ṛgvedic seer solemnly proclaims (X. 97.2, 4) gratitude to trees. It is interesting to note that such ancient texts as the *Ṛgveda* (X. 97.21), *Mahābhārata* (Śānti, 184) and *Manu-smṛti* (I. 49) reveal awareness about the consciousness of the plants - a fact which does not appear to have been known to the contemporary peoples of the East and the West. The ancient Indians were aware also of the sex of the trees and the process of procreation among them. The ancient Indians had some definite knowledge of the modes of treatment of plant diseases, as is evident from such works as the *Vṛkṣāyurveda* of Surapāla (11th cent. A.D.) and the *Vṛksāyurveda* section of the *Agnipurāṇa* (*c.* 9th century A.D.). Information on the following branches of botany can be gleaned from the different works of the ancient and medieval India :

Morphology (internal and external), plant physiology, Taxonomy and Ecology.

Such an early text as the *Taittirīya Saṃhitā* (V. 1.7.37) of the *Yajurveda* attests the knowledge of the rotation of crops.

Different methods of classification of the flora were known, *e.g.* Botanical classification, classification according to properties and classification based on food value. In accordance with the nature of the soil, in which trees grow, they are classified as *Jāṅgala* (arid) and *Anūpa* (marshy). Trees of the Mesophytes class have been mentioned as growing on common soil. The *Caraka-saṃhitā* (Sūtrasthāna - 28) classifies plants into six types in accordance with the food and drink yielded by them.

It is curious that botanical marvels of some sorts were produced in very remote ages. For instance, the *Upavanavinoda* chapter of the *Śārṅgadhara-paddhali* (13th cent.) lays down the process of producing fragrant flowers in plants producing flowers devoid of fragrance. We are also told that red cotton could be grown in trees yielding white cotton.

The Purāṇas reveal more advanced knowledge of botany. The *Vāyupurāṇa* (8.149-155) states seventeen types of *Oṣadhi* or annual plants withering away after the ripening of fruits. These are divided into three groups, viz. *grāmya* (rural), *āraṇya* (wild) and *grāmyāraṇya* (rural-cum-wild).

The *Mārkaṇḍeya Purāṇa* (49.67.68) also mentions seven varieties of *Oṣadhi*. The *Agni* (95.57-59) mentions the following kinds of *Vrīhi* (grains) :

godhūma, tila, māṣa, yava, nīvāra, śyāmāka.

The Purāṇas reflect intimate knowledge of ethnobotany.[49] The importance of plants has been stated in connection with the various necessaries of life, e.g. garment-making, cosmetics, and perfumes and beautifying materials, medicine for not only humans but also animals, military needs like weapon-making, religious rites, cleansing agents, gardens and bowers, furniture and other household appurtenances and building materials, food, alcoholic drinks, toxicological use, reproduction materials, materials for *Vaśīkaraṇa*, etc.

CHEMISTRY[50]

It developed mainly in connection with medical science. The medical chemists devoted themselves to the production of medicines to prolong life, aphrodisiacs, poison, drugs as antidotes to poison, alkalis, acids, metallic salts and intoxicants. They applied the chemical processes of calcination and distillation. Mercury was used to retard senile decay and as specific remedies for certain diseases. The celebrated Buddhist Nāgārjuna[51] (*c.* 2nd cent. A.D.) considerably advanced the knowledge of chemical compounds by preparations of mercury. A kind of gunpowder appears to have been discovered in ancient India.

Suśruta (later than Caraka who is believed to have flourished about the 2nd cent. A.D.) distinguishes two types of poison, viz. Vegetable and Animal. There was the knowledge about the formation of molecular qualities in chemical compounds and the chemistry of colours.

Varāhamihira (6th cent. A.D.), in his *Bṛhatsaṃhitā*, refers to several preparations of cement called *Vajralepa,* stated to last a thousand years (ch. LVI). He also refers to the composition of dyes and cosmetics (chs. XV, XVI). In ch. LXXVI on perfumery, he gives formulae for imitations of natural flowerscents.

In Sanskrit works, there are references to a chemical powder (*Yoga-cūrṇa*) inducing sleep, to a chemically prepared stick or wick which can generate light without fire (*Yogavartikā*), a powder paralysing the motor and sensory organs (*stambhanacūrṇa*).

Different writers mention composition and decomposition by chemical processes of calcination, distillation, sublimation, steaming, fixation, etc. Salt is either mineral or vegetable.

According to Caraka, colours, tastes, etc. of molecules of chemical compounds are the result of the collocation, in unequal proportion and unstable equilibrium, of the different forces latent in the atoms themselves. From the *Bṛhatsaṃhitā*, we learn of chimical processes for *Śilādāraṇ*, (cutting or crushing rocks), *Śastrapāna* (hardening of steel).

As regards the application of chemistry in connection with plants, we learn of the soil, chemically prepared, conducive to the growth of plants, general prophylactic, promotion of inflorescence and fructification by chemical processes.

Besides the *Rasaratnākara,* attributed to the aforesaid Nāgārjuna, there were several works on alchemy which was supposed to teach methods of turning base metals into gold and of rejuvenation, etc.

The Purāṇas vouchsafe for advanced knowledge of chemistry. Regarding the preparation of fragrant substances, as many as eight chemical processes have been laid down in the *Agnipurāṇa* (224.19-41). This Purāṇa (3-.12 ff) gives recipe for preparing some colours. Several kinds of wine are mentioned in some Purāṇas, e.g. *Matsya* (217.58), *Garuḍa* (174.77).

Some Purāṇas refer to several kinds of salt obtained from different sources. For example, the *Garuḍa* (174.18) mentions *pañcalavaṇa*. The *Matsya* also (217.60, 61) mentions some kinds of salt.

The *Garuḍa* (ch. 208), *Agni* (93) mention quite a number of chemical substances.

LIFE SCIENCE

There are divergent views as to how life came into being. According to the materialists, life is the result of peculiar chemical combinations of dead matter in organic forms. Sāṃkhya philosophy holds that life is not a *Vāyu* (bio-mechanical force) nor a mere mechanical motion resulting from the impelling force of *Vāyu*. It is a reflex activity, a resultant of the various concurrent activities of the *antaḥkaraṇas*. According to Vedānta, life is a kind of subtle rarefied ether-principle pervasive of the organism; it is not gross *Vāyu*, but a subtlised matter.

In the Purāṇas, living creatures have been classified according to different criteria. For example, the *Vāyu* (63/40) divides beings into two classes, viz. biped and quadruped. In accordance with their origin, creatures have been classified as *Jarāyuja* (born out of uterus), *Aṇḍaja* (born out of egg), *Svedaja* (born out of sweat, *i.e.* heat and moisture; *e.g.* ant, louse, etc.), *Udbhijja* (born out of plants and vegetables; *e.g.* firefly, tadpole, etc. (*Vāyu* 3/22).

Again, animals are divided as *Āraṇya* (wild) and *Grāmya* (rural) *Mārkaṇḍeya* 1.48/30; *Vāyu* 9/46-48.

Birds are classified as *Prasaha* (Preying upon other creatures and tearing them before eating), *Viṣkira* (eating grains etc. after scattering them), *Pratuda* (eating things after pecking them) *Vāyu* 69/336.

Aquatic creatures have been classified (*Vāyu* 294/297) as *Vṛtta* (full, circular), *Anuvrtta* (partly circular as frog), *Parāvṛtta* (slippery), *Śukti* (oyster), *Varāṭaka* (a kind of swan), *Śaṃkha* (conch), *Kālakūṭa* (aquatic poison), *Jalaukā* (leech), etc.

Among the creatures of the finny world are mentioned (*Vāyu* 69/292) :

Sahasradanta (thousand-toothed), *Makara* (shark), *Pāṭhīna* (a kind of fish), *Timi* (whale), *Rohita* (carp).

MATHEMATICS[52]

The two great factors, which led to the evolution of mathematics, were Vedic sacrifices and astronomy. The sacrifices required the construction of altars with absolute accuracy. This resulted in the development of geometry. The *Śulvasūtras,* a part of the Vedic *Kalpa* literature, are the earliest works on geometry not only in India, but, perhaps in the whole world. *Śulva* denotes the measuring string. These works originated several centuries before Christ, perhaps even before the Buddha. The *Āpastamba-Śulvasūtra* contains a generalised statement of what is known as the Pythagorean Theorem. It is not known whether or not the Indian mathematicians knew Pythagoras (6th cent. B.C.); but, the above idea was independent of Greek influence. The *Śulvasūtras* deal also with areas and volumes of a number of figures.

The greatest contribution of India to mathematics was the conception of zero (*śūnya*). The earliest reference to it was found in the Bakhshāli manuscript (400 A.D.). Its actual significance was probably realised sometime between the 8th and 9th century A.D.

The Vedic and Jain literatures distinguish between odd and even numbers, and classify the numbers, according to their values (*saṃkheya, Asaṃkheya* and *Ananta*). The extension of this classification led to the development of the position of numerals which proved to be an advantage in comparison with the Roman system, and gave rise to the decimal system of numbering. The above Bakhshāli manuscript, for the first time, expressed operation of fractions in terms of symbols. Bakhshāli manuscript and Āryabhaṭa[53] (b. 476 A.D.) refer to the rule of three. In the *Śulvasūtra,* surds are referred to.

One of the important discoveries was the determination of the value of π (*Pi*) Āryabhaṭa was the first to give the value of 3.1416 conveyed by the fraction 62832/20000. It was improved by later Indian mathematicians by correcting it to nine places of decimal.

Bhāskara[54] (b.*c.* 1114 A.D.) was the first to conceive and prove that X/0 is infinity.

The obligation to perform the Vedic rites at the precise point of time led to the rise of astronomy. This necessitated precise mathematical calculations.

METALLURGY

The knowledge of metallurgy as early as in prehistoric India is attested by the bronze sculptures, bands of gold etc., knives, axes, etc., unearthed in the site of the Indus Valley Civilisation.

The Vedic Saṃhitās also refer to ornaments and implements of metal.

From the passages, quoted in medieval works on medicine and *Rasāyana*, it appears that there was a science of metallurgy (*lohaśāstra*). The use of various metals an preparing Āyurvedic medicines presupposes a knowledge of calcination (*māraṇa*) and oxidisation (*jāraṇa*); knowledge of metallurgy was useful for making coins and various ornaments.

An engineering marvel, testifying to the ancient Indians' advanced knowledge of metallurgy is Sultānganj (Bihar) Buddha image made of copper cast in two layers over an inner core. Seventy feet high, weighing a ton, it dates back to about 400 A.D. Various articles in Indian bronze were made by what is called *Cire perdue* process.

Another engineering marvel is the Iron Pillar of Mehrauli near Delhi, which is over 1500 years old and is nearly 23 ft. in height. Consisting of a single piece, it is of an extraordinary size and weight.

In some works, we find instructions for making hard metals soft and for increasing the strength of metals.

PHYSICS

The elements of physics, known in ancient India, are as follows. Even at the time of the Buddha, or perhaps earlier, the objects of the universe were classified into several elements, viz. earth, air, fire and water. The orthodox Hindu schools and the Jainas added a fifth element, viz. ether (*ākāśa*). Most of the schools hold that the elements, other than ether, are composed of atoms (*paramāṇu*). According to the Jainas, all atoms are similar; the differences in the elements are due to the differences in the manner of the combination of the atoms. The atomic speculations are found in Vaiśeṣika philosophy.

In the field of acoustics, we find considerable development in Indian music. Quite early as many as 22 *Śrutis* or quarter tones were distinguished. Their proportions were measured with great precision. The Mīmāṃsaka philosophers distinguished three elements in the analysis of sound. These are *Nāda* (a quality of the air, which is the physical basis of audible sound), *Dhvani* (audible sound) and *Sphoṭa* (transcendental or intelligible sound).

According to the early writers on Nyāya philosophy, the sound-wave (*śabdasantāna*) has its substratum in ether (*ākāśa*) and not in air (*vāyu*). According to later writers, sound is not a mode of motion (*parispanda*), because ether, the substratum, is incapable of motion. In analysing vibratory motion, the writers hold that molecules of a bell vibrate when the bell is struck. Echo (*pratidhvani*) was considered to be a reflection of sound. Different kinds of sound were differentiated from one another by means of pitch (*tāra*-loud, high, shrill; *mandra*-low, etc.), intensity (*tīvra, manda,* etc.) and timbre (*asādhāraṇa dharma*). The pitch of a note was held to be inversely proportional to the length of a wire.

INDIAN EPIGRAPHY - A NOTE[55]

As we shall see in course of our study, Indian epigraphy spread abroad in many countries, *e.g.* Central Asia, Ceylon,

Burma, Siam (Thailand), Mālay Peninsula, Indonesia, Cambodia, South Annam. So, it is necessary to acquaint the reader with the history and nature of epigraphy in India.

Indian epigraphy has a long history harking way back to pre-Christian times. The earliest available inscription is the first Rock Edict of Aśoka (*c.* 273-32 B.C.), at Girnar, Junāgarh State, Kāthiāwād. (See D.C. Sircar, *Select Inscriptions*, I, p. 16). It is written in Prākrit language and Brāhmī script.

The existing epigraphic records fall broadly into two categories, viz. those issued by or on behalf of rulers and those issued on behalf of private individuals or organisations. The inscriptions of the first category may be classified as

(i) royal edicts,

(ii) those proclaiming some glorious deeds of kings in eulogies in the form of *Kāvya* or *Praśasti*,

(iii) those recording the grant of endowments to Brāhmaṇas or other deserving persons or officials or to religious institutions,

(iv) Miscellaneous.

As regards the manner, in which the inscriptions are written, generally an inscription begins and ends with an auspicious symbol or word or passage adoring a deity. The words *Siddham* and *Svasti* are commonly found in the beginning. In many inscriptions, *Siddham* was represented by a symbol. Some such symbols are *Svastika, Triratna* (trident-on-wheel), *Śrīvatsa*, the tree-in-railing; some symbols in early inscriptions are unidentified.

Generally, the names of the author, writer and engraver of a record are mentioned. Sometimes, inscriptions record the regnal year, season, month, day, fortnight, lunar mansion, etc.

As for materials, those used for writing or scratching consisted in Palmyra leaves, Birch and Aloe Bark, cloth and hide, paper and wood. Materials for engraving or embossing were stone, earthen objects, shells and other non-metallic objects, copper, gold, silver, bronze, iron and other metals.

The following languages were used in inscriptions :

Old and Middle Indo-Aryan - Sanskrit, Prākrit, Neo-Indo-Aryan-Mārāṭhī, Hindi and its dialects and allied languages, Gujarāṭi, Kashmiri and allied dialects, Oriya, Bengali, Assamese.

In the areas, where Neo-Indo-Aryan languages are in use, Sanskrit was generally used in records in the early medieval period. Independent Hindu rule was supplanted by the Muslims in wide areas. Wherever, in this area, independent or semindependent Hindu rulers flourished during the late medieval period, there was occasional use of the regional languages in their official records.

Of the Neo-Indo-Aryan languages, Mārāṭhī appears to have been the first to be used in epigraphs. One of the earliest specimens of the epigraphical use of this language is Marmuri Copper-plate grant (974 A.D.) of Cālukya prince Satyāśraya. See *Jour. Bom. Hist. Soc.*, II, p. 214.

Dravidian - Tamil, Kannada (Kanarese).

Some Tāmil records, dating from about the second and third centuries A.D., appear to be the earliest specimens of regional language used in inscription. (See D.C. Sircar, *Indian Epigraphy*, p. 46).

Telugu, Mālayālam and Ṭulu.

As regards script, both *Kharoṣṭhī* and *Brāhmī* are found in the inscriptions. *Kharoṣṭhī* was an Indian modification of the Aramaic script introduced in the region, now known as Peshawar and Hazara districts of Pakistan. An important inscription of Aśoka is the Kāndāhār bilingual epigraph in two versions, Greek and Aramaic.[56] It should be noted that Kharoṣṭhī ceased to be used in inscriptions before the 6th century A.D. in the north-western regions of India, as also in Afghanistan. The latest Kharoṣṭhī inscriptions are two Taxila records of about the 5th cent. A.D.[57] In later times, derivatives of the Brāhmī script, *e.g.* Nāgarī, Oriyā, Bengali, were used in the different regions.

The commonly used eras, found in Indian inscriptions, are those, reckoned according to the regnal years. These are *Vikrama, Śaka, Lakṣmaṇa Saṃvat.* A particular year is generally indicated by certain words standing for some figures which are to be read from the right to the left. Some words, which stand for particular numerals, are as follows :

0. *Gagana, Kha,* etc.
1. *Indu, bhū,* etc.
2. *Yama, netra,* etc.
3. *Rāma, guṇa,* etc.
4. *Veda, sāgara,* etc.
5. *Bāṇa, bhūta,* etc.
6. *Rasa, Kāraka, darśana*
7. *Nāga, aśva,* etc.
8. *Vasu, dikpāla,* etc.
9. *Dvāra, ratna,* etc.
10. *Diś, aṅguli,* etc.

It is interesting to note that, in some cases, mere letters were used to indicate numbers, a method introduced by Āryabhaṭa who composed his *Āryabhaṭīya* in 499 A.D. For example, the 25 consonants, from *Ka* to *Ma,* respectively indicate 1 to 25. The 8 letters, from *Ya* to *Ha* indicate respectively 30, 40, 50, 60, 70, 80, 90, 100.

Aśoka's inscriptions have been discovered in the Peshawar and Hazara districts of Pakistan. Among records from the Afghanistan region, mention may be made of the inscriptions of the times of Menander (reign *c.* 160-140 B.C.) and Vijayamitra found in the Bajaur tribal territory and the vase inscription of Huviska's (reign *c.* 162-180 A.D.) time from Khawat (Wardak) about 30 miles to the west of Kābul

In Indo-Muslim epigraphy, Arabic and Persian scripts were used. Such inscriptions are available from the last decade of the 12th century A.D. The largest number of Indo-Muslim inscriptions appear to have been written in the 16th and 17th centuries. Inscriptions of this kind are usually found on mosques, tombs and other religious buildings. These generally record the dates of their construction or repair often with the names of the reigning ruler, the builder or repairer.

Besides stone inscriptions, there are Indo-Muslim inscriptions on weapons, seals, signets, vases, vessels, precious stones, etc. A few copper plates with inscriptions have been found, but these were not many.

Most of the Indo-Muslim inscriptions are written in the Persian language, many are in Arabic while some are partly in Arabic, partly in Persian. In some cases, there is a mix of Arabic or Persian and Sanskrit or a regional language like Mārāṭhī, Kannada or Telugu. One trilingual inscription is also there. It is written in Persian, Sanskrit and Gujarāṭi (Vide *Bulletin of Baroda Museum*, 1953-55, p. 73 f.f.).

Barring a few, the Arabic inscriptions are in prose.

Arabic and Persian epigraphy in India are, besides being historically interesting, have importance from the point of view of palaeography and calligraphy. The usual scripts in the Muslim epigraphy are *Kufie, Nastal'liq* and *Naskh* including its variety called Thulth. Each of these was executed with fine penmanship.

BUDDHA AND BUDDHISM[58]

Among the great religions of the world, Buddhism ranks very high. Its architect, Gautama the Buddha (Enlightened one), has been regarded as one of the great men the world has ever seen.

Scion of a royal family, Gautama or Siddhārtha, was a boy with a difference. After his birth, the soothsayers predicted that he would renounce the world. Naturally worried, his royal father asked his men to keep the young Gautama, his only son and future successor, always involved in all the pleasures of life. But, destiny decreed otherwise. As he was going to the pleasure-garden in a chariot, some sights on the way created a stir in his soul, and an aversion to the luxuries of life. One day, he saw an old man, a decrepit, who could hardly move. On being told by the charioteer that this condition is inevitable in everyone's life, Gautama ordered him to drive back to the palace. On another occasion, he saw, on the way, a man afflicted with a fatal malady. The young Gautama, on learning that disease is unavoidable in life, went back. Again, he saw a dead man, and was told that death is the ineluctable end of human life. With a sense of disgust, he went back. On the fourth occasion, he met a wandering mendicant who renounced worldly life. This sight stirred his soul, and he found in ascetism the correct and peaceful way of life. One night, the prince, having left behind his wife, a paragon of beauty, and his little son, Rāhula, sneaked away from the palace in the stillness of night.

The prince, instead of being confined to the four walls of the palace, was now a free man in the free world. Urged by a burning desire to find out the means of averting the ills of life, he travelled widely meeting the wise and the learned people of the day. But, his restless soul found no peace. Then, he took to self-mortification abstaining from food and other practices essential for keeping the body and soul together. Emaciated and enfeebled by unwonted hardship, he realised that it was not the correct way of solving the problem that haunted him. He resumed the normal life, and started meditating under a tree. Long and absorbing meditation resulted in the dawning of enlightenment (*bodhi*); and he attained *Nirvāṇa* (extinction of anger, delusion, desire, etc.), the highest goal of life.

He started preaching his sermons. Soon he had a large number of followers. Thus, a Buddhist community was formed.

Though born in a family, following the Brāhmaṇical religion, yet the Buddha broke away from the conventional beliefs and practices. He was a dissident, a maverick. He raised a voice of protest against the traditional Brāhmaṇical order. He denied the authority of the Vedas, and the conventional rites and rituals, condemned animal-sacrifice. As regards God, he was agnostic. He urged his followers not to idle away time in the fruitless discussion on the indeterminable question of the existence of gods. He advised them to be rational, and used to say that the humans are the architects of their own destiny. Instead of rites and rituals, he preached certain ethical doctrines. Four noble truths (*Ārya satya*) form the corner-stone of the mighty edifice of Buddhism. These are in order *Duḥkha* (sorrow, misery), *Samudaya* (root or source), *Nirodha* (suppression), *Mārga* (way). The idea is that, having realised that earthly existence is full of misery, one should find out the source of suffering. Having ascertained the source, one should suppress it by the proper means.

The Master prescribed an ethical recipe designed to make a person's life peaceful and social life happy. The path, he pointed out, consists in eightfold practice (*aṣṭāṅgika mārga*). These eight are modes of disciplining one's *śīla* (conduct, character), *citta* (mind) and *prajñā* (intellect). The eightfold path is as follows :

Right (qualifies each of the following words)

Speech, action, occupation, effort, recollection, meditation, resolution, view.

According to the Buddha, the highest mental status and bliss can be acquired by practising the following :

Maitrī (love towards all), *Karuṇā* (compassion),
Muditā (to feel delight at others' happiness) and
Upekṣā (equanimity in favourable and adverse circumstances).

The term *Pañcaśīla,* which is now-a-days frequently heard in international politics,[59] originated in the Buddhist scripture. It includes the following five rules of daily conduct, prescribed by the Buddha, for the householders :

1. Abstention from the killing of creatures.
2. To desist from theft.
3. Avoidance of adultery.
4. Avoiding falsehood.
5. Not to use intoxicants.

Buddhism is essentially monastic. It requires its adherents to be devoted and loyal to *Triratna* or the three gems in the form of the Buddha, *Dharma* and *Saṃghà* (brotherhood of monks, the monastic order).

HĪNAYĀNA AND MAHĀYĀNA

The doctrine of the Buddhists of the Theravāda school was known as Hīnayāna. In course of time, there was a strong protest against this doctrine from a section of the Buddhists; this protestant faith came to be known as Mahāyāna. The date of origin of the Mahāyāna cannot be precisdy determined. Certain historical evidences point to its origin around the first century B.C. This doctrine made its first appearance in Andhra; this was a centre of the Mahāsāṅghikas. The Mahāyāna doctrine gradually earned popularity, and was recognised as a distinct form of Buddhism at the time of Kaniṣka. Within the second century A.D. it spread over the whole of north India and through the efforts of Nāgārjuna, Āryadeva, Asaṅga and Vasubandhu, was placed on a firm footing.

The broad differences between Hīnayāna and Mahāyāna are as follows. Some hold that, in the latter, there were certain secret teachings which the Buddha imparted only to a select group of pupils. Besides, in it some dogmas of the earlier school have been controverted. Both these are partly true. Certain dogmas of the Mahāyāna school are diametrically opposed to those contained in the Pāli canonical works. The jejune metaphysics of the Hīnayāna and the rigours of austerities taught in it failed to appeal to the heart of the masses.

To the Buddhists of the Mahāyāna school the Buddha was not a mere man; he was a superman, nay, an adorable deity. According to them, a man might be an Arhat by rigorous self-restraint and hard penance. The adherents of this school took Bodhisatta, the saviour of mankind, as a greater ideal than even an Arhat. Greater stress was laid by them on Karuṇā than on Paññā on which the earlier Buddhists put the greatest emphasis. The moral philosophy of a few Hīnayānists was turned into a universal religion by the Mahāyānists. The principal means of the new school was devotion (*Bhakti*) in place of the abstruse metaphysics of the earlier school. The eternal principles of the latter were negative while, in the hands of the former, these were positive. The edge of pessimism was considerably blunted in the Mahāyāna school; before the followers of this school there arose the prospect of a heaven full of bliss.

The Hīnayānists look down upon the other school. According to the former, the latter is a distortion of the teachings of the Buddha. The Mahāyānists look upon their point of view as supplementary to those of the Hīnayānists. The followers of Mahāyāna think that Hīnayāna is an incomplete form of Buddhism, and is meant for only those who are not fit for access into the inmost recesses of this religion.

The principal features of the Mahāyāna are as follows :

(i) Realisation of the falsity of the phenomenal world besides the emptiness of Puggala (i.e. the non-existence of things like Ātman).

(ii) Comprehension of innumerable Buddhas and Bodhisattas.

(iii) Worship of gods and godesses. The Buddhists have recognised many of the deities of the Brahmanical pantheon.

(iv) The utility of Mantras as a means of liberation.

(v) The superiority of mind, *i.e.* all is mind. Man is born from his thought and what he finds around him is mind-born.

The Spread of Buddhism

From an account of the travels of the Buddha with a view to preaching his doctrines it is clear that, in his lifetime, Buddhism spread from Kajaṅgala and Campā in the east to Verañja and Avanti in the West. Besides, this religion found followers from Rājagṛha and Vārāṇasī to Kosāmbī, Śrāvastī and Sāketa in the north. Various tribes at the foot of the Himalayas also embraced this religion.

At the time of Aśoka, after the third Buddhist council, Buddhism began to be preached over wide areas. It spread in the regions from Kashmir in the north-west to Mysore in the south. It found a large number of followers also in Ceylon and Suvarṇabhūmi. The latter, perhaps, indicated Burma or the lands in the Far East. It is noteworthy that this religion, along with Aśoka's message, was carried even to the distant lands under the occupation of the Greeks.

The nearest neighbour of India, viz, Tibet, was one of the regions which adopted Buddhism quite early. In course of time, it spread over the whole of south-east Asia. Siam, Cambodia, China and Japan became the strongholds of this religion. Even to-day most people of these lands are Buddhists.

As Buddhism progressed, it developed its own philosophy which did not conform either to the orthodox Brāhmaṇical systems of philosophy or to the heterodox systems of the Jainas and the Cārvāka schools, Buddhist philosophy grew into four distinct schools, viz. Vaibhāṣika, Sautrāntika, Mādhyamika and Yogācāra. The highlights of the systems are as follows.

Vaibhāṣika is so called as it is based on the *Abhidhamma-mahāvibhāṣā.* According to it, the Buddha was an ordinary human being. By dint of Buddhahood he attained *Nirvāṇa* and by death *Mahāparinirvāṇa.* His divinity lay in his realisation of Supreme Truth without the help of others. In this doctrine, the existence of both mind and external objects is recognised. The knowledge about the phenomenal world is obtained directly and not by inference.

The Sautrāntika derives its name from the *Suttapiṭaka* comprising many texts called *Suttanta.* It differs from the above in its view that knowledge about external objects is obtained by inference.

The Mādhyamika owes its name to the fact that it steers clear of both the extremes of the complete unreality and the complete reality of external objects; it adopts the middle course. According to it *Śūnyatā* (literally meaning emptiness, vacuity, void) does not mean absolute emptiness; it indicates only the unreality of the phenomenal world; all real objects are not regarded as *Śūnya.* By *Śūnya* it means the indescribable nature of the phenomenal world. It is a sort of relativity. It believes that the existence of the Supreme Force, underlying the external world, can be realised only by *Nirvāṇa.* This force has not been denied as such; what is denied is its comprehensibility by the senses.

The Yogācāra is so called as it lays stress on *Yoga* (meditation) and *Ācāra* (correct conduct). Its fundamental stand is that it recognises the existence of mind alone. It regards the perception of the phenomenal world as only a mental attitude or impression. External objects have no foundation in reality. This doctrine is called *Vijñānavāda.* This system believes that the controlled mind is capable of dispelling the delusion about the external world and also attachment to it.

Besides *Śūnyavāda,* referred to above, two other doctrines are prominent in Buddhist philosophy. One is *Pratītyasamutpāda* and the other *Sarvāstivāda.* According to the former, whatever arises has a cause; for it is called the doctrine of dependent origination. For example, an earthen jar required a material cause (earth) and an efficient cause (potter). According to the latter, the existence of both external and internal objects is recognised.

FOOTNOTES

1. See J. Marshall, *Mohenjo-daro and the Indus Civilisation.*
2. See R.C. Majumdar, *Advanced History of India.*
3. Our principal source is *Bhārater Jāti paricay* (in Bengali) by B.S. Guha, Calcutta, 1949 (India Govt.'s Deptt. of Anthropology Publication, Vernacular Series No.1).

4. For language, see Burrow, *Sanskrit Language.* For literature, see Winternitz, *History of Indian Literature,* Vols. I, II, III, S.K. De and S.N. Das Gupta, *History of Sanskrit Literature.*
5. Cf. Pāṇini, III.4.6.
6. Cf. Pāṇini, III.4.9.
7. Pāṇini II.4.39, II.4.73, II.4.76, III.2.88, V.2.122, VI.1.34, VII.1.8, VII.1.10, 103; VII.3.97, VII.4.78.
8. According to the orthodox view, the hymns were visualised by *Ṛṣis* or seers; i.e. they were revealed to certain people.
9. The two, called *Śākala* and *Vāṣkala,* are most well-known.
10. The hymns are also divided into eight *Aṣṭakas,* each *Aṣṭaka* comprising eight *Adhyāyas* each of which contains some *vargas,* each usually consisting of five *Ṛks.*
11. See Chronological table.
12. As Viśvanātha says, a sentence, of which the essence is *rasa* (delectable sentiment like comic, erotic, etc.), is a *Kāvya* (*vākyaṃ rasātmakaṃ kāvyam - Sāhityadarpaṇa).*

    Thus, in Sanskrit, *Kāvya* does not necessarily denote a poetical composition; even a prose work or a drama can be a *Kāvya* provided it fulfils the above condition.
13. See Radhakrishnan, *Indian Philosophy,* 2 vols.
14. See. S.C. Banerji, *A Companion to Middle Indo-Aryan Literature,* Calcutta, 1977.
15. Derived variously by different scholars :
    (i) From *paṃkti* (lines of the Buddhist canonical texts).
    (ii) From *palli* (village); according to this view, Pāli represents the rural language.
    (iii) From *Pāṭaliputra;* Pāṭali-Pali-Pāli.
    (iv) From Palāśa, older name of Magadha.
    (v) A grammarian observes - *saddatthaṃ pāletīti pāli;* Pāli is so called as it preserves the import of words.
16. Variously explained. According to one view, *prakṛtiḥ saṃskṛtam, tatra bhavaṃ tata āgataṃ vā prākṛtam;* the basic language or Prakṛti is Sanskrit, and Prākṛta is derived from it. According to others, *Prakṛti* means nature, and *Prākṛta* means the natural language of the people as distinguished from *Saṃskṛta* or the refined language.

17. The extant work is a Pāli translation, done in Ceylon, of a Sanskrit or Prākrit original, now lost. There is a Chinese translation dating back to a period between the fourth and the fifth century A.D.

18. A.H. Dani, *Indian Paleography*, R. B. Pandey, *Indian Paleography*; D.C. Sircar, *Indian Paleography*.

19. Invented by God Brahmā or the script in which the Brahma or Veda is preserved and which was mainly used by Brāhmaṇas.

20. Formed from *Khara* (ass) and *Oṣṭha* (lip). The following derivative meanings have been suggested :
    (i) The inventor of the script was called Kharoṣṭha.
    (ii) Used by barbarous people (*Kharoṣṭhas*) like Yavana, Śaka, Tuṣāra, etc. inhabiting the north-western boundaries of India.
    (iii) *Kharoṣṭha* is the Sanskrit form of Kashgar in Central Asia, which was the latest centre of the script.
    (iv) *Kharoṣṭha* is the Indian adaptation of the Iranian word *Kharosta* or *Kharaposta* (ass-skin); probably the script originally used to be written on ass-skin.
    (v) *Kharoṣṭha* is the form assumed in Sanskrit from the Aramaic word Kharoṭṭha used for this script.

21. By India we mean India, Pakistan and Bangladesh, *i.e.* the pre-independence India.

22. Taken from I.J.S. Taraporewala's *Elements of the Science of Language*. For the distribution of the languages and dialects, see the above book.

23. See Taraporewala, *Elements of the Science of Language*, 1962, p. 212.

24. This particular language has been chosen not because of the author's special predilection for it, but because the author, himself a Bengali, is most familiar with this language.

25. For history of Indian music, see Prajñānānanda, *Historical Development of Indian Music*.

26. See. M. Bose, *Classical Indian Dancing*.

27. See A.K. Coomaraswami, *The Painter in Ancient India*; W.G. Archer, *Central Indian Painting*, *Kangra Painting*;

K. Khandalavala, *Pāhāri Miniature Painting*; J.Bentley, *South Indian Paintings;* A.K. Bhattacharya, *Technique of Indian Painting.*

28. See J.N. Banerjee, *Development of Hindu Iconography*; A.K. Coomaraswamy, *Masterpieces of Indian Sculpture*; S. Kramrisch, *Indian Sculpture*; C. Sivaramamurti, *Indian Sculpture*; S. K. Saraswati, *A Survey of Indian Sculpture.*

29. For a historical account since the time of Indus Valley Civilisation, see A.K. Roy Chaudhuri, *Man Malady and Medicine.*

30. Vide, e.g., *Atharvaveda,* V. 13 which is a charm against snake venom. Some words, used in it, are non-Aryan; e.g. *Taimata* (stanza 6), *Āligi, Viligi* (both in stanza 7) *Urugulā, Asikni* (both in stanza 8), *Tabuva, Tastuva* (both in stanza 10).

31. According to Bloomfield, same as *Apaci,* found in medical works, and explained by commentators as *Gaṇḍamālā* (inflammation of the glands of the neck).

32. It deals with the magical rites of the *Atharvaveda* and the application of spells.

33. Ed. H.P. Sāstri, with Eng. trs., Asiatic Society, Calcutta, 1910.

34. For details, see P. Ray, *History of Chemistry in Ancient and Medieval India,* particularly the part dealing with the I atrochemical period.

35. See D.M. Bose and others: *A Concise History of Science in India.*

36. Rhys Davids, II, pp. 20 f.f.; Oldenberg, *Vinayapiṭaka* (Culla), V. 33.3.

37. See S.C. Banerji, *Kālidāsa Apocrypha,* pp. 205-206.

38. Vide, A.B. Keith, *Skt. Literature,* 1928, p. 534.

39. See T.P. Bhattacharya, *A Study on Vāstuvidyā.*

    For Muslim and Anglo-Indian architecture, see the section on Architecture in the chapter on Foreign influence in India.

40. It may denote monument, tomb-stone, place of worship, etc.

41. See T.P. Bhattacharya, *A Study on Vāstuvidyā,* p. 36, and our observations on Architecture in the chapter on Foreign Influence in India.

42. See our observations in connexion with architecture in the chapter on Foreign Influence in India.
43. Rectangular from the base to the top.
44. Base octagonal or hexagonal, but *Śikhara* rectangular.
45. Only the base is circular.
46. T.P. Bhattacharya, *op. cit.*
47. T.P. Bhattacharya, *op. cit.*, p. 291.
48. For details, see S.C. Banerji, *Flora and Fauna in Sanskrit Literature.*
49. For details, see P. Sen Sarma, *Plants in the Indian Purāṇas.*
50. For details, see S.C. Banerji, *A Companion to Skt. Lit.*, pp. 683, 684, 709-711 (2nd ed.).
51. There were other persons of this name.
52. For details, see S.C. Banerji, *A Companion to Sanskrit Literature,* pp. 685-686 (2nd ed.)
53. Another author of the same name is assigned to *c.* 950 A.D.
54. Another author of this name was born *c.* 600 A.D.
55. For details, see D.C. Sircar, *Indian Epigraphy* and *Select Inscriptions.*
56. See *Jour. Asiatique,* 1958, pp. 1 ff.; *Ep. Indica,* XXXIV, pp. 1 ff.
57. Marshall, *Taxila,* I, pp. 274 ff.; *Epi. Indica,* XXX. pp. 59 ff.
58. See T.W.R. Davids, *Buddhism, its History and Literature*; N. Datta, *Early History of the Spread of Buddhism and the Buddhist Schools*; H. Kern, *A Manual of Indian Buddhism*; Oldenberg, *Buddha, his Life, Doctrine and Order.*
59. The five principles of peaceful co-existence were first formulated in Sino-Indian treaty signed, in 1954, by Jawaharlal Nehru and Chou-En-Lai. These were mutual respect for each other's territorial integrity, mutual non-aggression, mutual non-interference in internal affairs, equality and mutual benefit, peaceful co-existence.

CHAPTER II

Links between India and Foreign Countries

India was never isolated from the rest of the world. It is true that there are huge geographical barriers both in the north and in the south. Nevertheless, people of various races defied the apparently insurmountable mountains and apparently uncrossable oceans. The eastern and western boundaries, however, were comparatively easy to cross. In remote antiquity, various races of people, *e.g.* Persians, Greeks, Arabians, Śakas, Hūṇas, Parthians, Mughals, etc. settled in parts of this country. In fact, this vast country was turned into one resort of the peoples of the world.

As early as in the neolithic age, India had links with South-East Asia and the Far East. There is no doubt about the connection of India with Middle and West Asia. The Drāviḍas and the Aryans were the two main architects of Indian civilization. It is not known whether or not Drāviḍas came from outside. But, most scholars are unanimous in their conjecture that the Aryans came to India from outside. If that be so, then it is but natural that they should maintain contact with the land of their origin.

There are evidences galore that there was close contact between India and the foreign lands in the historical age. This contact was not merely commercial or colonial. The most important factor was cultural contact. In this realm, India has given more than she has taken. The question of the give and take will be dealt with hereafter. In the cultural sphere, there was not mere contact; but India succeeded in acculturating some other countries. It is far more difficult to conquer a race culturally than to subjugate it forcibly by means of weapons; cultural conquest gives rise to far-reaching consequences. We shall briefly deal with the various modes of India's contact with foreign countries.

TRADE AND COMMERCE

It appears that trade continued for centuries down to the Buddhist Age from the mouth of the Indus to the Persian Gulf. There is evidence of maritime trade between the Phoenicians of Levant and Western India in 975 B.C. King Hiram of Tyre imported from India ivory, monkeys and peacocks in order to decorate his palace and the temple of king Solomon. Even in remote times commercial transactions took place between the Indus Valley and the Euphrates. The names of the Vedic deities Indra, Mitra, Varuṇa and Aśvin occur in the cuneiform inscription of Mittani's Hittite kings at Cappadocia. These inscriptions date back to the 16th or 15th century B.C. Some Hittite kings had Aryan names.[1]

The ancient name of Tamluk town in Midnapore district was Tāmralipti. It was in those times a great port very close to the sea. Among other littoral ports, noteworthy were Bhṛgukaccha (Broach), Śūrpāraka (Sopar, to the north of Bombay Sahajati (Central India), Kausāmbi (on the Yamunā river), Vārāṇasi, Campā (near Bhāgalpur) Pāṭaliputra (on the Ganges), Pattana (on the Sindhu river). Many of the land-routes started from Vārānasi and Śrāvasti (modern Set-Mahet in U.P.). Through the sea-routes there were commercial contacts between India and Burma, Mālay region (Suvarṇabhūmi), Siṃhala (Tāmraparṇī) and even with Babylon (Baberu).[2] The navigators used to move along huge rivers. Of such rivers, prominent were the Indus, Ganges and its tributaries. A huge route connected the principal centres of industry and crafts in the Ganges valley with the Middle and Western Asia; this route ran through the prosperous city of Taxila (Takṣaśilā). The long inland routes also helped trade with foreign lands. One very long route spread from

Rājagṛha in South Bihar up to the Godāvari river through Śrāvasti. Another difficult route lay through the desert areas of Rājputanā and reached Sauvīra (Multān and Jahrāvār) port in the Indus Valley and the port near the mouth of the Narmadā in North Deccan. The road, built by Sher Shāh (reign 1540-45), started from Sonārgāon in East Bengal, and ended in Sind; its length was 1500 *krośas* or 3000 miles. This road still exists connecting Calcutta with Amritsar in Punjab.

It was Vasco Da Gama who, by his discovery (1498 A.D.), opened up, for the European merchants, the sea route for trade with India. In 1509 A.D., the Portuguese occupied Goa. Columbus (*c.* 1446/51-1506), while looking out for India, chanced upon America. It was his object to grab Indian gold and to establish contact with India as a marketing centre. The people of the different countries of Europe fell out with one another for its possession. The result was war between the Portuguese, Spaniards, Dutch, French and the English. This culminated in the victory of the Englishmen. As early as 1757 A.D., Robert Clive, having vanquished the then Nawab of Bengal, named Sirāj Ud Dullāh, in the fateful field of Plassey (Palāśi), laid the foundation of British sujerainty over Bengal and eventually over India.

ENVOY

An important medium of India's contact with different foreign countries was the exchange of envoys. We shall briefly refer to some very noteworthy exchanges of envoys. In *c.* 302 B.C., Megasthenes was sent by the Greek King Seleucos to Candragupta Maurya at his capital, Pāṭaliputra. He traversed the entire North India from the North-Western frontier, and wrote an account, entitled *Indica.* The original account is lost. Fragments have been preserved by some later historians like Arrian, Diodoros etc. and collected by M'Crindle. This, indeed, is the oldest document about Maurya India. We learn from Strabo that an ambassador, named Deimachos, was sent by the Syrian king and son of Seleucos, named Antiochus

Soter I to the Maurya Emperor, Bindusāra (*c.* 300-273 B.C.). It is reported that Deimachos came to India several times. Strabo further informs us that the Indian king Poros (Puru) sent an ambassador in 20 B.C. to the Roman Emperor Augustus. With him went also a thinker who immolated himself in fire. After several centuries, India came into close contact with the Graeco-Roman world. Exchange of envoys took place between the kings of Magadha and Mālava on the one hand and the Hellenic world[3] on the other.

The Egyptian king, Ptolemy Philadelphos (285-247 B.C.) deputed Dionysios as ambassador to the Maurya king Bindusāra. In a rock-edict (13) it is stated that the propagation of Buddhism was successful in the kingdom of the aforesaid Ptolemy.

Greek Heliodoros came as an envoy to Vidiśā (Bhilsa) from the Bactrian king Antialkidas (*c.* 140-130 B.C.). Although he went from one place to another within India, yet being a Greek sent by a Greek his visit was not insignificant so far as Indo-Greek relation was concerned. Heliodoros was a great Vaiṣṇava devotee, and set up a monolithic pillar in honour of Vāsudeva. From an inscription on the body of the pillar we come to learn that some Greeks adopted Hinduism as early as the second century B.C.

In very remote times, Italy, particularly Rome came in close contact with India through trade and commerce. From Roman history we learn that Indian ambassadors visited the courts of the following Roman emperors :

Trajan (98-117 A.D.), Hadrian (117-138), Antoninus Pius (138-161), Marcus Aurelius (261-280), Heliogerelas (218-222), Julian (270-275), Constantine (323-353), Julian (361-363), Justinian (527-535). To the last-mentioned king Indian ambassadors perhaps came twice

India sent envoys to Syria between 218-222.

There is historical evidence of king Harṣavardhana (606-647) having established diplomatic relations with China. He sent an ambassador to that country in 641 A.D. In 1342 A.D.,

Sultān Muhammad Tughlak is known to have sent Ibn Batutā as an ambassador to China. At least two envoys are known to have been sent by China to India; the dates of their visits are 643-646 A.D. The ambassador was Wang-Liuentse. During his first visit Harṣavardhana was alive. At the time of the second visit, the Finance Minister of the dead Harṣavardhana, named Arjuna was on the throne. He resisted this embassy.[4] The ambassador came for the last time in 657 A.D. as a pilgrim. He performed some religious rites at Vaisāli and Bodhgayā.

History tells us that to the Persian King Khusru II an ambassador was sent in 625-26 A.D. by the Cālukya king, Pulakeśin II. In *c.* 627 A.D. the aforesaid Khusru sent an ambassador to the above Cālukya king. The ritual in connection with the submission of the credentials of this ambassador has been very beautifully depicted in the murals of Cave I at Ajantā. The Persian Sultān Shāhrukh sent to India Abdur Rajjak of Herat as an envoy in 1443 A.D. He came to Calicut first, and then proceeded to Vijaynagar. He left an interesting account of Vijaynagar. He writes that the land is so populous that one cannot have an idea of it from an ordinary book. He records that there are underground tunnels under the Treasury of the Government. In those places are stored lumps of molten gold. The rank and file among the people of this land wear ornaments studded with jewels and gilt ornaments in their ears, necks and fingers. From his account we learn that the entire kingdom contained 300 sea-ports. He notes that there was a Government Secretariat for the administration of the kingdom.

In 1615 A.D., Sir Thomas Roe came to the Court of the Indian emperor, Jāhāngir from James I, king of England. It was Roe's intention to extract some privileges in connection with trade.

INVASION

Among various means of contact between India and foreign lands, one was invasion by foreigners. Among the invaders, some came to conquer, while others aimed at plunder and pillage, while yet others wanted to amass fortune by trade and commerce. Of the invading countries Persia has to be mentioned first. Among the Asiatic countries, it was the closest to India to the North-West. Persia had consanguinity with the Aryan civilization of India. According to most scholars, the Aryans at first settled in Persia and then migrated to India. The precise time of the influx of the Aryans into India is not known. It can, perhaps, be said that this took place before the origin of the *Ṛgveda*, the earliest literature of the Aryans. But, the time of origin of the *Ṛgveda* is so controversial that no definite conclusion is possible about it. The commonly accepted view is that this Veda originated sometime between 1500 and 1200 B.C. Recently a Western scholar[5] has tried to prove, on various evidences, that this Veda came into being about 12,500 B.C.

A few centuries afterwards we find Persia as the conqueror of India. The Persian Emperor Cyrus (*c.* 558-530 B.C.) occupied the land between Kābul and the Indus. Darius (*c.* 522 B.C.-486 B.C.), the third emperor of the Achaemenian dynasty, brought the entire stretch of land between Gandhāra (the districts of Rawalpindi and Peshawar in Pakistan) and the Indus under his imperial sway. His naval invasion paved the way for the inclusion of the low-lying land on the Indus and the desert area of Rājasthān in the Persian empire. This region was the most populous satrapy under the Persian empire. This area yielded a huge amount by way of revenue. The army, engaged by Xerxes (486-465 B.C.), son of Darius, for an expedition to Greece, included Indian soldiers too. The domination of the later Persian emperor over this region declined about the middle of the fourth century A.D., and gradually petered out. An important cause of the decline and disappeạrance of Persian sway over India was the invasion of Alexander.

The second country to invade India was Greece under the leadership of Alexander in 327 B.C. Even many non-combatant

Greeks participated in this invasion. Soon after the invasion Alexander died. But, even after that contact between the two countries continued. In the wake of Alexander's death, Seleucos became the master of the occupied eastern territory. Soon after, Candragupta Maurya liberated the Indian territory conquered by Alexander. In order to recover it, Seleucos led an invasion sometime before 302 B.C., but was defeated by Candragupta. He, however came to be connected with Candragupta by matrimony. Candragupta's successor, Bindusāra maintained friendly relation with the Greek king of Syria. Aśoka (*c.* 273-232 B.C.) established friendship with the Greek kings of Syria, Egypt, Macedonia and Epirus. At some places in those regions, he caused hospitals to be established and medicinal herbs planted. Many Greeks were in the employ of Aśoka. Of them, one named Tusaspa was appointed Governor of Saurāṣṭra. As there were many Greeks among his subjects, he arranged for their moral training by means of bilingual inscriptions in Greek and Aramaic. After Aśoka's demise, in the north-west of his empire petty Greek kingdoms were established. These continued to exist till the assumption of power by Kaniṣka (first century A.D.). In this way, the two countries, India and Greece began to exercise influence on each other.

Antiochus III (close of third century B.C.), the Greek king of Syria and West Asia, crossed the Hindukush and mounted an attack on an Indian king named Subhagasena (Sophagasenas of the classical writers) who ruled over Kābul valley. The invader defeated the above king, and went away with enormous booty comprising a vast amount of money and a number of elephants.

Of all the invaders, the Arabs deserve special mention. Their main occupation was maritime trade. Their greedy eyes were attracted by the prosperous ports in the coastal regions of India and also by some places on the North-Western frontier. In 637 A.D., they led an expedition against Thānā near Bombay, but were repulsed. But, they desperately led another invasion into Broach, the Devala Gulf in Sind and also in the Kalat region. Towards the end of this century, they occupied Nakran in Bāluchistān. Gradually, they conquered Sind and Multān. With a view to expanding their territory, they often went on invading Cutch, Saurāṣṭra or Kāthiāwād and Western Gujarāṭ. But they were repulsed by the Cālukyas in the South, Pratihāras in the East and Karkoṭas on the North. As a result, their domination was limited to Sind alone. This kingdom continued up to 1175 A.D. when Sāhābuddin Ghuri defeated them. Sind passed under the domination of Delhi, and the hope of the Arabs' conquest of India was sealed for ever.

With the decline of the Caliphs of Baghdād, the ruler of Sind became almost independent. The Muslims set their foot on the Indian soil. Having started as merchants, they gradually exercised sway at various places, and, in course of time, succeeded in expanding their empire over the entire India. Their domination ceased in 1757 in the battlefield of Plassey. During this millenary or more they appeared in India as invaders, plunderers, travellers and rulers. Of the rulers, the Pāthāns and Mughals possessed central power.

Among the foreign invaders, noteworthy are the Śakas, Hūṇas, Pahlavas or Parthians and the Yue-chis or Kusānas. Śakas at first used to live on the Chinese border. Driven away from there, they settled in Bālhika (Balkh region of North Afghānistān). Displaced from there, they settled in Draṅgiana in the Pārada kingdom. Subsequently, they set up a colony, named Sakadvipa, in the lower Indus Valley. From there they proceeded towards Punjab, Mathurā and Ujjayinī. Towards the end of the first century B.C., they spread in Gandhāra, Punjab, Mathurā, Kāthiāwād and even up to Mahārāṣtra. At first, having assumed the title *Satrapa* (*Kṣatrapa*) they acknowledged the suzerainty of the Kusānas. Though dubbed as Yavanas, they were gradually assimilated into the Indian and the Hindu society. The last Śaka chief, Rudrasiṃha II was Mahāsatrapa of Ujjayinī. He was repulsed in *c.* 388 A.D. by the Gupta king Candragupta II.

The Pahlavas (distinct from the Pallavas of the Deccan) were basically Parthian. The people of this race came to India and, with the help of the Śakas, established some kingdoms in the North-West in the first century B.C.

The nomadic Hūṇas hailed from Central Asia. They started onslaught on India in the fifth century A.D. Their first attack was rendered futile by the Gupta king Skandagupta in 455 A.D. But, later on they came in larger hordes and mounted such fierce attack that the Gupta king was faced with financial stringency. They at first occupied Gandhāra. In course of time, the Hūṇa kingdom extended up to Madhya Pradesh. Their leader, Toramāna, was established as an independent king in Mālava in 500 A.D. His son, Mihiragula, having set up his capital in Siālkoṭ in Punjab, struck terror into the hearts of the people. But, the Mālava king, Yaśodharman and Bālāditya (perhaps the Gupta king Narasiṃha), jointly succeeded in defeating him in 528 A.D. The vanquished Hūṇas stayed on in India, and gradually embraced Hinduism. Among Rājput tribes, some appear to have been originally Hūṇas. A branch of the nomadic Yue-chis was called Kusāna. They, having settled in Bactria, suddenly invaded India in the first century B.C. In course of time, their leader, Kadphises laid the foundation of the Kusāna dynasty in this country. Their kingdom gradually expanded, and grew to be an empire. The kings of this empire continued to rule vigorously from *c.* 48 to 220 A.D. Of them, the foremost was Kaniska (78 or 120 to 144 A.D.) Scholars think that the Śaka era began to be counted in his time from 78 A.D.

The city of Ghazni in Afghānistān dealt blows to India again and again. Sultān Māhmud (997-1030) invaded India at least 17 times from 1001 A.D. At first he defeated the Shāhiya king of the Kābul valley near Peshawar and the neighbouring areas. Having occupied Punjab he began the plunder and pillage of Mathurā and Kanauj. In 1018 A.D. Māhmud laid waste Kanauj, and erased from the political map of India the powerful kingdom of the Pratihāras. In 1022-1023 A.D. Gwalior and Kālañjara acknowledged his suzerainty. The climax of his ruthlessness and greed was the invasion (1026) of Kāthiāwād (Saurāṣṭra) and the sack of the famous Somanātha temple. He also reduced the Mathurā temple to ashes. Having reduced the Śiva phallus into pieces and destroyed the temple, he took away all the wealth accumulated within the temple and in the city. The target of his last attack (1027) was Multān. Even with so much booty the rapacity of Ghazni was not satiated. Even after Māhmud some Sultāns of this place conducted invasions of this country. At one time, they caused havoc even in the holy city of Vārāṇasī.

According to the Muslim historians, Māhmud, having ruthlessly massacred a large number of people, returned home with fabulous wealth. It is estimated that from Nagarkoṭ alone he took away seven lakhs (at present more than a crore of rupees) golden *Dināras*, 700 maunds of sheets of gold and silver, 200 maunds of lumps of pure gold, corals, pearls, diamonds, rubies, etc.

In connection with invasions, the name of Chengiz must be mentioned. The real name of this man, born in 1162 A.D., was Tamuchin. This Mongol leader is well known by the Chinese official name Chengiz Khān. Having conquered a vast stretch of land in China and the famous Asian kingdoms, he defeated Jālāluddin, king of Khivā. The vanquished monarch sought refuge under Sultān Iltutmish who, however, did not grant him asylum. This wise decision of the emperor saved India from another holocaust. The intrepid Chengiz led expedition up to the river Indus. Extremely delighted by the above decision of the emperor, he did not proceed further, and directed his attention towards South-East Europe.

The very powerful and cruel military leader of Samarkand, named Taimurlang (1336 to 1405) invaded India in 1398 A.D. Having reduced the places on his way into a shambles and looted wealth, he arrived on the outskirts of Delhi.

Having slain one lakh Hindu prisoners, and defeated the last Tughlak Sultān Nāsiruddin, Taimur occupied Delhi. For a fortnight his predatory and destructive activities and massacre continued unabated in this city and the neighbourhood. On way back he conquered Meerut, Kāngrā, Jammu etc., and went away with his plunder. He left behind a legacy of anarchy, famine and epidemic. As a result, the very foundation of the Delhi Sultanate was shaken, and the way of its decline was paved.

Āhmed Shāh Ābdāli of Durāni extraction, who was a leader of the Āfghāns, was on the throne from 1747 to 1773 A.D. till his death. During this period, he invaded India as many as eight times. He occupied Punjab, and defeated the Mārāṭhās in the third battle of Pānipat (1761). But, his soldiers did not agree to invade Mathurā; because four years back they fell victims to fatal cholera and other diseases. A frustrated Ābdāli returned home. But, his invasion continued up to 1767, and considerably influenced Anglo-Indian politics.

The fabulous wealth of India attracted Persia many a time. Alexander's invasion marked the end of the Persian regime in north-western India. A little over two millenaries later, Persia's greedy eyes were again turned towards India. The Persian king, Nādir Shāh (accession 1736) started the invasion of India in 1739 A.D. Having proceeded unobstructed up to Karnāl, he defeated the Mughal army, and set foot in Delhi. The vanquished Mughal emperor, Muhammad Shāh welcomed the victor. But, some local people having attacked the soldiers of Nādir he angrily ordered the indiscriminate massacre of the people and the looting of their wealth. His soldiers burnt to ashes a large part of Delhi. Nādir occupied Kābul and the stretch of land to the west of the Indus, and brought it under his domination. After a blood-barth, he left the subjugated India no doubt, but took away with him 30 crores of rupees, abundant wealth, the renowned diamond Kohinoor and the Peacock Throne, 1000 elephants, 7000 horses, 10,000 camels, many exquisitely beautiful women of the Mughal harem, 200 architects, 100 masons, 200 carpenters, etc.

We now come to those invaders who settled in this country, and ruled over it. They belong to the races called Ghuri, Slave, Khalji, Tughlak, Lodi and Mughal. The founder of Muslim rule in India was Muhammad Ghuri (also known as Sihābuddin and Mainuddin). The Sultāns of Ghur were originally inhabitants of East Persia. Later on, they became Jāgirdārs under the Ghazni Sultanate. Sultān Ghiyāsuddin of Ghur appointed his brother, Muhammad Ghuri, as Sultān of the land under Ghazni. He conquered Multān in 1175 A.D. Being repulsed from Gujarāṭ in 1198 A.D., he occupied Punjab in 1186. Then he tried to proceed towards the fertile plains of north India. But, he was defeated by Pṛthvirāj in the first battle of Tarain in 1191 A.D. Again, he confronted the same adversary at the same place, and defeated and slew Pṛthvirāj. As a result, Ghuri became the king of the entire north Indian region up to the frontier of Delhi. In 1193 A.D., his slave and general occupied Delhi. In the following year, Ghuri defeated and killed Joycānd, king of Kanauj. For several years following Ghuri mostly lived in Ghazni. But, under the able administration of Kutbuddin and his subordinate, Muhammad Khalji, his victorious banner continued to flutter in the entire Gangetic Valley up to Bihār and Bengal. Unfortunately, his enjoyment of this kingdom did not last long. In 1206 A.D., the assassin's dagger put an end to his life. In the history of India, Ghuri's name is ever shining; because he was the founder of a durable Muslim regime in India, which lasted for the next long six centuries.

In connection with Muhammad Ghuri, we have mentioned Kutbuddin. This man, born in Turkestan, was purchased as a slave. At the behest of his master, he occupied the throne of Delhi and ruled (1206-1210) as the first Sultān. This dynasty was called Slave Dynasty. The kings of this dynasty ruled up to 1290 A.D.

Khalji was the name of a Turkish tribe. After the conquest

of north India by the Muslims, Khaljis came to live in India. Jālāluddin Khalji deposed the last king of the Slave Dynasty, and founded the Khalji Dynasty (1290-1320). Māhmud Khalji founded the Khalji Dynasty (1436-1531) in Mālava.

Ghiyāsuddin or Tughlak Shāh, son of the Turkish slave of Sultān Balban (1266-1286), founded the Tughlak Dynasty (1320-1413) of Delhi.

Bāhlol Lodi, who belonged to the Lodi tribe of Āfghānistān, founded the Lodi Dynasty (1451-1526) in Delhi. In the first battle of Pānipat (1526), Bābur defeated Ibrāhim Lodi, and sounded the deathknell of Lodi dynasty and founded the Mughal Dynasty (1526-1858). On his father's side, Bābur was a descendant of Taimurlang (1336-1405), Āmir of Samarkand. On his mother's side, he was a descendant of the Mongol leader, Chengiz Khān (1162-1227).

Through Persia and Arabia, particularly the latter, Europe learnt many things about India. In this way, some gems of the fund of Indian knowledge reached that continent. The wealth of India, too, tempted the West. To this country came, for the purpose of trade, the Portuguese (1498), Dutch (Dutch East India Company founded 1602), English (East India Company founded 1600) and the French (French East India Company founded 1664). Towards the close of the fifteenth century, Vasco da gama discovered the new sea-route, and set foot in Calicut port in 1498 A.D. This event is of great significance for the history of Indo-European relations. The founder of the Portuguese power in India, Albuquerque came to India, for the first time, in 1503. For the purpose of trade, the British came to India for the first time in 1593 A.D. In course of time, they became the master of India. The empire, that was founded virtually in 1757 A.D., came to an end in 1947, *i.e.* after long 190 years.

FOREIGN TRAVELLERS

There is evidence that many foreigners, besides envoys, travellers, religious preachers, etc. came to India in different periods. We shall see that Aśoka installed a foreigner in a high post.

Alexander was accompanied by many Greeks. Of them, many returned home, while others settled in this country permanently. We know that some Greek kingdoms were established in the north-western region.

Even before Fā-hien, Hiuen-tsang and I-tsing, many Chinese came to this country. Up to modern times, countless Chinese came to this country, carried on trade and commerce and are still living here.

Many Tibetan students came to India, and quite a few Indians, including the famous Atīśa Dīpaṅkara went to Tibet and settled there.

There is a tradition that Jesus Christ not only came to India, but also lived here for sometime. The Russian traveller, Nicholas Notovich, on the basis of a manuscript discovered in Tibet, wrote in his book, entitled Jesus Christ, that he spent twelve years in India. Western Christian priests frequented the Court of Ākbar. The Englishman, Thomas Roe, came to Jāhāngir's court (1615-18). There was advent of the British more than a century before they appeared here as merchants and then as rulers. Since the establishment of the East India Company, streams of Englishmen poured into this country as officials, soldiers, missionaries, etc.

COLONISATION

The Indians of ancient times built up some colonial kingdoms. In Indo-China, two powerful Hindu kingdoms were formed, one at Campā and the other in Cambodia. Campā included the whole of Vietnam. After a rule of thirteen centuries (150-1471), this kingdom was weakened by the repeated onslaughts of the people of Annam. In the sixteenth century, this Hindu kingdom became a target of Mongol invasion. In the first or second century A.D. the earliest Hindu kingdom was founded in Kambuja. The Hindu kingdom continued for long 900 years. In the fifteenth century, this kingdom became weak as a result of the attacks by the Annamese on the one hand, and the Thais on the other. In the heyday of this kingdom, it included the whole of Cambodia, Cochin, China, Laos, Siam, Burma and parts of Mālay Peninsula.

In the Mālay Peninsula and Indian islands, too, huge kingdoms arose. The first was founded in the eighth century by the Śailendra dynasty. It extended over Mālay Peninsula and almost the whole of the islands. In it were included Sumatra, Java, Bali and Borneo. The Śailendra kings ruled in full glory up to eleventh century. Subsequently, Rājendra Cola I, of the Deccan, conquered a large part of the Śailendra empire. About a century later, the Śailendra kings brought an end to Cola domination. But, as a result of an invasion of Ceylon in the thirteenth century, this kingdom fell.

In the early part of the fifteenth century, a fugitive and respected Hindu of Java founded the Malacca kingdom. This kingdom gradually became powerful, and grew into a notable trading emporium. The second king of this kingdom having embraced Islam, it became a stronghold of the Muslims. Gradually, they invaded Java. In the beginning of the sixteenth century, the Hindu king of Java was deposed. The expelled king and many Hindus took shelter in Bali where a Hindu colony continued for about a thousand years. The Hindu religion still exists there. Almost the rest of Mālay Peninsula adopted Islamic religion and culture.

An ancient colony existed in an island of Titicaca in Bolivia (America). The earliest inhabitants of this place were Indians nurtured in Harappā civilization. It is, however, not known whether or not they founded a kingdom.

It should be noted that some foreigners set up colonies in various parts of India. In this connection, the British, Portuguese and French deserve special mention. Of the British settlements (17th cent.) prominent were Masulipatam, Madras, Bombay, Surāṭ, the villages of Sutānaṭi, Kalikātā and Govindapur out of which developed Calcutta.

Goa, Daman, Diu were prominent Portuguese settlements early in the sixteenth century. Of the French settlements, prominent were Pondicherry, Surāṭ, Chandernagore (in West Bengal), Māhe (Malabar Coast), Kārikal (Coromandel Coast) in the 17th and 18th centuries.

Armenians also settled in different parts of India.[6]

RELIGION

Religion was a very firm bridge connecting India with the foreign countries. We shall deal, at the proper place, with the impact of Indian religion on the foreign countries and vice versa. The *Zehad* or crusade of the Muslims is a well-known historical fact. In connection with foreign influence on India, we shall discuss how Islam was propagated in this country. We shall discuss the spread of Christianity also.

Literature, sacred lore, science, music, etc. have brought India closer to some foreign countries. We shall discuss the matter at the proper place.

ACCOUNTS OF INDIA

Some foreigners wrote accounts of India. These accounts are, on the one hand, historical documents of the contemporary India and, on the other, sound evidence of India's contact with foreign lands. Of the writers of accounts, some were travellers while others were curious about this country. Of such accounts, some are partly or wholly lost. Among such writers, some never set foot on the soil of India. Some writings are full of geographical information. Most of them deal with the contemporary political, social and economic conditions. Some information about India is available in such works as are not written exclusively on India. Of those writers, who never came to India, the oldest is the Greek Herodotus (*c.* 484-425 B.C.), the famous father of history. Of those Greeks, who gave eye-witness accounts of India, the earliest, perhaps, is Scylax. He was engaged (*c.* 510 B.C.) by the Persian king, Darius for discovering the course of the Indus. He was a Captain of the navy (Herodotus, IV.44). The Greek Patrocles, having come as the commander of the navy of Seleucus, wrote an informative account of India. The ancient historian, Strabo wrote an account of the condition of India at the time of Alexander's invasion. In it, many excerpts of the *Indica* of Megasthenes have been quoted.

In addition to travellers, some wrote eye-witness accounts of this country Among them noteworthy are a few persons in the entourage of Alexander. Of them, prominent are Nearchos and Onesikritos. Nearchos was a general of Alexander's navy. He conducted the navy from the Jhelum up to the Indus, and later up to the Persian Gulf. He wrote from his experience gathered in the long sea-route. Onesikritos accompanied Alexander up to Takṣaśilā. He wrote an account of the Indian invasion by the Macedonian king. Fragments of this account exist in the writings of the later historians. Arrian has given us some information about India. At one place, he states that there is no slave in India. Perhaps he wrote this on the basis of the testimony of Megasthanes. From his writings we come to learn that, at that time (between the first quarter of the fourth century and the first quarter of the fifth) there were some autonomous cities. This is stated by Hegesandar also. Quintus Curtius was among the Greeks who wrote about India. From his writings we learn that the army of king Puru, while advancing towards the army of Alexander, kept in front a statue of Heracles. The Indian Heracles was, perhaps, Vāsudeva or Saṃkarṣaṇa. He has stated that the Indians used to write on barks of trees. From the account left by Athenaios, we learn, *inter alia,* that Amitrachates (Bindusāra) requested Antiochos, son of Seleucus and king of Syria, to purchase and send sweet wine, dry figs and a logician-professor. In reply, that king informed him that the sale of professors was not legal in Greece. What the above writer wrote about Bindusāra is corroborated by the account left by Hegesandar. Aelian writes that, in India, there was fight not only between man and man but also between elephants and other animals. He further writes that, in Pātaliputra, there was chariot-race with bulls and horses.

A dependable account of contact between India and the foreign lands is the *Periplus* (first century A.D.) written by the Greek sailors living in Egypt. Along the coasts of the Red Sea and Indian ocean he came by sea-route to India, and wrote this elaborate account. He attests the building of seagoing ships in India. He further informs us that the Indians used to go to some islands of the Arabian sea for trade.

Pliny was an ancient geographer. There is considerable information about the contemporary India in his natural history (*c.* 77 A.D.).

Of the foreign travellers in India, those from China deserve special mention. Many Chinese came to this country which was regarded as a place of pilgrimage being the birth-place of the Buddha. Some came with the object of collecting sacred texts, while others paid a visit out of curiosity. All of them did not write accounts. The first Chinese traveller was, perhaps, Chu-shihing who came probably in 290 A.D. Sung-i-un came in 518 A.D. Among others were Fa-ling, Chi and another not well-known. Of the Chinese travellers, who wrote accounts, the earliest was Fa-hien who stayed in this country from 401-410 A.D. His prime object was to collect authoritative manuscripts on the *Vinayapiṭaka.* He praised the efficiency of the Gupta administration which is stated as not too strict. The highlights of his accounts are as follows. At that time, people could move about at will, and there was no need of registration or visa. The usual penalty for serious crimes was fine. Capital punishment was not in vogue. Only recalcitrant rebels had their limbs mutilated. He has expressed satisfaction with the Magadhan cities, particularly Pātaliputra. In this city he stayed for full three years for learning Sanskrit and studying Buddhist scriptures. The people were mostly affluent. There were charitable institutions galore. Besides, there were rest-houses at intervals on roads. There was an admirable hospital for free treatment. He was charmed at the sight of the pomp and grandeur of the palace of Aśoka. He noted that the Buddhist holy places like Gayā and Buddhagayā were mostly vacant, or there were very few people in them. He has written that nobody kills animals, drinks wine and eats onion and garlic.

The next Chinese writer of note was Hiuen-tsang (600-664 A.D.). He lived in India from 630-643 A.D. His main object was the collection of Buddhist texts. He spent long eight years in the kingdom of Harṣavardhana. The king greeted him respectfully. Hiuen-tsang saw huge religious conferences at Kanauj and Allāhabād; in the latter place, the conference was for five years. His elaborate account throws a flood of light on the political, social and economic conditions of contemporary India. He resided for quite a few years at Nālandā Univesity as a student, and wrote an interesting report about the way of life of the teachers and the taught at the place. While going back, he took with him 150 relics of the Buddha's body, many images of the Buddha made of gold, silver and sandalwood and 657 separate works. The works are said to have been carried by 74 horses.

Another Chinese writer on India was I-tsing. Arriving in 657 A.D. he spent long 10 years at Nālandā University where he acquired deep knowledge about Sanskrit and Buddhist Śāstras. He wrote his celebrated account in 691 A.D. He has not written much about the political condition, but records valuable information about Buddhism and Sanskrit literature. He informs us that the Gupta king, Śrīgupta, built temples for the fellow-travellers accompanying those Chinese who came five centuries before him. From his writings we also come to learn that, in the second half of the seventh century, as many as 56 Chinese monks came for an Indian sojourn.

Besides the above trio, several Chinese wrote accounts of India. Noteworthy among them are Kiātān (785-805), Mā Huān (15th century) and Mā-toan Lin. Sheng-ching, too, wrote traveller's account. Hiuen-tā came to Tāmralipti by sea-route.[7]

Among the writers on India, the Arabians deserve respectful mention. The merchant-traveller Sulaiman was, perhaps, the first Arab to write an account (851 A.D.) of this country. He came to this country several times by sea. He was highly impressed by the power and prosperity of Amoghvarṣa I (*c.* 815-77). The most renowned of the Arabian travellers was Al-beruni (973-1048). His personal history will be found in connection with India-Arab-Baghadad. About Indian culture and civilization his *magnum opus* is the *Tahkik-i-Hind* (an enquiry into India). In it he has discussed, in 80 chapters, the Hindu religion, social order, customs and festivals, literature, philosophy, mathematics, astronomy and astrology, way of measuring time, legal works, geography, cosmology, medical science, etc. Another Arabian scholar-traveller was Māsudi (d. 956 A.D.) who wrote an account of India.

Let us now turn to Europe. The most noteworthy Italian traveller, Marco Polo (1254-1324), lived in India in 1288 and 1293, and left an interesting account of this country. He informs us about the righteous administration of the Pāṇḍya kingdom and the trade and commerce in that place. His account[8] throws considerable light on the *Devadāsī* (girls dedicated for dance and music in temples of deities) system prevailing in the Deccan, especially in Mālābār. The Italian traveller, Nicolo de Conti came to India in the fifteenth century A.D., and resided in Vijaynagar in 1420 A.D. in the reign of Devarāya II. From his account we learn that the king had many consorts and that *Satī* (self-immolation of widows in fire) prevailed in society and even among the queens. Another Italian traveller, Manucci, came to India, and lived almost throughout the reign of Aurangzeb (1658-1707). He has recorded his varied experience in the four volumes of his work entitled *Storia do Mogor.*

Mauhan visited Bengal in 1406 A.D. In his account he has lavishly praised the quality of the goods of this province.

Barthema lived in India from 1503-1508, and travelled from Gujarāṭ to Bengal. In his opinion, Bengal was renowned for cotton, sugar, corn and all kinds of meat etc. He has highly praised the industrial goods of Bengal.

The Jesuit traveller, Bārbosā, lived in India for five years from 1516 A.D. Besides Vijaynagar, he travelled also in North India, and came to Bengal in 1518. He has given a detailed account of Vijaynagar as a city and as a trade emporium. He tells us that the ships, used in South India, were built in Maldive islands. He also praised highly the goods produced in Bengal.

The Jesuit priest and author, Bartoli, visited India in the reign of Ākbar (1556-1605). He has described the *Din-i-Ilāhi,* introduced by Ākbar as an amalgam of the Muslim, Hindu and Christian religions.

The Portuguese traveller Paes came to Vijaynagar in 1522 A.D. when Kṛṣṇadevarāya (1509-1529 A.D.) was the ruling monarch. He wrote an informative account about the king and the social and economic conditions of the land. The Portuguese traveller, Fernao Nuniz, came to Vijaynagar in 1535 A.D., and left a detailed account of the kingdom.

The Jesuit scholar, Monserrate (perhaps a Portuguese) came (1580) to the court of Ākbar at his invitation, and being deputed by the Portuguese Government. The emperor engaged him for teaching his second son. Having spent a few years there, he wrote, in Latin, an excellent work about his Mission. It contains valuable information about contemporary events.

The English merchant, Ralph Fitch, came in 1583, and travelled widely in North India, Bengal, Burma, Malacca and Ceylon, and went back in 1591 A.D. His account was considered as an invaluable document for the mercantile activities of East India Company. The writings of Fitch were included, in the compilation, entitled *The Principal Navigations, Voyages and Discoveries of the English Nation,* written (1589) by Richard Hakluit, a scholar, diplomat and clergyman.

Of those foreigners, who wrote accounts of India without ever visiting this country, the most renowned, perhaps, was

Lāmā Tāranātha (b. 1573) of Tibet. The title of the account of India, which he wrote, in Tibetan, means history of Buddhist religion in India (1607). In it, he has described the events from Ajātaśatru (reign *c.* 516-489 B.C.) to the Sena kings of Bengal (*c.* 1095-1245 A.D.).

The Dutch Palsaert came at the time of Jāhāngir (1605-1627), and wrote an account. He was the Chief of the Dutch Factory of Āgrā. He has described the luxurious and amorous life of the richer section of the society. He refers to the production of and trade in indigo. He also states that, in parts of East Bengal, people were weavers, and the garments, made by them, were the most famous and best. He refers to many kinds of handicrafts made in Sind, which were exported through Goa and other Coastal cities.

In connection with embassy, we have referred to Thomas Roe. With him came (1615) Edward Terry as a priest. His account, entitled *Voyage to East India*, is a very reliable document about the contemporary people and events. He refers to many kinds of handicrafts made in the Mughal period.

The French traveller, Bernier (1620 or 1625-1688), visited India in 1656, and stayed on till 1668. He has given a pen-picture of contemporary India, towards the end of Sāhjāhān's reign and the beginning of the reign of Aurangzeb. Among other things, he records his delight at the prosperity of Bengal.

A fellow traveller of Bernier was Tavernier (1605-1690) who also wrote an account. From his account we learn that, about the middle of the seventeenth century, Bengal produced huge quantities of industrial goods many of which used to be exported by the Dutch.

Ibn Batutā, a scholar-traveller from Africa (1333), came to India at the time of Muhammad Tughlak (1325-51). His account is a valuable record about contemporary India.

Among the accounts of India, mention must be made of the *Voyage Beyond Three Seas* by the Russian Afanasy Nikitin, a merchant from Tver (present name Kalinin). His historic journey (1471-1474) went a long way in establishing direct contact between Russia and India. The Russians came to know of India through Iran and some western countries. Nikitin's work was the first first-hand account by a Russian. It was hailed widely; so much so that it was incorporated in *Sofiiskaya Chronicle.* After Nikitin's death at Smolensk, the manuscript was taken (1475) to Moscow; thus it was given state importance. Nikitin sailed to Iran via Astrakhan; this was the usual route of the Russian merchants to the East. He then followed the trade-route from Iran to India. During his journey he carefully recorded what grows and where, how much things cost, where was found plenty of pepper and incense, the price of horses, etc. The object of his journey was not merely commercial. He had a thirst for knowledge. He made a comparison of the Indian sculpture with the monument to emperor Justinian, in Tsargrad (Constantinople). His remarks on Indian religion and on the kingdoms of Vijaynagar and Bahmani are historically valuable; this is the first account of kingdoms by an European.

VARIOUS CULTURAL MEDIA

The scriptures, literature and inscriptions have connected India with various countries. In this connection, India has played the dual role of giver and receiver. The same remark applies also to architecture, sculpture and painting. The scripts of India influenced those of some other countries. There was give and take between India and foreign lands in various other cultural spheres also; *e.g.* music and dance and sports and pastimes. In the realm of language also, mutual influence is discernible.

From the point of view of ethnology also, contacts between India and other countries is proved. For instance, it may be pointed out that, from the ethnic similarity between the pre-historic Austro-Asiatic race of India and the races dwelling in Suvarṇabhūmi (South East Asia, Greater India), we can guess links between the two regions in very remote antiquity.

Some archaeological materials indicate India's contact with some other countries. For instance, among the things unearthed in places of the Philippines, there are Indian weapons, garlands, bangles, etc. In Kāshgar and Khotān etc. in Central Asia, many Sanskrit and Pāli works have been discovered underground. Of such works, the most noteworthy is the Bower manuscript. From the palaeographical evidence contained in the manuscripts discovered at Kāshgar in 1890, we can infer the fourth century as its date. It contains seven works ; viz.

I-III — Medical Science.
IV-V — Cubomancy.
VI-VII — Mahāmāyūrī Vidyā (supposed to be an antidote of snake-poison).

The date of Bakhsāli manuscript, discovered in village Bakhsāli near Peshawar in 1881 A.D., is supposed to be third-fourth century A.D., according to some and twelfth century according to others. It deals with Arithmetic, Algebra, Geometry, Mensuration and various other mathematical matters.

As at present education served as a link between India and some other countries in the remote past also. For example, Taxila (Takṣaśilā) had been a great centre of learning in the period from the seventh century B.C. to the third century A.D. It is learnt that many students from Greece, Central Asia, Kābul and the adjoining regions came to study there.

Another renowned seat of learning was the great University of Nālandā. Many scholars from the surrounding countries like China and S.E. Asia came to this University for higher studies. Hiuen Tsang studied there (672-688 A.D.). Visiting scholars from abroad participated in debates and discussions held here.

ROMANIES

The Romanies were a very important medium of contact between India and some foreign countries. We know that the people of the Gypsy class are homeless wanderers. Of them, some are snake-charmers, while others rear or sell dogs. It is amazing to think how they carried Indian language and ideas to other countries. It is not known when they infiltrated into Europe. Bataillard thinks that this event took place in pre-historic times. He is of the opinion that a Gypsy community used to live in Urjburg before 1400 A.D. In 1348 they are known to have lived in Serbia. There is evidence that the Gypsies lived in Middle Europe in the fifteenth century.[9] They lived in various parts of Europe from the fourteenth century to the sixteenth[10] e.g. Byzantium, Bohemia, Crete, Serbia, France, Denmark, Rome, Scotland, etc. In course of time, they became so turbulent that the government of every country, where they lived, had to control them. Though generally known as Gypsy,[11] Bohemian, Saracen, etc., yet they were known by other names in different countries; for example, they were called Assyrian or Ethiopian in England, Ismilite in Hungary and Romania, Tātern (Tartar?), Talatera in Sweden, Pagan in Bavaria, Philistine in Poland, Luri in Iraq, Karaki and Jangi in Persia, Karakuye and Romanishel in France, Chingharmes in Turkey and Syria, Katasivcloi in Greece, etc. Most of the designations hint at their foreign origin and irreligious nature.

They have considerable similarity with the Jews. Both are itinerant, and oppressed in many ways. Both had to struggle for survival. Some would identify the one with the other. But that is not proper, because their language and culture are different. Moreover, the Jews are not exactly nomadic. They did not leave a fixed place, and adapted themselves to the culture of the country where they lived.

Their provenance is controversial. According to some, they were the accursed descendants of Cain, eldest son of Adam (Bible, Genesis, IV). Others think that they were originally inhabitants of Egypt. According to one opinion, the Gypsies originally lived in Mesopotamia. There is, however, no dependable evidence in support of these theories. That they originally lived in India seems probable from their language.[12] It was, perhaps J. Bryant who, for the first time, discovered that the Gypsies hailed from India.[13] There is no definite evidence about the particular region of India where they lived. Some hold that the Gypsy language has resemblance with the languages Dard and Kafi. Some scholars have noticed some similarity between the Romany and the Pāhāri language of Western India. According to one opinion, their original habitat was in the land of the Jāṭs in North India. According to another opinion, there is similarity between the Gypsy language and Sindhi. Some have tried to show similarity between the Gypsy language and the language of Central India. It deserves notice that there is affinity between the Gypsy language and Hindī.

A few specimens of gypsy language are given below :

Dānt (Danta), Tu (you), Pāñj (pañca), Mānuṣa (Man), Kāma (Love), Lindrā (Nidrā) in the language of Albanian gypsies.

INDIAN LABOURERS IN FOREIGN COUNTRIES

The Indian labourers, living abroad, forged a noteworthy link between India and some foreign countries. Many labourers used to go, unwillingly or under compulsion, to work in British tea-gardens and other places. Some of them used to go to British Guiana, Fiji, Mauritius, etc. According to a computation, it appears that, in the period between 1834 and 1932, the number of Indian labourers living in different foreign countries, was two crores and eighty lakhs. They carried with them Indian language and culture.

FOOTNOTES

1. *Cambridge History of India*, 1922, Vol. I, p. 320.
2. Vide *Baberujātaka.*
3. R.C. Majumder, *Advanced History of India* , 1982, p. 135.
4. For details, see the chapter entitled Nature of contact between India and different countries.

5. D. Frawley, Astronomical Evidences etc., *Glory of India* (Quarterly Journal on Indology), V, Nos. 3 to 4, 1981, Motilal Banarsidass, Delhi.
6. See our observations on Armenia and India in Chapter III.
7. R.C. Majumder, Suvarṇadvīpa, I.7; II.350; I-tsing, *Record*, etc.
8. See Yule and Cordier, *The Book of Ser Marco Polo*, II, pp. 335, 345-46.
9. Winstedt. *Some Records of the Gypsies in Germany.*
10. Clebert, *the Gypsies.*
11. This word was current in West Europe, particularly Britain, because the people of those places thought that these people of dark or coppery complexion had come from Egypt. Gypsy appears to have been a corrupt form of Egyptian. Long before the advent of the Gypsies, the people of this class were known as Tinker. This word came into use in 1265 A.D. The word Gypsy got into English vocabulary in 1500 A.D.
12. *Vide The Gypsy Language* by Tataniya, English translation by S.S. Gitman, Nauka, Moscow.
13. Cf. J. Sampson, J. Bryant, *Journal of Gypsy Lore Society*, New Series, IV, 1910-11, pp. 162-940.

CHAPTER III

Nature of India's Contact with Particular Countries

We have already discussed the different media through which links between India and different countries were forged in a general way. In the present chapter, we shall see how and when India came into contact with particular countries. At first, we shall deal with India's contact with the neighbouring countries and then with other Asiatic countries. After that we shall look at the Western world. In doing so, we shall at first deal with Europe and then with America and Africa.

ASIATIC COUNTRIES

NEIGHBOURING COUNTRIES

India and Nepāl

In the third century B.C., Nepāl was a part of Aśoka's empire. In the fourth century A.D., this country acknowledged the suzerainty of Samudragupta. In the seventh century, Nepāl passed under the control of Tibet. In the eleventh century, this country was ruled by the kings of the Ṭhākuri dynasty. Then the dynasty of Nānyadeva of Mithilā nominally ruled over Nepāl. In reality, it was governed by the Malla kings of that country. Taking advantage of internal strife, the Gurkhā tribe of the West Himalayan region conquered Nepāl in 1768 A.D. This resulted in Gurkhā-British conflict in 1814-15 A.D. which ended with a treaty of peace. In terms of the treaty, a part of the Nepalese kingdom was ceded to the British, and the responsibility of determining the foreign policy of that country rested with the Indo-British government. As a result, subject to certain conditions, Nepāl figured as an independent state. Thus, we see the intimate and long relation between these two countries. Nepāl is perhaps mentioned, for the first time, in the *Arthaśāstra* (II. 11-30). Another evidence of early contact between these two countries is furnished by the mention of Nepāl in the *Rājataraṅgiṇī* (11th-12th century). From the Allāhābād inscription (verse 22) of Samudragupta (reign *c.* 330-380 A.D.) we learn that Nepāl used to pay tribute to the Gupta emperors. According to a tradition, the Indian artist Dhīmān and his son, Viṭapāla (ninth century), went over to Nepāl. The art of medieval Nepāl can be described as a branch of the Pāla art of Bengal.

The ancestors of the royal dynasties of Nepāl, viz. Licchavi, Thākuri, Karṇāṭa, Malla and Śāhi were migrant Hindus from India.

Nepāl is adjacent to India, and geographically an intergral part of it. Politically, however, Nepāl has maintained its status as an independent kingdom. This country was inhabited side by side by both Hindus and Buddhists. This is why the influence of both these religions is visible in the architecture, sculpture and painting of this country.

Indian influence began in Nepāl even before the Gupta Age. As a result of Muslim invasion in Bengal and Bihar, about the thirteenth century A.D., many Indian artists and scholars fled to Nepāl. This is how the way of development of arts and study of Śāstras was paved. The Nepāli kings also offered incentive to the development of arts and the cultivation of Śāstras. There was a revival of Nepāli arts at the time of king Pratāpmalla (1641-74 A.D.).

From Tibetan sources we learn that, en route to Tibet, Atīśa Dīpaṅkara (*c.* 983-1053) and other scholars lived in Nepāl for sometime.

India and Tibet

From Tibetan history we learn that Srongsan Gampo (reign 629-650 A.D.), king of that country and the founder

(639 A.D.) of the capital at Lhāsā, deputed a person, named Sambhoṭa, accompanied by 16 men, to India for studying Sanskrit. During the Pāla rule (750-1255), the cultural contact between the two countries was the closest. At that time, Bengal was flooded by Tāntric current. Through Tantra, particularly Buddhist Tantra, the contact between the two countries became closer. The Bengali Buddhist scholar, Atīśa Dīpaṅkara (10th to 11th century) went to Tibet at the invitation of the then king of Tibet in order to revitalise Buddhism. Even long before Atīśa, many Bengali scholars went over to that land of snow, lived there and wrote works. Prominent among them were Śīlabhadra (7th century), Śāntarakṣita (8th century), Kumāravajra, Padmasambhava (8th century), Jetāri (10th to 11th century), etc.

Towards the middle of the eleventh century, the Tibetan king sent two officers to India for inviting scholars to Tibet. The object of the invitation was revamping of Buddhism which became corrupt. The above officers came to Vikramaśila[1] monastery. But, with their mission unfulfilled, they went back home. The king again sent his messenger with costly presents to Vikramaśila to invite Dīpaṅkara. Rebuffed at this time also, the king, sometime before his death, sent his would-be successor to Dīpaṅkara. After the demise of the king, a man, with a letter from the deceassed king, was sent to Dīpaṅkara. The man was asked to invite the scholar occupying the next rank, if Dīpaṅkara did not agree. Dīpaṅkara, however, went to Tibet this time.

After Buddhism was firmly established in Tibet, India's relation with that country became closer, and many Indians living in Tibet started visiting the Buddhist centres of learning, particularly Nālandā.

Lāmā Tāranatha (b. 1573 A.D.) completed his history of Buddhism in India in 1607 or 1608. In it are described the events from Ajātaśatru (reign *c.* 516-489 B.C.), to the Sena regime in Bengal (*c.* 1095-1245 A.D.)

After the establishment of Lāmāism, there was far-reaching change in the national life of the Tibetans resulting in the fusion of Hīnayāna-Mahāyāna-Tantrayāna Buddhism. They were transformed from a martial race into a peace-loving religiously minded race. From among them there appeared spiritual preceptors, excellent scholars, proficient linguists and devotees engaged in meditation and penance. We shall see how numerous Sanskrit works were rendered into Tibetan by the joint efforts of Tibetan and Indian scholars.

The political relation between Tibetan and India was originally very close. In the Allāhābād Pillar Inscription, glorifying the conquests (*c.* 330-80 A.D.) of Samudragupta, there is mention of the allegiance of Nepāl, but there is no mention of Tibet. In the seventh century, Harṣavardhana sent an embassy to China through Tibet; a fact which tends to prove friendly relation with Tibet. After the times of Harṣa, his Minister, Arjuna, occupied the throne, and obstructed the Chinese emissary, Wang-hiuen-tse, who came to India. The insulted man went back to Tibet, and, with the help of the Tibetan king Srong San Gampo, defeated Arjuna, and occupied Tīrabhukti (Tirhut) in Bihar. In 1703 A.D., Tirhut broke away from Tibet resulting in the snapping of the political tie of India with that country. Of the Muslim conquerors in India, Ikhtiyār, son of Bakhtiyār, invaded Tibet in 1204 A.D., but was baffled. In the British regime, Warren Hastings, in 1774-75 A.D., sent an envoy to Tāshi Lāmā, the powerful spiritual leader of Tibet, for facility of trade. But, his attempt was futile; because ever since the beginning of the eighteenth century, Tibet had been owing allegiance to China, and two Chinese representatives resided in Lhāsā. China and Tibet offered joint resistance to the infiltration of the British power in India into Tibet up to the end of the nineteenth century. After the Burmese war in 1886 A.D., the British government entered into an agreement with China. The condition was that the British government would recognise Tibet as belonging to China. In exchange, China would not object to the British domination in Burma. In 1887 A.D., Tibet attacked the British protectorate of Sikkim, but was defeated. In 1890 A.D. there was a settlement between China and the British government with regard to the Tibet-Sikkim frontier. In 1893, though some advantage about trade in Tibet was given to the British, yet it was not effective. So, to the British, Tibet continued to be a prohibited country. A British subject, named Śarat Dās, for the first time, visited Lhāsā in 1879, and again in 1881. He, for the first time, translated into English the Tibetan chronicle, *Pag-Sam-Jon-Jang*. His book, *Indian Pandits in the Land of Snow*, informs us of the very important role of the Indian Buddhists in the religion and culture of that country. His *Tibetan and English dictionary* is still an authoritative work. He gathered much information about the political and religious conditions of that country. In the beginning of the present century, the then Dālāi Lāmā of Tibet, with a view to getting rid of the Chinese yoke, started negotiations with Russia. This made the British government of India apprehend that Tibet would pass under that country. In 1903 A.D., the British government, invaded Tibet, and, without any resistance whatsoever, defeated the army of Tibet. In 1904, the British army entered Lhāsā. At this juncture, Tibet was forced to enter into a treaty with the British. According to the terms, Tibet was obliged to give British government abundant money and trade facilities. In an agreement (1906) between England and China, England promised not to occupy any part of Tibet, and would not interfere in the internal administration of Tibet. In exchange, China was promise-bound not to allow any foreign power to interfere in the internal administration of Tibet and no part of Tibet would be ceded. In 1907, England and Russia made a contract that, in political matters relating to Tibet, everything would be done through China. Thus, the Chinese domination of Tibet became firm. As a result, China attacked Tibet, and compelled the Dālāi Lama to seek refuge in India. The British government protested. During this turmoil, the Tibetans denied (1918) allegience to China. After this, the relation of Tibet with India became cordial. But, in 1959, China attacked

Tibet, and the present Dālāi Lama fled the country, and got asylum in India.

India and Burma (Myanmar)

Geographically, Burma has been separated from India by a mountain range, dense forests and Bay of Bengal. Though politically a separate country, yet Burma was suffused with Indian culture, so much so that even some place-names were Sanskritic. Buddhist religion and culture were propagated in this country ever since the time of Aśoka (*c.* 273-232 B.C). The Burmese victorious flag fluttered even over Assam in 1816 A.D. At that time, in the British empire there was suspicion that Burma was aggressive. This resulted in as many as three Indo-Burmese wars. The victorious British annexed Burma to India in 1886. After 61 years, with the Independence of India Burma too became a self-governed State.

India and Ceylon (Sri Lankā)

Geologically Śrī Lankā is a land cut off from the Indian Peninsula. It had close relations with India. But, it was an independent political entity. This country had different names in different periods. For instance, in Pāli literature and Aśoka's inscriptions it was called Tāmraparṇī. The classical writers call it Taprobane. Though in Sanskrit it was called Siṃhala, yet in the *Rāmāyaṇa* it became the Laṅkā of the demon-king Rāvaṇa. In the West, it is called Ceylon. According to the tradition, a fugitive king of Bengal, Vijayasiṃha, conquered this island, and, to perpetuate his own name, he named it as Siṃhala.

India had intimate commercial intercourse with Ceylon. From the account of the sea-voyages of the Chinese priests in the second half of the seventh century A.D. (Beal, *Life*, pp. xli, xxx, ix) we learn that there was regular connection between Harikela and Siṃhapura (Siṃhala) by sea-route. According to the lexicon, *Kelpadrukoṣa* of Keśava, Harikela stood for Śrīhaṭṭa or Sylhet (*Śrīhaṭṭo Harikeliḥ syāt*). At one time, Harikela stood for Bengal; because, for some time, Bengal was a part of the Harikela kingdom (see *Epigraphia Indica*, vol. xxviii, pp.

338-389). In the third century B.C., Mahendra, being deputed by Aśoka, went to Ceylon, and converted the then king Devānaṃpıya Tissa, along with his family, to Buddhism. Ceylon, particularly Anurādhapura turned into a great centre of Buddhism. It was in this island that the Buddhist *Tripiṭaka,* for the first time, assumed the written form in 80 B.C. during the reign of Vaṭṭagāmani. Besides the entire Ceylon, Buddhism spread in most of South-East Asia. Even the Indian Buddhists used to go to Siṃhala to complete their studies.

In the domain of politics, as early as in the fourth century A.D. Meghavarna, king of Ceylon, established friendly relations with Samudragupta, and got his permission to complete a monastery at Bodhgayā for the facility of the Ceylonese pilgrims. In the sixth century, the Pallava kings Siṃhaviṣṇu and Narasiṃhavarman assumed the administrative charge of Ceylon. Again, in the tenth and eleventh centuries, the Cola kings Rājarāja and Rājendra I assumed the responsibility of ruling Ceylon. But, soon after this island regained its freedom. At this time, the Śailendra kings of Śrīvijaya kingdom led an unsuccessful expedition. In the beginning of the fifteenth century, Devarāya II, king of Vijayanagara (1425-47), occupied Ceylon. Within a short time, freedom was restored to the island. But, the unfavourable Goddess of Fortune pushed the island under the Portuguese domination in the middle of the sixteenth century. Most of the littoral regions passed under the occupation of the Portuguese settled (1510) at Goa. Fickle fortune embraced the Dutch in 1658 A.D. In course of time, the island passed from the Dutch to the British, and Ceylon virtually remained under British India. With the independence of India (1947), Ceylon snapped ties with India and came directly under the British empire. The Indian influence on the various aspects of Ceylonese culture will be discussed later on.

India and Afghānistān

Afghānistān has been connected with India through ages. But, the *Mahābhārata* states that Dhṛtarāṣṭra married a

Gandhāra princess; Gandhāra was the name of Kāndāhār. This country, conquered by Alexander, was occupied by his general, Seleucos who was compelled to cede it to Candragupta Maurya (accession 324 B.C.) Thus, what is now Pākistān, became an integral part of India. The discovery of Aśoka's inscriptions near Jālālābād and Kāndāhār clearly indicates the influence of Indian culture in that region. The country became a centre of Buddhism, and helped in its propagation in that region. Having been under Kusāna rule, this region, after the fall of this dynasty in the third century A.D., passed under the control of Persia. The Gupta kings failed to recover it. In course of time, Muslim rule was established in Afghānistān. The Pāṭhān Sultāns of Delhi could not keep that country under their control for a long time. The turbulent Mogols got a footing on this land, and started invading India. At last, Bābur, the future Mughal emperor, brought (1504) Afghānistān under his control. From Kābul he led an expedition to India in 1526. Having won the first battle on Pānipat, he established the Mughal empire in India. In 1595, Akbar, having conquered Kāndāhār, firmly established Mughal rule in this region. Eventually, Kāndāhār passed out of Mughal control. But, Kābul continued to remain under the Mughals. In 1739, the Persian king, Nādir Shāh, conquered Kābul. Thus, Afghānistān became isolated from India. In 1747, a powerful Afghān, Āhmed Shāh Ābdāli or Durrāni became the ruler of this country. Having created various disturbances to the Mughal empire, he conquered Punjab, and dealt a severe blow to the Mughal empire in the third battle of Pānipat (1761). Though he could not be the overlord in Delhi, yet Āfghānistān never again became a part of India.

Gandhāra

This was the name of the stretch of land on both sides of the Indus. It included the present districts of Rāwālpindi and Peshawar under Pakistān. The huge cities of Takṣaśilā and Puṣkalāvati were also included in Gandhāra. At one time, even Kashmir formed a part of Gandhāra. With this country India had a friendly relation. After the fall of the Maurya empire, Gandhāra was divided into petty kingdoms under the Indo-Bactrian kings. In course of time, Kusāna rule was established in this land. Gandhāra developed a distinct school of art and sculpture, which deeply influenced India. This school achieved so much reputation that, according to European scholars, it is the only school in ancient India that can claim a special position in the domain of art.

India and Persia (Irān)

The Aryan India has consanguinity with Persia. Historians think that it is through this country that the Aryans migrated to India. A branch of the Aryans is believed to have settled in Persia. There is close linguistic affinity between the Iranian religious treatise, entitled *Āvestā*, and the Indian Veda. Besides, some Indian deities appeared, in the *Āvestā*, with slight modifications of their names; *e.g.* Mithra (Mitra), Yima (Yama). The Vedic *Soma* is *Haoma* in the *Āvestā*. In the Persian pantheon appears Vaivasvata Manu.

The political relation of Persia with India dates back to the sixth century B.C. The Persian king, Cyrus (*c.* 558-530 B.C.), brought, under his imperial sway, the stretch of land between the river Kābul and the Indus. During the regime of the Persian king, Darius (*c.* 522-486 B.C.), the domination of Persia extended up to Gandhāra and the Indus, and continued up to the time of Xerxes (486-465 B.C.), son of Darius. His army, engaged for invading (480 B.C.) Greece, included soldiers collected from his Indian territory. The Persian kings divided their dominion in the North-Western frontier of India into some Satrapies or provinces. Each Satrapy was placed under a Satrap (Kṣatrapa). In the Kāshgarh inscription (2nd century A.D.) of Rudradāman, there is mention of the Yavana king, Tusaspa, appointed by Aśoka as a provincial Governor at Kāthiāwād (*Epigraphia, Indica*, VIII, p. 36). Tusaspa is regarded by some as a Persian.

The mural in Cave No.I at Ajantā bears witness to the fact that the political relation between India and Persia lasted long. It depicts the scene of the presentation of credentials by the emissaries sent (*c.* 627 A.D.) by Khusru II, king of Persia, to the Cālukya king Pulakeśin II (608-42).

India and Persia were closely related to each other during the regimes of the Achaemenians (6th to 4th cent. B.C. earlier half), the Parthians (1st cent. A.D.) and Sassanians (*c.* 226-641 A.D.)

The Persian influence on the script and architecture of India will be discussed in connection with the foreign influence on India.

In the seventh century A.D., the Arabians established sway in Persia and introduced Islam. As the Persians set more store by religion than the birth-place they came in hordes for refuge in India. The oppressive Muslims drove away the Zaroastrians from the motherland. Since then an Indian community, called Pārsis, grew in India. A Hindu king of India gave them asylum, and settled them.[2]

Bābur (reign 1526-30), born in Chinese Turkestan, with the help of Persia, succeeded, through many vicissitudes, in founding the Mughal empire in India. His son and successor, Humāyun (reign 1530-40, 1555-56), being defeated by Sher Shāh, fled away, and took shelter under the Persian king in 1544 A.D. With his help, he succeeded in regaining the throne of Delhi. After the fall of the Mughals, the British rulers appeared in the political scenario of India. From the foregoing account we find that India had been under foreign yoke for long 25 centuries and a half from the sixth century B.C. to 1947 A.D. Naturally, the dominating countries influenced India in various ways.

The firm establishment of Muslim rule in India resulted in the weakening of her relation with Persia. The main reason for this is that, while the Muslim conquerors of India were mostly Turkoman and Sunni, the Persian kings and subjects where Shiaite. But, the intrepid Persian Muslims used to frequent this country in quest of fortune. That their visits to this country were not futile is proved by Ādil Shāh, founder of the Ādilsāhi dynasty (1490-1673) in Bijāpur. After his invasion of India, the Persian king, Nādir Shāh (reign 1736-47) declared that the land, to the West of the Indus, belonged to Persia. As a result of the rise of Āhmad Shāh Durrāni (1747-73), the Persian sun set for ever in India.

The defeat of the Persian king, Darius III, by Alexander, in 331 B.C., initiated a new chapter in the history of India. As a result, almost the entire Indian empire of Persia passed under the Greeks. Even after the loss of Persia's political control over India, the commercial and cultural contacts between the two countries remained unaffected. The Sassanian dynasty of Persia established its sway over parts of north-west India after the fall of the Kushānas early in the third century A.D.

Some Persian works contain information about India. An important one is the geographical work, entitled *Hudud-Al-Alam* (982 A.D.).

India, Babylon, Chaldea

In the Old Testament (Isaiah, 47/1,5-759-710 B.C.), Babylon has been called daughter of Chaldea, and, in the thirteenth verse, mentions astrologers, star-gazers and monthly prognosticators. In the *Daniel* (4/7), there is mention of astrologers who came at the behest of Nebuchadnezzar (reign 1124-1103 B.C.). There was commercial contact between India and these countries ever since remote antiquity. In the *Baberu Jātaka*, there is mention of maritime trade. This *Jātaka*[3] states that a crow and a peacock were brought from India in a ship to Babylon. This contact took place in the seventh century B.C. According to some scholars, Babylon influenced Indian culture in the pre-historic period and early proto-historic period. Sayce is of the opinion that, in the third millenary B.C., Babylon had cultural and ethnic connection with Punjab. Communication appears to have been by the land; no clue about sea-route has been discovered.

We learn from the biography of Apollonius of Tyana, composed (first quarter of the third century A.D.) by Philostratus, that it was customary for the Indians to extend loving hospitality to the Babylonians. It is further stated that an Indian king presented to Apollonius seven rings, each containing the name of a planet; one ring each had to be worn on a day of the week.

Later writers like Porphyr have referred to a work written, about the Nāgā ascetics, by the Babylonian Gnostic Bardesanes (155-233). He is known to have gathered materials from Indian envoys sent (218-222) to Syria. He wrote an extensive and informative account about the way of life in Buddhist monasteries, a cave-temple seen by him in India, the discipline of the Brahmins and the Buddhists, etc. He wrote also about Indian anchorites. The question of Babylon's contribution to Indian astronomy will be discussed in connection with foreign influence on India.

Chaldea is one of the most ancient lands in the world. The culture and civilization of this country developed, nay reached the apogee centuries before Christ. The astrologers of this country were honoured personalities in the courts of Babylon and Assyria. From the *Book of Daniel* (chapter 2) it appears that the Chaldean interpreters of dreams used to frequent the court of the famous Nebuchadnezzar, referred to above. It cannot be definitely said to what extent Babylon was influenced by Chaldea in the realm of astronomy, and whether or not Chaldea had indirect influence on Indian astronomy. Strabo[4] (d. 24 A.D.) writes (16/1/6) that the Chaldeans are adepts in astronomy and the making of horoscopes.

India and Mongolia

Hordes of Mongols came to India at different times. Of them, a fairly large number settled in this country permanently. The Mongol leader Chengiz Khān (1162-1227) threatened Indian invasion. Another powerful Mongol, Taimur Lang (1336-1405), invaded India in 1398 A.D. Since then, the Mongols invaded India again and again. Even the powerful emperor Ālāuddin Khalji (1296-1316) found it difficult to resist them. The aforesaid invasion by Timur shook the throne of Delhi Sultanate, and paved the way for Mughal rule. The term Mongol stood for the non-Muslims of Mongolia. After conversion to Islam, they were designated as Mughal.

Indian culture appears to have produced an impact on the cultural life of Mongolia through Sanskrit. In some Shamanist works of that country, familiarity with Indian logic is noticeable. The influence of Sanskrit literature is visible in the Mongolian Epic ballads and Shamanist panegyrics. Among the Mongols such Sanskrit names as Sumeru, etc. are found.

Through Tibetan religious preachers, the Buddhist religion and Tibetan translation of Buddhist texts entered into Mongolia in the second half of the twelfth century.

In the Shaman hymns, composed in the period between the 14th and the 17th century, some Indian deities are named; *e.g.* Viṣṇu, Bisman Tugri (Vaiśravaṇadeva), Esruya (Brahma), etc. Among the Mongols we find also the word Garuḍa ; *e.g.* Gāruḍi, Temur Guruḍi (Iron Garuḍa), Olfei Garuḍi (fortunate Garuḍi), etc. According to a popular belief, the soul of the holy mountain to the south of the capital, Ulanbator, stands as Garuḍa with wings outstretched. The Sanskrit name Garuḍa appears as Kheredei of Khān Keredei in the Epic ballad current among the Buriyats of Irkutsk in Mongolia.

The doctrine of incarnation, occurring in Sanskrit works, appears to have had an impact on the Shāmānist doctrine. In an old Shāmānist prayer, Chengiz's youngest son and the wife of emperor Kublāi have been regarded as the incarnation respectively of Samantabhadra and Bodhisattvadhsattva (?) Tārā.

India and Mesopotamia

Mesopotamia is one of the ancient lands in the world. To this country Greek astronomy infiltrated as early as in the middle of the 2nd millenary B.C. Some influence of Mesopotamia on Greece is also noticeable. The celebrated Hipparchus (*c.* second century B.C.) does not seem to have been free from this influence. With Mesopotamia India came in contact in a remote age. This contact became closer in the wake of Alexander's invasion of India. According to some scholars, some influence of Mesopotamia is possible on the astronomy of the Vedic period. If Greek astronomy did influence Indian astronomy, then the indirect impact of Mesopotamia on the latter is not improbable. Dates a events began to be recorded from the time of the Mesopotamian king, Nabunassar (747 B.C.).

The place, called Maishān, in Mesopotamia, was the entrepot between that country and India. Some Indian tribes established colonies at this place.

Some scholars think that the earliest horoscope in the world was discovered in Mesopotamia. If that be so, then India, along with other countries, may be supposed to have learnt the making of horoscopes from Mesopotamia. There was an Indian temple in a local port. Sarton informs us that the date of the earliest horoscope is 29 th April, 410 B.C. Written in Cuneiform script, it is preserved in the Bodleian Library.[5] Neugabauer, however states[6] that the earliest horoscope, discovered in Mesopotamia, is dated 263 B.C. It may be noted that the word horoscope was derived from Greek horoscopos probably in the first century A.D. According to some scholars,[7] only seven horoscopes were found in Mesopotamia. Most of them belong to the Seleucidh, and the first one is dated 263 B.C. One of them is dated 28th February, 142 B.C.

In connection with the foreign contribution to Indian astronomy, the claim of Egypt deserves consideration. Some think that India owes her knowledge of the zodiacs to Egypt. But, there was no awareness of 12 zodiacs in the holy astronomy of that country.[8] Owing to Egypt's ignorance in this matter in the pre-Alexandrian age, it may be said that India cannot possibly be indebted for the knowledge of zodiacs to Egypt. The 27th chapter of the *Bṛhajjātaka* is named *Dreṣkāṇa.* In it, 36 presiding dates of Dreṣkāṇas have been described. In this matter, it seems that Egypt exercised some influence.[9] What Varāha has said, in verses 2-21 of this chapter, about *Dreṣkāṇa*, has nothing comparable in Ptolemy's *Tetrabibls.*

India and Bactria

The land between the Hindukush and the Oxus (Sanskrit Vaṅkṣu or Cakṣu) or Amudaria was called Bactria. This region was included in the Syrian empire of Seleucus. In *c.* 202 B.C., Bactria became a free Hellenic kingdom. Demetrios, ruler of this kingdom, having conquered Afghānistān and parts of Punjab, came to be known as the king of the Indians. In this way, North-West India came into close relation with Hellenic inhabitants of Bactria. Soon after, this part of India, being parcelled out into petty kingdoms, passed under the rule of the Indo-Bactrian kings. The most renowned of these kings, Menander[10] (Pāli Milinda), ruled over Punjab from *c.* 160-140 B.C. His coins have been found in an extensive area of North India, even up to the South of the Yamunā river. He is perhaps, that notorious Yavana king of the *Gārgīsaṃhitā*, who, having conquered Allāhābad, struck terror into the minds of the people of Kusumapura (Pāṭaliputra). According to a Buddhist tradition, he embraced Buddhism. The Pāli treatise, *Milindapañha* (*c.* between 100 and 200 A.D.) contains a dialogue between this king and the Buddhist ascetic, Nāgesena. There is evidence of the presence of the Buddhist Samanas in the first century B.C.

The contact with Bactria facilitated Greek influence on Indian art and sculpture, and led to the development of Gandhāra sculpture.

India and Asia Minor

Some archaeological materials, discovered at the place, called Bogozkeui or Boghaskyoi or Boghaz Keui, in Asia Minor, shed considerable light on Indian history. In some inscriptions (14th century B.C.), discovered here, there are Indian names, e.g. Daśaratha, Indra, Varuṇa, Mitra, etc. In the local archive, there is a manuscript dealing with the training of horses. In it, there are certain technical terms resembling Sanskrit words. All this tend to hint at the route by which the Aryans came.[11]

India, Arabia and Baghdad

Trade, expansion of kingdom and learning - mainly this threefold motive prompted the Arabians to come to India even from formidable distance. Extreme disparities in religion, manners and customs could not prevent the Arabs from coming over to India. Arabia did not rest content by learning various branches of knowledge from India, but took an active part in laying bare the storehouse of Indian knowledge before the Western world. Spain, conquered by Arabia, helped in disseminating Indian learning in the Western world. The relation of Arabia with India became so close that many Indians permanently settled in that country. Indian tribes like the Jāṭs settled in Arabia as early as in the times of the prophet, Mahammad (570-632 A.D.). Many Arabians, in their turn, made India their own land. Besides coming directly to India, many Arabians came through Persia with which country their close link was forged by geographical contiguity.

In the seventh century, Arabia, with considerable power at its command, established its control both over the land and sea routes to India. Since then trade and commerce between the two countries went on in full swing. From the accounts of Ibn Khurdadbih (9th cent., first half) and Al Idrisi (1100-1165) we learn that the place, called Samandar, was an important port and trade emporium. The hinterland of this large part comprised Assam, its neighbouring areas and the present Bāṅglādesh and West Bengal.

Māsudi (d. 956) writes that the navigators, having crossed Persian gulf, reached the Lāṭa Sāgar. Lāṭa stood for Southern Gujarāṭ. He has mentioned the following places on the coast: Saymur, Supara, Thānā, Sindan and Cambay. Saymur, Supara and Sindan indicated respectively Caula, *i.e.* Campāvati, Sopar or Śūrpāraka and Daman. From Lāṭ Sea the navigator reached Harkind Sea which, according to Arabian geographers, meant Bay of Bengal. Among the littoral cities, there is mention of Harkand in the treatise, entitled *Hudud Al-Alm.* Perhaps, Harkand became Harkin later on. Moticandra infers (*Trade and Trade-routes of Ancient India*, p. 201) that Harikela gave rise to the name Harkin. If that be so, then the great importance of Harikela, for maritime trade, can be inferred. It is stated in Marco Polo's account that "Bengala" (included in Harikela) acquired great celebrity in trade. It is due to this great commercial importance of this place that the ancient European travellers named the adjoining sea as Gulf of Bengala which is now called Bay of Bengal.

Tempted by the fabulous wealth of India, the Arabians, in 637 A.D., attacked the place, called Thānā, near Bombay, but were repulsed. Towards the end of the seventh century, they conquered Makran in Baluchistān. In 712 A.D. they conquered Sind. Established in Sind, they invaded Cutch, Surāṣṭra (or, Kāthiāwāḍ) and West Gujarāṭ. But, due to resistance in the south by the Cālukyas, in the East by the Pratihāras and in the North by the Karkoṭas, they were confined to Sind. In 1175 A.D., they were deprived, by Muhammad Ghuri, of their possessions in Sind.

From the writings of Māsudi (d. 956 A.D.) and Ibn Haukal, we come to learn that the Arabians in India lived in peace and amity with the Hindus. Some writers of Arabia left accounts of India.[12]

There is evidence that many Indian physicians went to Arabia, and adopted the medical profession. One of them was the Director of a big hospital there. He translated some Sanskrit works into Arabic and Persian. Ibn-Al-Nadim has written that Hārun-Al-Rasid, Caliph of Baghdad (786-803) once fell ill. The local physicians having failed to cure him, an Indian medical man, named Moneka (Mānik) healed him. Hārun gave him ample reward, and he settled in that country, and became connected with the hospital of the Barmaks.

From India Arabia got huge merchandise and rich cultural wealth. Both these passed to the Western countries through Arabia. What was merely Indian became universal.

India and Syria

There was brisk trade between these two countries. A landroute from India ran along the coast of the Mediterranean and the shores of the Caspian Sea, and extended up to Syria and Asia Minor. This road came into prominence in the wake of Alexander's invasion of India. In the early centuries of the Christian era, one of the main trade-centres was Palmyra in Syria.

In the seventh century A.D., the Syrian, Severus Sebokht, knew the depth and subtlety of Indian astronomy.[13]

India, Central Asia and Transbaikalian Siberia

Archaeological excavations have revealed contact between India and Central Asia since the Palaeolithic Age. Definite typological closeness between the cultures of southern Tajikistan and the Soan culture of north-western India. The existence of contact between the cities of Indus Valley and Bronze Age settlements in South Turkmenia has been established.[14] That central Asia was at one time considered to be an integral part of India is proved by the fact that this region was looked upon as a part of the ancient Uttarāpatha division of Bhāratavarṣa.[15]

In this region, in comparison with the Cultural conquest by India, commercial contact was rather insignificant. Thanks to the enthusiastic activities of the religious preachers and the political influence of the Kusāna kings, Buddhism spread in the extensive land lying between the Caspian Sea and the Chinese Great Wall as the universal religion of the nomads.

Around modern Khoṭān, hordes of Indians settled. As a result of excavations, in this region, the following have been discovered: numerous Buddhist *Stūpas,* monasteries, Buddhist and Hindu images, many manuscripts written in Indian language and scripts and documents. An important work is the *Bower manuscript* (*c.* 4th century A.D.), discovered at Kāshgarh in 1890 A.D.

Besides the aforesaid Khoṭān and Kāshgarh, there were other centres of Indian culture at Niyā, Kuchi or Kuchā, Turfān, Tun Hwang, Bamien, etc. In addition to the *Bower Manuscript*, referred to above, the German scholar, Grunwedel, and the French scholar, Paul Pelliot, collected many Sanskrit manuscripts from this region.

The Uigur Turks built up an empire in the ninth century A.D. This empire lasted up to eleventh century. In this period, Uigur literature, influenced by Sanskrit, developed. To the Turks it was an invaluable treasure and the oldest literature.

India and South-East Asia

There is mention of Suvarṇabhūmi and Suvarṇadvīpa in the following Buddhist and Hindu works: *Jātaka, Milindapañha* (*c.* 2nd century A.D.), *Arthāśāstra* (4th century B.C.; according to a recent opinion, 2nd century A.D.), *Kathsāsaritsāgara* (11th century). Suvarṇabhūmi included the later Indo-China, *i.e.* Cambodia or Kampuchea, Campā, Burmā, Siam and Mālay. Included in Suvarṇadvīpa were the later East Indies, *i.e.* Sumātrā, Jāvā, Borneo and Bali. Intimate contact of India with those countries is borne out, *inter alia*, by the word Viṣṇukrānta in the *Śaktimaṅgala* Tantra. This term indicates the vast land lying between the Vindhyas and Jāvā. Indian traders used to visit this country even in hoary antiquity. There are stories about kings, bereft of their kingdoms, attempting to found kingdoms in this region. Of the countries, with which trade relation of this area at the time of king Airlanga (1019-1049 A.D.) is stated, in a Javanese account, to have existed, there are Draviḍa, Karnāṭaka and Kalinga.[16] Even from before the Christian era, Indians used to visit this region. In course of time, some Indians lived there permanently, and had marital connection with the local people. In this way, gradually Indian colonies developed there.

Wales thinks that, in Greater India, the current of Indian culture flowed in five successive waves, viz.:

(1) Amarāvati (2nd-3rd century),
(2) Gupta (4th-6th century),
(3) Pallava (*c.* 550-750),
(4) Pāla (740-900),
(5) Later Pāla (12th-13th century).

In the first century A.D. was established Fu-nan or Kambuja kingdom, the oldest colonial kingdom. The ancient name of this kingdom was Śriśaila in Sanskrit. It is said that a certain Brāhmaṇa, named Kauṇḍinya, came to the coast of this country, defeated the queen and married her. After that he founded the kingdom. His descendants were known as Śailendras. The Śrīvijaya kingdom of Sumātrā, founded in the fourth century A.D., and the Śailendra empire of Suvarṇadvīpa, founded in the eighth century A.D., deserve special mention. In the Indian colonies there are numerous indications of Hindu culture in the following : temples, images of deities, customs and manners, inscriptions, literature and even in the language of certain regions. The influence of Sanskrit is visible. We are informed[17] that king Fanchan ti'en-chu Bā of Fu-nan sent an envoy, named Su-U (or Su-Bu), to India, about the middle of the third century A.D.

India and China

In view of the close contact between China and India, it will not be, perhaps, out of place to give a brief historical account of the former.

The agricultural civilisation of China was very old. Gradually, that great country came to be industrialised. The silk industry rose to a very high position in the world. We have seen how China silk came to be used in India in the hoary past.

According to sinologists, the Shiya royal dynasty was the first to rule China (*c.* 2205-1766 B.C.). During the rule of Chou dynasty (1122-249 B.C.), the feudal agrarian society came into existence. With the decline of the above dynasty about the eighth century B.C., China was divided into semi-independent states fighting with one another. In this period of turmoil, many memorable religious preachers and philosophers appeared in the country. It was in this period that the renowned philosophers, Confucius and Lao-tse gave a new dimension to Chinese civilisation and culture by their philosophical doctrines and literature.

During the succeeding regime of the Chin dynasty (221-207), according to which the country was called Cīna (China), feudalism gave way to the imperial sway over a unified kingdom. This dynasty was succeeded by the Han regime (206 B.C. to 220 A.D.). The kingdom was extended considerably on the west; relations were established with many foreign kingdoms including Rome. There was revival of literature and arts, etc.

After the fall of the Han dynasty, the country was again divided into small states. Moreover, the country fell a victim to the predatory invasions of foreigners in the north and the west. The then emperors established Ü kingdom in central and south China with their capital in Nanking. In the wake of disruption, following political disintegration, Confucian influence was on the wane thus paving the way for Buddhism which came to be firmlyestablished.

The above kingdom was supplanted by that of the Sui (590-618 A.D.) which was followed by T'ang rule (618-906 A.D.). In the latter regime, poetry and painting attained a high degree of development.

For centuries Confucianism, Taoism (preached by Lao-tse) and Buddhism have been prevailing in China. The religion of the masses is an amalgam of these great religious doctrines.

The highlights of the religion, preached by Confucius (551-479 B.C.), are as follows.

This religion has a human basis, it does not recognise supernatural elements. Love of humanity is a holy act. Confucius did not set much store by metaphysics and logic. He was empiricist and a great realist. It was his belief that there could be no happiness of the man unless the mass of humanity lives as one family.

Towards the ninth century, as a result of the growing

influence of Tao and Buddhist doctrines, Confucianism lost its vigour. About the middle of the same century, due to some antogonistic forces, Confucianism was revived, and betrayed some influence of Tao and Buddhist metaphysics. Confucianism again waned in the tenth century.

Taoism, founded by Lao-tse (6th century B.C.), is a sort of philosophical supersensualness. The term 'Tao' means the way by which one can reach the beginning of a thing. It is supposed to be the eternal divine path. It is that path through which everything in the world is being carried. It is the single internal force that activates the world and all that is in it. Itself unmanifest, it has no beginning nor end, and is changeless. It is formless, soundless, imperceptible, beyond speech and mind. In human mind, it is the ever-active conscious principle existing as the power of discrimination. This doctrine prevailed, almost in its pristine form, till the secome century B.C. Thenceforward, it became a potpourri of different theories, and was reduced to a religion to be practised. Then, various superstitious, even magic and sexual practices infiltrated into it, and thus diverted it of its sublime philosophy.

The civilization, in these two vast countries of Asia, is very old. The mutual contact of these two countries, perhaps, dates back to pre-Christian times. China silk is mentioned in the *Arthaśāstra* (*c.* 4th century B.C.).[18] In Sanskrit dictionaries, a kind of gourd is called *Cīnakarkarikā*. A kind of camphor is called Chinese *Karpūra*. The word *Cīnaja* denotes steel. A kind of lead is called *Cīnapiṣṭa*. The word *Cīnāṅga* also denotes lead. In verse 2383 of the *Kathāsaritsāgara* (1063-1082 A.D.), things, made of red lead, are referred to as *Cīnamaya*. That fine silk used to be imported from China in ancient times is proved by certain literary references. For example, the pre-Kālidāsa (*c.* 5th century A.D.) dramatist, Bhāsa, used the word *Cīnasicaya* to denote cloth made of such silk. The word *Cīnāṃśuka* (cloth made of China silk) is mentioned in the Harivaṃśa (1274-5), regarded as a supplement to the *Mahābhārata* (present form, *c.* 4th century A.D.), Kālidāsa's

Abhijñanśakuntala (1/31), Daṇḍin's (7th century) *Daśakumāracarita* and *Amarakoṣa* (4th century A.D.). The word *Cīnapaṭṭa* (Chinese cloth) occurs in lexicons. The word *Cīnaka* occurs in the *Mahābhārata* (8/236). The word *Cīna* is used to denote Chinese people in the *Manusaṃhitā* (10/44) the present form of which is generally believed to have originated sometime between the second century B.C. and the second century A.D. This word occurs also in the *Rāmāyaṇa* (4/44/14) the present form of which is generally believed to have originated about second century A.D., *Carakasaṃhitā* (1st or 2nd century A.D.), Varāhamihira's *Bṛhatsaṃhitā* (5th to 6th century A.D.), etc. The word *Cīna* is used to denote a herb in Bāṇabhaṭṭa's (7th century A.D.) *Harṣacarita* and some dictionaries. It is stated, in the *Harṣacarita*, that the generals of the armies of Harṣa used to put on Chinese chest-guards. The *Javā* flower is called Chinese rose in English. May be that this flower, regarded as most suitable for Śakti-worship, was imported from that country.

China is supposed by some to have been the original home of Tantra. There is mention of *Cīnācāra* in some Tantras.

In the Buddhist literature, the tree of the fruit, called pear, is called *Cīnarājaputra*. In this literature, there is also mention of *Cīnapati* as the name of a kingdom, as well as of the word *Mahācīna*. In the *Śaktimaṅgalatantra*, the term *Rathakrānta* stands for the vast stretch of land from the *Vindhyas* to *Mahācīna* including Nepāl. There is a treatise, entitled *Mahācīnācāratantra*.

Both sea and land-routes were used for trade between these two countries. The land routes were older. The main route ran through North-Western India. It extended through Afghānistān and Western Tibet up to Russian Turkestan and Chinese Turkestan. Intersecting Afghānistān it ran through the Kābul valley and reached Bamiyan valley. Another route lay from Kashmir through Gilgit, and joined another route extending up to Kāshgarh in Central Asia. The Indian,

Chinese and Western traders together turned this region into a trade emporium in the ancient world. From Kāshgarh two routes extended up to the Chinese border. These routes were opened in *c.* second century B.C. But, long before that time, two more routes existed between these two countries. One of them was from Pāṭaliputra (Pātnā) to Assām and North Burmā. The other one ran through Nepāl and Tibet. In the second half of the seventh century, many Chinese monks came to India by this route. The route, used by the Chinese Kiyātān (785-805 A.D.), ran from Tonkin to Kāmarūpa. This route crossed the river Karatoyā, and along Puṇḍravardhana, crossed the Ganges, and ended in Magadha through Kajangala (near Rājmahal).

The sea-route ran through South-East Asia which served as a connecting link between the cultures of the two countries. The Indianised kingdoms of South-East Asia served as a medium of transmission of Indian culture and Buddhism in China. There is evidence of maritime trade between these two countries during the reign of the Tang dynasty (618-906 A.D.) of China. Some coins of the kings of this dynasty have been discovered in South India. Indian merchantmen used to carry merchandise to the port of Canton.

As early as the beginning of the Christian era, cultural contact between these two countries took place and continued for a long millenary. From the account (Beal, *Life*, pp. xli, xxxix) of the sea-voyage of the Chinese priests in the second half of the seventh century A.D., China appears to have had contact, through sea-route, with Harikela the identity of which has been discussed in connection with India and Ceylon.

Besides Chinese envoys visiting India, some Chinese travellers also came to this country. At the request of the Chinese emperor, the Indian king sent a Brāhmaṇa follower of Tantra, named Nārāyanasvāmī, to China. This man claimed that he could increase the longevity of people. But, this claim proved empty, when the Chinese emperor died a premature death. After this, his son sent this man back to India.

Besides exchange of envoys, there were other kinds of political relationship between the two countries. A military dispute arose between the Kusāna king Kadphises II (*c.* 78-110 A.D.) and the Chinese emperor, Ho-ti (89-105 A.D.). In the battle Kadphises was defeated, and was forced to cede considerable land in the frontier. To avenge the defeat of his father, Kaniska (*c.* 120-162), the greatest of the Kusāna kings plunged into war with the Chinese, defeated them and recovered the lost territory. Like spring following winter, a peaceful chapter followed the battle. The cultural give and take between these two countries continued for over a thousand years.

With the introduction of Muslim rule in India and in the region of the North-West of this country, the connection with China virtually came to an end. Trade between India and China was resumed after the establishment of the East India Company (1600 A.D.) in India. But, at this time, the relation between China and India was subservient to the British commercial and imperialistic interest. Real friendly relation between China and India was restored in the wake of the freedom of India. Envoys have been exchanged between the two countries. There was also cultural contact. There was exchange of visits by the Prime Ministers of the two countries, and agreements between the two were signed (1954) on the basis of *Pañcaśīla* between Jawaharlāl Nehru and Chou-En-Lāi. The five principles were *(i)* Mutual respect for each other's territorial integrity, *(ii)* Mutual non-aggression, *(iii)* Mutual non-interference in each other's internal affairs, *(iv)* Cultural and Mutual benefit and *(v)* peaceful co-existence.

India and Japan

It is known that, long before the Buddhist age, a branch of the Indian Aryans set up colonies in Japan. As a result of the spread of Buddhism, these two countries came close to each other. The influence of Indian religion, scriptures and scripts in Japan will be discussed in the chapter on Indian influence in foreign countries.

India and Korea[19]

With the introduction of Buddhism in China, parts of South India started contact with various parts of Korea. In the early part of the eighth century A.D., the Korean religious leader, Bhikṣu Hiy-chi, accompanied by many disciples, came to India, and lived for a long time. He gathered several hundred images of the Buddha and manuscripts, and visited Vārāṇasī, Kurukṣetra and Kāshmir. Then, along with Indian merchants, he returned home by the route leading to China. The Cola-Cela kings are known to have exchanged ambassadors with Korea. The coins of the Cola-Cela kings have been found among the archaeólogical materials discovered in Korea.

There is historical evidence that an extensive Indian colony grew up in Sangwan the capital of ancient Korea. Many Indians, having married Korean girls, settled there permanently.

EUROPE

INDIA AND ENGLAND

At least 200 years before the establishment of the British Indian empire, Christians came to India for various purposes. Christianity infiltrated, for the first time, into this country, perhaps, during the time of the Parthian ruler, Gondophernes (sometime between 20 and 48 A.D.) of the North Western frontier. From certain inscriptions and contemporary literature we come to learn that there were Christians in Vijaynagar (Deccan) in the fourteenth and fifteenth centuries. Christian missionaries used to visit the court of Ākbar (1556-1605). His *Din-i-Ilāhi* contained elements of Christianity too. His son, Jāhāngir, looked upon this religion with regard. In his court, the Englishman, Sir Thomas Roe, lived from the close of 1615 A.D. He was an envoy of the British king, James. In the regime of Shāhjāhān (1628-58), the Portuguese Christians used to abduct the orphan Hindu and Muslim boys and girls, converted them to Christianity, and carried on slave trade with them. The Jesuit missionaries, too, used to convert Indians. Sivāji (b. 1627 or 1630) had respect for Christianity.

In 1593 A.D., an Englishman arrived at Cape Comorin by sea route. In 1600 A.D., the British East India Company got the charter for monopoly trade in the East. In 1757 A.D., Clive, having defeated the Nawāb of Bengal in the fateful battle of Plassey, laid the foundation of British rule in India. In 1947 A.D. (15th August), India gained complete freedom. During these 200 years, India learnt many things from the British, particularly in Science and Technology. Through them lofty ideas and scientific outlook of the Europeans led to renaissance of the Indian literature and culture. As a result of English education, and the methods introduced by the British, the Indians have found new horizons in the domain of knowledge.

After the commercial and political contacts of India with England, the Englishmen, and through them, the Germans, French etc. got the opportunity of knowing about and understanding India. They considered themselves fortunate after getting a taste of the ancient Indian literature and culture. The British scholar, William Jones (1746-1794), founded (1784) the Calcutta Asiatic Society for the facility of the cultivation of Oriental knowledge and science. It was Jones who, having translated many Sanskrit treatises into English, paved the way for the propagation of Sanskrit learning in Europe. In the domain of science, we have learnt many things from Europe, especially from England.

INDIA AND FRANCE

India came into contact with France in the second half of the seventeenth century. Pondicherry was a prominent French centre. From 1718 A.D. the French scholars came to know intimately of the Indian culture, and started collecting manuscripts of the Veda, Nyāyaśāstra, etc.

In 1658 A.D., Bernier (1620 or 1625-1688) came to Surat

as a representative of the then French Minister. In 1663 A.D. he went to Delhi, and was engaged as the residential physician of Aurangzeb and subsequently in other posts. Having travelled over a wide area, including Bengal, he returned home and wrote a travelogue. Another renowned French globe-trotter was Tavernier (1605-1690 ?). He lived in this country in 1638-1642 (?) for the purpose of trade. His account of world-wide travel is an illuminating document about the contemporary India—political condition, value of coin, economic condition, mineral resources like diamond etc., roads, vehicles, the manners and customs of both the Hindus and the Muslims, religious rites, public usage, etc., in short, all the information about India.

INDIA AND PORTUGAL

The Portuguese Vasco-da-gama came, via Cape of Good Hope, to Calicut in India in May, 1498. This was the first advent of the Portuguese in India. The local Zamorin or Hindu Zamindar respectfully welcomed him. But, understandably, the Arabian Muslims did not take kindly to him, and tried to create various obstacles to him. Gama, however, having visited Cochin and Cannanore safely returned to Lisbon in 1499 A.D. It was he who discovered the direct sea-route between Europe and India. Of the European merchants, who came to India, the Portuguese were, perhaps, the first. In 1500 Pedro Alvares Cabral came to an Indian coastal port with 13 seagoing vessels. Albuquerque came to India in 1503 and laid the foundation of Portuguese possessions in this country. In course of time, he became the Governor (1509-15) of the Portuguese territory in India. The contact between this country and Portugal resulted in the infiltration of some Portuguese words into the vocabulary of Bengali.[20] The Portuguese established the first Indian press at Goa in 1556. They imported some new fruits and flowers into this country. The Portuguese Barbosa came to India (1516), and wrote an account of this country.

INDIA AND HOLLAND

The Dutch first came to India for trade early in the seventeenth century. Palsaert came from Portugal to India at the time of Jāhāngir (1605-27), and wrote an eye-witness account.

INDIA AND ITALY

The curiosity and respect for India were aroused among the Italians in the pre-Christian period. In course of time, some Italians came to this country, and wrote accounts of India. With Rome India's contact was intimate. Pliny (first century A.D.) writes that every year, for the price of luxury goods, India pays to Rome ten lakh sesterces (Roman coins). This is corroborated by the discovery of many Roman coins in India. An evidence of close contact between the two countries is that a Pāṇḍya king sent (*c.* 26 B.C.) a mission to the Roman emperor, Augustus. The main business of the Indians, who went to Rome, was to discuss commercial matters. Strabo informs us (*Geography*, XV, 73) that a certain Indian king sent a man to Augustus asking for help in a good work. Subsequently, to different Roman emperors as many as seven missions were sent. Exchange of envoys took place between Rome and the two Indian states, Magadha and Mālava. Commercial transactions between India and Rome and other western countries took place through the port of Alexandria. The goods used to be sent to the European countries by sea route up to the coast of the Red Sea. A route ran from India through Persia to the Mediterranean sea along the coast of the Caspian Sea. This route extended up to Syria and Asia Minor up to a few centuries after Christ; Palmyra in Syria was a centre of this trade.

There was cultural contact also between India and Rome. The relation between India and the west became close at the times of the Roman emperors Augustus (reign 31 B.C.-14 A.D.), Trajan (reign 98-117 A.D.) and Marcus Aurelius (reign 161-180 A.D.). Some writers (e.g. Horace, *Carm.* IV. 14; Virgil,

Aeneid VIII. 680 ff.) mention, among others, the Indians and state that there was arrangement of state security for them. From the testament of Augustus we come to learn that letters used to come from Indian kings. The aforesaid Pliny writes (*Natural History*, VI. 24) that an Indian ambassador came to the Roman emperor, Claudius (reign 41-54 A.D.).

The Italian Marco Polo (1254-1324) came to Bengal in 1290, and returned via Burma. His travelogue mentions details about India, particularly Bengal. According to some, he mistook Pegu in Burma for Bengal. Some, however, think that, to him, Bengal meant the districts of Noākhāli, Chitagong and Tripurā, the first two included in the present Banglādesh and the third belonging to India. The account by Polo himself is lost. The present work was written by a person engaged by him. In the same year, he visited the Coromondal coast. He has left much information about the *Devadāsīs*[21] of the Deccan.[22]

Another Italian, Manucci, wrote an account of the social condition and the activities of emperor Aurangzeb (1659-1707). In 1704, Manucci wrote about the political and military matters under the above emperor, and about his relation with the Marāṭhās. This writer wrote in detail also about the *Kotwāl* or the protector of the city.

INDIA, GREECE AND OTHER HELLENIC REGIONS

In remote times, the word *Yavana* denoted Greek or Ionian. In fact, the word Ionia has some phonetic similarity with *Yavana*. This was originally a hilly coastal strip twenty to thirty miles wide in Asia Minor. Some think that India's contact with Greece began in the time of Alexander's invasion (326 B.C.). The word *Yavana* occurs, perhaps for the first time, in Pāṇini's grammar (4/1/49). There is no evidence to prove that Pāṇini, by this word, meant the Greeks who accompanied Alexander. Besides, Pāṇini is believed to have flourished before Alexander.

There is mention of India by Homer (*c.* 9th century B.C.). He states that the Greeks used Indian commodities in remote antiquity. Among such things were Kassiteros or Tin and Elephas or Ivory. According to the Greek orator, Chrysostom (*c.* 80 B.C.), a certain Indian translated Homer's poem, and, for this reason, the Indian connoisseurs of poetry knew the anguish of Priam, the lament of Andromache and Hecuba as well as the heroic exploits of Achilles and Hector. By this remark is hinted some similarity between Homer's *Odyssey* and the Indian *Rāmāyaṇa* and *Mahābhārata.* Some scholars have noticed similarity between the Vedic society and that of Homer's *Iliad* and *Odyssey.*

According to the testimony of Herodotus (*c.* 484-425 B.C.), the father of history, a certain Greek, named Scylax, came to India for the first time in 500 B.C. The Persian king, Darius (*c.* 522-486 B.C.) engaged him for surveying the region that lay beyond the Indus. On this Scylax, perhaps, wrote an account which is now lost. The Greeks could know some facts about India from the writings of Hecateus, a contemporary historian of Scylax and that father of Greek geography. Before this, they thought that India was situated in the end of the world, and was inhabited by barbarous primitive peoples.

At the time when, in the debating assembly of Magadha, Mahāvīra and Gautama Buddha, both belonging to the sixth century B.C., were busy establishing their own views about cosmology, the Greek Heraclitos (*c.* 540-480 B.C.) had been analysing fundamental materials and solipsism in the precincts of an Indian temple. Almost contemporaneously the Greek Pythagoras had been discussing unity in diversity, and established a society in which meat-eating was prohibited.

A certain Greek, named Ktesias, lived for twenty years (418-398 B.C.). As a physician of the then Persian emperor, gathered materials for an account of India. His account, entitled *Indica* (*c.* 400 B.C.), is available in fragments.

Indian philosophers, merchants, and adventurers used

to mix with the intelligentsia of Athens, and frequent markets of Alexandria. It is on record that a certain Indian philosopher discussed philosophical matters in Athens with Socrates (469-399 B.C.). We are told by Aristoxanus (*c.* 330 B.C.), disciple of Aristotle, that one of the Athenian scholars asked Socrates-what is the subject matter of philosophy. The reply of Socrates — curiosity about man. Eusarius (315 A.D.) has referred to this tradition.[23] We learn about the presence of the Indians in Athens also from the remnants of the lost writings of Aristotle.[24] Plato's friend, the astronomer Eudoxus, was enthusiastic about Indian thought.[25] Candragupta Maurya, founder (*c.* 324-321 B.C.) of the Maurya Dynasty, was connected matrimonially with a Greek king. His son, Bindusāra (*c.* 300-273 B.C.), established friendship with the rulers of some Hellenic kingdoms, and wanted to engage a Greek professor of logic in his own kingdom. Aśoka gave to a *Yavana* Chief the administrative responsibility of a province and also the charge of an important irrigation project. Besides, in Greece, he propagated Buddhism and was responsible for many kinds of work of public utility. It appears that Kaniska (reign *c.* 120-144 A.D.), the greatest Kusāna king, engaged Greek engineers in India. It is said that Apollonius (*c.* 50 A.D.) came to Takṣaśilā to acquire learning from Brāhmaṇa teachers. It is also said that Plato came to the bank of the Ganges. It is understood that, out of regard for Indian philosophy and religion, the Greek philosopher, Demetrius, renounced his earthly possessions, came to India to live with the Brāhmaṇas till death (Toxaris, 34).

That the Yavanas or Greeks were held in esteem in this country is proved, *inter alia*, by the *Mahābhārata* the present form of which is generally believed to have been completed by about fourth century A.D. It is stated, in this work (Karṇa, 45/36), that the Yavanas are omniscient, brave and different from the other Mlecchas. The word *Mleccha* denotes any foreign non-Aryan race beyond the pale of the system of castes and the stages of life (*Varṇāśrama*). The Greeks were perhaps differentiated from the other *Mlecchas* owing to their superior knowledge.

Alexander, having defeated the ruling Persian king, invaded India in 327 B.C. His object was to conquer the Persian territory of India. Āmbhi, king of Takṣaśilā, welcomed him. But, Puru (Porus), king of the region between the Jhelum and Chenab, resisted the Yavana king, but was vanquished. The magnanimous victor returned to the vanquished the kingdom lost by him. Alexander conquered the petty principalities of Punjab and the area occupied by the tribes. Then he brought the petty kingdoms of Sind under his control. Having parcelled out the occupied area into small units like the Persian Satrapies, engaged a Persian or a Macedonian as a ruler of each of these units. He reduced the kings of certain places to the status of feudatory chiefs. He established some new cities too with a view to facilitating trade in the land of Five Rivers and movement along sea-routes. Candragupta, however, having founded the Maurya dynasty in Magadha, removed the last vestiges of the foreigners from the Punjab and Sind.

The invasions by Persians and the Macedonians were not, however, an unmixed evil. Indian soldiers fought (480 B.C.) for the Persians in the battlefields of Europe. This resulted in the greedy eyes of Hellas being directed towards India inhabited by strange people and possessed of unprecedented wealth. Consequently, Alexander invaded India, and Greek kingdoms were established in the North-West. As a result of the planned sea voyage of Alexander and his invasion, the geographical outlook of the contemporary Indians was broadened. They became conscious of new horizons, and became acquainted with new trade-routes by land and sea. The dream of Alexander to build up a chunk of Hellas in western and the central wild areas of India resulted in intimate contact between the two countries. Many Greeks became versed in Indian language, and many of them became Indianised, and settled in this country.[26] Some Greek authors made eulogistic remarks about Indian sages. Many among the Hellenic rulers and some politicians used to hear the Indian philosophers with respectful attention. In connection with Indian influence in foreign countries, we have referred to the famous Indo-Greek king, Menandar, and also to his deep reverence for Buddhism. The Greeks could learn many things from the writings of eye-witness accounts of historians and geographers like Herodotus (*c.* 484-425 B.C.), Hecateus (589-486 B.C.) and visitors like Megasthenes. Perhaps, through these writings some Indian learning reached Greece.

In the place, called Memphis, skulls like those of Indians in c. fifth century B.C. have been found. So, contact between the two countries even in that remote age is certain.

ARMENIA AND INDIA[27]

It is possible that India had some relation with Armenia as far back as the middle of the first millennium B.C.; because Armenia and parts of India belonged to the same Achaemenian kingdom. This relation was maintained in the Greek period also. An Armenian tradition refers to an Indian colony in that country. Armenian literature contained facts about India. Indubitable proofs of the relation between these two countries are furnished by the Armenian colonies in different parts of India, *e.g.* Gwalior, Lahore, Dacca, Delhi, Lucknow, Pondicherry, etc. A spurt in the influx of Armenians into India took place after the Christians began to be persecuted in Iran. After the East India Company was firmly established in India, the British started harassing the Armenian merchants; this spelt the ruin of them.

A number of books on India came to be written in Armenia in the 17th and 18th centuries. One such book was the Textbook for *Commercial Schools* by K. Joughayetsi. Besides printed books, some Armenian manuscripts throw light on India—economic life, religion, manners and customs, etc. Some eminent Armenians visited India, and thus gathered first-hand facts about this country. One such notable man was

Danila Atanasov who came in 1790s. Another distinguished traveller was Danibegashvili who left an illuminating account of India.

INDIA AND HUNGARY

Hungary is one of those European countries which, despite geographical distance, came very close to India culturally. Certain factors evoked the interest of the Hungarians in India, her culture, literature and art. The strongest urge among the people of Hungary was the quest of their origin and early history. They migrated from the East to their present country as early as the 9th century A.D. Hungarian explorers started towards Asia in the 13th century. The basic facts were established by the end of the 19th century. But, details about the early history of Hungary and the origins of the Hungarian language, the Asiatic affinities of Hungary's folk-culture and folklore remained unknown. So, oriental studies are regarded as a part of "national studies" which lead to a better understanding of the Hungarians' past and present.

Another factor, responsible for Hungary's interest in India, was sympathy for an oppressed nation trying to shake off the foreign yoke. For centuries, the political and economic condition of Hungary was very much akin to that of Asian nations struggling against colonial rule. After the liberation of Hungary and of India, this mutual sympathy led to a multi faceted cooperation. This gave an impetus to the cultivation of Indology in Hungary.

The richness and variety of Indian literary tradition, philosophy, religion and art have evoked the admiration of the Hungarians. Some of them, impelled by a strong desire to have a first-hand knowledge of Indian life and wisdom, visited India, while others settled here permanently. Travelogues, works on Yoga, art, etc., relating to India, appeared in Hungary. Of late, visiting Indian music and dance troupes have forged close links between the two countries. The most famous

Hungarian, who visited India, was Alexander Csoma de Koros about whose work we have written in connection with India's influence abroad.

A strong Indo-Hungarian link has been forged by the Gypsies. It has now been proved that this class of people started leaving India, in successive waves, in the tenth century A.D. Researches on Gypsy language, folklore and ethnography have revealed their Indian origin. Their language has affinity with north Indian languages. They still follow certain Indian customs. Many Gypsies have been living in Hungary since the 15th century. Gypsy musicians have associated themselves with folk-music in Hungary and other countries.

Theodore Duke, the renowned biographer of Csoma de Koros, was a member of the Asiatic Society of Bengal, and came to India in 1854 to serve as an army doctor. He played some role in bringing Indian and Hungarian scholars close to one another. He recommended Rājendralal Mitra for honorary membership of the Hungarian Academy of Sciences. He also helped the renowned scholar Aurel Stein (1862-1943) to come and work in India.

Another potent factor resulting in close contact of Hungary with India was Rabindranath's visit to Hungary in 1926.

The growing demand for translations of Indian classics and contemporary best-sellers in various Indian languages has given a fillip to Indological studies in Hungary.

The growing contacts in politics, economics, trade and culture have led to new demands. The urge for a better understanding of the India of to-day has stimulated studies in contemporary Indian history, economy and sociology.

The works[28] of the Hungarian E. Baktay (1890-1963) went a long way in making India known to the people of Hungary.

G.W. Leitner (1840-1899), born to an Austrian family, and residing in Hungary, travelled widely in India while carrying out anthropological and sociological studies. His travel accounts, articles and monographs[29] are replete with material relating to the north-western region of India during 1864-1886; the studies are particularly valuable for anthropological research. He published (1882) a separate study on the indigenous education system of Punjab. He was one of the founders of Punjab University.[30]

The Hungarians' thirst for information about India was not quenched by translations of Indian classical works as also of eminent works of modern writers and by works on Gandhi and Subhās Bose. The result was the publication of over a dozen travelogues relating to India. Some of the travelogue-writers were Count Apponyi, Cholonky, Takacs, Germanus, Stein, etc. Several books on India were translated from other languages also. Some of the authors of such works were Bromfield, Brunton, Forster (the noted book, entitled *A Passage of India*), Wegener, etc. Kipling's books on India, especially his *Jungle Book,* are very popular in Hungary.

It is not much known that the Hungarian traveller, Mano Andrasy, published, in 1853, a book laying down the events of a journey in the East (including Bengal).[31]

J.M. Honigberger, a Transsylvania Saxon by birth, residing in Hungary, spent many years from 1829 in the court of Ranjit Singh (1780 -1839) of Punjab as his physician. In his travel-account (*Thirty-five years in the East*), he has given historical sketches of Punjab and Kashmir in connexion with medicine, botany, pharmacy and culture (London, 1852, new ed., Calcutta, 1905; in German, Vienna, 1861). The work, besides vividly describing the daily life of Lahore, gives an account of Ranjit in a human perfection.[32]

After the liberation of Hungary in 1945, the contacts between that country and India have increased in the political, cultural, technological and economic fields.

Stephanus Tomosko, a Slovak by birth, residing in Hungary, wrote, in Latin, a study on the cases of the Sanskrit language. (*De Causis linguae Sanscritae,* Pozsony, 1831).[33]

INDIA AND RUSSIA[34]

In current international politics, we find these two countries very close to each other. It is interesting to note that this contact is not one of convenience nor a temporary affair. India and Russia have known each other for centuries. The most striking fact about their relations is that they have ethnic affinity. Modern research has proved that the region, originally occupied by the Indo-Europeans, included some parts of what goes by the name Soviet Union. After the Aryan (Indo-Iranian) community came into being, Aryan people continued to dwell in the regions forming parts of the erst while USSR.

Besides ethnic affinity, there is linguistic affinity too. Many peoples of Russia speak languages belonging to the Iranian family.

From the ethnic, linguistic and cultural data we find that the origin of the Indo-Aryans is bound up with the prehistory of the European part of the USSR.

Russia came to know of India from two main sources, direct and indirect. Trade, travel etc. provided means of direct contact. Literary sources were indirectly instrumental in the Russian's acquiring knowledge about India.

We shall briefly deal with the principal literary sources. In the early centuries following conversion to Christianity, Greek and Bulgarian literary works flooded Russia. In the translations of Christian works, there appeared in Russia Indian names, topics and motifs as also Indian ideas which already took shape a few centuries earlier in Byzantium. Byzantium got these from the writers of the "Church Fathers" and the writers of the Roman Empire in the 4th and 5th centuries. In these were incorporated, *inter alia*, extracts from the notes of those who took part in the invasions of Alexander.

The ancient collection, entitled *Physiologus*, and similar works went a long way in acquainting Russia with India, its animal kingdom. Another such work was the *Christian Topography* by Indicopleustes (6th cent.). A very important work in this connection was the Romance of Barlaam and

Joasaph, a transposition of the legendary life of the Buddha, which laid down India's ideal of renunciation.

Indian literary motifs and stories infiltrated into Russia partly through the west and partly through Iran. For example, the Indian text on the origin of castes (*varṇa*) probably came to Russian folklore tradition through the Iranian Manichaeans and Christian heretics of the first centuries A.D., and then through Byzantine and Bulgarian literatures.

Among the important literary media, through which knowledge about India poured into Russia, were also the following works :

The Narrative of Macarius of Rome,
Visit of Zosima to the Rahmans,
Narrative of Methodius of Patara,

The story of the Indian kingdom (based on the story of a letter from the Indian priest king John to Greek ruler Manuel Comnenus. The letter in Greek appeared in the middle of 12th cent., Russian version appeared early in the 13th cent.

Alexandria (Alexander Romance) by pseudo-Callisthenes (Based on notes by contemporaries of Alexander and folk-legends). Of many Russian versions, the earliest one dates from 11th-12th cent.

Fables of Indian origin - Stephanitus and Ihnelates (as old as *Pañcatantra*).

Geographical works - Polish *Chronicle of the Whole World* by M. Bielski, Italian *Cosmographia* by G. Botero, Flemish *Cosmographia* by G. Mercator.

Archaeological finds like goods and coins indicate relations between Kievan Russia and the Orient including India, in the 8th and 9th centuries. It seems that connections with India arose through the Khazan capital, Itil-Khazaran, situated at the mouth of the Volga. Arab sources refer to contacts between Russians and Indians in Itil and other cities in the 9th and 10th centuries.

There is evidence of a trade-route, via river Volga and the Caspian Sea, linking Russia with Central Asia and north

India, in the 10th and 11th centuries. The Russian *Chronicle of Times Past* mentions a route to some regions which include India.

In the 14th cent., the Sultāns of India maintained trade relations with Russia. Indian gold coins of the 14th cent. have been found in the Volga region. Al-Omari states that Russian fabrics were a great luxury in India. From a number of sources we learn of the presence of Russians in India in the above century. Āmir Khusro Dehalevi refers to Russian women as "as cold as ice." The *Tughlakhāmā* testifies to the service of Russians in the army of Ghiās-ud-dn Tughlak (reign 1320-25).

The Nikonovskaya Chronicle refers to the fact that, in 1532, an ambassador, Khozya-Hussein (Khwaja Hussain), came from Babur to the Russian king, Vasily Ivanovich.

Russian interest in India was great in the middle of the 16th cent. during the regime of Ivan the Terrible (1533-1584). Indian goods reached Moscow mainly through Persia. Ivan made attempts to establish trade relations with India. Russian merchants reached India. The British traveller, Ralph Fitch, heard of them in the 1580s. Indian merchants appeared in the Russian market. A bronze vessel, with an inscription in Indian *Gurumukhī* script, probably dating back to the 16th cent., has been found in Orsk (South Urals). The 17th cent. saw a spurt of the supply of Indian goods to Russia. The commodities included precious stones, incense and medicines. Indian merchants appeared in Astrakhan between 1615-1616. Gradually they settled there permanently. It is interesting to note that the Indian merchants amassed money also by money-lending, and enslaved many local people.

In a bid to establish direct diplomatic relations with India and to facilitate trade between the two countries, a Russian mission was sent to Shāhjāhān. In 1675 another embassy was sent to Aurangzeb. Twenty years later, another Russian embassy was sent to the above emperor.

In the eighteenth century, India and Russia came closer

to each other through trade. During the time of Peter the Great (1689-1725) attempts were made to improve trade relations. Such attempts continued even afterwards, and new routes were found. The intimate commercial relations resulted in the settlement of Indian traders at some places in Russia, *e.g.* Astrakhan, Kizlyar.

Gradually, the Russians developed also an academic interest in India. Oriental antiquities began to be collected. Some Russians tried to learn Indian languages and scripts. G.J. Kher started work on Indian languages. Some works, composed in Russia, threw light on India. One such important work was *A Historical Description of Russian Commerce* by M. Chulkov. *Comparative Dictionary of World Languages* by P. Pallas is also noteworthy. Some West European works also acquainted the Russians about Indian life. One such work was A *Short and General Explanation and Discourse on the Manners, Habits, Language, Faith and Philosophy of the Indians* (1789).

In the second half of the 18th cent., some Russian journals also dealt with Indian topics. A noteworthy Journal was the *Prazdnoye vremya v polzu upo treblennoye* (Issue No. XVIII, 1759).

The Indological activities of the Asiatic Society, Calcutta, generated the interest of Europeans, including Russians, in Indian culture and literature.

The great and firm link between the two countries was forged by the noted Russian, Lebedev (1749-1817). In course of his peregrinations, he came to Madras in 1785, and learnt something of the Tāmil language. In Calcutta he studied Bengali, Hindustāni and learnt the elements of Sanskrit. Lebedev wrote extensively on India, her peoples, religion, philosophy, etc. His basic work on India was *An Impartial Review of the Systems of the East-Indian Brahmins, Their Sacred Rites and National Customs* (1805).

In the beginning of the 19th cent., the Russians read about India mainly in the works of German, French and English Indologists.

Indo-Russian cultural contacts date back to a remote past. Archaeological finds have established beyond doubt such contacts with regions of Central Asia, which constitute the territories of the Soviet republics. One unifying factor was that parts of India and the above regions belonged to the same Achaemenian State. For example, the Central Asian satrapies of Bactria, Sogdiana and Khorezm and Indian Gandhāra and some other regions were included in the above kingdom. Two examples will suffice to show the closeness of India and the above regions. The Sanskrit word *Sārtha* (merchant) came to be used to designate the settled Iranian population of Central Asia (the Sārthas). According to Vasily Barhold, the city-name Bukhara comes from the Indian word *Vihāra.*

Subsequently, the eastern state of Alexander, that of the Seleucids and the Graeco-Bactrian kingdom facilitated such contacts.

In the Muslim period, particularly in the 13th and 14th centuries, lively contacts between India and Central Asia were established. The reason was that the noblemen of the Delhi Sultanate were connected with Central Asia by origin, blood relation and religion. Noted Central Asian poets, Navoi, Jami, etc. maintained intimate links with Indian poets of the 15th cent.

Contacts between India and Transcaucasia also date back to far-off ages. Strabo testifies to a commercial route through Causasian Albania by which Indian commodities reached the Black Sea.

INDIA AND AMERICA

For a long time there was an impression that Columbus (*c.* 1446/51-1506 A.D.) first discovered America. Ireland also claims this credit. Again, Iceland claims to have first discovered this continent.

Chamanlal (*Hindu America*), on the authority of Poindexter, one-time U.S. ambassador in Peru, holds that, from the point of view of race and culture, America is only an extended form of Asia. Poindexter said that, by designating the people of the new world as Indians, Columbus did the right thing. On the authority of *History of Mexico*, published from the Foreign Affairs Department of Mexico, Chamanlal has written that it was Indians who had first colonized America. Pomponius, a contemporary of Julius Caesar (100-40 B.C.) and a writer of Roman history, wrote that, when Metallus Celer was Pro-Consul (62 B.C.) in Gaul, he was given some Indians as presents from king Suevans.

The Indians used to go to the west by sea-route in quest of minerals. In Peru the first cultivation of cotton took place in 3600 B.C. and in Mexico in 3400 B.C. In that age, cotton was an Indian commodity. It is a historical fact that there was brisk trade between Calcutta and Salem and other East Coast cities of America between 1785 and 1865. Salem, one of the flourishing ports in America, and Boston, in Massachusetts, benefited by an expanding Indo-U.S. trade. The commodities, chiefly imported from Calcutta, were, besides cotton, silk, salt petre, linseed and spices. The one thing, exported to Calcutta, Bombay and Madras, was ice. The first consignment left Boston in May, 1803. The export of ice was referred to by Thoreau in his work, entitled *Walden*.[35]

AFRICA

INDIA, EGYPT AND OTHER AFRICAN COUNTRIES

One of the earliest civilizations of the world developed in Egypt. There are many evidences of her close commercial contact with India. One such evidence is Indian colony in Egypt and Egyptian colony in India. In the *Chāndogya Upaniṣad* (8/8/5),[36] dating back to the pre-Christian times (may be pre-Buddhist), some surmise a hint about the Egyptian mummy. We get references to Indian women, dogs, cows and Indian spices loaded on camels' backs, in the procession of the Egyptian king, Ptolemy Philadelphos (reign 285-247 B.C.). This king sent Dionysios as ambassador to the Maurya king, Bindusāra. It is learnt that a chamber of the pleasure-boat of Ptolemy Philopator (221 B.C.) was studded with Indian jewels. The discovery of Indian images at Memphos, perhaps indicates an Indian colony in that region. The marks of *Cakra* (wheel) and *Triśūla* (trident) on the tomb-stone of Ptolemy are significant. The consecration,[37] by an Indian, in honour of the deity Pan of a temple of Rhodesia on the desert route towards the Red Sea, indicates contact between the two countries. Hultzsch informs us that, in a market at Bangalore, silver coins of the time of the Egyptian king, Ptolemy Soter (from 305 B.C.), have been discovered. Rostovtze seeks to show the similarity between the economic structure in the administration of king Ptolemy in Egypt and the economic provisions in the *Arthaśāstra*. For example, it may be stated that, in both these countries, there was monopoly trade in oil, salt and mines, and the administrative measures in this connection were also similar. Besides, state-socialism in both these countries was considerably similar.[38]

The scientist-geographer, Ptolemy, composed world geography (*Guide to Geography*) in about 150 A.D. He lived in Alexandria in the second century A.D. He gathered materials from those Indians who migrated and settled there. Ptolemy's book, *Tetrobibls* mentions different countries supposed to be under particular zodiacs. India was stated to be under Makara (Capricornus). The ancestors of the renowned traveller, Ibn Batutā (Indian tour 1333 A.D.) were Africans.

In the domain of astronomy, the 360-day year (twelve months of thirty days each) was recognised in Egypt as in India and Mesopotemia.

In the second half of the first century A.D., an Egyptian navigator came to India by sea-route along the coasts of the Red Sea and the Arabian Sea. He recorded his experience in the *Periplus of the Erythrean Sea.* It throws considerable light on India's trade with the west. Quite a few littoral ports also have been mentioned. It further states that ships, made in India, carrying various commodities, left these ports for the western world. Among the commodities were pearls, costly stones, spices, articles for decoration and muslin. There was ample demand for these things in the western countries. These were carried to the ports through roads. We also learn from the *Periplus* that some Indians used to live in certain islands of the Arabian Sea for commercial purposes. There was a regular colony of the Indian merchants in the islands of Socotra.

Alexandria[39] was a big port and centre of trade in Egypt. Alexander selected this place for building a city. In this city, there was a meeting of eastern and western cultures. Through this place was carried on India's trade with Rome and other western countries. The commercial commodities used to be brought to the Red Sea by sea-route. Then these were sent to the destination either by land-route or along the Nile for a thousand years. This city had been a centre of trade and of the intellectuals; because, it was a meeting place of the Jews, Syrians and the Greeks. In the Pāli work, *Milindapañha* (*c.* 2nd cent. A.D.), Alexandria has been mentioned as a place where Indians regularly lived. This is corroborated by Chrysostom and Ptolemy. In the times of Kusānas (*c.* 48-120 A.D.) many Brāhmin philosophers used to live here.

The impact of Indian culture on the Greeks of Egypt is borne out by the *Oxyrhynchus Papyri.*

An Egyptian merchant travelled in India and Ceylon and became a monk (first half of sixth century A.D.).

Cosmas Indicopleustes, or the 'Indian Navigator' as he was known in Greek, wrote in Greek an account of his travels describing the countries he had visited, including India and Ethiopia.[40]

The political history of India reveals that some Sultāns of Delhi were actively connected with the ruler of Egypt. When Muhammad Tughlak (reign 1325-1351) dreamt of world-conquest, he established friendship with the Sultān of Egypt. But, the Egyptian ruler was more concerned with the expansion of his kingdom than with action as a friend of

Muhammad. Muhammad's dream, however, proved to be utopian. Firuz Shāh Tughlak (reign 1351-1388) looked upon the Caliph of Egypt with great regard. In Muslim India Firuz, for the first time, declared himself as a representative of the aforesaid Caliph. During the first six years of Firuz's reign, he twice received directions about administration from the Caliph, and got from him royal dress as a mark of respect. The coins of Firuz contained the name of Caliph along with his own. Sultān Māhmud Khalji (reign 1436-1469) of Mālava received recognition of his kingship from the Caliph of Egypt. Sultān Ābu Said of Khurāsān sent envoys to Māhmud. Sultān Māhmud Begad of Gujarāṭ, towards the close of his reign, allied with the Egyptian Sultān, jointly tried to resist the growing power of the Portuguese in the Indian ocean. The joint venture of the Egyptian navy and the Indian army succeeded in defeating the Portuguese. But, in 1509, the Portuguese completely routed the united Muslim navy. The Turko-Afghan Sultāns of Delhi at times used to owe allegiance formally to the Caliphs of Baghdād. But, the rulers of Delhi were themselves quite powerful. During Turko-Afghan rule in Delhi, the aristrocratic Muslims used to serve as generals or administrators of the kingdoms. They also played an important part in installing a man as a king. To this respectable community belonged the Egyptian Muslims too among others. Some countries tried to utilise Egypt for curbing British power in India. This motive prompted Napolean (1769-1821) to resolve to lead an expedition against Egypt. This, along with the plan of the establishment of French power in Egypt, was a cause of headache to the English bureaucrats. They apprehended that the powerful adversary, having actually occupied Egypt, might invade India.

In Egypt, there lived some ascetics given to meditation. Both Hindu and Buddhist influence is noticeable in their saintly lifestyle, physical hardship and pure meditation.[41]

India's connexion with Africa, particularly Egypt and Ethiopia, dates back to pre-Christian times.[42]

An European Sanskrit scholar, Francis Wilford, claimed[43] in 1794, on the alleged authority of the *Padma* and *Skandapurāṇas,* that ancient Indians knew of Egypt and the lands near the sources of the Nile. It was subsequently proved that the above scholar was misled and misinformed about his source. So, his statement was rejected. The fact, however, seems that about 1200 B.C., some seafaring people invaded Egypt from where they were repulsed and came to India.

The earliest definite contact between India and Egypt and Ethiopia took place during the Achaemenian regime of Persia. In this period, the Egyptians, Ethiopians and Indians were fellow-subjects under the same empire. In the Persepolis sculptures, there are bas-reliefs of representatives of all subject -nations of the Achaemenian empire bringing tributes to the monarch. Among the nations, there are both Indians and Ethiopians. The army of Xerxes, organised for the invasion of Greece, included Indians, Egyptians and Ethiopians.

Definite historical record of India's contact with Africa dates back to about 250 B.C. when Aśoka sent Buddhist missionaries to Egypt and to some other countries like Syria.

The Arabs and Indians appear to have opened up a sea-route from South Arabia at the junction of the Red Sea and the Arabian Sea about 1000 B.C. Maritime trade flourished after South Arabians formed the State of Ethiopia (Abyssinia) in Africa. Indian goods appear to have been exported by this sea-route through the Red Sea, to Egypt. South Arabian and Indian merchants monopolised this trade. Cinnamon, malabathrum, other spices, precious stones, cotton and silk textiles, objects of iron and other metals used to be exported to Aksum (Ethiopia) and to Nubia in Egypt. The discovery of the Red Sea Arabian Sea-route to India, by the Greek and Egyptian navigators in the first century A.D., gave a fillip to this trade. The *Periplus* (*c.* 60 A.D.) gives the oldest and most reliable account of the commercial and cultural ties between India and Ethiopia.

It has been suggested[44] that king Tārkṣya, mentioned in

the *Śatapatha Brāhmaṇa* (XIII.4.3) was the Egyptian Pharaoh Taharqa. If the identification is correct, then it may be presumed that some sort of contact existed between India and Africa as early as the seventh century B.C., the probable age of the above Brāhmaṇa text.

It has been reasonably established that, about 2000 years ago, sea-traffic existed between India and Ethiopia. This trade relation continued down to the present century. In course of time, this relation became so intimate that Indian merchants developed into an influential community in Eastern and Central Africa up to Uganda and beyond.[45] There were links between the Indians in Ethiopia and other Indians higher up in Egypt from at least the third century B.C. when Aśoka sent Buddhist missionaries to Egypt. By the time of Christ, maritime and overland commerce brought India close to Ethiopia and Egypt. Naturally, cultural exchange followed.

As stated earlier, the *Periplus* testifies to flourishing commercial and cultural contacts between India and Ethiopia. Among the articles, exported by India, were iron, steel, cotton cloth, muslin, coats of skin, girdles, coloured lac, wheat, rice, clarified butter, sesame oil, honey.[46]

It is interesting to note that some loan-words from India to Ethiopian[47] (Amharic, etc.) bear testimony to close relation between the two countries. The following old Ethiopian words may be noted :

Nage (elephant) = Skt. *Nāga*
Sokar (sugar) = Pkt. *Sakkarā* = Skt. *Śarkarā*
Nisk (musk) = Skt. *Muṣka*
Santarai (game of chess) = Skt. *Caturaṅga*

H. Schoff notes (*Periplus*, pp. 64-65) that, before the conversion of the Abyssinians to Christianity about 330 A.D., "their strongest outside influence may have been Buddhism."

Christianity was introduced in Ethiopia early in the fourth century A.D. by Syrian merchants who participated in the commerce between Egypt and India. King 'Ezana (d. *c.* 330

A.D.) of Ethiopia embraced Christianity which went some way in closely linking up that country with the Syrian Christian world of South India in Kerala. This community was connected with Indian trade.

Besides Indian merchants from Western India, some Buddhists, Jains and Brahmins also probably lived in Ethiopia. Buddhist missionaries were sent by Aśoka to Egypt in the middle of the third century B.C. It is likely that Buddhist ideas and ideals travelled to Ethiopia too.

In the wake of expansion of Arab power, following the establishment of Islam in Arabia in the seventh century A.D., from Sind in India to Spain in Europe, direct commercial and other kinds of connexion between Christian Ethiopia and Hindu India declined, and were finally snapped. Muslim Arabs now became dominant. Nevertheless, Indian merchants, both Hindu and Muslim , were still active in Ethiopia, Arabian and East African trade-centres even during the troubled times of the 16th and 17th centuries; this is known from the Portuguese records left by Manoel de Almeida, a missionary who lived and travelled in Ethiopia and India from 1602 till his death in 1646.[48]

Ras Tafari, at first Regent (1916-1930) under Queen Zauditu of Ethiopia, later became (1936) Emperor Haile Selassie I of the independent and sovereign country. The history of Ethiopia from the second decade of the present century was marked by Italian aggression supported by some western powers. After the outbreak of World War II, the British supported Ethiopia. Indian soldiers were engaged in fighting the Italian army in Ethiopia. Eventually, Ethiopia regained freedom and became grateful to India. India has been helping Ethiopia in her reconstruction work. The intimate contact of the two countries was marked by Emperor Selassie's visit to India in 1956 and the then Indian President's visit to Ethiopia in 1966.

No account of Indo-Ethiopian relation can be complete without a reference to the Hābshis. They were the Abyssinian or Ethiopian slaves. Among them, there was a class of enunchs. Ethiopia came to be known as a supplier of Hābshi slaves, particularly enunchs, for Muslim countries, especially in the courts and harems of Muslim rulers. In India, Hābshi Khojās (Abyssinian eunuchs) were appointed, in the harems of Muslim kings, as guards and as servants in charge of the women. Queen Rāziāh (1236-40) had such a slave to whom she showed special favours. He was raised to the position of Master of the Stables.

From the account of Ibn Batutā (middle of the 14th century) we learn of the presence of a number of Hābshi mercenaries in the Indian mainland and in the Indian seas. In the Bāhmani kingdom of the Deccan (1347-1518), armies of slaves and mercenaries of Hābshis used to be recruited. Hābshis were present in the military and civil services of the various States, *e.g.* those of Ādil Shāh Dynasty of Bijāpur, Nizām Shāhi Dynasty of Āhmadnagar, Quli Qutb Shāhi House of Golcondā, Imad Shāhis of Berar, etc. Some of these Hābshis rose to prominent positions. For instance, Mālik Ambar (*c.* 1615), a Hābshi, became a Minister of Āhmadnagar at the time of Jahāngir. Other Hābshis played prominent roles in the Deccan states in the 16th-17th centuries. Thousands of Hābshi mercenaries took sides in political struggles. Some Muslims of India intermarried with the Hābshis.

Hābshi slaves figured also in the courts of the Muslim Sultāns of Bengal. Sultān Ruknuddin Barbak (1459-74) is said to have inducted, into his court, a host of Hābshi guards and soldiers. In course of time, these pampered slaves grew in power; so much so that they threatened the stability of the State. In fact, the Hābshis dominated and ruled over Bengal for six years (1487-93). Mālik Andil or Andiyal (*c.* 1490) distinguished himself as a loyal Hābshi commander of forces.

The Ethiopians, who came to India through centuries, were gradually Indianised as a section of the Indian Muslim community. The Hābshis formed part of the naval defence forces of different independent States from the 17th century.

The Hābshis, who were known by the honourable sobriquet of *Sidis* (Masters), built up, for themselves, a small state, Janjira, on the Bombay coast.

FOOTNOTES

1. Established, in Bhāgalpur district in Bihār, by the Bengal king Devapāla (*c.* 810-850).
2. Karaka, *History of the Parsis,* 1884, I, p. xv.
3. Translation of Jātakas by Francis and Neil, vol. III, p. 83 (Jātaka no. 339).
4. *Loeb Classical Literary Series,* vol. VII, p. 203.
5. Kane, *History of Dharmaśāstra,* V, pt. 1, p. 596.
6. *Journal of Near Eastern Studies,* IV, p. 16
7. Neugabauer, *op. cit.*; Maclean, *Babylonian Astrology and Its Relation to the Old Testament,* p. 7, note 3.
8. The *Nile and Egyptian Civilization,* p. 453.
9. Kanc, *op. cit.* ; p. 582 and footnote 869.
10. Probably to be distinguished from the dramatist of this name. For the dramatist, see Keith, *Sanskrit Drama,* 1924, p. 60, f.n.3.
11. Hall, *Ancient History of the Near East.*
12. See S.M.H. Nainar, *Arab Geographers' Knowledge of Southern India.*
13. See Basham, *The Wonder that was India,* Preface.
14. See Bongard-Levin and Vigasin, *The Image of India,* Ch. VI (Ancient Indian Civilisation in the Light of New Archaeological Excavations in Soviet Central Asia).
15. See. D. C Sircar, *Indian Epigraphy,* p. 202.
16. See Radharaman Ray's article, Jābhār Viṣṇu Avatār, *Ānandabājār Patrikā,* dated 19/2/84 A.D.
17. Liyang-Shu, 54, 22 etc.
18. According to a modern scholar, it is a compilation of the second century A.D., made from several works.
19. See Amitabha Chakraborty, *Korīya Upadvīpe Bhārata-Sabhyatā,* Bengali *Ānandabājār Patrikā,* dated 14/10/84 A.D.
20. See discussion on Literature and Language under Foreign Influence on India.

21. Girls engaged for dancing and singing before deities in temples.
22. Vide Yule and Cordier, *The Book of Ser Marco Polo*, II, pp. 345-46. For the places, visited by Polo, see p. 335 of this book.
23. *Praeparatio Evangelica*, XI, 3.
24. Werner, J., Greeks and Jews, *Journal of Religion*, April, 1938, p. 128.
25. Pliny, *Natural History*, XXX.3.
26. W.W. Tarn, *Greeks in Bactria and India*, pp. 313-14, 380-81, 390-91.
27. For details, see Bongard-Levin and Vigasin, *The Image of India*.
28. See the section "Miscellaneous".
29. E.g. Graeco-Buddhist Sculptures, *Asiatic Qrly. Review*, Sr. II. Vol. VII, 1894; *Indian Antiquary*, II, 1873.
30. See Bethlenfalvy, *India in Hungarian Learning and Literature*, p. 13.
31. *Ibid.*
32. *Ibid.*
33. *Ibid.*
34. For details, see Bongard-Levin and Vigasin *The Image of India*.
35. For information about commercial relations between India and America from the late eighteenth century to the mid-nineteenth century, see the article, entitled The American Connection, published in the daily newspaper, *Telegraph*, Calcutta, 17.3.90.
36. C.f. *tasmāt... pretasya śarīram bhikṣayā vasanenālaṃkāreṇeti saṃskurvantyetena...*
37. Charlesworth, *Trade-Routes and Commerce of the Roman Empire*, p. 59.
38. Cambode, *American History*, VII. 154.
39. For invasion in India, Alexander set up two colonies which also were named Alexandria. One of them was in Afghānistān near Kābul, and the other was at the confluence of the Chenab and the Indus in Sind. Both these cities succumbed to the ravages of time.
40. Vide S.K. Chatterji, *India and Ethiopia*, p. 32.
41. D. Mansel, *The Gnostic Heresies of the First and Second Centuries*, 1857, p. 32.

42. For details, see S.K. Chatterji, *India and Ethiopia.*
43. Paper in the *Asiatick Researches,* Calcutta, Reprinted, London, 1801.
44. By H.K. Deb (d. 1966) in his paper, Vedic India and the Near East, published in *Jour. of Royal Asiatic Society of Bengal,* XIV.2, 1948. This suggestion has been endorsed by S.K. Chatterji in his monograph, *India and Ethiopia,* Calcutta, 1968.
45. J.H. Speke, *Jour. of the Discovery of the Sources of the Nile,* London, 1863.
46. *Periplus,* Schof's ed., 1912, pp. 6, 14.
47. E. Littmann, Indien und Abessinen, *Festgabe Hermann Jacobi,* Bonn, 1926.
48. See S.K. Chatterji, *op. cit.,* p. 58.

CHAPTER IV

Influence of India in Foreign Countries

We have already noticed that India had various kinds of contact with different countries ever since the Vedic age. We have also seen how and when India came in contact with those countries. In this chapter, we shall discuss the different matters in which India influenced other countries, and shall assess the extent of this influence. Our discussion will include also the manner in which Indian ideas were imbibed by the foreigners living in India.

The spheres of influence are as follows:

(*a*) Science and Technology,
(*b*) Scriputure, Literature and Philosophy
(*c*) Religion,
(*d*) Architecture, Sculpture, Painting, etc.
(*e*) Script,
(*f*) Language and Grammar,
(*g*) Cultural Influence,
(*h*) Music (vocal, instrumental) and Dance,
(*i*) Law, Politics and Statecraft,
(*j*) Geographical names,
(*k*) Sports and Amusements,
(*l*) Inscriptions and Coins,
(*m*) Miscellaneous.

Before discussing the subject of this chapter, we state below the opinions of some highly intellectual Western scholars about the influence of Indian culture in the West.

There is a growing interest in Great Britain and other western countries in the cultural heritage of India. For several centuries past Indian culture has been attracting the western people in various ways. But, in the present century, their attitude is respectful. They are minutely analysing the contrast between Indian culture and their own. In order to comprehend Indian thought, one has to know thoroughly Vivekānanda, Rabindranāth and Mahātmā Gāndhi; because their ideas are rooted in ancient Indian culture. Vivekānanda emphasised two elements of Indian culture, viz *Prajñā* (wisdom) and *Karuṇā* (compassion). The essence of Rabindranāth's teaching is universal fraternity and the negation of discrimination in all spheres of life. Gāndhiji stressed non-violence which has been recognised in recent times in the west. In Great Britain books on Indian culture are being avidly studied and the film on Gāndhiji's life has, in many ways, satisfied the curiosity of the people of that country.[1]

What has been said by another renowned Western scholar[2] is briefly as follows:

Time was when the western people did not set much store by researches about Oriental subjects; because, there was an impression that such subjects were full of mysticism and had no connection with the mainstream of education. But at present, Oriental learning has got its proper place in the educational set up of the west, free from prejudice and pre-conceived notions. Now the students of Oriental learning are competing with the students of vocational subjects. The current thinking is that, for international contact, there is nothing comparable to historical research about the Asian people. The scholar said that William Jones (1746-94), by his devotion to Oriental learning, aimed at the sublimation of human mind. On the above occasion, another distinguished scholar,[3] professor at King's College, London, while tracing the background of the foundation of the Society, said that a twofold motive prompted its foundation; one was respect for Indian culture and the other its decadence in the close of the eighteenth century and early in the nineteenth century.

Will Durant, a leading historian of the present times, says:-

India was the motherland of our race, and Sanskrit the mother of Europe's language. She was the mother of our philosophy; mother through the Arabs of much of our mathematics, mother through the Buddha of the ideals embodied in Christianity. Mother India is in many ways the mother of us all.

A. SCIENCE AND TECHNOLOGY

This topic will be discussed under the following heads :
1. Mathematics, 2. Astronomy, 3. Medical Science,
4. Mineralogy and Metallurgy, 5. Physics,
6. Chemistry, 7. Technology.

(I) MATHEMATICS

China[4]

In this subject, China has unequivocally acknowledged her debt to India. In a list, prepared during the rule of the Sui Dynasty of China (581-618 A.D.), a number of scientific Sanskrit treatises has been mentioned; e.g. *Po-Lo-Men Suyanf* (Indian method of counting; three treatises), *Po-Lo-Men-Wen Ching* (Indian astronomy-21 works) and some more astronomical works. *Po-Lo-Men* means Brāhmaṇas. The object of the astronomical school founded (seventh century) at Chang-Nan was the dissemination of Indian astronomy and the revamping of the almanac in accordance with the Hindu method. Similarity between China and India is noticeable in the determination of the area of a circle, and of the approximate value of π (3.1415925636...) etc. It cannot, however, be asserted that, in every case, there is borrowing from India. The area of a segment of a circle, as laid down in China's earliest arithmetic (second century B.C.), is found in the treatise of Mahāvīra (*c.* 830 A.D.) of India. The solution of indeterminate equation of the first degree occurs in the work of Āryabhaṭa (fourth century A.D.). This is found in China's works of a much later date.

Arabia

Some Arabians were engaged to translate into Arabic the *Brāhmasphuṭasiddhānta* and *Khaṇḍakhādyaka* of Brahmagupta (b. 598 A.D.)

With the assistance of Hindu scholars, Al Fazari (d. 796 or 806) and Yakub Ibn Tārik (d. 796) completed this translation. Such translations resulted in the introduction of the Indian methods of writing number in Arabia, as some scholars think. In the ninth century, Al Kindi wrote a book, entitled *Hisābul Hindi* about the Indian system of counting. That Arabia was indebted, in this respect, to India is proved by the fact that, in that country, it is called *Hindisat* or Indian knowledge. Al khwārizmi, for the first time, introduced numbers in the place of letters indicating numbers. In his Algebra, he has utilised Indian works among his sources. The Arabian scholar, Al Battani (877-918) has taken ratio, sine and tangent from the geometry of Āryabhaṭa (b. 476 A.D.).

The rise and spread of Islam as well as the political supremacy of the Muslims helped the dissemination of Indian mathematics, astronomy etc. in foreign countries, especially West Asia, North Africa and Spain.

EUROPE, PARTICULARLY GREECE

In course of time, this system got into other places. According to some scholars, *e.g.* Schroeder (1851-1920) and Garbe (1857-1927), the Geometry of Greek Pythagoras (*c.* 580-500 B.C.), was, to some extent, influenced by Hindu geometry. The Vedic *Śulvasūtra,* dating back to centuries before Christ possibly even before Pythagoras might have inspired Greece in this respect. This opinion is, however, not accepted by scholars like Keith.[5] Some think that Diophants (third century) of Alexandria, the earliest algebra-knowing man and the father of this branch of knowledge in Europe, got inspiration from India. Up to the sixteenth century, Binomial Theorem was unknown in Europe. In this also India was, perhaps, the pioneer. About the thirteenth century A.D., before which the decimal system was not known in Europe, the Indian decimal system was introduced, and gradually spread all over the world.

Around fourth century A.D., the highest number was myriad, *i.e.* 10^4, and, in Rome, it was mille or thousand. It was India that thought out the higher number called *Parārdha*, *i.e.* 10^{12}. In the classical age, the highest number was 10^{53}. These great numbers Europe learnt perhaps from India. The civilized world got the idea of zero from India. The book on the Hindu system of counting, composed by the aforesaid Al Khwarizmi (d. *c.* 844 A.D.), was translated into Latin under the title *De numero indico.* According to Cajori, both the form and content of modern arithmetic and algebra are basically Indian.[6]

(II) ASTRONOMY
ASIATIC COUNTRIES

South-East Asia

Certain Cambodian inscriptions mentioned Horāśāstra. The *Siddhānta* treatises of Indian astronomical science were included among the subjects to be learnt by the princes. In Indo-China and Indonesia, *Sūryasiddhānta* was adopted as an epitome of astronomy. There is deep influence of Sanskrit treatises in the Wariga literature of Bali.

MONGOLIA

All the twenty-eight asterisms (*nakṣatra*) have been accepted in Mongolia under the term *Nagsadar.* The Mongolian Susaga (from Susakha ?) appears to have been a local term for Viśākhā.

CEYLON

Anomabassi, author of the astronomical work, *Daivajñakāmadhenu*, was, according to *Mahāvaṃśa*, a contemporary of Parākramabāhu (1236-71 A.D.). In this work, the author seeks, in 2618 verses, to epitomise the authoritative astronomical works of Varāhmahira (*c.* 475-550 A.D.), Bhoja (11th cent. -first half) and Parāśara; these names occur in this work.

CHINA

Several works on astronomy, written during the rule of Sui Dynasty (7th cent. A.D.) are mentioned. Of these, noteworthy are :

1. *Po-Lo-Men Tien-Wen-Ching-it* is a work on Indian astronomy in twenty-one volumes.
2. *Po-Lo-Men Chie Chie Sien-Jen-Wen-Suo* had discussed the activities of the Brāhmaṇa, named Chie Chie, in thirty volumes.
3. *Po-Lo-Men Tien-Wen*—it is a single volume on astronomy.
4. *Po-Lo-Men-Yin Iand Suyan Ching*—it contains a discussion on the determination of time according to Indian system, in one volume.

We have stated earlier that *Po-Lo-Men* denotes Brāhmaṇa.

Details about the contents of the works are not known. But, from the titles and their mention in the list of Royal Dynasty, it is clear that, even in that far-off age, curiosity about Indian astronomy was aroused among the Chinese scholars.

It is learnt that, in seventh century, Indian *Siddhāntas*, associated with Gautama, Kaśyapa and Kumāra, were taught at the place, called Changnan. The names of astronomers like Gautama (Chu-Tan) are known from the records of the Thang dynasty. It is known that Chu-Tan Hasita (Gautama Siddha or Siddhārtha), an astronomer of the Thang regime (eighth century) translated the Indian almanac under the title *Chiu-Chi-Li.* From about this time the Indian planets, Rāhu (ascending node of the moon) and Ketu (descending node), in relation to eclipse and some other matters were incorporated into Chinese astronomy. It is said that a Tāntric-Buddhist, named I Hāsing, of the Thang regime, was ordered by the emperor to study the arcana of Indian astronomy current in China.

With Buddhism Indian astronomy, too, entered China. Some Indian incantations, connected with this science, were also current in China. Indian astronomers were included among those who formed an astronomical community under the Chinese government. The astronomical treatise, *Navagrahasiddhānta,* is preserved even today in the collection dating back to the Tang regime.

ARABIA

The curiosity of the Arabians about astronomy was aroused by the Persian treatise *Ziz-assrahariyar.* In the Sassanian regime (*c.* 226-641 A.D.) the Tables, based on astronomical observations, were written. In this work, which reveals the influence of Indian astronomy, the Arabian scholar, Al Beruni[7] (973-1048) was conversant with Brahmagupta's (b. 598) *Brāhmāsphuṭasiddhānta* (628), the lost commentary by Balabhadra (*c.* eighth century) and the fragmentary exposition by Pṛthūdakasvāmin (sometime before 864 A.D.). He knew the *Āryabhaṭīya* also (*Al Beruni's India,* I, p. 158). He translated into Arabic the *Laghujātaka, Khaṇḍakhādyaka* and *Karaṇatilaka.* In his account of India, he has quoted from the above work of Brahmagupta, particularly from its twenty-first chapter. Ibn Tārik, in his treatise, called *Tarkib Al Aflak,* reveals the influence of Sanskrit astronomy. He has mentioned the terms *Saura, Sāvana, Cāndra* and *Nakṣatra* denoting various methods of measuring time. Āmir Khasru (1324 or 1325) writes that the astronomer, Ābu Māshār, studied astronomy at Vārānasi for ten years.

When Sind was under Caliph Mansur (753-74), some Indian scholars took manuscripts of Brahmagupta's *Brāhmasiddhānta* and *Khaṇḍakhādyaka* to Baghdad. These two works were translated into Arabic by Al Fajari and also probably by Yākub Ibn Tārik. These two works were called respectively *Sindhind* and *Al Barkand.* Āryabhaṭa's works also were translated into Arabic or adapted. Al Khwarijmi (850) prepared his astronomical Tables, called *Ziz* on the basis of Al Fajari's translation.

It is reported[8] that a book, called *Manuṣyajātaka,* on astrology, written in Arabic and in Devanāgarī scripts with a Sanskrit commentary, has been discovered.

The Arabians, perhaps, got the idea of *Nakṣatras* (asterisms) from India. Āryabhaṭa's discovery that the earth is round influenced Arabia. His *Sūryasiddhānta* exercised profound influence in the neighbouring countries.

SYRIA

See the chapter on the nature of India's contact with different countries.

EUROPEAN COUNTRIES

Some technical terms of this science were, perhaps, learnt by Europe from India; *e.g.* the word *aux* is derived from the Sanskrit word *ucca.* In a Latin manuscript on astronomy, discovered by Thorndike in England, the Hindu system has been followed. It reveals the influence of Brahmagupta's *Khaṇḍakhādyaka* and *Dhyānopadeśa.*[9]

In connection with foreign influence in India, we shall see that some technical terms are similar in Greek and Indian science. Of these words, some are undoubtedly Greek. But others are Sanskrit. So, in the case of these words, mutual influence cannot be ruled out. According to some,[10] after Alexander's invasion of India some Greek scholars lived in this country. Some of them composed Sanskrit works. Kane points out[11] that two big works on astrology were composed by Sphujidhvaja and Mīnarāja both of whom claimed to have been Yavana kings. Among the Greeks, many learnt the Indian language and many were Indianized.[12] At Besnagar (a city in old Mālava) the inscription of the Greek Heliodoros has been written in Sanskrit.

In the thirteenth century, the *Āryabhaṭīya* was translated into Latin. Horace(d. 8 B.C.), in his *Ode to Maecenas,* has referred to the zodiacs Tulā (Libra), Vṛścika (Scorpio) and Karkaṭa and the evil influence of Śani (Saturn) in his horoscope.[13] Thus the influence of Indian astronomy is obvious.

(III) MEDICAL SCIENCE

The germs of this science in India are found in the Veda, especially the *Atharvaveda*. This science appeared in a systematic form long before Christ. Surgery also was developed. Of the medical works, the earliest extant one is the *Caraka-saṃhitā* (1st and 2nd cent. A.D.). The earliest available authoritative work on surgery is the *Suśruta-saṃhitā*. India is one of the ancient lands in which etiology and physiology were developed to a great extent. The other two countries are China and Greece.

TIBET, MONGOLIA, RUSSIA

It is known that the people of ancient Tibet were accustomed to Indian drugs. It is also learnt that the *Yogaśataka* of Nāgārjuna or Vararuci of uncertain date were translated into Tibetan. The Sanskrit medical work, *Amṛtahṛdaya* (four volumes) was translated into that language in the eighth century; the original work is lost. There is a Tibetan exposition of this work. Its Tibetan exposition was translated into Mongolian under the title *Dorben Undusun* which was brought to Russia. The Mongol work *Rasiyan* known as *Amṛtahṛdaya Aṣṭāṅga*. There are Mongol names of certain Indian drugs. The wellknown Tibetan work *Tanjur* contains, among other Āyurvedic treatises, translation of Vāgbhaṭa's (*c.* 7th cent. A.D.) *Aṣṭāṅgahṛdaya* with two commentaries. Indian veterinary science also was included in the *Tanjur*. The medical system of Tibet was based mainly on *Āyurveda*.[14] This Tibetan system was adopted by various hill tribes of the Himalayas, near Tibet. In it there is mention also of Śālihotra's *Asvāyurveda*. These works were rendered from Tibetan into Mongolian. This Mongolian translation was partly published, with Russian translation, by Pozdnevev. India was the homeland of the

Āyurveda treatises fragments of which have been discovered in Mongolia.

CEYLON[15]

Indian drugs, introduced by Buddhist missionaries, were entirely adopted in Ceylon. The manuscripts of the bilingual *Yogaśataka* (summary of the Āyurvedic Aṣṭāṅga) existed in Tibetan translation up to the end of the nineteenth century. Of the Sanskrit medical works, composed in this country, the *Sārārthasaṃgraha* is stated, in the *Mahāvaṃśa* (37/108-11, 145), to have been composed by king Buddhadāsa (accession 338 A.D.). The oldest medical treatise, *Yogārṇava*, belongs to the thirteenth century.[16]

BURMA (MYANMAR)

The people of Burma adotped the Āyurvedic system to a great extent. The Burmese technical terms in medical science were derived from Sanskrit.

BAGHDAD

During the regime of Hārun Al Rashid (786-803), for translating the works of Caraka, Suśruta and Vāgbhaṭa into Arabic, Indian scholars were appointed. During the period from the seventh century to the ninth, the name of Caraka was highly esteemed in the region of Saracenic and Latin world.

ARABIA

Indian medical science has been discussed in the Arabic work *Kitāb-Al-Hawi* of Al Rhazi (d. 932). Caraka has been mentioned several times in the Latin translation of this work by Farachi (*c.* thirteenth century). The aforesaid Al Rhazi, who was an Arabian physician, has recognised the works of Caraka and Suśruta as authoritative. The Latin translation of Avicenna's medical work had been authoritative in Europe up to the seventeenth century. In this work, Indian Āyurveda has been copiously used. The famous Barmaki family played the leading role in introducing the Indian works on Āyurveda and Toxicology.

In connection with Suśruta, the following method has been mentioned. If there is any injury to the intestine, the Indian surgeon holds together the split parts, and places big ants over the affected place. When those ants bite the affected place, these are killed and their lips are mixed with the wound so that they get mixed with the body. If there is any injury to a side of one's lower abdomen, the affected part is stitched. The Arabians learnt this method which was transmitted to the west. This method still prevails in the Somali coast.

It is interesting to note that an emigrant Indian medical scholar succeeded in curing the long-standing stomach-ailment of his royal patron (Hārun al-Rashid) and became the physician-in-Chief of the state dispensary. He translated the *Suśruta-saṃhitā* into Arabic under the title *Kilal-Samural-hind-i* of Susrud. Ali ibn Zain translated the *Carakasaṃhitā* as the treatise of 'Sarag'. In later times, Mādhava's *Nidāna* was translated under the title Badan and the *Aṣṭāṅgahṛdaya* as *Astankar.* The *Siddhayoga* was also translated into Arabic.

PERSIA

In 850 A.D., Rabbun, a physician of Tabari in Persia, elaborately described Indian drugs in his work, entitled *Firdaus Ul Hikmat.* The Arabic translations of Āyurvedic treatises were translated into Persian. The autobiography of Burzūya, a physician under the Iranian king, Chosroes I (531-579 A.D.), contains a summary of embryology. According to Hertel, it contains characteristically Indian ideas. There is definite evidence of Indian influence on the renowned medical school established (fifth cent. A.D.) at Gundesapur in Suriana by the Greek Nestorians expelled from the Byzantine Empire.[17] In this connexion, it may be noted that the *Caraka-saṃhitā* mentions, in the chapter on the functions of the 'wind', the presence of Kāṅkāyana, a physician from

Bāhlika (*bāhlikabhiṣaj*), in the company of the learned men around Master Ātreya.[18] Bāhlīka or Bactria, on the other side of the Hindu Kush mountains, was a part of the territory of the aforesaid Chosroes I.

The Indian Hakims, who practised the Unāni system of treatment, are known to have made considerable contribution to the medical literature of Persia.[19]

CENTRAL ASIA

Āyurveda travelled to this region along with Buddhism and Indian culture. A considerable portion of the *Bower Manuscript* (*c.* fourth century A.D.), discovered (1890) at Kāshgarh, deals partly with Indian medical science. Of the three medical treatises, contained in it, one deals with the curative properties of *laśuna,* other roots and herbs, particularly relating to optical diseases.

Another treatise, the *Navanītaka,* is a huge work in fourteen chapters. The third one contains medical formulae in seventy-two verses. Of a semi-medical character is the third one containing spells and charms to counteract the effect of snake-bite.[20]

The Kuchean translation of a collection of Sanskrit medical texts and a part of *Yogaśataka,* attributed to Nāgāruna or Vararuci, with Kuchean rendering; have also been discovered.[21]

Some Uigurian manuscripts on medical science, based on original Sanskrit texts, have been published.

An extensive area of Asia is inhabited by people speaking the Turkish language. Fragments of some Āyurvedic works, *e.g.*, Ravigupta's *Siddhasāra,* are preserved in old Turkish language.

SIBERIA

Many Āyurvedic works are preserved in the libraries of Siberia. It is learnt that some reputed physicians used to follow Āyurveda in their treatment.

CAMBODIA (KAMPUCHEA)

In some manuscripts of this place, the name of Suśruta occurs. Besides, there are lists of the Sanskrit names of drugs presented to different temples during the reign of king Jayavarman VII (*c.* 1181-1281). The king is known to have established 102 hospitals (*ārogya-śālās*). An inscription contains 23 Sanskrit verses giving the account of diet and medicinal herbs supplied to these hospitals. Suśruta's work is mentioned in an inscription of the last decade of the ninth century A.D.

CHINA

This country came to know of Āyurveda in the fifth century A.D. The pediatric text, called *Rāvaṇakumāratantra*, was translated into Chinese in the eleventh century. The Chinese work on the diseases and treatment of pregnant women is, perhaps, a translation of the *Kaśyapasaṃhitā*. In medical science, there is some similarity between India and China. According to Needham, the Indian *Cāülmogrā* and some other drugs have found a place in the list of Chinese medicines for several centuries. It is stated in the earliest biography (233-296 A.D.) of the famous Chinese surgeon, Huā, that his surgical skill was only an imitation of the methods practised by the Āyurvedic physician Jīvaka, a contemporary of the Buddha. We are informed that Huā used to operate on a person after rendering the affected part benumbed. He used to apply surgical instruments in the intestine, and could operate upon the head.

JAPAN AND KOREA

The influence of Indian medical science on that of Japan is obvious. In Sho Sho-In, a considerable number of drugs, with their Indian names, have been preserved since the eighth century A.D. It is the main provincial temple in Japan, generally known as Todaiji, and was founded by the then emperor at Nara in 745 A.D. It was a temple of the Royal family, and the largest and strongest monastery. The main store of this temple is called Sho Sho-In. It still exists and contains many valuable articles.

Indian drugs were current in Korea also.

GREECE

The idea that breath pervades the whole body is common to Āyurveda and the Greek *Hippocratic Collection*. The various kinds of wind like *Prāṇa*, contained within the body, are wellknown in Āyurveda. In this respect, it is not known whether or not the Vedic thought spread in the countries influenced by Greece. As in the Āyurveda, the idea of *Tridoṣa*, i.e. derangement of the three humours, called *Vāyu* (wind), *Pitta* (bile) and *Kapha* (phlegm), occurs in the Greek *Timaeus*. This idea is found even in the Vedic literature dating back to at least 1500 B.C. So, Indian influence on the *Timaeus* of Plato (428-348 B.C.) is not unlikely. Perhaps this idea reached Greece through Persia. From the aforesaid *Hippocratic Collection* (*c.* 460 B.C.) the indebtedness of Greece in certain medicines and some basic medical principles can be inferred. In connection with breath, the Greek writer holds that disease is a natural occurrence. Similar statement is found in the Indian School of Ātreya, and, in connection with wind, in some Vedic works. From the similarity in the medical science of these two countries some think that India is the borrower. But, though India admits Greek influence in astronomy, there is no such admission in the case of medical science. The Indian medical science does not contain any term that may indicate foreign influence. On the other hand, the statements of Hippocrates, on the following matters, agree with Indian medical science:

Emphasis on prognosis, greater importance of diet than medicine, four faults in respect of *rakta* (blood), *Śleṣmā* (phlegm), *śvetapitta* (white bile), *pītapitta* (yellow bile), their change with the change of seasons, etc. His writings about medicine appear to hint at his familiarity with black pepper, ginger, etc. mentioned in Āyurveda. These reasons lead us to suppose that Greece was the borrower. This surmise is not unreasonable in view of the fact that Āyurveda was older.

The theory that diseases are caused by the derangement of the three humours, viz. *Vāta, Pitta, Kapha,* is common to India and Greece. This concept, merely indicated in the *Ṛgveda,* appears in the *Atharvaveda* which clearly enumerates the three humours. The *Atharvaveda-pariśiṣṭa* shows the clear formulation of the theory. It emerges as a comprehensive theory of causation, symptoms and treatment of diseases in the *Bhela-saṃhitā* which is not posterior to the Hippocratic tracts. Might be that the idea arose in Greece independently. But, in view of the fact that the Indian concept was much older, and that communication between the two countries, dates back to a period even earlier than Alexander's invasion (327 or 326 B.C.), there is possibility of borrowing on the part of Greece.

Megasthenes (Indian visit *c.* 302 B.C.) gives recipes for curing elephant-diseases, which betray clear borrowing from the *Hastyayurveda* of Pālakāpya.[22] The Āyurvedic dry *pippalī* (long pepper), used in prescriptions for eyes, was adopted in Greece under the name Median (Indian) medicine *peperi.*

Arrian writes that the Greeks did not know the antidote of snake-poison. So, Alexander appointed Indian physicians for this purpose. Some of them accompanied his army in its return journey to Greece. Nearchos (4th cent. B.C.) also writes about the Indian expertise in this respect. Strabo refers to Indian physicians. Elements of *Āyurveda,* perhaps, found their way to Greece even earlier through Persia, and the trade-routes by sea. This inference is warranted by the fact that, besides black pepper and ginger, noted above, cardamoms, musk-root plant, indigo and cane-sugar, indigenous to India at that time, figured among the earliest exports of India to Greek ports.

ROME

The famous Roman physician, Celsus (*c.* first century A.D.), in his medical treatise, has referred to Lithotomy (removal, by surgery, of kidney-stone) current in ancient India. It is understood that the Roman physicians were engaged in search of Indian drugs. The above physician has acknowledged his debt to India in respect of eye-ointment and the Indian method of plastering. Galen (131-201 A.D.) of Pergamum has acknowledged his debt to India in respect of the things mentioned by the aforesaid Celsus.

ENGLAND

According to the great Indologist, Basham,[23] the English people learnt the art of plastic surgery, particularly Rhinoplastic surgery and the method of reshaping broken ears and lips from India in the eighteenth century under the English East India Company. In recent times, the efficacy of certain methods, taught in the Yogaśāstra of ancient India in respect of the management of various physical and mental maladies, has been recognised in western countries.

The close relation of body and mind was taken into consideration by the Indian physicians in treatment. The method of curing certain diseases by hypnotism was discovered in India. At present, this method prevails in the foreign countries also. Braid, Esdaile and Elliotson of England learnt this method in India.

Suśruta has mentioned 760 herbal medicines. Many of these are found in the list of western drugs. In the *Bower Manuscript*, referred to earlier, there is praise of garlic. Now-a-days, its efficacy has been recognised in various countries. In India, *Sarpagandhā* (*Raulfia serpentina*) is used for soothing the nerves. At present, this is being used in many countries for curing mental diseases.

(IV) MINERALOGY AND METALLURGY

From the *Periplus* we learn that, in the first century, Indian iron and steel used to be exported to Africa, particularly Ethiopia. The Romans, Egyptians and the Arabians highly praised the skill of the Indian metallurgists in extracting metals from ores. The skill of the Indians in casting metals earned praise. It is believed that the art of bending thin rods of steel, art of making a sort of blades etc. were learnt by other countries from India.[24] The Persians considered Indian swords to be the best. *Jabāb I Hind* (Indian answer) meant stroke of an Indian sword of steel. There is evidence of the export of Indian steel in about the fifth century A.D. Al Kindi (ninth century) writes that steel used to be exported from India to Arabia.[25]

According to some scholars, notably Martlet, the foundation of European metallurgy was laid by the nomadic immigrants who were, perhaps, Gypsies. P. Batailard (1814-1894) thinks that the Gypsies introduced bronze into Europe.[26] In support of his view he has referred to a discovery. In the weapons and jewellery, discovered in the Baltic Coast, there is the Indian sign of *Svastika*. In connection with this, it may be noted that, at a place in Vienna, a golden broach of about 400 A.D. has been discovered. A coloured stone is set on it. It appears that the practice of setting stones on metallic things started in India.[27]

(V) PHYSICS

Certain ideas of this science appeared to have been discovered in India. According to the atomic theory, found in the Vaiśeṣika philosophy, *aṇu* (molecule) is just a point, it has position, but no magnitude. There is reason to believe that the ideas about elasticity, cohesion, impenetrability, viscosity, fluidity, porosity, etc. originated in India. The Indian scientists came to the conclusion that atoms cannot exist in a disintegrated manner.

Molecules are microscopic, eternal and fundamental. The Jainas used to think that Umāsvāti analysed the mutual attraction and repulsion of atoms in the formation of molecudes, and matter cannot be inflinitely divisible. So, we see that, for the initial knowledge of physics, the world is indebted to India. The time of Kaṇāda, founder of Vaiśeṣika philosophy, is uncertain. Generally he is supposed to have been a contemporary of the Buddha (sixth-fifth century B.C.).

(VI) CHEMISTRY

In India, chemistry arose as a handmaid of Āyurdeva. It originated out of the necessity of preparing Āyurvedic medicines, calcination etc. of metals, preparation of various kinds of wine, etc. At first, it appeared as pure alchemy. The prevalence of this branch of knowledge as early as the Indus Valley Civilization can be inferred from painted pottery.

Indian chemistry exercised some influence in Arabia and China.

The dawn of Āyurveda in India took place as early as the Vedic age, particularly in the *Atharvaveda*. There is reference to this science in the *Mahābhāṣya* of Patañjali (*c.* second century B.C.). There is evidence of the cultivation of this science in the Buddhist *Vinayapiṭaka* of pre-Christian times. Caraka (*c.* first or second century A.D.) was, perhaps, the first man to write a treatise on this science.

(VII) TECHNOLOGY

Now-a-days Indians are visiting foreign countries in droves for learning technology. It should be noted that technology, in however rudimentary a form, was not unknown in ancient India. India's contribution to world technology is not insignificant. The spinning wheel arose in India. The stirrup, used by horse-riders, originated in India as early as the second century B.C. The use of horse in war had been prevalent from remote antiquity. Besides, this animal was widely used by kings, in hunting excursions and for joy-ride. So, it is natural that the necessary appurtenances were known to the people since early times. Air-guns were, perhaps, made for the first time in Europe in the sixteenth century A.D. The Indian *Nalika* (pipe-gun ?) was, perhaps, its precursor; from it small arrows or iron bullets could be hurled.

Bhāskara (b. 1114 A.D.) was its founder, and Europe and Arabia were the borrowers.

D.K. Kanjilal's researches led him to the conclusion that, in ancient India, probably a kind of aeroplane and a sort of submarine used to be built.[28] In the western countries, such things began to be built long after that.

"Bangalore, Sept. 4(P T I)

It was an Indian who first manufactured and demonstrated an aeroplane to the world, a Bangalore-based photo journalist has claimed.

According to Mr. Regret Iyer, who has written to the London-based *Guinness Book of World Records*, Talpade, a scholar in Vedas and Sanskrit from Dukkarwadi Chirrah Bazar in Bombay, manufactured an aeroplane, exhibited it at Bombay Art Society and gave a demonstration flight on the Chowpathy beach of the city in 1895 eight years before the Wright brothers took off with their machine.

Talpade's experiments were based on the Rigveda and the aeronautical treatise of Maharishi Bharadwaj, according to Mr. Iyer.

Talpade's aeroplane, named Marut-sakha, conformed to the Vedic references to aeroplanes".

Calcutta Daily Newspaper, *Telegraph* 5.9.95

B. SCRIPTURE, LITERATURE AND PHILOSOPHY

Before taking up India's influence in different foreign countries, we, should state that Rabindranatha's works produced a great impact on the world at large. The award of Nobel Prize for his English version of the *Gītāñjali* is an index to the appreciation of his literary merit in the west. Many of his works have been translated into various languages of the world.

Culturally, Nepāl and Mithilā were closely connected. The Buddhist and Brāhmanical works in Sanskrit exercised profound influence on the literature and culture of Nepāl. A version of the *Bṛhatkathā* was composed in Nepāl under the title *Bṛhatkathā-śloka-saṃgraha* by Budhasvāmin (fifth or sixth century; according to some eighth or ninth century). Many Sanskrit works were rendered into Nepāli. A version of the

Cāṇakya-nīti-saṃgraha was, perhaps, composed in this country. The national epic of Nepāl, entitled *Rāmāyaṇa*, by Bhānubhakta, bears eloquent testimony to Indian influence.

In the twelfth century A.D., Muslim invasion and administration in Bengal and Bihar helped the spread of Indian culture and literature in Nepāl. A sense of insecurity stemming from the persecution by the Muslims drove the orthodox Buddhists and Brāhmins, particularly the scholars among them, to flee with their precious possessions in the shape of manuscripts and to seek refuge in Nepāl. As a result, that country turned to be a veritable repositary of manuscripts. Among these, there are some the originals of which are lost in India. Such a work is the *Saddharma-puṇḍarīka*. The *Caryāpada* (*c.* tenth century), the earliest available Bengali work, was discovered in Nepāl.

TIBET[29]

In connection with the nature of link between India and Tibet, we have seen that many Bengali Buddhist scholars went over to that country. Of them, some rendered into Tibetan quite a few Sanskrit works, particularly on Tantra. These translations alone survived; the originals are lost. It is learnt that, ever since the time of Sambhoṭa up to the present century, there is reference to the significance and sanctity of the Indian concept of *Śabdabrahman* (words conceived as the eternal Brahman). Many Sanskrit idioms and imageries from Sanskrit literature have been adopted in the Tibetan literature. Quite a few Sanskrit words have been incorporated into the Tibetan vocabulary; e.g. *om, maṇi, padma, ārya, dharma, paṇḍita, ratna, vajra,* etc. The orthography and pronunciation of these words, have, of course, undergone considerable change. Approximately, as many as 700 Tibetan vocables are derived from Sanskrit. Up to the time of P. Namgayal (1642 A.D.), the administrative documents used to be written in Sanskrit. There are, however, some linguistic changes. The Tibetan *Tanjur* contains, besides Tāntric works, Tibetan translations of the following works :

Kāvyādarśa of Daṇḍin (eighth century), the *Meghadūta* of Kālidāsa (*c.* fifth century), the *Chandoratnākara,* a treatise on prosody.

It may be noted that some Sanskrit inscriptions have been found in Tibet.

A Tibetan version of the Bengali scholar (10th-11th cent.), Jñānaśrīmitra's *Kārya-kāraṇa-bhāva-siddhi,* a work on Buddhist logic, is available.

Tibet appears to have been profoundly influenced by the *Yoga* philosophy. Systematic knowledge of *Yoga* was, perhaps, imparted to the Tibetans by the Bengali scholar, Dīpaṃkara Atīśa (10th-11th cent.) who settled there. Tsoṅg-kh-Pa's *The Yoga of Tibetans, Tantra in Tibet,* Chang's *Teachings Tibetan Yoga* and *Six Yogas of Naropā* throw a flood of light on *Yoga* as adopted in that country. Of the four sets of Tibetan Tantra, two are concerned with *Yoga*; one is called Yoga-tantra and the other Highest Yoga Tantra. In the highest *Yoga,* there is no external activity, and the practitioner is able to generate the *Yoga* than which nothing higher exists. In yogatantra, the practitioner mainly relies on meditative stabilisation, and resorts to only a few external rites. The other two kinds of *Yoga* are called *Action Yoga* and *Performance Yoga.*

"In Action and Performance Tantras, a Truth Body which is said to be thoroughly pure in the sense of being free of all dualistic elaborations, is achieved through the *Yoga* of singleness—meditation on emptiness - and a Form Body, which is said to be impure in the sense that it is involved in duality, is achieved through the *yoga* wits signs-*deity yoga.*

BURMA[30]

Sanskrit didactic works have exercised influence on some didactic works of Burma. Some stories of the *Hitopodeśa* (sometime between 900 and 1373 A.D.) were widely current in this country. The king, Hsinbyushin, invited some Brāhmaṇas from Kāśī (Vārāṇasi) for translating different Indian scriptures. King Botuwpaya (eighteenth-nineteenth century) looted many Sanskrit treatises from Ārākān, and got them translated. Certain Pāli works, e.g. *Gaṇḍavyūha* (seventeenth century) were composed in this country. Some *Subhāṣitas* from the Sanskrit narrative literature were quoted in the Pāli *Suttavaddhananiti*, current in this country, and in its Burmese translation.[31] Wise sayings from Sanskrit *Subhāṣita* literature have been incorporated into parts II and III of the *Lokasāra*, the popular Pāli anthology. In the fifth century, Buddhist scriptures used to be studied. The influence of Pāli literature in this country was so deep that it played an important role in forming the mother-tongue of the people of this country. Besides commentaries on Buddhist religious texts, the scholars of this country wrote also on Indian philosophy, grammar, prosody, rhetoric, jurisprudence and didactic matters.

SOUTH-EAST ASIA[32]

It is learnt that at least four Tantras, viz. *Śiraścheda, Sammoha, Vinayaśīla* and *Nayottara*, were current in Cambodia (present Kampuchea) in *c.* 800 A.D. It is said that a certain Brāhmaṇa taught this Tantra to Śivakaivalya, preceptor of Jayavarman, king of this country. There is reference to the daily recitation of Purāṇa at certain places.

Tāntric influence is noticed in Java also. The most noteworthy Javanese work, influenced by Tantra, is *Tattva Sang Hiyang Mahājnana.* Written in the same vein is another Tāntric work called *Sang Hiyang Kamaha Yanikan.* In Bali, the Tāntric *Bījas, Hrīṃ, Krīṃ* and their significance were known.

In the work, *Bṛhaspatitattva.*[33] discovered in Java, there are 74 Sanskrit verses along with their Javanese translation. No such work has been found in India. The above verses, in the same form, are not known to occur in any Sanskrit work. In this work, Śaiva philosophy has been discussed. Another philosophical work, discovered in this country, is *Gaṇapatitattva.*[34] No work of this title is known in India. In the *Vratiśāsana,*[35] written in old Javanese, there are Sanskrit verses interspersed. It appears to have been a short-cut for the use of ascetics. It reveals profound respect for the sublime Indian ideal about ascetism. From this region Sanskrit works of some other types, relating to Hindu and Buddhist religion and religious rites, have been recovered.[36]

The Javanese *Tantu Pangelaron* was composed between the fourteenth and the sixteenth century A.D. In it, cosmogony, myths and legends about deities, etc. have been described in the Purānic manner. The *Agastyaparvan*, though written in Javanese, quotes Sanskrit verses. The Wayang literature in this country is, in many respects, like Sanskrit shadow-play. It reveals the influence of the *Rāmāyaṇa* and *Mahābhārata*. Some scholars have noticed the influence of Sanskrit literature on the written and unwritten legends prevailing in Java.

The profound impact of the Sanskrit *Pañcatantra* and the *Hitopodeśa* can be discerned in the *Tantrikāmandaka*, in other works of the *Tantri* class as well as those of the *Kancil* class, in fables and in stories. Ideas from Sanskrit works appear to have been adopted in the *Nāgarakṛtāgama* and also in other historical works.

Quite a few Hindu kingdoms were founded in Java. Four Sanskrit inscriptions, found in West Java, indicate the spread of Indian culture in that country. The Chinese traveller, I-tsing (seventh century) testifies to the regular cultivation of Sanskrit in Heling, the most renowned Hindu kingdom. There is influence of the following Sanskrit works on the literary works of Java, composed from 925-140 A.D.:

Veda, Purāna, Āgama, Dharmaśāstra, *Nīti* literature, grammar, rhetoric, prosody, astronomy, history, etc. The two Javanese works on prosody are the *Vṛttasañcaya* (*c.* 1200 A.D.) and the *Vṛttāyana*. There is an old Javanese version of the Sanskrit lexicon, *Amaramālā*.

There is influence of Sanskrit lexicons on the Javanese lexical works, *Ādisvara, Ekalavya, Kṛtavasa* and *Caṇṭakaparva*. The most prominent work of this class is the Sanskrit-Kawi[37] dictionary preserved in the Batavian Society of Arts and Sciences.

There is Javanese translation of the *Mahābhārata*. Besides, there are the works entitled *Arjunavivāha* (eleventh century) and *Sang Satyavān*. Yogīśvara's *Rāmāyaṇa Kakawin*[38] is a noted work. There are *Rāmāyaṇa* paintings of the ninth century A.D. at the place called Prambanan in West Java. In the fourteenth century scenes from the *Rāmāyaṇa* were painted at Pantaran in East Java.

The themes of most of the poetical works in old Javanese have been taken from Sanskrit literature. These contain copious Sanskrit metres, words and verses. The most renowned work of this class is the *Bhāratayuddha* (1157 A.D.) by Mpu Seda. Almost contemporaneous with it is the poetical work, *Harivaṃśa.*[39] Other noteworthy poetical works are *Smaradahana* (1185), *Bhomakāvya, Nāgarakṛtāgama* (1365) by Prapañca and *Kṛṣṇāyana* (1104), *Kṛṣṇāntaka, Sumanasāntaka, Arjuna-vijaya, Harisraya.*

The *Nītiśāstra Kakawin* of Java has been modelled on the Sanskrit *Nītiśataka, Pañcatantra, Cāṇakyaśloka,* etc. Some of its verses are obviously translation of Sanskrit verses. The didactic *Kuñjarakarṇa* echoes the doctrines of rebirth and Karman of Sanskrit scriptures. The *Kāmandakarājanīti* is modelled on the Sanskrit *Kāmandakīya Nītiśara.* Portions of the Javanese work *Nītipraya* remind one of the Sanskrit *Arthaśāstra.*

Among the religious texts, the *Sūryasevana* and *Gāruḍeyamantra,* both composed in old Javanese, are especially noteworthy. The *Bhuvanakośa* and *Bhuvansaṃkṣepa* are renowned Śaiva works. The *Caturpakṣopadeśa,* dealing with spiritual matters, bears the impress of Sanskrit religious literature.

The Javanese *Brahmāṇḍapurāṇa* is written mainly in the manner of an Indian *Purāṇa.* It has a prose version, called *Pṛthuvijaya* as well as a poetical version called *Brahmāṇḍapurāṇa.* In the *Agastyaparva,* composed in Javanese, Agastya is represented as describing the creation of the world in the Purāṇic manner with Sanskrit quotations. This indicates the popularity of the Indian sage Agastya. The *Ādipurāṇa* and *Bhuvanapurāṇa* deal with well-known Purāṇic legends, but we do not know of any Sanskrit work on which it might be based. The *Bhuvanapurāṇa* contains a number of verses written in corrupt Sanskrit.

Some Javanese works betray the influence of Kālidāsa. The Javanese *Smaradahana* was inspired by Kālidāsa's *Kumārasambhava.*

The influence of the *Manusmṛti* is perceived in some legal treatises in Pāli in Burma. In some Javanese works, the indebtedness to Manu has been clearly acknowledged.[40] The very titles of the *Śivaśāsana* and *Pūrvādigama* indicate Indian influence. Into the theme of the work Indian ideas are interwoven. In Indonesia, the Sanskrit word *Āgama* is used to indicate legal treatises. There are Sanskrit verses in the *Kramaning Sākṣī.* Here also the adherence to Manu's views is clear. Most of the *Sārasamuccaya* is written in Sanskrit verses. The *Svarajambu* is only a version of the major portion of the eighth chapter of *Manusmṛti.* It appears that the law in Siam (or Thailand) follows the *Manusmṛti.* The very title of the *Fra Dharmaśāstra* indicates the influence of Hindu *Dharmaśāstra.* Manu's image, established in the Philippines, is a mute witness to the high esteem of the people of that region for Manu. This image is in the Art Gallery in the Senate Chamber of the Philippine Republic.[41]

The language, in which some inscriptions (ninth century) of Bali[42] are written, is a pot-pourri of Sanskrit and the old language of Bali. Some works of this country are called Veda, though they have no connection with the Veda so far as the subject is concerned, *e.g.* Buddha Veda. Some Sanskrit works of Java, e.g. *Mahābhārata* and *Brahmāṇḍapurāṇa,* are popular in Bali also. The Sanskrit compositions of this country are mostly of an eulogistic type. Of such literary compositions, the *Rāmakavaca* is prominent. The people of this country believe in the Indian deities Viṣṇu, Śiva, Varuṇa, etc. Their religious rites are influenced by the Brāhmanical religion and Tantra. In the dictionary, called *Svarasaṃhitā,* a work of this country, there are quite a few Sanskrit words with their meanings.

The inscriptions testify to the fact that the *Rāmāyaṇa* story was current in Indo-China and Indonesia already in the first half of the first millennium of the Christian era. The name of the popular *Rāmāyaṇa* in Siam (Thailand) is *Rāmakira* or *Rāmakien* (exploits of Rāma). One of the sources of this work was the *Nārāyaṇasippam* of that country; it describes the ten incarnation of Nārāyaṇa. The *Cāṇakya-nītiśāstra* was translated into the language of this country. The literature of Thailand is deeply influenced by Sanskrit.[43] The *Kathāsaritsāgara* and some other Indian narrative works in Sanskrit were translated into the Thāi language.[44] In the present century, the Sanskrit *Vyāsasubhāṣita-saṃgraha* was known, in this country, as *Vyākaraśataka* perhaps through the medium of the *Vyāsakarāya* of Ceylon.[45] Many *Subhāṣitas* in the Pāli *Lokanīti* have been taken from Sanskrit. This work was very popular in Burma. It was very renowned also in Thailand where it ran into several editions. One of them is entitled *Suphasit Lokanīti Klam Klong*. The most well known *Subhāṣita* work of this country is *Phrah Ruang* which is connected with *Suphasit*; the author was, perhaps, a king of the thirteenth century. This work also contains some *Subhāṣitas* which are substantially derived from Sanskrit *Subhāṣita* works. Pip 'hekśon and the Sönnön, the former an anthology of Thailand and the latter a Pāli work of this country, contained instructions derived from the *Rāmāyaṇa*. The metrical translations, in Thāi language, of Sanskrit *Abhijñāna-śakuntala* and *Meghadūta* exist. The *Nang Tantrai* is the most noteworthy work in the translation literature of this country. This reminds one of the *Tantrikāmandaka* of old Java. Quite a few dramas of this country were based on *Jātaka* stories. In the early part of the present century, one, Chua Langkarna by name, tried to present the *Jātaka* stories to the populace in the native language. The dramatic literature of Thailand draws upon the *Rāmāyaṇa* story. Instead of *Vālmīki-Rāmāyaṇa*, however, the *Daśarathajātaka* and the popular story of the *Rāmāyaṇa* have provided the source. The *Rāmakathā* is the basis of the shadow-play, called *Nang*, of this country dating back to the eighteenth century. The dialogues of Bāli-Sugrīva and Daśaratha-Rāma have provided the source of some of the Thāi poetical works.

Noteworthy among the Javanese works, influenced by Indian or Sanskrit literature, are: (in Devanāgarī alphabetical order)

Aṣṭādaśa-Vyavahāra — on law.
Ādigama — revealing the impact of the *Manusaṃhitā*.
Ṛṣiśāsana — relating to religious sects.

Kāmandakarājanīti,

Kārakasamgraha,

Kālayavanāntaka — another name of *Kṛṣṇavijaya*.

Kuṭāramānava — mostly follows the *Manusaṃhitā*.

Kṛṣṇavijaya — fight between Kṛṣṇa and Kaṃsa.

Caṇḍakaraṇa — dictionary (Sanskrit - old Javanese).

Devadaṇḍa — legal treatise.

Nītivrata — title indicates contents.

Pālutuka — didactic.

Puruṣadasanta,

Bhuvana-tattva-paricaya — story of the previous births of two Yakṣas.

Raṇayajña — didactic.

Rājapatiguṇḍala — on politics (*c.* thirteenth century).

Sārasammuccaya — didactic; contains more than 500 verses culled from the *Mahābhārata, Pañcatantra* and *Hitopodeśa*.

Sukṣavasa,

Svarajambu — follows chapter 8 of the *Manusaṃhita*.

Svaravyañjana — grammatical.

Some Buddhist works also were written in Java. The earliest portion of the work, entitled *Sang Hyang Kamahāyānikan* is a sort of exposition of a Sanskrit text, and is written for the Vajrayānists. It contains verses in corrupt Sanskrit. The work, *Sang Hyang Kamahāyanan Mantranaya* contains about 42 Sanskrit verses. Its theme is the mystical elements of *Vajrayāna*.

The influence of Sanskrit in Kambuja or Cambodia (Kampuchea) was widespread.[46] This country's version of the *Rāmāyaṇa* is called *Rāmakerti* or *Rāmakera*. It is a metrical version of the *Rāmāyaṇa* story. It reveals a syncretism of Brāhmaṇism and Buddhism; Rāma is represented as *Bodhisattva*. It is a medley of Vālmīki's story and various folk stories. The dance-drama of this country was considerably influenced by the *Rāmāyaṇa*. The kings of this country were patrons of Sanskrit which was, at a time, the state language. The Pāli *Rājanīti*, popular in Burma, was translated into the language of this country. It contains wise sayings relating to politics in Sanskrit literature. The *Supa'hasita e bapsri* contains verses in Khmer language. Some of these verses are modelled on Sanskrit *Kāvya,* particularly *Amaruśataka.*

In comparison with Java, the vocabulary of this country contains a lesser number of Sanskrit words.

It appears that Sanskrit grammar was studied with great zeal. King Yaśovarman (887-900) is known to have written a commentary on the *Mahābhāṣya.* Some inscriptions quote a few rules of Pāṇini.

In Campā (South Annam) more than a hundred Sanskrit inscriptions are preserved even to-day. This indicates that, at least up to the tenth century A.D., the influence of Sanskrit language and literature, in this country, was wide and deep. The earliest inscription (third or fourth century A.D.) is composed in the metre *Vasantatilaka* and in a *Kavya* style of high order.

Sanskrit was, for sometime, the state language. Many Sanskrit treatises from India were brought to this country. Many works were composed in Sanskrit in this country also. From one inscription we learn that king Bhadravarman (fifth century A.D.) was *Caturvaidya,* i.e. versed in the four Vedas. The Vo-Canh Rock inscription (400 A.D.) refers to *Viśvjit*[47] sacrifice. King Indravarman III was conversant with Indian philosophy. Indravarman VII was versed in *Dharmaśāstra.* In this period, the Indian epics, *Manusaṃhitā, Nārada-smṛti,* Śaivite and Vaiṣṇavite literatures were widely studied. R.C. Majumdar points out that one inscription contains the word *Purāṇārtha* while another refers to *Arthapurāṇa-śāstra.* In his opinion, both these terms refer to a single work which might be an analysis of some Indian Purāṇa or a local edition of the same. Some inscriptions reveal close familiarity with the Indian prose and poetical literatures. The latest version of the *Rāmakathā,* in this country, has been composed on the basis of the Annamese version in the eighteenth century. Some of the kings of this country were versed in the scriptures like the Veda. There is reference also to their mastery over the philosophical systems like *Mimāṃsā,* There was the cultivation of Pāṇini's grammar and Buddhist scriptures. The *Rāmāyaṇa* and *Mahābhārata* were so popular that, at the place called Tra

Kien, an image of Vālmīki was set up. Another evidence of Indian influence is the practice of counting years by the Śaka era.

At Penang in Mālay country,[48] two inscriptions, written in a South Indian script, and dating back to the fourth century A.D., have been found. Both of them contain a few Sanskrit words. There are some more inscriptions of the fourth to fifth century A.D. One of them contains three Sanskrit verses. In another, there is reference to the great navigator, Buddhagupta, a resident of Raktamṛttikā.[49] From the Chinese account we learn that, at a time, Indian kings used to rule over this country, and used Sanskrit language.

The *Pañcatantra* and the *Hitopadeśa* were translated into the language of this country. The *Kathāsaritsāgara* provided the themes of at least two treatises of Mālay. The Sanskrit *Śukasaptati,* through its Persian version called *Tutināmā* (middle of fourteenth century), influenced Mālayan literature. The present form of the Mālayan treatise *Adat Temenggong* testifies to the influence of the Sanskrit works of Kauṭilya, Manu, Kāmandaka, etc. Elements of the folk stories of Mālay were derived from the *Rāmāyaṇa, Kathāsaritsāgara* and *Jātaka.* In the episodes of some romantic literature of this country, we meet with the Indian merchant, prince, ascetics, ghosts, sages and gods etc.

The Sanskrit word *Svasti* occurs in a stele of this country. Buddhagupta's inscription contains the word *Siddhyātrā.* There is indication of the popularity of the Śaivatantra at some time in this country. Figures of some *Rāmāyaṇa* characters are found in the pedestals of images, in old stands for water-bottles, etc. Many themes of dance, drama, puppet-play and shadow-play have been taken from the *Rāmāyaṇa* and *Mahābhārata.* The oldest manuscript of the *Rāmāyaṇa,* called *Hikāyat Serirāma* is based on a Tāmil exemplar. The Mālayan treatises, called *Hikayat Perang, Pāṇḍavajaya* and the *Hikāyat Mahārāja Boma* are based on the *Mahābhārata.* According to some, Indian elements were incorporated into the Mālayan literature in the twelfth century A.D. Stories from the Tāmil work, *Manimekalai*, were translated into the language of this country.

The Chinese accounts tell us that Sanskrit works were widely studied in the Śrīvijaya kingdom in Sumātrā. The Ligor inscription (755 A.D.) sheds considerable light on this kingdom. There is evidence of the cultivation of Indian literature in this country before the advent of the Muslims.

An inscription of this country, dating back to about second half of the fifth century A.D., bears testimony to the intimate knowledge of Brāhmanical culture and works. It begins with salutation to Brahmā, Viṣṇu and Śiva. Then there is mention of Mahārājādhirāja Devānīka who has been compared with Yudhiṣṭhira, Indra, Dhanañjaya, etc. There is reference also to a sacrifice performed by the above king. From that inscription we learn that, in accordance with the faith that merit accrues as a result of birth or death in a great place of pilgrimage, that king planned the establishment of a holy place called Nava Kurukṣetra. The above inscription contains three verses from the *Mahābhārata* and one from the *Matsyapurāṇa.*

The Pāli *Lokanīti* is well-known in this region. It contains many *Subhāṣitas* based on Sanskrit *Subhāṣitas.* The version of the *Lokanīti,* belonging to this country, appears to have originated in India.

Four Sanskrit inscriptions (fourth century A.D.), discovered in Borneo, testify to the fact that, in this country, there was, at a time, a Hindu kingdom and that Sanskrit religious and secular treatises exercised influence. In some inscriptions the following Sanskrit words occur :

Bahudāna, Jīvadāna, Kalpavṛkṣadāna, Bhūmidāna, etc.

The literature of Laos clearly reflects the impact of Sanskrit grammar, lexicon and prosody.[50] In fact, the classical *Kāvya* literature of this country is constituted by the translation of Sanskrit *Kāvyas.* The didactic and satrical literature and fables of Laos have been inspired by Sanskrit literature. The

Pañcatantra of this region has been enriched by the ideas contained in the Sanskrit *Pañcatantra.* The title of a collection of stories of this province is *Mullatantai.* This name comes from the Sanskrit *Mula Tantra.* The bulk of the Laotian literature is only another form of the literature of Thailand. Fifty didactic Jātaka stories are current in this country. The *Maṅgalasutta,* written in this country, earned popularity in Burma. The *Śāsanavaṃśa* refers to it.

PHILIPPINES[51]

The influence of India on the legends and stories of the Philippines is obvious. For instance, the subject-matter and characterisation in the longest poetical work of this land, entitled *Darangon,* are basically Indian. The reader of the *Ifugao Ralituk* is reminded of the story of Arjuna's collecting water from the mountain, pierced with arrow, for Bhīṣma about to die of thirst. The impact of Sanskrit literature on the non-Christian people of this island is clear. It is curious that the *Bantugan,* though a great poetical work of the Muslims, is mainly based on the *Mahābhārata.* In it, the characters, called *Bakaramata* and *Bhāratamātā* are local forms of the Indian *Viśvakarman* and *Bhārātamātā* respectively. In some Muslim folk-songs, we find some corrupt forms of Vedic hymns. The words *Maharadiya* and *Laoyana* are derived from Sanskrit *Mahārājā* and *Rāvaṇa* respectively.

CEYLON[52]

Indo-Ceylon Sanskrit works were imported in four different periods. At first, the impact of Sanskrit went on till 1017 A.D., *i.e.* at the time of the conquest of Ceylon by the Coḷas. The second period extended up to the sixteenth century when the Portuguese conquered the stretch of land along the coast of Ceylon. The third period saw the import of the above books up to 1815 A.D. (Kandyan Age). The fourth period started in 1815. There was Tāntric influence in this island. On the Ceylonese literature and language the influence of Sanskrit was considerable. The *Rājadharma*, laid down by Manu, has been repeatedly referred to in the Ceylonese Buddhist historical work *Culavaṃśa*. In matters relating to property, marriage, adoption, etc. there is similarity between Kandy and India. In about 1245 A.D., one Rāmacandra Kavibhāratī of Gauḍa went to Ceylon, and was converted to Buddhism.

According to a Ceylonese tradition, the great poet Kumārdāsa (Kumārabhaṭṭa or Bhaṭṭakumāra) was a king (*c.* 517-26 A.D.) of that country. There is a tradition that he was a friend of Kālidāsa. The *Jānakīharaṇa*, a great poetical work, is associated with his name. The earlier *Anuruddhaśataka*, by Anuruddha, is an eulogy of the Buddha. Written in the manner of the Indian *Śataka*, it is the earliest and foremost of the *Śataka-Kāvyas* of this land. Another work of this type is the *Nāmāṣṭaśataka*. This anonymous work contains an eulogy glorifying the Buddha's exploits. The verses in the anonymous *Buddhagadya* have some similarity with Jayadeva's (twelfth century) *Gītagovinda*.

Of the 69 words in the beginning of this country's *Katikāvata* or rules about the Buddhist order, all excepting 21 are Sanskrit. The influence of Kālidāsa, Bhāravi, etc. is noticed in the form and subject-matter and style of the three renowned Ceylonese poetical works called *Sasadā*, *Muvedevā* and *Kavasi Luminā*. The impress of Sanskrit *Dūtakāvya* is clear in the message-poems (*Sandeśakāvya*) written in this country from the sixteenth century onwards. The titles of two such works are *Tisvasandeśa* and *Mayūrasandeśa*.

The influence of the Sanskrit rhetorical works is noticeable in the work, *Siyavasalakara* associated with the name of king Sena IV (accession 954 A.D.). The oldest of the present rhetorical works of Ceylon is modelled on the *Kāvyādarśa* of Daṇḍin (8th cent. A.D.).

In Ceylon some anthologies of Sanskrit verses have been compiled. Besides, in the Ceylonese *Subhāṣita* collection, there are quotations from Sanskrit works. Some Ceylonese verses reveal the indebtedness to Sanskrit. Of such Ceylonese works, noteworthy are *Subhāṣitaya, Lokopakāraya, Anurāgamālaya, Upāratnamalaya.* The poetical work, entitled *Vedaṃkabipota* testifies to the influence of Sanskrit in this country.

CHINA

W. Budge, formerly of British Museum, London, informed that he found the mention of Manu's Law in a manuscript found in China.[53] In connection with religion, we have seen that many Indian scholars went to China, settled there, and either translated Buddhist religious texts into Chinese or helped the local scholars in such translations. The Khotānese scholar, Śikṣānanda (652-710), went to China, and translated into Chinese the Sanskrit work *Buddhāvataṃsaka,* which is lost. The originals of many Buddhist Sanskrit works are lost; only their Chinese translations are available. Noteworthy among such works are the *Brahmajālasūtra,* the *Mahāyāna* works *Prajñāpāramitā* and *Ratnakūṭa.* Quite a few Sanskrit works, written by Śīlabhadra (d. 654 A.D.), the Head of the Great Nālandā monastery, are lost. These survive only in Chinese translation. Towards the second half of the fourth century A.D., the renowned Chinese scholar, Tāo-Nagn, besides exposition of Buddhist scripture, composed a work on India. Portions of the *Rāmāyaṇa* and the *Mahābhārata* were translated into Chinese.

It is interesting to note that Zen Buddhism, well-known in Japan, is said to have originated in China under the instructions of a Buddhist teacher, said to have been named Bodhidharma, from India.[54] The two important Zen text-books are the *Pi-Yen-Chi*[55] or *Pi-Yen-Lu*[56] and the *Wu-Men-Kuan. Zen* stands for *dhyāna,* one of the accessories of *Yoga* (*Yogāṅga*), according to Patañjali's *Yoga Sūtra* (ii.29). Sūtra iii.2 defines *dhyāna,* The *Pi-Yen-Chi* consists of Hsüch-tou's poetical comments on the text mostly comprising selections from the history of Zen *mantras,* entitled *The Transmission of the Lamp* and of Yuan-Wu's additional notes. Hsüch-tou was a great exponent of the

Yün-men school, and flourished early in the Sung regime (980-1052).

The *Wu-men-Kuan* is one man's work, being attributed to Hui-K'ai (1183-1260). He flourished in the latter part of the Sung rule.

JAPAN

Long long before the Buddha, a band of Indian Aryans, settled in Japan. Perhaps they introduced some Indian scriptures, particularly the *Manusaṃhitā* in that country.[57]

Indian philosophy of *Yoga* influenced *Zen* Buddhism of Japan. As we have seen, *Zen* originated in China. One Dogen, the founder of the Söto school of *Zen* in Japan, is reported to have first brought the *Pi-yen-chi* or *Pi-yen-lu* an authoritative Chinese work on *Zen* into this country in the thirteenth century. Early in the fifteenth century, a Japanese edition of the work was prepared. The two Chinese text-books on *Zen*, entitled *Pi-yen-chi* or Lu and *Wu-men-Kuan* were known in Japan as *Hekiganshu* or *Heki-ganroka* and *Mu-mon-Kwan* respectively.

KOREA

The stories of Indian *Pañcatantra* reached Korea from Tibet. This became very popular in Korea. The Korean literature reveals the influence of Pāli and Prākṛta literatures. Many Korean scholars used to give instructions to their pupils about Sanskrit and Pāli literatures. Many students from that country used to visit Takṣasilā and Nālandā in order to study Dharmaśāstra. The religious leader, Bhikṣu (monk) Hiyecho was the first Korean to translate Buddhist Pāli works directly into the Korean language.

CENTRAL ASIA[58]

There is a Khotanese translation of the *Rāmāyaṇa.* Fragments of the Khotanese Buddhist work, entitled *Vajracchedikā Prajñāpāramitā* have been found. There are several Buddhist texts in the language of Khotan, belonging probably to the eight to tenth centuries.[59] German-Turfan researches have resulted in the discovery of the *Laghucāṇakya*. A truncated version of Cāṇakya's sayings has been discovered in East Turkestan.

PERSIA,[60] ARABIA,[61] BAGHDAD, MONGOLIA[62]

The earliest translation of the *Pañcatantra* was made in Persia in the fourth century A.D. during the time of Nasr Ibn Āhmad Samani at the behest of his Minister, Belami. Firdausi has mentioned it in the *Shāhnāmā*. Almost contemporaneously, Rudaki composed a poetical version of it. The first translation is lost. The second one is scattered in a poetical form in some works. Ābdulmāli's work was polished; it was revised by Husain Baij Kashefi in Hizri ninth century. In accordance with the name of Sheikh Āhmad Suhaili, minister of Sultān Hussain, it was named *Ānwār-I-Suhaili*. The simpler name of the *Āyār-I-Dūnish* was *Nigar-I-Dānish*. From the *Kabushnāmā* we learn that Kabushbin Wayashamgar (tenth century), king of Khurarjam, asked his son to read the Persian translation of the *Pañcatantra* for acquiring knowledge. In the introduction to the *Shāhnāmā* of Firdausi, this work has been characterised as a mine of knowledge. I. Sekhara directly translated the *Pañcatantra* into Persian.

From the introduction to the *Shāhnāmā* and from the *Kabushnāmā* we learn that Cāṇakya was very popular in Persia.

Jainul Abedin (fifteenth century), king of Kashmir, got the *Mahābhārata* translated into Persian. Dārā, brother of Aurangzeb (1659-1707), translated the *Yogavāśiṣṭha* and *Gītā* into Persian. In his *Majmaul Baharain* (*Samudrasaṅgama*), there is a discussion on similar thoughts of the Hindus and and the Muslims. Indusekhar Hāssān and Hekmat rendered into Persian the drama, *Abhijñānaśakuntala* of Kālidāsa, into Persian. The aforesaid Dārā translated into Persian as many as 50 *Upaniṣads* in his work, *Sirre Ākbar*. Through this translation the western countries became familiar with the *Upaniṣads*.

Not only in Persia, in India also several Persian works were composed on the basis of Sanskrit works. Akbar's (1556-1605) Prime Minister, Sheikh Ābul Fazl, translated the *Gītāsāra* into Persian. Under the patronage of this emperor, some Muslim scholars rendered the *Rāmāyaṇa* and the *Mahābhārata* into Persian.

Fayzi (d. 1595) translated the mathematical work, *Līlāvatī* into Persian. The Persian scholar, Ferishtā (*c.* 1570-1612), came to India, and, at the behest of Sultān Ibrāhim Ādil Shāh II, composed (1609) the *Tārikh-I-Ferishtā*,[63] dealing with the history of Muslim rule in India. The main Sanskrit works, translated into Persian, are listed below along with the names of their translators.

(The names of works are in Sanskrit Alphabetical Order):

WORKS	*TRANSLATORS*
Amaracarita	Rāmprasād
Upaniṣad (50 or 52)	Dārā Shuko
Nala Damayantī	Faizi
Pañcatantra	Induśekhara
Brahmasūtra Śāṅkarabhāṣya	(Summary) Amarnāth, Lachminārāyaṇ.
Bhagavadgītā	Ābul Fazl, Faizi, Dārā, Ābbās, Śāntāprasād, Madhos.
Bhāgavatapurāṇa	Todarmal and Laksminārāyaṇa Sarur.
Mahābhārata	Al Beruni, Abul Fazl, Badauni, Jainul Ābedin.
Rāmāyaṇa	Bedil, Badauni, Nehnārayana, Mākhanlāl, Devidās, Amarsingh, Āmānat Rāi, Ānandaghana,

	Mohār Singh, Sādullāh Maisihi Pānipati, Misr Rāmādās, etc.
Vikramorvaśīya	Ābidi
Veda	Badauni
Śaṅkaradigvijaya	Lakṣminārāyaṇ
Śakuntalā	Hāssān Indusekhar Hekmat.

Of the other Sanskrit works, translated into Persian, the following deserve mention[64] :

Kathāsaritsāgara	Bījagaṇita
Kāśīkhaṇḍa (included in the Skandapurāṇa)	Bṛhatsaṃhitā
Kośaśāstra (Sexual Science)	Brahmavaivartapurāṇa
Pārijātaka (on music)	Yogavāśiṣṭha
Purāṇārthaprakāśa (Chronology and creation of the world)	Rājataraṅgiṇī
Prabodhacandrodaya (drama)	Vāyupurāṇa
Viṣṇupurāṇa	
Vedāntasāra	
Śālihotra	
Śivapurāṇa	
Śukasaptati	
Siṃhāsanadvātriṃśikā	
Harivaṃśa	

One of the deities in the Persian pantheon is *Vaivasvata Manu*. Considerable influence of the *Manusaṃhitā* is noticeable in the life of the Iranians. It is learnt that, under emperor Darius (sixth-fifth century B.C.) law was formulated, for the administration of the empire, on the basis of the *Manusaṃhitā*. Through the devotees of Zoroaster the worship of Manu and the study of his *Dharmaśāstra* were introduced in Western Asia and the Occident.

Most of the Sufi poets and writers of Persia were influenced by Sanskrit literature. Of them, the following deserve special mention : Sanai, Attar, Rumi, Irāki Hamdani, Auladi, Kirmāni, etc. The Sufi literature contains some words having the meaning of Sanskrit words. A few instances are cited below :

Words in Sufi Literature	*Corresponding Sanskrit Words*
Tohid	Advaita
Jat-E-Mutlak	Brahma
Ālam	Brahmaloka
Marifat	Jñāna
Su'ur	Buddhi
Khudi	Ahaṅkāra
Nafs	Mana (s)
Fikr	Cit

The *Wayahdat-Ul-Ojud* of Ibn-E-Ārabi has similarity with the *Advaitavāda* of Śaṅkara 's Vedānta. Such sentences as *An-Al-Hak* (I am God), *Laisa-Fi-Jubbati Sioyā Āllāh* (under my cloak there is none other than God) are current among the Sufis. These compare well with the Vedāntic doctrine *Ahaṃ Brahmāsmi.* In the Vedānta, five stages of salvation have been laid down. Curiously enough, the different stages of emancipation are set forth in the renowned work, *Mathnavi,* by the celebrated Sufi poet of Iran, Rumi. Like the Vedānta, Sufi philosophy also considers the phenomenal world as illusion.

ARABIA

Indian scriptures and literature were cultivated in Arabia. In c. 750 A.D., the Arabian scholar, Muquafā, translated the Pahlavi version (sixth century A.D.) of the *Pañcatantra.* Contemporaneously with Muqafa, or sometime after, Ābānal Laheki composed an Arabic poem based on the *Pañcatantra.*

Ābdullā Ibn Hilāl Al Ābbāji translated into Arabic the Pahlavi version of the above work.[65] The aforesaid Muqāfa also did the same thing. Stories of the *Pañcatantra* have found place in different Arabic prose and poetical works. The *Pañcatantra* has been imitated in the Arabic language, and works have been composed on the basis of its stories. The Arabian writer, Māsudi (d. 956 A.D.) has stated that the introductory part of the Arabic work, *Sindbād* is similar to that of the *Pañcatantra.*

From Al Biruni's (973-1048) *India,* we learn that he was familiar with many branches of Sanskrit literature and scriptures. He introduced the *Bhagavadgītā* to the Muslim world.

MONGOLIA[66]

The Buddhist works, *Pañcarakṣā,* etc. were translated into the Mongolian language under the patronage of emperor Kaisam Kulug (Sanskrit name Āyurpapata—1307-1311 A.D.). There are translations also of the *Vajracchedikā Prajñāpāramitā.* Among other works, translated into that language, is the *Meghadūta*; the Tibetan poetic version of this work was translated in prose. The *Rāmakathā* has a Mongolian version. Besides, the shadow-play of the Rāma legend was very popular. Those, who used to sing the Mongolian epic ballads, were familiar with the *Kāvyādarśa* of Daṇḍin (eighth century). For the elegance of the literary and verbal forms of those ballads, Dandin's work used to be consulted. The Mongolian scholars of the earlier generation used to study the *Bodhicaryāvatāra* of Śāntideva (seventh century), as well as the Mongolian version of the Tibetan *Tanjur.* The first work was, for the first time, translated into the Mongolian language in 1305 A.D., and the original was incorporated into the printed text of the Mongolian *Tanjur.* Between the fourteenth century and the nineteenth, the aforesaid work of Śāntideva was translated into Mongolian, and explained several times. The philosophical thought in the above poetical work and the Tāntric songs in the *Tanjur* influenced the Mongolian *Uriu-Yin-Dagun* (everlasting songs composed by Mongolian scholars). The *Subhāṣita-ratnakoṣa* of Tibet was translated into Mongolian more than once; this Tibetan work contained translations of many Sanskrit *Subhāṣitas.* On the basis of this Mongolian translation or the Tibetan version was composed the East Mongolian *Buriyat* by Lāmā Irdini (second half of nineteenth century to the twentieth, earlier half). In it *Subhāṣitas* have been culled from the *Pañcatantra* and the *Hitopadeśa.* The *Subhāṣita* collection of this country contained either translation of Sanskrit *Subhāṣitas* or their ideas.

There is a Mongolian translation of the Arabic translation of the *Pañcatantra.* It is attributed to Ābu Nāsr (d. 1280 A.D.). There is evidence of the Mongolians' familiarity with the *Vetālapañcaviṃśati, Vikramacarita* and *Śukasaptati.* In the language of the Kālmuks, a branch of the Mongolians, there are versions of many Indian vampire-stories. It was, perhaps, as a result of intimate contact with India, that the idea of writing works on *Nīti* originated among the Mongolians. Over a portion of Europe the Mongols exercised their domination for about 200 years. It was, perhaps, through them that the aforesaid Indian works got into Europe.

ENGLAND[67]

William Jones (1746-1794), founder (1784) of Calcutta Asiatic Society, had profound knowledge of Sanskrit scriptures and literature. His hymns (1784-1788) to Kāmadeva, Prakṛti (in the forms of Durgā and Bhavānī), Indra, Sūrya, Lakṣmī, Nārāyaṇa, Sarasvatī and Gaṅgā, are full of references to Sanskrit myths and legends and literature in general, and mute witnesses to his scholarship. He translated the *Rātrisūkta* (X. 127) of the *Ṛgveda.* He was conversant with Indian philosophy also. For example, he looked upon the world as the manifestation in form of the formless God, regarded the phenomenal world as the illusory appearance of God, and thought of the transcendental Supreme Being.

We quote below some Sanskrit verses composed by English scholars to prove their proficiency in Sanskrit language and literature. The Sanskrit scholars of the Government Sanskrit College of Calcutta were extremely unnerved when Macaulay proposed (1835) to abolish this College. As a representative of those scholars, Prem Candra Tarkavāgīśa sent a letter to Wilson (1786-1860), founder of the above college, then residing at Oxford.

Wilson replied :

niṣpiṣṭāpi paraṃ padāhatiśataiḥ śaśvad bahuprāṇinām
santaptāpi karaiḥ sahasrakiraṇenāgnisphuliṅgopamaiḥ /
chāgādyaiśca vicarvitāpi satataṃ mṛṣṭāpi kuddālakair
dūrvā na mriyate kvāpi nitarāṃ dhāturdayā durbale //

[Even a thin blade of grass, being always trampled hundreds of times by many creatures, being scorched by sun-rays like sparks of fire, always chewed by goats, etc., being pressed by spades, does not die. God has compassion for the weak.]

In the wake of Sepoy Mutiny (1857), the wounded soldiers had to be accommodated in Calcutta Sanskrit College for medical treatment. At that time, the college was shifted to Bow Bazar. In 1860 the college was shifted to its own building. On this occasion, Principal Cowell (1826-1903) wrote the following verse to express his joy :

vidyālayaḥ svālayametya sāmprataṃ
samṛddhakīrtir-bhuvane bhaviṣyati /
tathāhi sānau malayasya nānyato
manoharaścandana eva rohati //

[Now coming to its own place, the college will be very much famous in the world; because sandal-wood, delightful to the mind, grows on the Malaya mountain alone, not elsewhere.]

In 1864, Cowell wrote the following verse on the occasion of the retirement of Premcandra Tarkavāgīśa :-

āśāḥ sarvāstimiravalitā antarlīno'ṃśumālī
tūtkaṇṭhādho mukulitadṛśo' pyākulāyā nalinyāḥ/
antaḥpuṣpaṃ pratinidhirabhūt svarṇavarṇābhareṇu
ścintārūḍhā virahihṛdaye proṣitasyeva mūrtiḥ //

[All the directions were enveloped in darkness, the sun set when this painful situation arose, the lotus had its eyes closed and became very much perturbed. At that time, the gold-like pollens inside the flower became the representative of the sun in the heart of the beloved in separation, like the husband, afflicted with anxiety, living abroad.]

The English poets Byron (1788-1824), Keats (1795-1821), Southey (1774-1843), etc.were familiar with the teachings of Manu.[68]

Some of the celebrated English scholars, who enriched Indology by their valuable contributions, were as followos.

Ballantyne (1813-64), Cunningham (1814-93), Halhed (1751-1830), Jones (1746-94), Kielhorn (1840-1908), Muir (1809-82), Peterson (1846-99), Wilkins (1750-1836), Williams (1819-99), Wilson (1786-1860).

FRANCE[69]

According to Voltaire (1694-1778), the *Manusaṃhitā* was the best of all the works of the east which travelled to the west. It is learnt that those, who composed the Napoleanic Code, studied *Manusaṃhitā.*

The celebrated scholar, Victor Hugo (1802-1885), in his work, entitled *Suprematic,* has imitated an *Upaniṣad.* La Martin (1790-1869) has written about Sanskrit epics, dramas and poetical compositions. Comte's (d. 1857) positivism,[70] according to some,[71] is nothing but Buddhism adapted to modern civilization; it can be characterized as philosophical Buddhism in a new garb. There was a host of scholars of this country who were not only interested in Sanskrit literature, but also made substantial contribution to it by translation and study .

In recent times, Louis Renou and J. Filliozat were towering Indologists of this country; their contributions to Indology are rich and varied.

Among the French scholars, who made notable contributions to Indology by translations of texts and studies, renowened were Duperron (1731-1805), Bopp (1791-1867), Burnouf (1801-52), Chezy (1773-1832), to mention only a few.

GREECE

The Greeks were familiar with Manu and his *Dharmaśāstra*. The Arabic version of the *Pañcatantra* was translated into Greek. This is the first translation of this work in an European language. The *Aesop's Fables* of Greece reveals remarkable similarity with some stories of the *Pañcatantra*; the possibility of Greece having been the borrower in this respect cannot be ruled out. In the realm of novels, the similarity of ideas in the two countries is marked; who the borrower was cannot, however, be determined. In the drama, *Suppliant Woman* of Æschylus (500 B.C.), there is a brief pen-picture of Indian life-style.

There is considerable similarity about the nature of reality between the *Upaniṣad* and the Eleatic doctrine. The similarity in the outlook of Empedocles (*c.* 490-430 B.C.) and Anaxogoras and the Sāṃkhya doctrine is striking. The first exponent of Sāṃkhya philosophy, Kapila, is believed to have preceded the Buddha (*c.* 563-483 B.C.) by several generations. The early *Upaniṣads* belonged to the pre-Buddhistic age. There is no chronological difficulty in the assumption of Indian influence in Greece. But there is no certain evidence in this regard. As great men think alike, the ideas concerned may have developed independently in the two countries.

There is striking similarity of thought about creation between the ideas of ancient Indian writers and the line of Greek Orphic thinking. The veteran Indologist, Barnett has noticed some similarity between Orphic literature and the Indian scriptures. Similar thoughts are found in respect of the theory of rebirth, the imperishability of the soul, etc.[72]

Like the Indians of old, Pythagoras (6th cent. B.C.) believed that it is the souls of the holy men that get refuge in the regions of the sun and the moon. In the *Upaniṣad,* the moon has been characterised as the abode of souls. The biographer of Pythagoras states that this philosopher travelled widely, and learnt many things from the Brāhmaṇas, among others, living in Egypt. According to Rawlinson, the above Greek scholar was influenced more by India than by Egypt.[73] Gompez thinks that when there was an intellectual ferment, the above Greek philosopher, contemporaneous with the Buddha, acquired profound knowledge in oriental learning through Persia.[74] About this the following scholars, *inter alia,* are unanimous : Winternitz (*Viśvabhāratī Quarterly,* 1937, February), William Jones *(Works,* III, 236), Colebrooke (*Miscellaneous Essays,* I, 436 ff.), Schroeder (Pythagoras Die Inder), Garbe (*Philosophy of Ancient India,* pp. 39 ff.), Hopkins (*Religions of India,* pp. 559-560), Macdonell (*Sanskrit Literature,* p. 421). Keith, however, does not accept this view (*JRAS,* 1909, pp. 569 ff.).

The influence of the *Upaniṣad* on Plato can be inferred. Like the *Upaniṣad,* Plato, in his *Republic,* refers to the Supreme Being. In his *Timaeus,* he, like the *Upaniṣad,* recognises one world-soul. Like the Indian triad of qualities, viz. *Sattva, Rajas* and *Tamas,* he recognises *Logistikon, Thumos* and *Epithumia* respectively. The divine origin of soul, its existence before the birth of the mortal body, confinement within the physical frame, speculation about the condition of the soul after one's death, the rebirth of the soul in a man or animal according to the deeds of the person concerned in the previous life, the final emancipation of the soul from the cycle of the rebirths and its return to God - these ideas of Indian philosophy were imbibed by Plato and Empedocles who, probably, in their turn, propagated these ideas among the Greeks. These ideas originated in India even before the sixth century B.C. and appeared in Greece in later times. Stutfield, in his *Mysticism and Catholecism* (1925, p. 74), has admitted the possibility of the influence of India on Plato.

Weber, in *History of Indian Literature* (1852), holds that the originals of many Greek fables are found in the Indian. This view was endorsed by A. Wagener in his *Essai sur la ..... apologues de l'inde et les apologues de la Grece-Latin.* Subsequently, Weber rejected (*Ind. Stud.*, III, p. 327) the idea of Indian origin. On the contrary, he came to believe that it was the Indians who borrowed through the Buddhists. The latter view was opposed by O. Keller in his *History of the Greek fables* (1862). He believed in Indian origin and borrowing through Assyrian connecting links.

ITALY

Rome appears to have been familiar with Manu through Greece. The influence of India is noticed in the *Philosophoumena,* composed by Hippolytus (*c.* 170-235 A.D.) or a contemporary writer. It contains a brief description of the doctrines of the Brāhmaṇas living at Tagavena (Tungavena or Tuṅgabhadrā). The French Indologist, Filliozat, has pointed out that this work contains the Upaniṣadic doctrine followed by the Brāhmaṇas living on the bank of the Tuṅgabhadrā in South India. The influence of the Upaniṣad on the philosophy of Plotinus has been proved.

Among the Sanskrit works, translated into Latin, the *Pañcatantra* deserves special mention. The *Gesta Romanoram* reveals the impact of narratives in Sanskrit works. In the sixteenth century, an Italian, named Sasseti, came to India, and made notable efforts to familiarise his countrymen with Sanskrit. This was, perhaps, the first stepping stone to the familiarity of the west with Sanskrit literature.

Gorresio (1808-91) edited and translated the *Rāmāyaṇa.*

HOLLAND

A priest of this country, named Abraham Rogerius (1609-?) published his *Open Door to Hidden Heathendom* in 1651 A.D. It contains Dutch translation of 200 verses from the Sanskrit *Nītiśataka* and *Vairāgyaśataka.* This is the first translation of a Sanskrit text into an European language. Palsaert of Holland came to India at the time of Jahāngir (1605-1627). He left an eyewitness account of India.

Brockhaus (1806-77), Caland (1859-1932) were some of the outstanding Dutch indologists.

HUNGARY

Hungary's literary contact with India dates back to the 14th century A.D. Many visionary stories like the 'Visio Philberti', 'Visio Tnugdali' and the well-known story of Lorinc Tar are intimately connected with Indian examples.[75] This type developed in the 14th century Hungary. The Hungarians' zeal for Indian literature led to the successive translations of the *Pañcatantra* in 1678-82, 1781 and 1784. Among other Sanskrit works translated, partly or wholly, into Hungarian were the folloiwng :

Amaruśataka, Arthaśāstra, Atharvaveda, Bhagavadgītā, Buddhacarita, Cāṇakya, Chāndogya, Daśakumāra-carita, Gītagovinda, Hitopadeśa, Kālidāsa, Kāmasūtra, Kathāsaritsāgara, Kāvyādarśa, Mahābhārata, Manusmṛti, Mohamudgara, Mṛcchakaṭika, Nalopākhyāna, Rāmāyaṇa, Ṛgveda, (Śaṃkarācārya), Śatakatrayī (Bhartṛhari), Śuksapatati, Upaniṣad, Vetālapañcaviṃśatikā.

The noteworthy Buddhist work, to be translated, was the Pāli *Dhammapada.* The Prākrit *Gāthāsaptaśatī* (*Sattsaī*) was also translated.

The life-story of the Buddha came to be familiar with the Hungarians about the 15th century through the Latin version of the Buddha legend, called *Barlaam and Josaphat.* Its Hungarian translation was done in the 16th cent. In the 16th and 17th centuries, a popular Hungarian story was the *Poncianus historiaja* which is a translation of the Sindbād stories (Greek *Syntipas* or the Story of the Seven Vazirs) originating from India where it is lost in its original form. Dodsley's 'The Oeconomy of Human Life' (1751) was translated into Hungarian, under titles like *The Wise Indian,* by different writers. F. Verseghy (1757-1822) was the first to write about Indian history.

Among the Hungarians, who were deeply influenced by ancient Indian literature, and made notable contribution to Indology, the name of Alexander Csoma de Koros (1784-1842)[76] is a glowing one. He came to Calcutua, and, with the patronage of Asiatic Society, made an extensive study of ancient works. His contribution to Indology consists, *inter alia*, in an English rendering of the Sanskrit and Tibetan Buddhist terminological dictionary, called *Mahāvyutpatti* (3rd-4th cent. A.D.), a catalogue and survey of the *Tripiṭaka* in Tibetan. The value of his contribution has been clearly laid down by Lokesh Chandra in the following words :

"He opened up a vast vista of this treasures of art and thought, literature and philosophy, grammar and lexicography, medicine and metallurgy, astronomy and alchemy and other branches of learning of India hidden in the Tibetan language. The dark recess of India's history shone afresh by the dedicated and pioneering efforts of Csoma."[77]

Another noteworthy Hungarian, J. Schmidt (1868-1933), wrote a *History of Sanskrit Literature* (1923), and two other books, one (1921) dealing with Indian epic literature and the other on the works of Kālidāsa. He was the author of a monograph on the activities of the Buddha and Buddhist literature. He published (1923) also a *History of Indian Philosophy*.

Among the noteworthy modern Indians, whose works have been rendered into Hungarian, Rabindranath is the most towering figure. Some of the other modern Indian writers are as follows :

Ahananuru (Tāmil writer), Amṛta, Annadāsankar Rōy, Khuswant Singh, Mahātmā Gāndhi, Mānik Bandyopādhyāy, Mulk Rāj Ānand, Nārāyan Gangopādhyāy, Premchand, Pritam, Tārāsankar Bandyopādhyāy.

A noteworthy feature of the Indological studies in Hungary is the study of Gypsy-lore which is regarded as a branch of Indology. We have written about the Gypsies in Hungary in chapter III.

The Gypsies were popular in the Hungarian literature of the closing decades of the 19th century. For example, the Gypsy frequently appears in the novels of Mor Jakai. Janos Army's *The Gypsies of Nagyida* deserves mention in this connexion.

A very distinguished Hungarian Indologist was Aurel Stein (1862-1943). His most outstanding contribution to Sanskrit literature was an edition (Bombay 1892) of the *Rājataraṅgiṇī* and its English translation (London, 1900).

Stephanus Tamasko, a Slovak living in Hungary, translated some verses of the *Ṛgveda* and the Buddhist work, *Dhammapada.* What is remarkable is that he wrote an ode in Sanskrit.[78]

Indological studies have got a boost in the post-independence (1945) Hungary as a result of more brisk contact with India. The Department of Indo-European Linguistics in Eotvos Lorand University of Budapest has become the main centre of classical Indological training, studies and research. Arrangements for studies in other fields of Indology have been made in other institutions. The above Department has introduced a full-fledged course in Indology (B.A., M.A., M. Phil). Janoj Harmatta (b. 1917), Head of the above Department, has published learned treatises, e.g. *Ancient Indian Literature* (Budapest, 1952), *History of the Indus Culture in the light of new excavation,* To the History of the *Śukasaptati* (1963), New Evidences for the *History of Early Medieval North-Western India* (1966), To the History of Greeks in Bactria and India (1966), Researches on various classical Sanskrit texts, e.g. *Śukasaptati, Kathāsaritsāgara, Hitopodeśa, Daśakumāracarita,* etc. have been carried on enthusiastically. Some important texts have been translated. Some of the outstanding Indologists of this period are Gyula Woftilla (b. 1945), Jozsef Vekerdi (b. 1927), etc.

In this period, Gypsy studies also have progressed considerably. The aforesaid Vekerdi's works, *The Gypsy Folk-Tale.* His work on Gypsy dialects of Hungary is reported to have been in press. Gypsy songs have also been studied. Some

Hungarian short stories and novels have been based on Gypsy themes. M. Lakatos, himself a Gypsy, has written a very popular novel.

A remarkable event in the annals of Indological research in Russia is the explorations in Central Asia. These resulted in the recovery of Buddhist texts and art-objects. Explorations in this region have facilitated research relating to Indian literature, religion and history. Some of the Hungarian Orientalists, connected with operations in Central Asia, in the post-independence period, are Louis Ligeti (b. 1902), Alice Sarkozi, Geza, Bethlenfalvy (b. 1936), Jozsef Terjek (b. 1939), George Hazal, Margit Koves.

GERMANY

Schiller, a friend of the great litterateur, Goethe (1749-1832), imitated the theme of the *Meghadūta* in his *Maria Stuart.* In the *Meghadūta,* the exiled Yakṣa chose cloud as messenger to his beloved. In Schiller's work, the captive queen sends message to her lover through the cloud. Goethe was so profoundly impressed by the *Abhijñāna-śakuntala* that he recorded his appreciation in glowing terms; he saw the heaven and the earth combined in the sole name of Śakuntalā.

J. Grimm maintains (Reinhart Fuchs, pp. Cclx-1xv) that Beast Fable originated in primitive Indo-Germanic folklore; the agreement of German Beast fables with Greek and Indian could be through the primitive relationship of these peoples.

According to a scholar, "the fidelity with which the Greek and German tales adhere to their original Indian framework, is indeed astonishing."[79] A remarkable coincidence is the story of the Dog and the Sparrow in Grimm's Collection, as compared with an episode in the *Baital Pachisi,* viz. the story of the Nautch-girl and the parrot.[80] In earlier Greek literature, only eight complete fables are known, with a dozen others only referred to; the latter, however, include The Ass's Heart, The Countryman and the Snake, The Dog and the

Shadow—all of which can be traced to India before Alexander's invasion (327/326 B.C.).

The German scholar, Max Müller (1823-1900) rescued from oblivion the Veda, the oldest treasure of India. Some other German scholars were also deeply interested in Sanskrit literature and philosophy.

Adelung (1768-1843), Aufrecht (1822-1907), Benfey (1809-81), Böhlen (1796-1840), Böhtlingk (1815-1904), Bopp (1791-1867), Bühler (1837-98), Deussen (1845-1919), Eggeling (1842-1918), Goldstücker (1821-72), Hiuobrandt (1853-1927), Humboldt (1767-1835), Lüders (1869-1943), Oldenburg (1854-1920), Pischel (1849-1908), Roth (1610-68), —these were some of the outstanding Indologists who either translated Sanskrit texts or wrote studies on different aspects of Indology.

AMERICA

Lopez, in his *Les Races Aryans de Peru*, states that there is the influence of the *Rāmāyaṇa* and *Mahābhārata* on the poetical literature of Peru. According to Chamanlāl, the *Ṛgveda* is a source of some poetical works of Inca.

Whitney (1827-94) was a very distinguished American scholar who dedicated himself to cause of Indology.

RUSSIA

Systematic Sanskrit studies began in this country in the earlier half of the 19th century.[81] Even before that the *Bhagavadgītā* was translated into Russian in 1788. It was followed by a partial translation of the *Śakuntalā*, which appeared in 1792. In some Russian Universities, the study of Oriental languages and literatures, including Sanskrit, was introduced. Books were written on the common origin of Russian and Sanskrit. Comparative dictionary of these two languages was written. Bibliographical works relating to Sanskrit literature were composed. Buddhism provided a great impetus to the study of Sanskrit works relating to that religion.

Some of the outstanding Russian Indologists were as follows. Böhtlingk (1815-1904), besides editing Pāṇini's grammar (1839-40), *Śakuntalā*, etc., compiled, in collaboration with other scholars, the monumental *Great St. Petersburg Dictionary* (1852-1857). Vasily Vasilyev (1818-1900) was a very distinguished Buddhist scholar. His most important work was *Buddhism, its Doctrines, History and Literature* (pt. I, 1858, pt. III, 1869). Another renowned Russian Indologist, who specialised in Buddhism, was Oldenburg.

The foremost among the Russian Orientalists was Minayev (1840-1890) who was the founder of the Russian school of Indology and Buddhist studies. He began with investigations into the *Ṛgveda*. He studied Buddhism and Jainism also. He travelled (1874) in the East, his intinerary including India, Nepāl and Ceylon. His *Travel Notes* resulted in the publication of *Studies of Ceylon and India*. He paid two more visits to India. His *Buddhism, Researches and Materials* (1887) entitles him to an exalted place in the galaxy of western scholars dealing with Buddhism. Among the Buddhist Sanskrit texts, edited by him, the most important was an edition (1889) of the philosophical-poetical work *Bodhicaryāvatāra* of Śāntideva (7th cent.). His survey of Sanskrit literature embraced Vedic, Buddhist, epic literatures, classical *kāvya* and folk literature. His scholarly activities were not confined to Sanskrit literature alone. His work *"On the phonetics and Morphology of the Pāli language"* (1872) was an outstanding one which was translated into French (1874) and English (1875). Among his posthumous publications, relating to Pāli texts, were the translations of the *Petavatthu, Suttanipāta* and *Mahāvagga*.

Now we come to the Indological studies in Russia at the end of the 19th cent. and the begnning of the 20th. During this period, the two most outstanding figures were Oldenburg (1863-1934) and Scherbatsky (1866-1942), both pupils of Minayev. A major work of Oldenburg was *Buddhist Legends* (1894) which deals with the literature relating to such legends in Sanskrit, Prākrit and Pāli. He had a profound knowledge not only of Buddhism and Buddhist literature, but also of Buddhist art. Some of his noteworthy publications, besides the above, were *A Collection of Sinhalese Tales* (1931), *Material on Buddhist Iconography* (1901), *An Album of Buddhist Representations from the Kazan Ecclesiastical Academy* (1903), *Modern Organisation of the study of the Fine Arts and Their Technique in India* (1931). The monumental *Bibliotheca Buddhica* (begun in 1897), an international undertaking, in the production of which a galaxy of scholars of different countries participated, was the result of Oldenburg's initiative. In fact, entitled *A Collection of Original and Translated Buddhist Texts,* its aim was to present the original and translated Buddhist writings connected with Northern Buddhism.

In view of the bulk and quality of the above studies, the following remark of Oldenburg, Scherbatsky and Tubyansky seems to be prefectly justified:

"Russian Buddhist studies must be considered first in the ranks of European Buddhist studies."

Scherbatsky had a profound knowledge of both Brāhmanical and Buddhist works. He published the historical poem *Haihayendracarita* (1900). He published papers on the history of poetry in India, particularly on the *dhvani* theory. His outstanding work was the two-volume treatise, *Theory of Knowledge* and *Logic According to Later Buddhists.* The first volume (1903) included a translation of Dharmakīrti's (7th cent.) *Nyāyabindu-prakaraṇa* and Dharmottara's *Nyāyabinduṭīkā.* The second volume (on perception and inference) appeared in 1909. German and French translations of the work are an index to its high appreciation in the scholarly world. His two works, though small, deserve mention. One was the *Logic in Ancient India* (1902) and the other, *The Central Conception of Buddhism and the Making of the Word Dharma.* These stimulated interest in Buddhistic studies. His two-volume *Buddhist Logic* (1930-32) was acclaimed by the distinguished British Buddhologist, Conze, as "a masterpiece of the first order". His work, relating to Buddhism and

Buddhist literature, fully justifies the fact that he was regarded, both in the East and the West, as the leading figure in world Buddhology.

This versatile scholar also translated into Russian Daṇḍin's *Daśakumāracarita*, parts of the *Arthaśāstra*, the *Laghusiddhāntakaumudī* of Varadarāja. Science in ancient India also attracted his attention. He published (1924) an article, entitled Scientific Achievements of Ancient India. He was interested also in Indian materialism, and published (1927) his article, 'History of Materialism in India'.

He was also a brilliant teacher of Sanskrit, and produced a set of distinguished scholars, *e.g.* Obermiller, Tubiansky, Vostrikov, Semichov, Kalyanov. The following epitaph succinctly indicates the mission of Scherbatsky's life :

He explained the wisdom of ancient Indian thinkers to his own country.

Indological reasearch in Russia, in the present century, can be divided into some well-defined stages. The period between 1917 and 1920, following the Great Revoluton, was one of great cultural activity, a sort of revival of the cultural life which was in disarry during the socialist Revolution. Some of the outstanding publications in this period were subsequent issues of the *Bibliotheca Buddhica*, mentioned earlier, Rosenburg's two-volume *Introduction to the study of Buddhism Through Japanese and Chinese Sources* (1919), *Literature of the East* (with a Survey of Indian Literature by Oldenburg), 1919. Tsybikov's *A Buddhist Pilgrim in the Holy places of Tibet* (1919), etc.

The period from 1920s to 1930s witnessed Oriental studies set on new lines. The teaching and study of Sanskrit sources started vigorously in several cities besides Petrograd, *e.g.* Moscow, Tbilisi, Kharkov, etc. Sanskrit came to be recognised as an indispensable discipline for the comparative historical study of the Indo-European languages. Urdu, Bengali and Tāmil also began to be studied. Marxists historiography began to concentrate on the history of the ancient orient.

Noteworthy publications, during the period, were Reisner's *Ideologies of the East, Studies in Eastern Theocracy* (1927), with a large part on ancient India, the magazine *Vostok* (The East), Baranikov's translation of Āryaśūra's *Jātakamālā*, Larin's translation of Vāmana's work on poetics, Obermiller's translation of Buston's *Tibetan History of Buddhism* (2 vols), edition of *Abhisamayālaṃkāra*, translation of Sumpakhanpo's *A Chronicle of Buddhism in India, Tibet and Mongolia*, the translation of the *Arthaśāstra*, Shor's translation of *Pañcatantra* (1930) and *Vetālapañcaviṃśatikā* (1939).

In the post-war period (1940s-1950s), the history of ancient India was studied analytically. Some of the note worthy publications of this period were Osipov's *Short Study in India's History up to 10th century* (1948), Barannikov's translation of Tulsi Das's *Rāmāyaṇa* (1948), translation of portions of the *Mahābhārata*, Vorobyov-Desyatovsky's (1927-1956) monographs on the development of personal pronouns in Indo-Aryan languages, translation of *Mṛcchakaṭika* (1956).

In the 1950s, India and Russia came into intimate contact with each other. The keen interest of the Russians in India is evident from the translation of a number of works by Indian scholars, *e.g.* Nehru's *Discovery of India* (1955), Radakrishnan's *Indian Philosophy* (1956-56), Y.N. Roerich's[82] (1902-1960) unpublished huge Tibetan-Sanskrit-English-Russian dictionary.

In very recent times, work on a complete academic translation of the *Mahābhārata* is going on. Indian manuscripts are being vigorously studied. Work on different aspects of Indology is proceeding apace. Indological journals are being published. Soviet scholars have evinced keen interest in Indian national historiography. *Ancient India, A Historical Survey* by Bongard-Levin and Ilyin (1969) is a noteworthy work.

Some of the important recent works on Indian languages are : Ivanov and Toporov's *Sanskrit*, Yelizarenkova and

Toporov's *The Pāli Language*, Vertogradova's *Prākrits* (1978), Andronov's *Dravidian Languages* (1965), Zaliznyak's *Grammatical Study of Sanskrit.*

Russian Indologists have been interested also in Indian philosophy. Mention may be made of Anikeyev's *On Materialist Traditions in Indian Philosophy* (1965). Indian philosophy, both heterodox and orthodox, is being avidly studied in Russia.

Indian religion, too, has attracted the attention of Soviet Indologists. As examples we can mention Guseva's *Hinduism* (1977) and *Jainism* (1968).

Soviet Indologists have tried to encompass the totality of Indian culture. They have not left out Indian art. A noteworthy Russian work in this field is Tulayev's *Art of India*, 1968. Some of them are working on the art of painting according to the *Viṣṇudharmottara.*

Among the Sanskrit works, translated into Russian, very renowned are, besides the *Bhagavadgītā*, the *Manusmṛti*, Aśvaghoṣa's *Buddhacarita* and Kālidāsa's dramas.

No account of the impact of Indian literature on Russia is complete without a reference to Tolstoy (1828-1910). He was deeply interested in the Buddha and Buddhist Sanskrit literature. He was interested in Indian philosophy, the life and teachings of Rāmakṛṣṇa and Vivekānanda. He wanted to publish a translation of Abhedānanda's works. In the last years of his life, he planned to write a book on the Buddha, and edited Boulanger's *The Life and Teachings of Siddhārtha Gautama,* called the Buddha (1911).

Rabindranāth (1861-1941) made a tremendous impression on the Russian intellectuals.[83] Russian translations of his poems, were frequently published. Russian poets perceived a kindred spirit in Tagore's works. Poet Bryusov wrote verses in imitation of Tagore. M. I. Tubyansky (1893-1943) made a thorough study of Rabindranātha's works. He composed a work entitled *Rabīndranāth O Tār Viśvavīkṣā* which was hitherto unknown.[84]

THEMES OF INDIAN NARRATIVES IN FOREIGN COUNTRIES[85]

Literature and culture do not keep to geographical boundaries. As a flowing river surmounts all obstacles, meets the ocean and is merged in it beyond recognition, so also the stream of culture gets over the narrow barriers of race and religion, and gets lost in the great ocean of humanity. Many Indian narratives have become part of the narrative literature of the world. For the present we shall take into account only the Sanskrit narratives and their diffusion in foreign countries. In this chapter, we have used Penzer's ten-volume Indian edition of the English translation, by Tawney, of Somadeva's *Kaṭhāsaritsāgara*, entitled *Ocean of Story*.

CHANGE OF FORM

In the *Śatapatha Brāhmaṇa*, Urvaśī, having forsaken king Purūravas, assumed the form of a female swan. In the *Rāmāyaṇa*, Ahalyā, as a result of her adultery with Indra, disguised as Gautama, was reduced, by the curse of her husband, Gautama, into a heap of ashes. Demon Mārīca assumed the form of a golden deer for tempting Sītā. In the *Mahābhārata*, Kindama,having assumed the form of a deer, cohabited with a female deer. In the Śalyaparvan (9/52), we find that a boy was transformed into a girl for one night. In the above cases, the cause of transformation was the transgression of prohibition.

In the *Daśakumāracarita*, a nymph was transformed into a silver chain. In the *Kādambarī* (Pūrvabhāga), Kapiñjala, having bathed in the Acchoda Lake, was released from his equestrian form, and was restored to his normal condition. A famous example of transformation is provided by the story of a rat being transformed successively into the form of a cat, a dog and a tiger and finally reduced to its own form (*Hitopodeśa*, Nirṇayasāgara ed. p. 115).

In some other countries, too, the idea of transformation occurs in some narratives . In the *Household Tales*, there is the

Tale of Two Brothers, in which a person is represented as transformed, at the touch of the magic wand, into a stone-image. The motif of transformation occurs also in the story of seven magicians and two brothers, contained in the *Folklore and Legend Oriental.*

MAGIC WAR OR STRUGGLE OF TRANSFORMATION

This is a very old theme. Among the examples that we have, the events are as follows : at first, a person is reduced to an animal, and sold to a person who pays the highest price. Generally, the seller is the father of that person. He should never sell the rope which is tied to the neck of the animal; because, if one parts with it, then he will have to remain in the form of the animal concerned. Secondly, eventually magic war takes place between the hero and the magician (mostly father of the hero) or between the rescuer of the hero and the magician.

In the *Kathāsaritsāgara* (37), it is stated that, due to the presence of a rope in the neck of a person, named Bhavaśarman, he is reduced to a bull. When some sympathetic person, out of kindness, throws away the rope from the neck, he is restored to his original human form.

Similar motif is found in the *Nights.* As illustrations may be cited the second Kalenders' Tale (Burton, vol. I, pp. 134-35), Sidi Nu Uman (Burton, Supp., vol. III, p. 325). For similar motifs in the east and the west, the following, *inter alia,* may be consulted :

Oesterley, *Baitāl Pachisi,* pp. 174-175.

Busk, *Sagas from the Far East,* p. 4.

Gibb, *History of the Forty Vezirs,* pp. 253-56.

Mialtovic *Serbian Folklore.*

Ralston, *Russian Folktales,* p. 229.

BITCH AND PEPPER

It occurs in the second part of the story of Devasmitā (*Ocean of Story*, Ch. XIII). A female ascetic, trying to enter the private apartment of Devasmitā, was prevented by a bitch. She, however, managed to enter with the help of a maid servant. Then she tried to create Devasmitā's confidence in her, and went away. On another day, she came and gave the bitch a piece of meat mixed with the powder of pepper. The bitch ate it up. As a result, tears began to roll down from her eyes. She showed this to Devasmitā, and said that the bitch, remembering her (ascetic) as its companion in the previous life, was shedding tears. The crafty ascetic also said that the bitch and she had been co-wives of a Brāhmaṇa in the previous life. She further said that, during the absence of her husband, she used to have sexual gratification by living with another man. Consequently, she had been born in this life as an ascetic. On the other hand, her co-wife had been born as a bitch, because she tried to maintain her chastity.

The transformation of a woman into a bitch occurs in the *Disciplina Clericalis* (vide Wilson, *Essays on Sanskrit Literature*) and in *Le Grande as La vieille qui suduisit la jeune fille*, iii. 148 (ed. III, vol. IV. 50). The theme occurs in the story of the Old Woman and her Dog in the *Gesta Romanorum.* Besides, this theme is found in the Persian Sindibad Nāmā, Syriac Sinban, Greek Syntipas and the Libro des los Engernos and Hebrew Sandabar. A similar story occurs in the Arabic story, The Wife's Device to Cheat Her Husband (*Nights*, Burton, vi, pp. 152-156).

In this connection, mention may be made of the story of Nastagio and the Spectre Horseman (vide *Decameron*, Fifth Day, Eighth Novel). In it, a person tries to persuade a woman to accept a lover after convincing her of the suffering a woman had to undergo for having refused her lover in the previous life.

EAVESDROPPING

Eavesdropping or trying to hear secret conversation from a place of hiding occurs in several Indian stories. For example, one may cite the *Kathākośa* (vide Tawney, *Oriental Translation Fund*, New Series, ii, 1895). A similar story occurs in Frere's *Old Deccan Days* (stories no. 5,7 and 9). In this connection, we may mention also Bernhard Julg's *Mongolische Märchen* etc. (Innsbruch, 1868, Tale 15, p. 147). For another instance, see Bloomfield, *Life and Stories of Pārśvanātha*, p. 185. For a Jewish version, see Gaster, *Example of the Rabbis*, nos. 110, 447, 449. For further instances, see Coxwell, *Siberian Folk tales*, p. 163; Bolte and Polivka *Anmerkungen zu den kimderund Hausmärchen der Brüder Grimm*, Leipzig, 1913, I, p. 53 n.

A KNOW-ALL MAN

In the *Kathāsaritsāgara* (Ch. 30) one Hariśarman appears as omniscient; he is considered to be a repository of supernatural knowledge. After a theft in the Royal palace, he has been summoned to find out a clue for the recovery of the stolen goods. He used to boast of his power to do so, but, in fact, he had no power. So he takes time, but feels very uneasy mentally. The story of Allwissened in the *Grimm's Tales* has considerable similarity with this story.

Versions of these stories, sometimes with a little variation, are found in various eastern and western countries. As an instance, the Mongolian version, called *Siddikur*, of the Sanskrit *Vetāla-pañcaviṃśati* can be mentioned. The story, almost in its entirety, occurs in Schleicher's *Lithuanian Legends*. A version of it occurs in Henricus Belius's *Facetioe*. Some similarity of this story is found also in the *Nights* (vide Burton, Supp., Vol. 1, pp. 282-287). Also see Coxwell, *Siberian Folktales*, p. 193 and elsewhere; Wesselski, *Märchen des Mittelalteres*, pp. 242-243.

FAITHFUL SERVANT

The story of the faithful servant, Vīravara, occurs in the Sanskrit *Vetāla-pañcaviṃśati*[86] (no.4) and *Kathāsaritsāgara* (no.

70, Ch. 53). Vīravara was ready to sacrifice his life for the welfare of his master. A similar story occurs in the Persian *Tutināmā*[87] and the Turkish *Tutināmā*.[88] The closest similarity of the Indian story is found in Grimm's *Der getrene Johannes* (no. 6). In this connection, mention may be made of the story of Two perfect Friends in Peter Alphonse's *Disciplina Clericalis*. In course of time, the story has been included in the seven Sages of Rome. It also got into the French literature and connected with the Carolingian Cycle[89] in Chanson de geste of Amis et Amiles (12th cent.).

CIPHER LANGUAGE[90]

This method is present in the narratives of both the east and the west. May be that the west learnt it from the east. In the literature of the east, the person, to whom this language is used, does not understand it. A third person explains it to him. In some cases, one sign language is answered by another sign language.

This device occurs in Puṣpadanta's narrative in the *Kathāsaritsāgara* (Penzer's ed., I, no. 3). A person, named Devadatta, finds a princess in the window, and falls in love with her. The princess sends a message to him in sign language. This method has been adopted in a story of *Arzi Borzi Khān*, the Mongolian version of the *Siṃhāsanadvātriṃśikā*. It has been rendered into German by Jülg (*Mongolische Märchen-Sammlung*, Innsbrück, 1868, p. 240). Its English rendering has been done by Busk (*Sagas from the Far East*, pp. 315-23), and Coxwell (*Siberian Tales*, pp. 227-31). It appears as the sub-story in Lady's Ninth Story included in *The Forty Vezirs* (Gibb, p. 116).

DISGUISED HUSBAND

This motif occurs in the ancient Indian narrative literature. In the *Rāmāyaṇa*, (present form, *c.* second or third century A.D.) Indra, disguised as Gautama, enjoyed Gautama's wife, Ahalyā. In the *Kathāsaritsāgara* (33), a Vidyādhara-Prince, disguised as king of Vatsa, married Kaliṅgasenā. Benfey has pointed out different forms of this motif in *Kalila and Dimna*, John of Capua, *Śukasaptati*, *Ānwār-I-Suhaili* and *Bahār-I-Dānish*, etc. as well as in the European Collections, called *Le Livre des Lumieres*, *Cabinet des Fees*, *Decameron*, etc. Excepting in the *Rāmāyaṇa* and *Kathāsaritsāgara*, this trick has been played by humans. In the work of Herodotus, however, a superhuman being is involved in this matter. Almost everywhere the woman has been represented as innocent.

POISON-DAMSEL
(*Viṣakanyā*)

The idea of poison-damsel, perhaps, originated in India, although examples of it are rare in Sanskrit literature.

The practice was to slowly poison a girl till her whole system became charged with poison; so much so that her breath, kiss, embrace, and even her glance used to poison a man who came into physical contact with her. Such women were employed against enemies. The most noteworthy example of such a woman occurs in Viśākhadatta's (*c.* seventh century A.D.) political drama, entitled *Mudrārākṣasa*. In this work, Rākṣasa, Minister of the Nanda King, tried to kill Maurya Candragupta with the help of a poison-damsel (*Viṣakanyā*). In the *Pariśiṣṭaparvan*, king Nanda is represented as having gradually poisoned a girl.

In the *Kathāsaritsāgara* (19), we find king Brahmadatta's Minister, Yogakaraṇḍaka, sending a few *Viṣakanyās* as dancers among the attendants of king of Vatsa.

Latin *Secretum Secretorum* is a version of an Arabic work. It contains Aristotle's warning about *Viṣakanyā* to Alexander coming to India. Through the translations of the above work, in different languages of Europe, the idea of *Viṣakanyā* spread in Spain, Italy, Holland, France, England, etc. The occurrence of the motif of *Viṣakanyā* in the *Gesta Romanorum* further paved the way of its dissemination in different countries.

A modern version of the story of *Viṣakanyā* occurs in *Rappacini's Daughter* by the American poet, Hawthorne. The story is this. A doctor, ever since the birth of his daughter, trained her to inhale the smell of the poisonous plants in his garden. After a few years, the girl became so much charged with poison that whatever flower was touched by her withered away. A young man fell in love with her. A colleague of the girl's father, for the safety of that lover, prepared, for the girl, a potion by drinking which one could counteract the effect of poison. But, the poison was so much absorbed in her system that the sudden use of the potion led to her death.

CHANGED BRIDE

This motif occurs in the narrative literature of both the east and the west.

It is found in the story of Kamalākara and Haṃsāvalī in the *Kathāsaritsāgara* (no. 163 C, vol. VI, p. 40). It appears also in Grimm's *Kinderund Haus Märchen*, no. 89 (Die Gänsemagd). In this connexion, Vide B. Schmidt, *Griechicche Märchen*, p. 100; Gonzenfach, *Sicilianische Märchen*, no. 33, 34, Introduction to Basila's Pentamerone (Burton, i, p. 5)

For details about this subject, see :

P. Arfert, *Das Motiv Vonder....Erzählung-Litterateur*.... 1897, pp. 8-71;

Cosquin, *Contes Indiens et 1' Occident*, 1922, pp. 61 ff.

P. Saimtyves, *Les contes de Perrault*, 1923, pp. 48, 50-52.

SPURNED LOVE OF WOMAN

In ancient Indian literature, there are several instances of the revengefulness of women as a result of unrequited love. In the *Rāmāyaṇa* Rāvaṇa's sister, Śūrpaṇakhā, offered her love first to Rāma and then to Lakṣmaṇa. Far from entertaining her, Lakṣmaṇa chopped off her nose. To avenge the insult and injury, she inflicted injury on the body of the "human being" that had spurned her love. She did not rest content by doing this much. She instigated the fellow-Rākṣasas to destroy him. In the *Mahābhārata,* Ambā, frustrated in her desire to get the love of Bhīṣma, performed severe penance designed to cause his death.

In the *Pāla-Gopāla-Kathānaka* of the Jain Jinakīrti (fifteenth century, first half), a woman, having failed to seduce a young man, resolved to take revenge. So, she brought a false charge against the young man that he had tried to violate her chastity.

In a palm-leaf manuscript,[91] written in Telugu language, of the *Śārṅgadhara-carita,* prince Śārṅgadhara's step-mother is stated to have fallen in love with him. The prince refused her. The irate lady complained to the king that the prince had attempted to violate her chastity. The king, blinded by anger, inflicted severe punishment on the son. In the *Kumārarāmacarita,*[92] we find that the queen was attached to her youngest son. As the prince did not fulfil the amorous desire of his mother, she lodged a similar complaint to the king. The hen-pecked king, extremely enraged, sentenced the son to death.

Similar instances occur in Persian and Arabic novels. The book of *Sindibad* (the story of the king, his son, the damsel and the seven Vazirs) is its best example. In this connection, mention may be made of "The Craft and Malice of Women"[93] in the *Nights* and in the Persian *Bakhtyār Nāmā.* In a Turkish version, a man's mother-in-law has been depicted as the instigator.[94]

Let us conclude this topic with a reference to the *Arabian Nights* which has become a part of the world literature entertaining generations of readers, male and female. The following observations of S.K. Chatterji[95] are very pertinent in this connexion :

"The romantic story-telling of India, made more romantic by the spirit of Persia, and broadened by the realism of the Muslim Arab world, gave to world that great work of imagination, the *Arabian Nights* which quickly was transformed into a world classic".

PHILOSOPHY

The impact of Indian philosophy is found in some countries of South-East Asia. In an inscription (seventh century A.D.) of Cambodia, of the time of king Mahendravarman, Śiva has been considered as identical with Paramātman of the *Upaniṣad.* The six Indian systems of philosophy were among the subjects to be learnt by the kings of that country. King Bhavavarman's officer, Vidyāpuṣpa, was familiar with Nyāya and Vaiśeṣika systems of philosophy. King Īśānavarman's officer, Vidyāviśeṣa, was also versed in the above systems. It is learnt that Indravarman's preceptor, Śivasoma, learnt philosophy from Śaṃkarācārya. We are informed that Śrīsvāmin, protégé of king Jayavarman II, had profound knowledge of Indian philosophy, particularly in Nyāya philosophy, Two philosophical treatises, *Bṛhaspatitattva* and *Ganapatitattva,* have been found in Java. The Sanskrit originals are lost.

Some Buddhist philosophical works were rendered into Chinese. Among them especially noteworthy are the following:

Mādhyamikaśāstra, Saddharmapuṇḍarīka, Daśabhūmikasūtra, Yogācārabhūmi and *Abhidharmakośa.*

Chinese translation alone is available of some Buddhist works, their Sanskrit originals are lost. Noteworthy among them are the *Brahmajālasūtra, Ratnakūṭa* and *Mahāsannipāta.*

In Japan, some Buddhist philosophical works were published. Of these, the most well-known is the *Sukhāvatīvyūhanāma Mahāyānasūtra.* Of the Sanskrit manuscripts, discovered in this country, the principal one is the *Aṣṭasāhasrikāprajñāpāramitā.* There is profound influence of Buddhism on the philosophy of Nshida Kitaro (1870-1945). He introduced Buddhist Nihilism[96] by a combination of Buddhist philosophy and western ideas.

In Korea was published the *Mahādharmakośa.* The Mongols burnt it, and the next edition was published in 1236 A.D.; this is the earliest of the extant editions.

Indian philosophy deeply influenced western thought for a long time. Not only western philosophers, but also poets could not escape this influence.

After reading translation of the *Upaniṣad*, the German savant, Schopenhauer (1788-1860) was overwhelmed, and said—the *Upaniṣad* has been the solace of my life, and will be the solace of my death. The Upaniṣadic doctrine of salvation and the Buddhist doctrine of *Nirvāna* (suppression of desires) produced a great impact on his mind. Indian philosophy seems to have been the foundation of the pessimistic doctrine of this scholar as well as of Hartmann. It seems, Eckhart (*c.* 1260-1327 or 1328) and Tauler, exponents of Christian mysticism, were influenced by the Ātman-Brahman doctrine of the *Upaṇisads.* The Upaniṣadic idea of the unity of Brahman may have been the foundation of the Monism of Fichte (1762-1814) and Hegel (1770-1836). Certain statements of Fichte, made in his *Anweisung... Leben,* seem to echo the nondualistic Vedānta. Some scholars have found some similarity between the philosophy of Kant (1712-1804) and Indian philosophy. Perhaps, he was influenced by the doctrines of *Māyā* (illusion) and rebirth. There were writings on Indian aesthetics even before his *Aesthetics.* May be, that he was indebted to India in this respect also. Besides, like Buddhist philosophy Kant also used to think that some problems could be solved; *e.g.* what was the origin of the world ? Is the world limited or eternal ? Deussen (1845-1919) translated the *Vedāntasūtra* and some *Upaniṣads,* and highly praised Vedānta philosophy. Nietzsche (1844-1900) also lavishly praised the *Upaniṣads.* The Nobel-Laureate, Hess, was charmed by the philosophy of life adumbrated in the *Bhagavadgītā. Yoga* and the doctrine of *Māyā* influenced his thought. Bethoven (1770-1827) not only translated the *Gītā* and portions of the *Upaniṣads,* but also adopted the ideas contained in them. The Indian idea of Monism appears to have influenced the concluding song (chorus) at the end of the second part of the *Faust* (1797) of Goethe. According to Humboldt (1767-1835), the Gītā is the only truly philosophical poem in all the literatures of the world. He used to consider himself blessed for getting the opportunity of studying the *Gītā.*

The French scholar, Victor Hugo (1832-1885), has imitated an *Upaniṣad* in his poetical work *Suprematic.* The Romanian Eminescu (1850-1889) composed a poetical work, entitled *Tattvamasi.* In it has been discussed the unity of Ātman and Brahman. The Russian stalwart, Tolstoy (1828-1910), in a letter to Mahātmā Gāndhi, quoted the *Upaniṣad* and the *Gītā.*

The *Gītā,* particularly its doctrine of desireless action (*Niṣkāmakarman*) inspired many an English poet. The very title of Matthew Arnold's *Disinterested Endeavour* is an index to the influence of the above doctrine. In the compositions of Blake (1757-1827), Keats (1795-1821), Jones (1746-1794), Huxley, etc. there is influence of the Gītā.

In *The Dry Salvages* (Section 3), Elliot has written the substance of Kṛṣṇa's message in the *Gītā.* In the writings of Isherwood, Hard, Jung, etc. we find Hindu ideas. Yeats (1865-1939) and Russell were influenced by the *Upaniṣad* and the *Gitā.* The title *Razor's Edge* of Somerset Maugham's book is clearly translation of the words *'Kṣurasya dhāra'* of the *Upaniṣad.* His *Writers' Note-book* (1938) is a witness to his indebtedness to the *Upaniṣad.* The One, who is mentioned in Wordsworth's *Tintern Abbey* as the driving force behind all sentient beings, is the counterpart of the Upaniṣadic Brahman. The idea of divine consciousness in everybody, according to Coleridge, echoes the Vedāntic idea.

The influence of Indian philosophy is inferred in the Monism and the idealistic philosophy of America in the nineteenth century. Emerson's doctrine that the phenomenal world is a manifestation of the One, and of rebirth, etc. reflect Indian philosophical ideas. He himself has particularly mentioned the Veda, *Gītā* and *Viṣṇupurāṇa.* Thoreau's writings reveal considerable impact of the *Upaniṣad.* Whitman's theory of Transcendentalism indicates the influence of Indian philosophy. In his *Passage to India,* he has written that his soul is identical with the universal soul; this idea is typically Indian.

Glimpses of Indian non-dualism are noticed in Steinbeck's *To A God Unknown and the Grapes of Wrath.* Attachment alone is not renunciation - this view of his is Indian in origin. His *Cannery Row* echoes the Indian theory of illusion (*Māyā*).

The pioneers of the Christian Movement used to think that matter and sorrow have no real existence; this perception is indispensable for freedom from sorrow.

Some Greek writers have respectfully referred to Indian sages. The Greek rulers and statesmen looked upon Indian philosophy with regard.

The doctrine of rebirth, according to the Greek philosopher, Pythagoras (*c.* 580-500 B.C.) may have been based on the *Upaniṣad.* Some think that he was influenced by Sāṃkhya philosophy. It was, perhaps, under the influence of the Upaniṣad that philosophers like Xenophanes sought unity behind all diversities. Urwick observes that each and every doctrine of Pythagoras is almost entirely a repetition[97] of the original doctrines laid down in Yogaśāstra. According to a Greek tradition, Thales, Empedocles (b.*c.* 490 B.C.) and some other Greek scholars came to the east for studying philosophy. Enfield says that Pythagoras, Anexordes, Pyrrho, Democritus (d.*c.* 370 B.C.) and several other Greek philosophers came to India.

The stratification of consciousness, according to Plato (428-348 B.C.), reminds one of the stages of the mind called *Jāgrat, Svapna* and *Suṣupti.* The three qualities of *Sattva, Rajas* and *Tamas,* recognised in Indian *Śāstras,* have the corresponding terms *Logistikon, Thumos* and *Epithumia* respectively according to Plato. *Plato's Dialogue* echoes the Upaniṣadic prayer for being led from the unreal (*asat*) to the real (*sat*), from darkness to light and from death to immortality. Plato's view that asceticism is the best means for the soul's emancipation from the bondage of the body indicates Indian idea. The main Orphic doctrine about emancipation of the soul from the body appears to be Indian in origin. The Greek idea of *Logos* corresponds to the Vedic idea of *Vāc; Vāc* is like Latin *Vox*. The Greek Thales (sixth century B.C.) used to think that water is the material cause of all things. In the Veda, too, water is at the root of the creation of the universe. It was Garbe, who, for the first time, pointed out the similarity between the two views. The Eleatic doctrine about the unity of all things is akin to the Upaniṣadic doctrine of universal unity. The admission of *Sat* and *Cit* as the only reality, the illusory appearance of everything, the difference between the apparent and the real—these ideas of Parmenides (b. *c.* 515 B.C.), founder of the above philosophy, are similar to Upaniṣadic attitudes as explained by Śaṅkarācārya.[98] Ranade characterises Śaṅkara as the Indian Parmenides. Parmenides, too, can be called Greek Śaṅkara. Gompez has noticed that Melisus' Joyful, effortless, powerless pristine existence is akin to that Vedāntic doctrine according to which the world is considered to be an illusion and the central existence is of the nature of the existent (*sat*) conscious (*cit*) and blissful[99] (*ānanda*). The propounders of the atomic doctrine, Leuciplus (fifth century B.C.) and Democritus (*c.* 460-370 B.C.) are known to have widely travelled in the east, and perhaps met the Indians in Persia. Urwick thinks that the substance of Plato's thought in the *Republic* is written in Indian works. According to him, Plato and the Indian sages had similar thoughts, similar faith and similar dreams. Inspired by the same intellectual ideal they thought in a sublime manner.[100] He further says that there is similarity between Hindu scriptures and Plato's ideas, reasoning and conclusion. Some technical terms of psychology and ethics, current in that country, are almost translations of Sanskrit words.[101] Like the Brāhmanical caste divisions, Plato has divided the state into three categories; *e.g.* guardian, concomitant and artist.[102] The difference between common knowledge and wisdom, according to Plato, is like the difference between knowledge (*vidyā*) and spiritual knowledge (*adhyātmavidyā*). The higher state of the soul, called *nous* according to him, is the *Ātman* or spiritual consciousness of the Vedānta. His *dikaiosune* is *dharma* of Indian philosophy. His doctrine of *anamnesis* is similar to the origin of all *dharmas.*

The Greeks, perhaps, learnt the theory of incarnation from India. The idea of incarnation, along with other Indian ideas, were known in Greece.

In the *Symposium,* Athanasius reminds one of the Upaniṣadic doctrine of salvation. The similarity between Neo-Platonism on the one hand, Vedānta and Yoga on the other, is noteworthy. The similarity consists in the following: belief in rebirth, doctrine of *Karman,* Monism, the highest goal of life is freedom from rebirth, self-realization through knowledge, *dhyāna* (meditation).

In support of the tradition that Socrates (*c.* 469-399 B.C.) knew Indian philosophy we may cite the testimony furnished by Aristoxenus (*c.* 330 B.C.). According to him, some Indian scholars went to Athens. Among them, one asked Socrates what, according to him, was the subject-matter of philosophy. There is evidence that Indian philosophers had access to the circle of the intellectuals of Athens. The Hellenic rulers and politicians used to listen respectfully to what the Indian philosophers said. The foreign concepts of substances, five gross elements (*Pañcabhūta*), motion, molecule, etc. appear to have influenced Greek philosophers like Aristotle (385-322 B.C.). According to Schlegel (1772-1829), the Greek atomic theory was influenced by the contemporary Vaiśeṣika doctrine of India. According to Garbe (1857-1927), Sāṃkhya philosophy moulded the philosophy of the Greek Heraclitus (*c.* 540-480 B.C.), Empedocles (*c.* 490-430 B.C.), etc. According to a Greek tradition, these philosophers came to travel in the east. According to scholars like Winternitz (1863-1937), the Greek philosopher, Pythagoras, was influenced by Sāṃkhya philosophy. He is also said to have visited India. The existence of One behind the phenomenal world according to

Xenophanes (*c.* 560-478 B.C.), Parmenides (b.*c.* 515 B.C.), etc. is like the Upaniṣadic ideas.

In Italy a work, entitled *Katá Pason Aireseon Elenchos or Philosophumena,* was discovered in 234 A.D. This work, by Hippolytus (*c.* 170-235) or a contemporary author, is an account of the doctrines of the Brāhmaṇas living in Tagavena (Tungavena or Tuṅgabhadrā) in South India. It is learnt that it contains the Upaniṣadic doctrines of the ascetics living in the Deccan. The influence of the following *Upaniṣads* is clear:

Aitareya (1/1-4, 2/1-4), *Chāndogya* (3/1/37-38, 8/12/1-3), Kaṭha (2/2/15), *Muṇḍaka* (2/2/11), *Bṛhadāraṇyaka* (3/79/14), *Taittirīya* (2/5/1).

There is definite evidence of the fact that the Romans acquired profound knowledge of the Upaniṣadic philosophy at least in the third century A.D. Careful summary of the Upaniṣadic doctrines appears in the *Elenchos*; this proves how popular the *Upaniṣad* was in Rome.

While supporting Christianity, Hippolytus has attacked the Upaniṣadic doctrine. This is an evidence of the fact that the Romans were familiar with the doctrines imported from India.[103]

Radhakrishnan has discussed the similarity of ideas between the Gnostic philosophy and the *Upaniṣad.* According to him, the relation between philosophy and religion, found in Gnostic philosophy, is a characteristic of Hindu thought. The doctrines of rebirth and *Karman,* according to Plotinus (205-270 A.D.) seem to echo Indian philosophy. Man's destiny is determined by his quest of truth, beauty, and honesty; otherwise man has a fall—this doctrine is typically Indian.[104] The Logos doctrine, similar to the Vedic *Vāc,* in which words are stated to be possessed of divine power, has got into the Fourth Book of the *Bible.*

Some Gnostic doctrines have similarity with Upaniṣadic doctrines.[105] Kennedy goes so far as to characterise the Gnostic philosophy as oriental doctrine in a Hellenic garb. The Gnostic doctrine of many heavens is basically Indian; it has three qualities corresponding to the triad of qualities according to Sāṃkhya. Similarity between the Gnostic ideas and Mahāyāna Buddhism has been noticed. There is an account of how the Gnostic ideas spread from India through trade.[106] The famous Gnostic teacher, Bardesanes (155-233 A.D.), learnt many things about it from an Indian ambassador to Syria.

Among the philosophical works, written in Turkish, are the *Yogācārabhūmiśāstra, Abhidharmakośa* and an epistle of Nāgārjuna,[107] preserved in the Peking National Library. Parts of Āamas have been found in *Seven Hedin Collection* in Stockholm.

The atomic theory of Arabia, propounded by Al Rhazi (865-926) reflects the deep influence of Nyāya-Vaiśeṣika philosophy. Al Beruni (tenth-eleventh century) acquainted the Islamic world with Indian philosophy.

There is considerable similarity between Sufism and Vedāntic thought. It is understood that the Sufis got inspiration from wandering Indian ascetics. Some important points of similarity are as follows : according to the Āijudiyā Sufis, Paramātman has his manifestation in everything; the individual soul and Paramātman are identical. This concept was advocated by Śaṅkarācārya. The Suhudiyā Sufis believe that everything emanates from Paramātman. This outlook is in consonance with Rāmānuja's qualified Monism. It is believed that the Bhāgavata doctrine helped the formulation of the Sufi doctrine. Emperor Jāhāngir (1605-1627) pointed out the similarity between Vedānta and Sufism.

The exposition of Indian philosophy by Rāḍhākrishnān generated great enthusiasm among the scholars of both the east and the west. His gift of the gab and facile pen evoked a new awareness in the west, particularly in Europe, about Indian philosophy. As a result of Vivekānanda's(1863-1902)persuasive preaching and Rādhākrishnān's oratory, the Vedānta doctrine has become the warp and woof of the life of some people there. The two works of Isherwood, viz. *Vedānta for Western World* and *Vedānta for Modern Man*, are an index to the popularity of Vedānta in the west. One of the leading Indologists of modern times, Basham, expresses his deep regard for ancient Indian philosophy in the following superb manner :

The sages who meditated in the jungles of Ganges Valley 600 years or more before Christ are still forces in the world. *The Wonder that was India*, 1967, p. 487.

C. RELIGION[108]

Indian religion, particularly Buddhism appealed to the heart of the people of various countries. Rādhākrishnān rightly says[109] that a large part of the world received religious education from India. Curiously enough, the *Manusaṃhitā*, dating back to hoary antiquity, made the following prediction :

Etaddeśaprasūtasya sakāśādagrajanmanaḥ /
Svaṃ svaṃ caritraṃ śikṣeran pṛthivyāṃ sarvamānavāḥ / /II.2

[All people of the world should learn their respective conduct from the Brāhmaṇa(s) born in this country.]

NEPĀL

This country, the nearest neighbour of India, was flooded by the twin currents of Hinduism and Buddhism. In the sixteenth century, Vaiṣṇavism, preached by Caitanya, spread to Nepāl.

It was Vasubandhu (fourth or fifth century A.D.) who was at the root of the diffusion of Mahāyāna Buddhism in that country. To some Bengali Buddhists belongs the credit of the spread of Vajrayāna in that country. Of them, the most prominent was Atīśa Dīpaṃkara (*c.* 980-1053). They exercised their influence in Nepāl *en route* to Tibet (1042). The monasteries at Nālandā, Vikramaśila, Odantapurī and Jagaddala, provided inspiration in Nepāl.

In that country, devotion to Gaṇeśa is profound. The worship of this deity started in the tenth century A.D. Since then, the elephant-faced deity has been enjoying great popularity there. On the occasion of harvest, the two sons of Pārvatī, Gaṇeśa and Kārtikeya, are worshipped.

TIBET

The Tibetan king, Srong-Tsan-Gampo (*c.* 629-98), embraced Buddhism, and preached it among his people. It is said that this king initiated the subjects to the *mantra* "Oṃ Maṇipadme Hūm".[110] The famous sandalwood image of the Buddha Avalokiteśvara, used to be worshipped in the Potālā palace of Dālāi Lāmā, was, perhaps, taken from India by Sambhoṭa, deputed by the above king. As a result of the Indo-Tibetan cultural contact, Lāmāism came into vogue in Tibet. The result was a fusion of Hīnayāna, Mahāyāna and Tantrayāna Buddhism. In this country, too, Gaṇeśa has found a respectable niche in the pantheon.

From the *Blue Annals* we learn that the above king, as the protector of religion, acquainted the people with many religious works. To the devout Tibetans this king and his two queens were human incarnations of *Avalokiteśvara* and Goddess Tārā respectively. It was their belief that this God and this Goddess came to Tibet as the king and the queen in order to introduce Buddhism in that country.

King Khri-Sron Ide-Btsan (755-780) was bent upon the diffusion of Buddhism in that country.[111] He established temples in Central Tibet, and set up many images of the Akṣobhya Buddha and Tārā. King Ral-pa-can (814-836) played an active part in the spreading of this religion even at the cost of his life. From the Tibetan chronicles we learn that, due to extreme attachment to Buddhism, this king lost his life at the hands of an assassin. After this, Tibetan Buddhism stagnated. A group of reactionaries stood in the way of the progress of this religion. After the advent (1042) of the great Atīśa Dīpaṃkara, a new chapter began in the history of Tibetan Buddhism, and for that matter, in the history of Tibet.

BURMA

Buddhist religion and culture struck such a deep root in this country that the majority of the Burmese are still Buddhists. At the time of the decadence of Buddhism is India, many Buddhist monks went to Burma, settled there and introduced Tantric Buddhism.

The sphere of Sanskrit Buddhism in Burma comprised :

(a) Lower Burma with its political centre at fly capital of Prome and later on at the Talaing capital of Thaton,

(b) Upper Burma with its centre at Pagan.

The earliest form of Sanskrit Buddhism in that country was, perhaps, Mūlasarvāstivāda-nikāya which was, in all probability, introduced sometime before the seventh century. By about the ninth century, or still earlier in ancient Prome Theravāda Buddhism got a firm footing. Approximately by the middle of the eleventh century, Thaton city turned into a stronger centre of the above form of Buddhism.

We have it, on the testimony of Tāranātha, that Mahāyāna Buddhism made its way into Pagan and other centres of Upper Burma at least in the fifth century A.D. The above historian tells us that the school of Buddhism existed in Pegu and Ārākān also. The flourshing period of Mahāyāna in Burma was roughly between 1057 and 1300 A.D.

The Burmese claim to have received their culture through a Śākyan migration from Madhyadeśa of India. The kings of Burma are said to have originally descended from the Sūryavaṃśa.

There is the tradition of Aśoka's spreading the message of Buddhism. There is hardly any doubt about the existence of Buddhism in Burma in the third century A.D. Epigraphic testimony is available about the fact that it was in a flourishing condition in the seventh and eighth centuries in Lower Burma. There is corroborative evidence of the archaeological finds. We learn of the heyday of monastic scholarship. Grammar, logic, medicine, astronomy, philosophy, polity, law, prosody, even military science were vigorously cultivated.

The Buddhists made a deep impact on the life and culture of Burma; in fact, they succeeded in ridding that country of primitive heathenism. Buddhism exercised civilising influence on the rough and rude semi-civilised people of the country. It also served as a unifying force when the Burmese had no common identity. Buddhist culture played a considerable part in the growth of Burmese language and literature too. Pāli, the language of Theravāda Buddhism, was the sole guide in this respect. The members of the Buddhist Saṃgha did not live in the cloistered isolation of monasteries. There was a relation of love and respect between them and the laity.

- Certain Hindu deities, *e.g.* Gaṇeśa, Durgā, etc. appeared in this country. Since the time of Aśoka (*c.* 273-232 B.C.), Hindu priests were appointed to high posts under the Buddhist kings. They used to worship Nārāyaṇa at the time of coronation, and the foundation of houses. Viṣṇu has been described as a sage. The Vaiṣṇava Temple at Pagan is a mute witness to the popularity of Vaiṣṇavism there. Prome or Hmawza was known, in ancient times, as Bissunamyo which is equivalent to Viṣṇupura. Some images of this place are Viṣṇuite in character. Viṣṇu as Nārāyaṇa seems to have been known to the Hindu colonists of Burma. Another major Hindu deity in Burma is Śiva. According to the Burmese text, *Mahayazawin*, Viṣṇu presided at the foundation of the city of Hmawza (old Prome), and was helped by Gavāmpati, Indra, Nāga, Garuḍa, Caṇḍī, Parameśvara (Śiva). Several images have been found there. Of the divine Trinity of the Brāhmanical religion, Brahmā is also not absent, although he plays no significant part. In *Anantaśayyā* reliefs from Thaton and Hmawza, He is represented as associated with Viṣṇu and Śiva. Independent images of Brahmā are rare. Among other Brāhmanical deities, we meet with Gaṇeśa and Sūrya.

The images of the Brāhmanical deities in Burma may be assigned to the following three periods :

(1) Early period - 9th to 13th cent.

(2) Medieval period - 9th to 13th cent.

(3) Late or decadent period - 14th to 15th cent.

The Brāhmanical element came to be prominent in Burma at least in the sixth century A.D., and continued till at least the fourteenth. This element was more or less confined to the Indian section of the population. In early times, Brāhmanical influence was, perhaps, confined to Ārākān on one side and Lower Burma (Kingdom of Hmawza) on the other.

According to numismatic evidence, kings of Brāhmanical descent, whose names ended in Cantra, ruled over Ārākān from at least the fifth to the eleventh century A.D.

Sanskrit inscriptions palaeographically dated from seventh to tenth century A.D.

Brāhmanism, however, could not replace or supersede Buddhism.

MALDIVES

In this country, Hinduism and Buddhism prevailed before the influence of the Muslims. Many people used to worship Śiva, Viṣṇu, Brahmā and Indra. Buddhism, perhaps, travelled from Ceylon to Burma. At one place in the island, a Sun-temple and an image of the Sun have been found. In the national festival, women, through music and dance, worship the Sun who is, indeed, the most popular deity. The last king of this region was a Buddhist.

AFGHĀNISTĀN AND GANDHĀRA[112]

Śaivite archaeological materials (seventh-eighth century) have been unearthed in the place called Tagao and Gardeja. Hiuen Tsang (seventh century) has referred to the famous temple of Goddess Bhīmā, consort of Śiva, in the Gandhāra region. The so-called Trimūrti is a beautiful example of the prevalence of Śaivism in this country. It was discovered at Akhun Dheri. In the middle is Śiva. The Śiva-murals at Piyanjikel testify to the popularity of Śaivism.

IRAN (PERSIA)

The religious sentiment of Iran was generally influenced by Hinduism. The Buddhist monks, sent by Aśoka to preach Buddhism in the countries to the west of India, passed through Persia, and exercised some influence on the strong Manichaeism. The pious Mani (b. 215), belonging to this country, introduced this religion. Perhaps due to the influence of Buddhism, animal-sacrifice has been prohibited in this religion. Both the Veda and the *Āvestā* have glorified the deity called Mitra. There is no doubt about the identity of Vedic Mitra with the Iranian Mithra. The presence of Buddhist *samanas* in western Persia, in the second century B.C., has been proved.

TURKESTAN

Some archaeological materials, discovered at Dandan-Ulik and the neighbouring area, indicate the prevalence of Śaivism in East Turkestan. The Panel no. D X.8 is a proof of the worship of Śiva-Śakti.

CEYLON AND SOUTH-EAST ASIA

For preaching Buddhism in Ceylon, Aśoka is said to have sent his sister, Saṅghamitrā and brother (according to some, son) Mahendra (or Mahindra) in 251 B.C. They preached this religion there, and converted king Tissa and other members of the royal family. Among the subjects also many embraced Buddhism. The name of Mahendra does not appear in any inscription of Aśoka. But, that such a person did the noble work in Ceylon is proved by the works *Dīpavaṃsa* and *Mahāvaṃsa*, composed in that country, as well as by a memorial column built by the Ceylonese in his honour at Anurādhapura. We learn from the *Mahāvaṃsa* and *Cūlavaṃsa*, that, before Aśoka, there was influence of the Brāhmanical religion in Ceylon. In that country, there are many images of Gaṇeśa and the pantheon includes Śiva, Viṣṇu and Skanda; Viṣṇu is extremely popular.

According to a Ceylonese tradition, some people were sent to Suvarṇabhūmi[113] for preaching Buddhism.

The existence of many images of Gaṇeśa in Thailand, Cambodia (Kampuchea), Campā (Vietnam), Jāvā, Sumātrā, Bali and Borneo, testifies to the popularity of this deity in those countries. Besides images of Gaṇeśa, there are references to this deity in some inscriptions of Cambodia. The image of Gaṇeśa, found at Srah Taset (Angkor), has two heads. He is seated in *Padmāsana.*[114] with a round sweetmeat in his left hand, perhaps a rosary in his right hand and a serpent hanging like a sacred thread. His tusk has touched his belly, head is covered, and there is a serpent-bangle in his left hand. There is a three-headed and six-armed Gaṇeśa-image in a temple. In Cambodia, the magnificent temple, Angkor Vāt,[115] originally dedicated to Viṣṇu, stands as a mute witness to the diffusion of Brāhmanical religion in that region. As in India, in that country also, it was considered to be a pious act to distribute free copies of the *Rāmāyaṇa, Mahābhārata* and Purāṇas among worthy persons. The inscriptions indicate the influence of Pāśupata Śaivism and Pañcarātra Vaiṣṇavism in this country. Buddhism also was there, though not as pervasive as Hinduism. Some Pāli inscriptions indicate that, towards the end of the glorious period of that country, Hīnayāna Buddhism exercised considerable influence on the kings.

In Bali, many Hindu and Buddhist ritualistic works have been discovered.[116] Śaivism and Buddhism are still there.

Śiva used to be worshipped in Laos. Among the didactic and religious texts in this country, the most noteworthy is the collection of fifty stories of the *Jātaka,* made by an unknown person. The work, *Maṅgalasutta* was also very famous.

Hinduism and Buddhism (both Hīnayāna and Mahāyāna) existed side by side in Mālay.

In Jāvā, Viṣṇu was the famous deity. The popular king, Airlanga (1019-1042 or 1049), was regarded as an incarnation of Viṣṇu. At a place, called Belahan, a beautiful Viṣṇu image, mounted on Garuḍa, has been found. Generally, it is supposed by people to be an image of Airlanga.

In Thailand, there are images or paintings of some Hindu deities. Some murals depict *Rāmāyaṇa* scenes.

The discovery, in Cambodia, of four Tantras, called *Nayottara*, etc. indicates the popularity of Tāntricism in that country. At one time, there was prominence of religion in the main walks of life. This religion was mainly Purāṇic, and the greatest deity was Śiva worshipped as a phallus. Śiva was considered to be the fortune-giver to kings. The Kampuchean Hindu king, Jayavarman II (802-815), established a Śiva-phallus, called Devarāja, at the place, called Phnom Kulen. This phallus was regarded as the palladium of the royal dynasty. The Brāhmaṇa *Gurus* used to perform *Koṭihoma* and Vedic sacrifices. Śaivism exercised the greatest influence in the ninth-tenth centuries. In the twelfth century, Vaiṣṇavism was very strong. Buddhism also prevailed in this country.

The influence of Hinduism was not negligible in Campā too. The people of this country adopted certain cultural matters of India during the reign of king Bhadravarman, the real founder of this kingdom. We are informed that a king, named Gaṅgārāja, renounced kingship, and lived on the Ganges the sight of which is reported to have been very delightful to him. King Indravarman II, out of regard for Buddhism, built temples and monasteries in honour of the Buddha. He, however, was not antagonistic to Hinduism; rather he was respectful to the traditional Śaiva faith of the kings of Campā.

MESOPOTAMIA

People of the Mandean sect used to live in the port called Maisan. Their spiritual and mystic path of knowledge was full of Indian ideas. Through the above port there was trade between the two countries. Here some Indian tribes set up a colony.[117]

BABYLON

It is understood that the Babylonian Bardesanes (155-233) wrote a work about Indian religious thought. He gathered materials from two persons sent as envoys to the Roman emperor, Antoninus Pius (158-181). The materials, gathered by him, have been preserved in the work, *Abstinence,* of prophyry. Bardesanes has referred to Brāhmaṇas and Buddhists. He mastered considerable information about the life-style of the Hindu and Buddhist preceptors and about the education imparted by them.

CHINA

Hinduism, to some extent, and Buddhism, to a great extent, spread in China. As in many other Asiatic countries, Gaṇeśa infiltrated into China also; the great Chinese Wall could not resis this access. This deity appeared in this country as early as the sixth century A.D. A dual image, called Kangitem, has been found in China.

Some Indian scholars like Kumārajīva, Paramārtha (fifth-sixth century), and Bodhidharma (sixth century) helped in the Chinese translation of many Buddhist treatises. The Chinese, in large number, embraced Buddhism. They regarded India, the motherland of the Buddha, adored by them, as the greatest holy place. Many Chinese came to India on pilgrimage. Their object was to acquire knowledge about Buddhist doctrines from Indian scholars, to acquaint themselves with the Buddhist doctrine, to know about Buddhist customs, collection of Buddhist texts, acquisition of relics of the Buddha's body, and to acquire merit by visiting the Buddha's land.

From the history of China, we learn that, in the sixties of the first century A.D., Buddhism was officially welcomed. In that decade, a Buddhist work (an aphoristic work comprising 42 sections) was compiled in China, and a temple was built in honour of the Buddha.

In about 67 A.D., the Indian Buddhist monks Kāśyapa,

Mataṅga and Dharmarakṣa, visited the court of the Chinese emperor Ming-Ti (58-75 A.D.). The emperor, believed their exposition of Buddhism, built a temple for their residence and meditation. The above two persons translated several Buddhist Sanskrit works, and converted many people to Buddhism. Many other Indian Buddhist monks went to China, and successfully preached Buddhism and initiated people to this religion. In the fourth century A.D., the Chinese emperor, U-Ti, embraced this religion. Like Confucianism and Taoism, Buddhism, too, was recognised as a religion of China. In this way, intimate cultural intercourse between the two countries continued for over a millennium. Mahāyāna Buddhism acquired wide popularity in China. The Chinese gave it a new form. They laid greater emphasis on the Bodhisattva, particularly the ideal of Amitābha than on the Buddha's message that the cessation of *Taṇhā* (thirst or desire), is the *summum bonum* of life.

The Lokapālas of Hindu pantheon got inextricably mixed up with the deities of the Buddhist pantheon. Dhṛtarāṣṭra, Virudhaka, Virūpākṣa and Vaiśravaṇa— these four Lokapālas have been converted into four Mahārājas of the Buddhists.

JAPAN

Japan, a predominantly Buddhist country, accepted Gaṇeśa after the ninth century A.D. Most of his images are two-armed, four-armed or six-armed. In one image, there are three heads (each with three eyes), and four hands with a sword, a radish, a round sweetmeat and royal sceptre. He was supposed to be an elephant-king, seated on a mountain. The names of about 900 Indian deities figure in the arts and place names of this country. In the Shingon pantheon, there are, besides Gaṇeśa, the following Indian deities :

Indra, Agni, Yama, Sarasvatī, Varuṇa, Vāyu, Īśāna, Brahmā, Pṛthvī, Sun and Moon. Shintoism of this country is, according to some, another form of Hinduism.[118] Varuṇa is worshipped as Sui-ten in Tokyo. Sarasvatī appears as Benten.

Śiva is found under the name of Daikuku in the Shikoko island. In the temple of Kotohi, the sailors worshipped God Kompira which is derived from Sanskrit Kumbhīra. Viśvakarman is the deity of carpenters, bearing the name Visukatasuma. In Japan also, king Yama is a terrifying deity under the name Emm. In Japanese art, nearly 900 Indian deities appeared.

A wide area of Japan welcomed Buddhism. Time was when most of the Japanese were Buddhists. Buddhism entered Japan in the first quarter of the sixth century A.D. through China and Korea. From certain ancient works of this country, we learn that a South Indian Brāhmaṇa, having turned into a Buddhist monk, went to Japan, and spent the rest of his life there. It is said that a considerable number of Japanese monks learnt Sanskrit from him. The Japanese way of *Sādhana*, called *Zen*, was inspired by Buddhism. Its role in the religious life of Japan is very important. The word *Zen* (Prākṛta Jhāṇa) is derived from Sanskrit *Dhyāna*. In the second half of the fifth century A.D., an Indian religious preceptor, named Bodhidharma, went to China where he preached Buddhism. It is he who is regarded as the propounder of Zen Buddhism which is influenced by Tāoism of China. The sum and substance of this doctrine is that success in *Sādhana* cannot be achieved by external rites and rituals nor by logical reasoning. The truth can be realised or *Bodhi* (enlightenment) can be obtained only when one's consciousness is lost in the calm and tranquillity of the void through meditation.

KOREA[119]

Despite communism in North Korea, and America-dominated administration in the South, Mahāyāna Buddhism, at places underlying Vajrayāna, is the only State religion. According to a tradition, in the first century A.D., Li-Tho, a prince of the Li dynasty, having completed his studies in Buddhism in India, married a Cola princess of South India. A few years back, in a Buddhist conference held in Seol, capital of South Korea, an edition of the Pāli *Tipiṭaka* and an illustrated edition of the *Jātaka* stories were published. The former president of Cambodia and a leader of the Buddhists, Prince Narodom Sihānouk, while residing (1980-82) in Piyang-Iyáng, capital of North Korea, wrote a book, in French, containing an elaborate discussion in detail about the Buddhist pagodas and temples there. President Kim-Il-Sung is himself son of a Buddhist scholar. He declared 2000 Buddhist temples in Korea to be government property. There is a Minister exclusively for matters relating to Buddhism in Korea. On the door of each Buddhist shrine is inscribed, in Devanāgarī characters, the words *Om Maṇipadme*. Buddha's message is inscribed both inside and outside the shrines. The Korean emperor, in the first century A.D., accorded to Buddhism the honoured position of the State religion. Bronze and stone images, showing various *Mudrās* (hand-poses), of Tathāgata and Mañjuśrī have been discovered in caves and river-valleys. Some people of this country believe that Tathāgata himself came to Korea for preaching his doctrine.

In the Hindu temples of this country, mainly Śiva and Viṣṇu used to be worshipped. Images of Lakṣmī and Nṛsiṃha (Man-lion incarnation of Viṣṇu) have also been found. Four deities were believed to live on the peak of the mountain Taeung in the North. They were Svayambhu Śiva, Brahmā, Maitreya and Viṣṇu. Beside their feet were seated the two demon-servants, Śumbha and Niśumbha. The image of the Korean Goddess, Cisinvalgi, is similar to that of Indian Durgā.

PALESTINE

Two centuries before Christ, Buddhism flourished in this country.

SYRIA

Religious preachers, sent by Aśoka, went to Antiochos Theos (261-246 B.C.), the Greek king of West Asia and Syria.

There is mention of this king in a rock-inscription (13) of Aśoka.

CENTRAL ASIA

There is mention of Mithra (Mitra), *i.e.* the Sun-God, Viṣṇu and Śiva in the Tocharian inscription[120] on a seal. From this it seems that the mixed cult of these three deities prevailed in this region in about 500 A.D. There is abundant evidence of the popularity of Śaivism in Central Asia. It is believed that the Buddhist philosopher, Asaṅga, brought about a syncretism of Śaiva and Buddhist religions. The image of Mahākāla, found in this region, deserves special notice. In it, we find a demon's head, the opening of the mouth, flaming red hairs and elephant-skin in upper hand, blazing sword in the middle right hand (left hand missing). Though the lower hands are absent, yet the trident and the thunderbolt are visible. In the lower part, there are the image of Kārtikeya and the scene of the carrying away of nectar by Garuḍa. Signs of Brahmā-worship are present in the caves of Kucha region. In a fragmentary mural at Balabast, there is the figure of Indra. Vaiṣṇavite influence has been noticed in a Buddha-image in the Domoke region.

In Khoṭān, there are many bronze plates and painted wooden slabs showing Gaṇeśa. The figures of Gaṇeśa and Kārtikeya appear in the paintings of Tun-Huang and some other places.

This elephant-faced God made his way into Mongolia also. The names of some Indian deities, in Mongolian forms, are found in the Shamanist hymns of the period from the fourteenth century A.D. to the seventeenth. In this country, Garuḍa is very popular, and is regarded as a symbol of Shamanist soul of the holy mountain, named Bagdokhan Aula. In the Mahākāvya-songs of the Buriyats of Irktik, Garuḍa can be recognised as Kheredei or Khan Keredei. Buddhism reached Mongolia through Tibetan translation. The Tibetan preachers took this religion to that country in the twelfth century A.D.

SIBERIA

Buddhism was, perhaps, preached among the Buriyats of Siberia in the seventeenth century A.D.

ARMENIA

Kṛṣṇa and Balarama (Demetar) crossed the Indian border as early as in the 2nd century B.C. Their influence is noticed in Armenia in that century.

ASIA MINOR

In Boghaz Kyoi, a fragmentary work, dealing with chariot-driving, has been discovered. In it, some words, denoting the motion of chariots, appear to be like Sanskrit; e.g. *Aikavartanna* (*Eka āvartana*), *Teravattanna* (*Tri āvartana*).

The Phoenicians of Levant were connected with India through trade.

GREECE

Aśoka sent missionaries to several foreign countries for propagating Buddhism. Among his contemporary Greek kings and the kings of the various Hellenic countries, prominent were Antiochos II Theos (261-246 B.C.) of Syria, Ptolemy Philadelphos (285-247 B.C.) of Egypt, Antigonos Gonatas (277-239 B.C.) of Macedon, Magas (300-250 B.C.) of Cyrene and Alexander (252-244 B.C.) of Corinth. In some of their kingdoms, Aśoka set up centres for preaching universal love.

The Indo-Greek (or Bactrian) king, of Sākala (Sialkot in Punjab), Menander (reign *c.* 160-140 B.C.), embraced Buddhism. His dialogue with the Buddhist ascetic, Nāgasena, is recorded in the Pāli treatise, *Milindapañha* (original form, first half of first century A.D.).

Heliodoros (first half of the second century B.C.) of Takṣaśilā, though Greek, was a follower of the *Bhāgavata* religion. He built a monolithic Garuḍa column at Besnagar[121] in Madhya Pradesh, in honour of Vāsudeva.

Some Kharoṣṭhī inscriptions mention that Greek *meridarchs* used to establish Buddha-relics and sanctuaries.[122]

The Gnostic doctrine is a syncretism of Greek (Platonic) and Hindu religions.[123] The following among the main characteristics of this doctrine are, according to some, derived from the Upaniṣadic doctrine and traditional Greek mysticism :

1. God is beyond description, infinite and above all thoughts and languages. He is different from Creator-God. He is separate from His inherent quality, beyond reason and truth. He is eternal silence.
2. If God is beyond space and time, if He is perfect, then how is creation possible, how can evil remain in it ?

En passant, it may be mentioned that Apollonius of Tyana was a famous Gnostic. Philostratus writes that he came to India, and lived in the monasteries of the wise for about four months.[124] Inspired by Indian (Buddhist) ideas, he abhorred animal-sacrifice, and became a vegetarian. According to him, under no circumstances should one shed others' blood. He laid great stress on prayer and meditation. Renunciation was, according to him, the highest ideal. The western scholar, King, is certain[125] that, in the annals of Christianity, India is the source of every idea that was, in course of time, condemned as heretical. How much of what is rightist or conventional has been derived from India it is difficult to say.

According to Eusebius, Numenius sought support of the philosophical doctrine of Pythagoras and Plato among Brāhmaṇas, Magis and Egyptians.[126] Numenius had considerable influence on Plotinus (205-270). The similarity between the Neoplationism of Plotinus and Vedānta philosophy is well-known.[127] Ritter has given the title 'Diffusion of Oriental Modes of Thought among the Greeks' to the introduction of his account of Neoplatonic philosophy.[128] We have it from Rādhākrishnān that, according to Vacherot, Zellar and Brehier, Indian influence on the above philosophy is beyond doubt. As instances, we may point out that, according to Plotinus, the phenomenal world originated from the Supreme God. Nondualistic Vedānta, too, considers it as the illusion of Brahman. According to the *Taittirīya Upaniṣad*, human soul is a replica of the universe; in it there are matter, life, consciousness, intellect and spiritual bliss. In a similar vein, Plotinus holds that the soul has, in it, unity, pure intellect, elan vital and matter. According to him, it is a universal principle that the disembodied soul gets to the place if deserves. Thus, he subscribes to the doctrine of *Karman*. Like the Hindu scriptures, Neoplatonism believes in spiritual consciousness. According to it, by meditation, the soul can be freed from bondage and communion with the Supreme is possible. Like the Upaniṣadic realisation of Brahman, the advocates of the above doctrine believe that, in *Samādhi* (perfect absorption of thought into the one object of meditation, *i.e.* Supreme Spirit), one can get *Pratyādeśa* (divine direction). In the theology of Plotinus, God is unknowable. In the Upaniṣad also, the formless Brahman is beyond knowledge, and can only be realised or perceived.

Some similarity can be noticed between Greek and Indian deities. In India, the mountain Himālaya is *devatātmā* (divine). In Greece, the mountain Olympus is believed to be an abode of gods. Indian Indra and Greek Zeus, etc. occasionally came down to the earth, and assumed disguise to gain woman's love. Homeric deities move about in chariots drawn by horses. Indian gods also are supposed to do the same; the Sun's chariot is drawn by as many as seven horses (*saptasapti*). Both the countries have similarity about the language of the gods.[129]

In Greece, asceticism was added to the mystic school of the religious system. In this, we can infer the influence of India directly or through Persia. According to Inge, in the Platonic outlook on life, developed in Greece, religion played the rôle of philosophical, moral and mental education. Such a condition at first developed in Asia, particularly in the *Upaniṣad* and Buddhism.[130] Professor Dodds has no doubt that Greek culture arose against the background of the

Orient.[131] According to Meyer,[132] the Greek world had been imbued with Egyptian, Persian and Indian cultures since remote antiquity.

AMERICA

There is similarity between the Indian Trinity (Brahmā-Viṣṇu-Śiva) and the Mexican Ho-Huijilopoktali-tlyalok. Despite the local characteristics of the Viṣṇu image of Mexico, the mace and wheel indicate its Indian origin. The Ananta-śayyā (bed in the form of the serpent called Ananta) of Viṣṇu appears in a piece of sculpture (sixth century A.D.) found at La Venta (Tābasco). The appearance of Indian Gaṇeśa is found in the Chak images in the temples of Mayas. In Mexico, there was no elephant. So, the idea of the elephant-faced deity, perhaps, originated from such a person as was experienced about elephants. Besides, at the place, called Coatzumalhuapa, in Guatemala, young Chak is found to be looking at an older deity like Śiva. With matted locks and a serpent on the neck. In Mexico, the *Svastika* sign is sometimes associated with Chak; we find in India Gaṇeśa with the *Svastika* sign. The Mayas were, perhaps, worshippers of the Śiva-phallus. At places like Uxmal, Kābā, etc. stone phalluses are still found. At the summit of the Tikala temple in Mexico, the human figure of Śiva, with matted locks, exists. At Kampache, there is the image (fifth or sixth century A.D.) of the dancing Śiva; it reminds one of the Indian Śiva as Naṭarāja. The signs of the hand-poses of the Mayas, occurring in manuscripts like the *Dresden Codex*, are like Indian hand-poses. In many images of Mexico, the Indian Kaṭakāmukha[133] *mudrā* has been noticed; it indicates advice. At the places, called Uxmal, Chichen Itza, etc. there are temples of the Dwarf deity which reminds one of Viṣṇu's Dwarf incarnation. The Maya Goddess 1.X Tub Tun, vomiting out precious jewels, has the characteristics of the Indian Nāginī of Kubera.[134] The similarity in the classification of the deities is found between the Indians and the Mayas.[135]

Like the Indians the people of that country circumambulate the images of deities. Oblation to fire and sun, and dance in honour of the sun prevailed in both the countries. This dance festival is called *Caḍaka* festival in India, Voladores De Papantala in Mexico and Wiwangay Wachipi among the Sioux Indians living at the place, called Dakota, included in the United States of America. In it, there are everywhere the practices of inflicting injury on one's own body and of the gift of blood.

Among the Mayan images, there is a sort of Kālī image in what is called Coatlicue. In it, two serpents constitute the head of the Goddess; this may be the precursor of the Kālī image. On the earthen vessels (*c.* 400 A.D.) of Nazca, there is the figure like that of Indian Kālī with its dark complexion, lolling tongue and a garland of human skulls. The figure of a similar Goddess appears in the earthen images (*c.* 200 A.D.) of the Moche valley. Beneath her feet is a male figure like Śiva, holding a begging bowl.

Ancient Andeans revered a deity named Viracoca. There was an Indian king having almost the same name (Vīracorcha). As an evidence we may refer to a copper-plate inscription of the Pallava king, Nandivarman (ninth century) of the Deccan. In its sixth verse, there is mention of the king, Vīracorca. It is further stated that he married a Nāga princess. The inhabitants of America, named as Pātāla (nether region), were designated as Nāgas. This king might have been the deity Viracocha worshipped by the ancient Pallavas.

The inhabitants of Peru used to worship an omnipotent invisible Paramātman. He was regarded as the creator and protector of the world. Such an idea is typically Indian.

The Incas of America descended from the common proto-Aryan ancestors of the Indo-Aryan Brāhmaṇas and Kṣatriyas. The Incas were Sun-worshippers and believers in the Supreme Brahman regarded as the omnipotent creator and ruler of the world. They used to think that everything emanates from Him, and into Him again everything is merged at the end. In this idea, the Indian element is obvious.

Of the deities, worshipped in Central and South America, there are Śiva, Gaṇeśa, Indra, Sūrya, Hanumān, Viṣṇu and His Kūrma incarnation. In the pantheon of Central America, the chief deities were Sun, Moon and God of rain. It seems that the civilisation was rooted in India.

EGYPT

Aśoka sent preachers of Buddhism to Egypt. In one of his rock-inscriptions (13) there is mention of Egyptian king Ptolemy (Philadelphos) as one in whose kingdom Buddhism was preached. D. Milman is certain that, in the west, pure Indian mysticism or *Maramiyā* doctrine was, for the first time, established in the deserts of Egypt.[136] Flinders Petri noticed Persian and Indian influence on the Egyptian work, *Hermetica.*[137] It was this influence that formed the foundation of the Jewish and Greek religions.[138]

RUSSIA

Buddha images, dating back to the pre-Mongol age, have been discovered in South Russia. That devotion to Nārāyaṇa became prominent in Soviet Central Asia is proved by the fact that the name of Nārāyaṇa occurs in a fragmentary inscription of Tarikistan, dating back to the second-first century B.C.

ISLAM AND INDIA

Arabia is the place of origin of Islam. From there it spread in different countries. Islamic *Zuhad* or opposition to physical mortification, perhaps, owes itself to Buddhism. Sufism[139] is a form of Islam with considerable modification. In connection with philosophy, we have mentioned some similarities in the philosophy of Vedānta and Sufism. According to Nicholson and some other scholars, the idea of Sufis about *Fana* (destruction of creatures) was derived from India, and has some similarity with the Buddhist *Nirvāṇa*. The Sufi doctrines of *Tauhid* (unity of gods) and *hak-ik* (ultimate truth) are akin to the tenets of Vedānta. Even the language of the Sufi *Yazid* is like that of Hindu philosophy. The Sufi word, denoting 'that' (referring to God), is similar to *Tat* of Indian philosophy. The Sufi phrase *Takunu Antadhak* is literal translation of the Upaniṣadic *Tat Tvamasi.* The monism of *Yazid,* and the concept of the world as illusion appear to be carbon copies of Śaṇkarācārya's non-dualism (*advaita*) and the doctrine of illusion (*Māyā*). Zachner thinks[140] that Sufism is nothing but Vedānta in Islamic garb. The Sufi doctrine of *Anal Haq* is akin to Vedāntic idea *Ahaṃ Brahmāsmi.* Such a concept is absolutely opposed to Islam. An outstanding exponent of Sufism was Jālāl-uddin Rumi (d. 1273). In his treatise, *Mathnavi,* he introduced a kind of devotional dance called *Sama.* It is like the *Kīrtana* song of the Hindus. His teaching is that man's heart is the mirror of divinity, and man is a replica of God. Individual soul is identical with the eternal soul which, indeed, is God to whom individual souls have to go back. These ideas irresistibly remind one of Indian philosophy, particularly Vedānta.

India was the source of many of the mystic rites of the Sufis. Their *Pasp Anjas* may have been taken from the *Prāṇāyāma*[141] of Yogaśāstra. Sufi *Dhikr* and *Tasbih* are similar to *Japa* (muttering or mentally repeating a *mantra* or the name of a deity) and *Mālā* (rosary) of the Hindus. Like the Hindus, particularly the followers of Tantra, the Sufis also believe that, for God-realisation, love alone is not enough; what is also required is devotion to *Guru* (preceptor). According to a parable, current among the Sufis, prince Adhama (d. 777) of Balkh went astray in youth. Once, in a hunting excursion, an aerial voice reprimanded him. Thenceforward he led a disciplined life. This story has been compared by some with that of the early life of Gautama Buddha. The above similarities cannot be dismissed just as accidental. Vedānta arose centuries before the rise of Sufism so that Indian influence on it is not improbable. May be that Sufism originated independently. It may be presumed that, as a river, while flowing, gathers silt from various places, so also Sufism, as it became popular and a living faith, imbibed ideas from India. This religious system arose in Iran with which India had intimate political, commercial and cultural contact through centuries.

In course of time, Buddhist literature got inextricably mixed with Islamic and, for that matter, Sufi literature.[142] About the eighth century A.D., some Buddhist and other Indian treatises were translated into Arabic. The Arabic version of the story of Barlaam and Josaphat became a part of the Arabic literature. The Buddhist story of the elephant and the blind men occurs in the writings of Jalāluddin Rumi and others. The moral of the story is that, as a blind man can feel only a part of the elephant but cannot have the idea about the animal as a whole, so also the different religions, due to spiritual blindness, cannot comprehend the whole truth, but can know only a part of it. Dogmatism about religion has been condemned by both the Hindus and the Buddhists.

CHRISTIANITY AND INDIA

Some similarities are noticeable between some Christian doctrines and Indian religions and philosophy. Considering India's contact with Arabia and various western countries since long before the Christian era, and the greater antiquity of Indian culture, India's influence in those foreign lands does not appear to be improbable. The way in which gradual spiritual uplift has been described in the treatise, *Enoch*, reminds one of the *Kauṣītaki Upaniṣad.* The qualities of God, according to the former work, are present in the Upaniṣad. Eschatology of the Christians is, to some extent, similar to Aryan thought. The instructions of Jesus relating to self-restraint and mortification have parallels in Buddhism and the Upaniṣad. The presentation of the relics of the Lord's body and Confession, etc. are, probably the result of Buddhist influence which is not improbable in view of the fact that Buddhism arose some five centuries before Christ, and spread in various countries. If it is true that Christ came to India, and lived there for long twelve years,[143] then Indian influence on the religion, taught by him, seems to be more than probable. It should also be borne in mind that the followers of the *Gnostic* doctrine, who influenced Christianity, were, to a great extent, indebted to Indian thought. Some of the ideas, contained in the Christian religion, are not found in Judaism and Greek culture which went a long way in constituting it, but in Hindu religion and philosophy. Some of the similarities, occurring in Greek mysticism and Indian thought, influenced Christianity. These are awareness of sin, need for absolution, post mortem reward or punishment resulting from good or bad deeds done in the previous life, repressive and purgatorial punishment, utility of sacrament for a blissful life in the other world, need for moral and ritual purification.

In Greece, the Eleusinian, Pythagorean and Orphic organisations and the Platonic school were chiefly Indian in character and contents. These, in their turn, became the precursors of some elements of the later Platonic doctrine and Catholic theology.[144]

Considerable affinity between Kṛṣṇa and Christ meets the eye. These are as follows :

1. Tradition is that, before delivering Kṛṣṇa, mother Devakī was surrounded by an astonishing halo. It is said that, before the delivery of Christ, mother Mary was encircled by a supernatural ring of light.

2. It is said that, before the birth of both, an indescribably joyful atmosphere prevailed everywhere in nature.

3. After the birth of Kṛṣṇa, sage Nārada warned Kaṃsa that the eighth son of Devakī would kill him (*Harivaṃsa*, II, 56). After this, Ksṃsa put to death the seven sons of Devakī, one after another. On hearing that a "King", named Jesus, had been born, king Herod asked the wise man - where is he who is born as the king of the Jews ? (*Matthew*, II.4). Saying this, he ordered the assassination of all the new-born male children.

4. A demon, surrogate of Kṛṣṇa, as son of Yaśodā, taunted Kaṃsa (*Harivaṃśa*, II. 59). The aforesaid wise people laughed at Herod (*Matthew*, II.16).

5. On the pretext of paying tax, Nanda went to Devakī at Mathurā with the baby Kṛṣṇa. Similarly, Joseph went, with Jesus, to Mary in Bethleham.

6. Kṛṣṇa's departure to Vraja (Vṛndāvana) is almost similar to Jesus' escape to Egypt.

Due to the above points of similarity, some think that the Kṛṣṇa legend had an imapct on the account of Jesus. But, there is no evidence about it. Nevertheless, so many similarities cannot, perhaps, be dismissed as just accidental.

According to C. Elliot (1862-1931), there is similarity in the rituals of both the Tāntric religion and Christian religion. In the Anglican Church, in initiation, the sprinkling of water on the initiate is like Tāntric *Abhiṣeka.* Woodroffe, who dived deep into Tantra, was of the opinion that the Christian Cross is like Tāntric *Nyāsa.*[145] In Christian initiation, incantations, similar to those in the Tāntric ritual, are recited. The belief is that, by initiation, one can attain heaven; but the ultimate condition of the uninitiated is deplorable. Tantra also believes that, by physical rites, progress in the spiritual path is possible. In the Roman Church, one rite is concerned with exorcism; in it, salt, oil and light are used. There is such a Tāntric rite too.

In later times, Buddhism was confused with the Christian religion. Manichaeanism is a syncretism of Buddhism, Zoroastrianism and Christianity. Christian and Buddhist legends were mixed up in Islam. The Buddhist-Christian romance *Barlam and Joasoph,* while travelling from the west in the sixth century A.D., finally reduced the Buddha to a Catholic saint. The name Joasaph is supposed to be derived from Bodhisattva. In the eighth century China, there was mixing up of the two religions systems.[146]

Basilides (2nd cent. A.D., 1st half) caused the infiltration of Hindu and Buddhist ideas into Christianity. He used to think that God transcends country, time and consciousness. He should be worshipped silently. His conception of God does not agree with the outlook of the common Christians.[147]

According to Albertus Magnus, communion with God is the ultimate goal of life, and meditation is the way to it. In ordinary life, the mind is engrossed with the objects of sense. If the mind can be detached from the objects of sense, then one can, through the medium of pure intellect, attain union with God. This Indian conception reached the west[148] through the medium of the Arabians who were versed in metaphysics. The following characteristics of the Jewish *Kabbala* (analysis of secret mystic matters) do not occur in the original religion. These are found in the *Upaniṣad* and *Tantra.* The characteristics are as follows :

power of letters, used in *Mantra* and talismans, created things originated from God and not from the void, similarity between the cosmos and the body, doctrine of rebirth, pantheism.

Buddha condemned mortification devoid of joy, current from earlier times. The emphasis, laid by John the Baptist on rites and mortification, is not inconsistent with the doctrine of Jesus. Jesus discouraged people about ritualsitic religion, and emphasized initiation and faith; faith in the pious is better even than sacrifice. The Buddha said—the lotus grows in the water, developes in water, but is not polluted by water; it remains above water. In a similar manner, *Tathāgata* grows up in the world, but gross worldliness does not touch him (*Saṃyuttanikāya,* 22/94). Jesus said, I am not of the world (John, XVII. 14-16).

Blessing one who curses, to do good to one who hates, to give one's cloak to a person who has taken his coat, giving everything to the suitor—these are teachings of Jesus. These ethical principles have been declared in Buddhism. In the *Jātaka* sources, we find that the Buddha, in his many past lives, rigidly followed them.[149] The moral narratives are found in both the religions not only as edification but also as a medium of education.

Rhys Davids has shown[150] that there is remarkable similarity between the moral principles, taught by the Buddha, and the moral teachings of the *Bible.*[151] Praise of gift, condemnation of stratagem, purity, modesty, courtesy, truth and love — instructions about these are common to both. It is, however, difficult to determine whether or not, in this respect, Christianity is indebted to Buddhism, and, if indebted, to what extent.

There are some remarkable similarities in the history of both the above religions. The Buddha was betrayed by his cousin brother (or, own younger brother, according to some). Judas played false with Jesus (*Matthew,* 26/48). Māra (Satan) tried to allure the Buddha to go astray. We hear of Jesus also tempted by Satan (*Matthew,* 4). In this connection, mention may be made also of the story of the attempt of Yama to tempt Naciketā, as narrated in the *Kaṭhopaniṣad.*

A comparison of Buddhism with Christianity reveals remarkable similarities in respect of the founder's authority, community and discipline.[152] Both the Buddha and Christ were founders of their respective communities with powerful authority over them. Both had soteriological patterns as saviours, as teachers of righteousness and as spiritual kings of their communities. Both of them had innumerable disciples. Both believed that it was their mission to establish righteousness. Each founded a community on teacher-disciple pattern; each community was soteriologically criented. The stories of the birth of both have similarity. Each is said to have been extremely precocious during the early years of their lives. Each of them renounced material wealth and power for salvation of not only of themselves, but also of suffering humanity. We have already referred to attempts at their temptation which was overcome by both. Both became spiritual and not secular leaders of their followers. Both tried to save and protect their people not by force but by setting moral example by their conduct.

In matters of doctrine, ethics and discipline the commandments (tenfold) of Christ and of the Buddha (in the form of eightfold path — *aṣṭāṅgika mārga*) were accepted as binding by all members of the community. This led to the pursuit of common ideals and goals among the adherents. Discipline in outer as well as inner life was insisted in both the religions. For the preservation of the communities, for which there was great concern in both the systems, both the Buddhist and Christian systems prescribed punishments for wrong-doers, the severest punishment for the gravest offence having been excommunication. The part, played by James and the Apostolic Council in restoring unity when dissension arose between the Jewish and Gentile Christians, is similar to Sāriputta's (Buddha's close disciple) reconciling the secessionist followers of the truculent Devadatta with the Buddhist community.

Discipline was of prime concern in both the communities. In the *Pātimokkha* of the Buddhist community, the Buddhist monks had to confess their sins before an assembly which had the right to condone or forgive. In the early Christian community, too, one had to make confessions and secure pardon. In both communities, disciplinary authority was derived from the founders. Discipline was more inwardly directed than in earlier societies. In both communities, there were elements of asceticism in life-style; the purposes of discipline were mainly extra-worldly in their outlook. Both the systems had similarity in that both emphasised the common possession of all properties.

RĀMKRISHNA AND THE WEST

Rāmkrishna's (1836-1886) religion was composite. He used to believe in the underlying truth of all religions . He would say that the ultimate aim of religions is the same. According to him, Āllāh, Hari, Kṛṣṇa, Christ, etc. are but different names of one God. His teaching was that man's duty is selfless service of the people; it is through service of humanity that God is served. According to some, Rāmkrishna's position in the Indian renaissance was similar to the place of Socrates (*c.* 469-399 B.C.) in Greek mind. This great man deeply influenced the west through Vivekānanda, his most intimate disciple, and through the preachings of the Rāmkrishna Mission. Max Müller (1823) remarked that, compared with the so-called uneducated Rāmkrishna, the greatest intellectuals of Europe are simply groping in the dark for realising the truth. The French scholar, Romain Rolland (1866-1944), was a devotee of Rāmkrishna. Rolland's profound regard for him has been fervently expressed in his *Life of Ramakrishna.* According to Isherwood, Rāmkrishna was an incarnation of Śiva.

D. ARCHITECTURE, SCULPTURE, PAINTING, ETC.

Before dealing with these subjects, we should note that the arts were not of the same type throughout India. Different styles arose in different regions. Of the different types, those of Amarāvatī, Gupta, Pallava and Pāla schools exercised considerable influence in South-East Asia. The Gandhāra school also deserves mention. The schools, which followed Gandhāra and Amarāvatī in inspiring the above region, are successively as follows :

Gupta (320-600), Pallava (600-800), Eastern (800-1200).

The Eastern school is also known as Pāla and Sena schools. Of the above, the Eastern school, particularly that of the Pāla period (*c.* 750-1155) made the greatest contribution in South-East Asia. Within its ambit came also Nepāl, Tibet, Burma, and, to some extent, Ceylon.

NEPĀL

The architecture of Nepāl may be characterised as an edition of Indian architecture. The *Viṣṇudharmottarapurāṇa* was the guide-book of Nepāl architecture. The best and oldest example of Indian influence in this country is the *Stūpas.* It seems, Aśoka introduced architectural skill in Nepāl. There is epigraphical evidence about this. Sārnāth and Mathurā, which may be characterised as the centres of Buddhist art, played an important part in introducing Indian art and architecture in Nepāl. Works like the *Prajñāpāramitā*, *Guhyasamāja* and *Mañjuśrī Mūlakalpa* inspired the Buddhist art in this country. The works *Jñānasiddhi, Sukhāvatīvyūha* gave Nepāl the idea of *Dhyānī Buddha* (Buddha in meditation). The skill of casting molten metals was highly developed in India in the Pāla period (*c.* 750-1155). This was responsible for the Nepāli art of making bronze images. After the introduction (twelfth century) of Muslim rule in India, many of the rulers started demolishing temples and shrines. This resulted in a setback in sculpture and architecture. In Nepāl, too, the influence of Indian arts declined to a considerable extent. As a result, Nepāl developed its own style.

Like architecture, the sculpture also of this country can be characterised as a branch of the Indian sculpture of the Pāla period (*c.* 750-1155). There are many images of Kṛṣṇa-Rādhā in this country. Besides, Kṛṣṇa's exploits, as described in the *Bhāgavata* and *Gītagovinda,* have been represented in sculpture. Due to Buddhist influence, images of *Dhyānī Buddha* (Buddha in meditation) are found. In Nepāli bronze sculpture also Indian influence is obvious. Many images of the Buddha are scattered in this country. Indian influence is noticeable in the image of the Bodhisattva, reduced to a dying condition as a result of abjuring food.

TIBET

It is learnt that Srong-Tsan-Gampo, king (seventh century) of this country, encouraged Indian architectural style. We are further informed that this king established twelve temples, each with a Buddha image, in order to propagate Buddhism.[153] It is understood that he built several monasteries also. His two queens also are stated to have established monasteries.[154]

It is learnt[155] that king Srong Tsan Gampo (7th cent.) brought an image of Avalokiteśvara, with eleven faces, from South India. Besides, he established twelve temples, each with a Buddha image.

AFGHĀNISTĀN

Though at one time, a part of India, it later on became an independent kingdom. Some examples of Indian sculpture there are marble representations of Śiva's head, destruction of buffalo-demon by Durgā, Sun-god, Gaṇeśa, etc. In the sculpture of this country, there are characteristics of the art of the Gupta and Kashmirian styles. Śaivism was highly popular here. There are figures of Śiva on the coins. The Chinese travellers saw temples at many places, particularly of Śiva. Stone images of Śiva-Pārvatī, mounted on a bull, six-armed Śiva-image, terracotta Śiva image, etc. testify to the wide popularity of Śaivism. Besides marble, ivory has also been used in making images. Śaivite influence is noticeable in wood-work also. The dancing pose is a rare specimen. Many rock-hewn Buddha images are found in Swat and the frontier of Afghānistān. Noteworthy is the twin image of Śiva-Viṣṇu. Viṣṇu appears separately also. Besides them are Indra, Brahmā and Skanda Kārttikeya.

IRAN

The art of ivory-carving was learnt by Iran from India in the early centuries of the Christian era. The elephants in the Sassanian art, as revealed in the bas-reliefs depicting hunting scenes, were copies of the Indian figures of elephants.

CENTRAL ASIA

There are the figures of Kubera and Gaṇeśa in some seals found in Endere, Niyā, etc. in Central Asia. The images of Śiva and Viṣṇu are also there. There is a host of Buddha images in this region. The story of the *Vessantarajātaka*, has been delineated in a Stūpa at Miran. In one part of it, there are figures of a winged nymph and Cupid (Kāmadeva).

Ruins of Buddhist shrines (7th-8th cent.) have been discovered by digging in Uzbekistān and Tajakistān. The rockcut caves of Kumtura show Buddhist influence.

BURMA

The Burmese Buddhist architecture is, to a great extent, indebted to India. The very name of Śrīkṣetra, capital of the Piu dynasty, is Indian. Besides, it was built in accordance with the Indian belief about cosmology. It is an imitation of Indra's Amarāvatī. In it, there are thirty-two main gates and a golden palace at the centre. Pagan's *Ānanda* temple is an important place of interest in Burma. In the costruction of this temple, the contribution of the Indian architects or of the followers of the Indian style is considerable. An inscription states that the traders built a Viṣṇu temple, and the Mālābārī merchants (thirteenth century) contributed money for this purpose.

The influence of Bengal is discerned in the Burmese paintings. In it, we find the imitation of paintings in illustrated palm-leaf manuscripts. As instances, the wall-paintings of Kubaukkyia, Abeyadana and Thanbula with the paintings in the Bengal manuscripts of *Aṣṭasāhasrikā-prajñāpāramitā* and *Pañcarakṣā*. In some murals of the biggest temple of Jāvā, there are paintings of the scenes of the Rāma legend.

CEYLON

There is similarity between the fresco painting, dating back to the end of the fifth century A.D., at the place, called Sigiriya, in Ceylon, and the Ajantā paintings (fifth century to seventh century A.D.). In the architecture of Anurādhapura, the imitation of the styles of Sānchi and Amarāvatī has been inferred. The art of the Andhra region influenced Ceylon. The imitation of the Pallava style (sixth century-ninth century) is greater. The imitation of the structures of Cola period (*c.* 100 A.D. to 11 century) is also found; *e.g.* Śiva temple of Polonnaruva. The Sanskrit treatise, *Sāriputrīya*, dealing with architecture, was very popular in Ceylon.

Generally, Ceylonese sculpture is based on Indian models. Indian influence is obvious in many Buddha images of this island. The earlier images were made in accordance with the style of the Andhra school. In some cases, there are also the chracteristics of Gupta and Pallava sculpture. The human images of the Panel reveal similarity with the images at Sānchi. In Ceylon, the images representing dance and an engraved work in stone and ivory indicate Indian impact on the art of dance in Ceylon. Bharatanāṭya reached Ceylon from South India.

MALDIVES

There was widespread influence of Indian architecture and sculpture in this country. The Sun-temple, Ajidha or Forulun, discovered in the Hubhadhu region, is the oldest of its kind in the world. At one place an image of blackstone has been found. On the body of the temple various postures and hand-poses of the Sun are engraved on stone. At the place, called Hadadahumati, bronze images of Viṣṇu and Buddha have been discovered. The Buddha image, found in the island Ari-Tho-Du, is huge. It is not known whether the architects and sculptors of the Hindu and Buddhist temples and images were Indian or not. But, in conception and delineation Indian influence is beyond doubt.

SOUTH-EAST ASIA

There is imitation of the *Śikhara* of the Pallava and Drāvida styles of Indian temples in the temples of Jāvā, Cambodia and Annam. The difference is that the temple-columns of South India are not found in the temples of the above countries. A cluster of Hindu temples, near Barabudur, the famous temple of Jāvā, is known as the Prambanan Group. The biggest and the most beautiful temple is called Larazonprang. It was built in *c.* 860 A.D., and dedicated to Śiva. There are temples also in the names of Viṣṇu and Brahmā. The largest temple has been named after Durgā, slayer of the buffalo-Demon, inside it. The entrance in the main gate is decorated. The architecture of this place imitated the Indian model. The *Gopuram* of the Indian temples, in a modified form, is found in the temples of Jāvā (tenth-fifteenth century). According to Coomaraswamy, there is influence of the Gupta, Pallava and ancient Cālukya styles on the architecture of Jāvā. The model of Bengal has been followed in the temples, built in tier upon tier, of Jāvā and Bali as well as in the small monolithic temples. The influence of Eastern India is visible in the sculpture also of Jāvā. This influence is very pronounced in the Kingdoms of Jangala and Kediri in East Jāvā. In embellishment and effusive expression, etc. there is the impact of the Sena style of Bengal. According to Grousset (*L'Art Pāla and Sena*, p. 284), the natural poise and tranquillity, found in the images of deities of the Kadiri period, indicates the influence of the Sena Age. In some later (*c.* 1250 A.D.) images of East Jāvā, we find proto-Bengali script. It seems, these were made by Bengali sculptors of the East Indian School. After the demolition of Buddhist monasteries in Bengal and Bihar by the Muslims, many Buddhists of these two provinces took asylum in that country.

Many buildings in the kingdom of Funan reveal Gupta and post-Gupta styles. Śaivite and Vaiṣṇavite temples have been discovered in Campā.

The architectural pattern of the Śrīdeva temple in Thailand is like that of Hindu temples. East Indian influence reached this country rather late, and was not very widespread. Some scholars think that king Aniruddha (1044-77) of Burma engaged architects experienced in the East Indian style, and this resulted in the introduction of the Pāla style in Siam.

Of over twenty-thousand temples in Bali, many reveal Indian characteristics. Śaivite and Vaiṣṇavite influence marks the architecture and sculpture of Borneo. Some similarity with Indian mausoleums is found among the ruins of the Śiva temples of Keda in Mālay. The impact of the Pāla school can be discerned in the Buddhist monastery (*c.* 99 A.D.) at Dong Duang in Campā. Its plan reminds one of the Pāhārpur temple in East Bengal (Bangladesh).

In this region, Indian influence was the greatest under the Śailendra kings (8th-13th cent.). The Vat Fra That temple, dating back to the Śrīvijaya period (13th - 14th cent.), was built in accordance with Indian *Śilpaśāstra.* In most of the South-East Asian countries, for the foundation sandstone and limestone were used as in India. In Indonesia, hard stone was used in the structures of Pallava-Pāṇḍya Cola styles, and the Indian pattern was followed in the construction of buildings. The spacious spaces for circumambulation, in Barabudur, Prambanam and Angkor are in the pattern of those provided in Indian temples. The egg-shaped domes of the *Stūpas* are in the pattern that was in vogue in north, west and south India. The tower-like roofs in those countries are in the Indian pattern. The decoration towards the base of platform is also Indian. This pattern has been in vogue since the Gupta Age (*c.* 320-510). The *Gopuram*[158] of the South-Indian temples has been adopted in Indonesia with a slight variation of the name as *Gapuram.* Examples of this are found in the temples of Zedong and Plousan, as also in Angkor. The site-plans of the Indian temples are square, rectangular, octagonal or circular. In South-east Asia, the square and rectangular shapes have been largely adopted. At Bayon and Angkor[157] (1049-1066), there are Pañcāyatana plans. The end-portion of the topmost storey of the Indonesian temple is like a *Stūpa* or *Kalaśa* (pitcher).

In Sumātrā, architecture of Pāla style is not found in abundance. There are some structures which are marked by the impact of Bengal school of the Pāla Age. Stutterheim has pointed out (*Studies in Indonesian Archaeology,* p. 23, fn. 32) that there is similarity between the Nalagai *Stūpa* and the Giryek Stūpa of the Pāla Age.

The sculpture of the Gupta Age (*c.* 320-570) was accepted as a model in the Indian colonies in this region. The impact of this art is wide in Mālay, Sumātrā, Jāvā, Annam, Cambodia, Celebes, etc. The best example of sculpture in the Funan kingdom is the one made by the Hindu king Rudravarman.

In this region, there are many Buddha images as well as those of the Hindu deities like Viṣṇnu and Śiva. There are many seals containing Sanskrit inscriptions. A Buddha-head, having the characteristics of the Gandhāra art, has been found at Bā. This is, perhaps, the earliest Indian article. The images of Harihara and Ardhanārīśvara, found in South Funan, are glittering specimens of the sculpture of this country.

The magnificent Bayon temple stands in the middle of the city of Angkorthom. It looks like a pyramid; the number of the high columns is nearly forty. The central column is about 150 ft. high. Around every column, there are beautifully engraved human faces. This is the face of Avalokiteśvara. In reality, these represented faces of the deified king Jayavarman.

A bronze statue of the Buddha in Campā is the oldest and a very good example of the Amarāvatī art. In some images, the Gupta model has been followed. The images of Harihara, Umā and Lakṣmī in Cambodia, bear testimony to the Indian art. Among other things, a tree, resembling the Indian *Kalpavṛkṣa* (wish-yielding tree), is inscribed in this temple. There are many scenes from the *Rāmāyaṇa, Mahābhārata* and *Harivaṃśa.* In the temple, there are images of Yama and Citragupta. These are full of about 750 Apsarases. There are different kinds of beautiful head-dress in the hand of each.

In some temples of this land, there are scenes from the *Rāmāyaṇa.* As instances, we can mention the following :

The rock-temple of Bafoun, Prasat An temple, Bante Srei temple, etc.

At the foot there are leafy decorations. Some human figures of the *Rāmāyaṇa* adorned old water-bottles, etc. Bronze Buddha images of the Gupta period exist at the place, called Kutei, in Kota Bangum. On the Kombeng hill, there is a considerable number of images of Hindu and Buddhist deities. There are, in Cambodia, images of Śiva containing the characteristics of the Śiva image in a Pāhārpur temple in East Bengal (Bangladesh); it holds, in its right hand, the handle of an umbrella which is made of peacock-feathers. At different places in Borneo, there are golden images of Viṣṇu and images of Śiva and Gaṇeśa. Some influence of Indian art is seen in the sculpture of Sumātrā. In an engraved dancing figure at Padang Lawas, there is imitation of the East Indian art. It has been noticed (Schnitger, *The Archaeology of Hindu Sumātrā,* Pls. XXXIII - XXXV) that, in the image of the Vajrayāna deity Heruka, found in Sumātrā, there is similarity with the *Nairātma* image (tenth century) of Bihar.

At Keda in Mālay, there is a Buddha image of bronze containing the characteristics of the Amarāvatī style. At Perak, there is a Buddha image (fifth century) made in the Gupta style. A bronze image of Avalokiteśvara, having Tāntric characteristics, is a witness to the Pāla style (eight-ninth century). A bronze statue at Perak is like the Indian sage Agastya. There are innumerable statues of this sage in South India.

The influence of Pāla Bengal is noticeable in the sculpture of Jāvā. According to Grousset,[158] this influence is very much vivid in the Prambanan art of the middle of the ninth-century. It seems that some ideas of the sculptors of Pāhārpur in East Bengal were adopted in the case of the bas-relief panel at Mendu in Central Jāvā, in some reliefs of Barabudur. In some pieces in the collection of Nusee guimet there is resemblance of the Kuvera image and the Jambhala image of Vikramapura (in present Bangladesh). In the Bodhisattva images of Prambanan and Plousan and of some other places, there is similarity with some images preserved in Calcutta Museum and the Museums of Dacca and Lucknow. In this connection, we should mention also the Mañjuśrī images of Plousan and Calcutta Museums. According to the aforesaid Grousset,[159] the natural calm and tranquillity of the images of the deities of the Kadiri Age of Jāvā reflected the influence of the Sena (*c.* 1060-1200) art of Bengal. He thinks that the statue of King Airlanga, mounted on Garuḍa, and of queen Dedes, in the form of Prajñāpāramitā, may be compared with some images of India. In some comparatively late (*c.* middle of thirteenth century) images of East Jāvā, there are mystic writings in old Javanese and proto-Bengali script. It seems that, in this case, the sculptor belonged to the East Bengal school.

The influence of the Pallava art of South India and the Gupta art of North India is seen in the stone images attached to some temples of Burma, and in some terracotta pieces. There are images of the ten Incarnations of the Hindus (with the Buddha as the ninth) in the Bidagat Tail Library (twelfth century).

In some Buddhist and Brahmanical images of this country, there is the influence of the East Indian art. From the point of view of art and sculpture, Brāhmanical elements entered into this country at least in the sixth century A.D., and continued till the fourteenth. As an example, we can mention Viṣṇu's *Ananta-Śayyā* (the Serpent King forming a bed) in the Rangoon Museum. In this connection, images of Vaiṣṇava deities, etc. in some temples of Pagan sould also be mentioned.

MAURITIUS

The Mauritian Government has passed the Āyurvedic Bill granting to Āyurveda a status equal to that of allopathy.[160]

KOREA[161]

Outside Yakṣa Hall, there is an image of the Buddha in deep slumber on a fully bloomed lotus. It reminds one of the *Anantaśayyā* (Serpent-King as bed) of Viṣṇu. It was produced by the joint effort of the Indian and Korean sculptors in the sixth century. There are many images, made in India, in several pagodas of Korea. Besides Buddha images, there are many Hindu images also in this country. Among the gods and goddesses, whose images have been discovered, are Śiva, Viṣṇu, Lakṣmī, Sarasvatī, Nṛsiṃha and Indra.

The shape of the Swagawang Pagoda, resting on two pillars, in the province of Kasan, built in the Koguriyo regime, is like a match-box. It seems to be an imitation of the Venkaṭeśvara temple of Ellora.

JAPAN, CHINA

Considerable influence of India is revealed by Japanese temples. Jainism and Buddhism had deep impact on Japanese architecture. Reflection of Zen outlook is visible in common houses.

Indian influence in China is not so marked. The temples of the pagoda-type appear to have had Indian models.

In Japan, the representation of the images of nearly nine hundred deities is an evidence of how deep and intimate was the Indian influence on the sculpture of this country. In some cases, however, the Japanese sculptors have introduced changes according to their own imagination. For example, the locks of hair of Sarasvatī are tied in a knot at the back as we find in the Japanese girls. In some Gaṇeśa images of Japan, the deity is represented as holding as axe and a radish.

As a result of religious and cultural exchange over a millennium, India has, to a great extent, influenced the Chinese sculpture and architecture. In certain places, *e.g.* Yan-King, Longmen, etc. rock-cut caves, Buddha images 60 or 70 ft. high, paintings on cave-walls and multi-storied Chinese temples built in the reign of the Sung dynasty bear testimony to this influence. The sculptural style of the Kusāna, particularly the Gandhāra art reached China through Chinese Turkestan. It seems, the Indian *Makara* (shark) has merged in the Chinese dragon.

EUROPE

Coomaraswamy has pointed out that, in the sculpture of medieval Europe, Makara (Shark) has appeared again and again.

In the Spanish church there are the Indian *Makara* and *Kīrtimukha.* The idea of *Kīrtimukha*, perhaps, reached England from France through Plantagenets. The original form of the figure, called Grisman, existing in some Romanesque[162] chruch, is Indian.

Roman architecture is, to some extent, indebted to India.[163] Some Greeks were influenced by Indian architecture and sculpture. We have stated, in connection with Religion, that Heliodoros (2nd cent. B.C.), envoy of the Greek king of Takṣaśilā, Antialkidas, built a Garuḍa column at Besnagar (Vidisā) in honour of Viṣṇu .

HUNGARY

Hungary's interest in India was not confined to Indian literature alone. Indian art also attracted the Hungarians. The Museum for Far Eastern Art in Budapest (1919) contained Indian objects also. The efforts of its first director, Z.F. Takacs, assisted by I. Schwaiger (1864-1940), enriched the collection of Indian artefacts, especially sculptures. Takacs also contributed the work, called *The Art of the East* (2nd ed., 1934). He wrote also a scholarly paper, Kushāna Art in F. Hopp Museum at Budapest, and some related Art Products, in the *Jour. of Indian Society of Oriental Art, Coomāraswāmy Vol.*, 1937. Baktay's work on Indian Art (Budapest, 1958, 1963) is a valuable contribution on the subject.

Early in the third decade of the present century, two Hungarian painters, Mrs. Saw-Brunner and her daughter Miss Elizabeth Brunner, came to Sāntiniketan. There they tried to incorporate, into their paintings, the traditions of Indian art, religion, philosophy and the characteristic features of the Bengal school. They settled in India. Their art reveals closer connexion with Indian art than to the Hungarian.[164]

Charles Fabri[165] (1899-1968) was a distinguished Hungarian who was deeply interested in Indian sculpture. He came to India in 1933 at the invitation of Rabindranāth, and lived here till his death. He wrote some books on Indian art. He suggested some novel ideas. For instance, he decried the iconographic approach, and emphasised the necessity of a purely artistic assessment.

He was keenly interested in the art of Mathurā, and propagated new ideas explaining the evolution of Mathurā art.[166] He proposed a new chronology for the sculptures of Mahābalipuram (Madras).[167] He wrote interesting papers on

Ajantā also. His work on the art of the Orissa region was one of the best books on the subject. It was Fabri who drew the attention of art-lovers to the terracotta art of Kashmir, which originated in Buddhist times.

His principal works on art are:

Indian Art : A New point of view, Delhi.

An Intro. to Indian Architecture, 1963.

Discovering Indian Sculpture, 1970.

History of the Art of Orissa, 1974.

Some of his important papers are:

The Temples of Khajurāho, *March of India*, V.12, No.4, Apr., 1960.

Gandhāra, Mathurā and Amarāvati Art, *Ibid.*, V. 13, No. 9, Sept., 1961.

In post-independence (1945) Hungary, interest in Indian art has got a new dimension. Hopp Ferena Museum, mentioned earlier, has become the centre of research in Indian art. Horvath, the new Director of the above Museum, visited India, and wrote about aspects of Indian art in his treatise, *The Art of Asia* (Budapest, 1954). Baktay wrote a valuable book on *Indian Art* (Budapest, 1958, 1963) covering Indian sculpture, painting and architecture. Incidentally, he instituted a comparison between Indian and European (particularly Greek) sculptures.

Vera Horvath (b. 1926), now in charge of the Indian Collection of the aforesaid Museum, published many papers[168] relating to the materials preserved in the Museum, *e.g.* Kashmiri shawls, Mauryan Mother-goddess figures, unpublished stone-figures from Gandhāra, etc. In her book, *Greek Gods in India* (Budapest, 1976), she discussed Gandhāra art. Her other book on Indian art is reported to be in press.

AMERICA

Many pyramid-like temples have been discovered in old America. Of the two famous temples, one is dedicated to Sun, and the other to Moon. According to some, the idea of such temples was got from Egypt. In fact, however, there are many differences between the two. Rather Cambodian temple pyramids have more similarity with the American temples; these remind one of the Hindu-Buddhist world. The influence of Cambodia is ruled out by the fact that the Sun-temple of Mexico was built at least one thousand years before the earliest temple-pyramid of Cambodia. Cambodia might have influenced Mexico since the third or fifth centuries A.D. Some similarity has been noticed between temples of South India and South-east Asia on the one hand and of ancient America on the other. In both, the temples are round, and a different colour has been applied in each of the four directions. In the pyramid of the Maya civilisation, Indian influence has been observed. Serpent-column, attached column, covered gallery, *Jāfri* (fence with holes), etc., these characteristics reflect Asian, particularly Indian influence. The Mayas belonged to the tribal civilisation of America of which relics have been found in Guatemala, British Honduras and Mexico. E.G. Squire has noticed similarity between the architectural style of South Indian Buddhist temples and those of ancient America. The *gopuram* of Mayan temples is like that of the temples of India, particularly South India. It seems that the architects of both the countries followed the Sanskrit text of the famous treatise on architecture, called *Mayamata.* A temple of Mexico was built in about 1600 A.D. In the primitive line-drawing of this temple there are figures of people, wearing turbans, who belonged to the third millennium B.C. The Ziggurat of the American civilisation appears to be a special characteristic of the eclesiastical architecture. Its origin can, perhaps, be traced in the Harappan civilisation.

There is a famous Cross at Palenque in Mexico. In it, there is the representation of a tree and a demon-face in its branch. It, perhaps, corresponds to the *Kalpavṛkṣa* (wish-yielding tree) grown on the Sumeru mountain, represented in Indian sculpture.

There is considerable Indian influence in Maya sculpture of which an excellent example is the pyramid-temple at Piedras Negras. In it, there is a Buddhist scene. It shows affinity with the engraved decoration, relating to *Jātaka*, in a *Stūpa* at Barabudur. In Maya sculpture, there are images of human beings seated on lotuses. Such pieces of sculpture are found in India, particularly in the Amarāvatī school. Indian influence is clear in some images, particularly in the reclining images holding lotus-stalks. In Indian sculpture, the lotus-stalk emerges from the mouth of Makara or of some fierce-looking maritime animal whose body is like a fish and trunk like that of an elephant. In the Maya sculpture, the lotus-stalk is flanked on both sides by fish. The face of the Indian Makara has similarity with Agnisarpa of Mexico. In both the places, there is the figure of a man that has emerged from the mouth of a fierce animal. The Atlantic image, that appeared in India since second century B.C., has been found at Tula in Mexico.

AFRICA (ETHIOPIA)

A new development in modern Ethiopian art is to illustrate a story in coloured pictures painted in skins or cloth, the different phases of the story being given in compartments, with legends for each compartment. The practice is of folk origin. It is very probably that, in this type of hagiographic or legendary story-telling through a series of pictures, there is influence of Indian Art.[169]

The monolithic columns of Axum (Ethiopia) are a prominent characteristic of pre-Christian Ethiopian art. They have outward similarity with Indian temple art with towers built in the first half of the first millennium A.D. The following observations of J. Fergusson[170] point to the Indian inspiration behind the great monolith of Axum:

"The idea is Egyptian, but the details are Indian".

He points out its similarity with such Indian temples as are in Bodh-Gayā. He aptly remarks "that curious marriage of Indian with Egyptian art which we would expect to find in the spot where the two peoples came in contact, and enlisted architecture to symbolise their commercial union".

In this connection, mention should be made of the churches and other edifices at Lalibela in Ethiopia, excavated out of the living rock. S.K. Chatterji remarks[171]: "A comparison of these rock-churches and other edifices with the Kailāsa at Ellorā and other rock-temples in India is irresistible". E. Littmann also suggests[172] the possibility of Indian influence on the Lalibela rock-churches.

It is very important to note that the Ethiopian script owes a deep debt of gratitude to India. It is the introduction of the vowel-marks into the basic consonantal letters of the Sabaean script. We quote below the observations of S.K. Chatterji[173] in this connexion :

"This great innovation undoubtedly came from the example of the Indian system of writing, the Brāhmī and the Kharoṣṭhī, and here the Indian merchants and residents at Adulis and Aksum,[174] in the third and fourth centuries A.D., might have been of help".

MUSLIM SCULPTURE

In some Muslim structures, we find a kind of the Indian *Kīrtimukha.* As an example, we can mention the ancient Talisman Gate of Baghdad.

E. SCRIPT

Not only in arts, language and literature, but also in script India considerably influenced some other countries. Barring the different original scripts,[175] the main scripts of India were two, viz., Brāhmī and Kharoṣṭhī. The prevailing alphabets of the majority of the South-East Asian countries are derivatives of the Brāhmī script.

There is an impression, among some scholars, that the alphabet, used in the early inscriptions found in Indonesia and Indochina, is Pallava Grantha. They think that Indo-Aryan culture spread in those countries from the Coromandel

Coast during the Pallava regime from about the middle of the fourth century A.D. to about the close of the ninth. D.C. Sircar puts forward cogent arguments[176] to prove that the above impression is erroneous. One of his arguments is that the alphabet, used in Pallava inscriptions from the 4th to 6th cent. A.D., and in most of the early epigraphs of the region beyond Bay of Bengal, cannot be labelled as Pallava Grantha. It is actually late Brāhmī common to southern and western parts of India. He comes to the conclusion that the peoples of different parts of India, particularly of the littoral areas, both eastern and western, played a role in spreading Indo-Aryan culture in S. E. Asia. Thus, the contribution of the Coromandel Coast in this respect was not exclusive, but a part and the part played by the western areas of the Deccan as also East India was also considerable.

NEPĀL

With Nepāl India's contact has been intimate through centuries. Though politically apart, Nepāl is culturally a part of India. The numerous Nepāli inscriptions in Gupta Brāhmī script bear eloquent testimony to the impact of Indian script. In this country, Devanāgarī was widely used. The use of the following also is found in different places:

Gurumukhī, Tāmil, Telugu, Śāradā, etc.

TIBET

The political and cultural contacts of India with Tibet were long and close. The great Tibetan scholar, Sambhoṭa came to India, learnt the language and script, and after returning home reformed the Tibetan script. The impact of the Western Gupta script of the seventh century is noticeable in this country.

TURKISH LANGUAGE

The Brāhmī script was used in the old Turkish language. The earliest example of Turkish works, written in this script, dates back to the ninth century. Similar compositions, numbering over hundred, are preserved in the Berlin Collection.

AFGHĀNISTĀN, CEYLON, SOUTH-EAST ASIA

The Brāhmī script was in vogue in the northern region of Afghānistān in the fifth century A.D. There are similarities with the contemporary Indian Brahmī script in the script used in Ceylon in the third century B.C. In the tenth century inscriptions of that country, a script, used in contemporary South India, was used. The influence of Grantha and Batteluttu scripts is noteworthy. Three votive records of Ceylon are written in Pallava-Grantha character, which may be palaeographically assigned to the seventh century A.D.[177] Also to be noted is the use of the East Indian Pāla script. Geographical proximity, commercial contact, invasion of Ceylon, etc. facilitated Indian influence in that island. The same reasons account for the evolution of scripts in Cambodia and Annam in like manner. In this region, the impact of Kanarese and Telugu is clear. Some scripts of Mālay reveal resemblance with Indian scripts. In this country, Indian script was current before the introduction of Arabic and Roman scripts. In the Ligor Inscription (8th century), the Brāhmī script was adopted. An inscription of Mūlavarman in Kulei in Borneo is similar to the Pallava script of South India. The inscriptions of Pūrṇvarman, too, show such similarity. Tibet was a medium through which Indian scripts exerted influence in South-East Asia. Attempts have been made to prove the influence of the South Indian Pallava script on that of the Philippine Islands. A script of Thailand originated in India. The alphabet of the country is derived from that of Kambuja, which, in its turn, was derived from Indian inscriptions of the sixth and eighth centuries. The alphabet of Sumātrā has followed that of Devanāgarī. The model of the earliest Korean script, Hangul, was Sanskrit; it was developed in the fourteenth century.

MALDIVES

The letters of Stone-inscriptions, found in this country, are pictorial, and bear resemblance with the Harappā-Mohenjodāro letters. Incidentally, it may be stated that there is Hieroglyphic script on a piece of coral stone preserved in the National Museum of Mal, the capital of the country.

In short, late Indian Brāhmī script was at the root of the principal scripts of South-East Asia, although their present forms are different to a considerable extent.[178] The time, when Indian scripts made their way into that region, is a matter of controversy. According to scholars, the Vo-Canh Inscription[179] of Funan[180] is the earliest specimen of South-East Asian script; it is written in late Brāhmī script. The date of this inscription is controversial, it being variously assigned to different dates from the second century to the fifth.

Late Brāhmī script having been adopted in Jāvā, the Indonesian Sundanese, Madurese and Balinese scripts evolved. The Barak script of Sumātrā also has the same history. It seems that the Bugi and Macasar scripts and Tagalog script of the Philippines have the same source.

The South-East Asian scripts may be classified as follows :

Gujarāṭ-Mālava script— *c.* 5th cent. A.D.
Southern script— *c.* 6th cent. and sometime later.
Mixed form of
Pallava and Western
Cālukya scripts - end of 6th century.
South Indian script—Do
Pallava script - *c.* 6th century.

CENTRAL ASIA

The influence of Indian scripts in this region is undoubted. In the Buddhist works, written in Khoṭān, Kāshgarh, Kucha, etc., in Sanskrit, Prākrit and local languages, Brāhmī and Kharoṣṭhī scripts have been used. Agnideśa is situated in the

..y between Kucha and Tun Huang. Brāhmī script was in vogue there. In the local library, many Sanskrit manuscripts were preserved. The principal reason of Indian influence in Central Asia was the spread of Buddhism.

JAPAN

The arrangement of scripts in Japan is associated with the name of Bodhisena. In that country, the Buddhist monks learnt the Sanskrit script named *Siddham.* The Japanese scholar, K. Daishi, devised an alphabet, called *Katakana,* consisting of fifty sounds. In the Japanese alphabet, the order of the vowels is like that in Devanāgarī. In the Irohanta song, composed by the Japanese Kukai, there are forty-seven letters. The Japanese alphabet contains fifty letters, each indicating a particular sound.

EUROPE

GREECE

James Prinsep holds that "the oldest Greek (written from right to left) was nothing more than Sanskrit turned topsy-turvey". The Brāhmī script of India used to be originally written from right to left.[181]

AMERICA

Some tablets in Peru contain writings in a script that resembles the Harappan script.

F . LANGUAGE AND GRAMMAR

LANGUAGE

NEPĀL

Nepāli or Newāri language has been deeply influenced by Sanskrit, Pāli and Prākrit. The impact of Maithilī, Bengali and Hindī is also great.

AFGHĀNISTĀN, PERSIA

The intrusion of Sanskrit words into the vocabulary of

Afghānistān has been noticed. The linguistic affinity between Sanskrit and the language of the Persian *Āvestā*[182] is so close that some words of the *Āvestā,* with a little modification, become Sanskrit; *e.g.* Yasan (Skt. Yajña), Haoma (Skt. Soma), Gos (Skt. Gauḥ), Verethraghna (Skt. Vṛtraghna). The close similarity between the language of the *Āvestā* and Sanskrit is but natural; because the Aryans are believed by many historians to have settled in Persia before coming over to India. For this reason, Sanskrit is called Indo-Iranian. The similarity between Persian and Sanskrit is also quite considerable. This phenomenon cannot be taken as an example of India's influence in Persia; because this similarity was perhaps there before the Aryans migrated to India.

There are, however, certain Iranian vocables which appear to have been borrowed from the Indian Language.

TIBET

It is learnt that some Tibetans were sent to India with the object of producing a written form of the Tibetan language by adapting the Sanskrit alphabet with the phonetic characteristics of Tibetans.[183] The present Tibetan grammar has been modelled on Sanskrit grammar. In the Tibetan language, there are some Sanskrit words; e.g. *Om, Maṇi, Padma, Ārya, Dharma, Paṇḍita, Ratna, Vajra,* etc. Into the vocabulary of this country some Sanskrit words, with a little variation, have crept. It is believed that as many as 700 Tibetan words were derived from Sanskrit. At the instance of king Gampo (reign 629-650), translation of Sanskrit works into Tibetan started, and continued in the regime of his successor. As a result, the crude Tibetan was transformed into a polished literary language.

CENTRAL ASIA

The language of Khoṭān became a literary language under the influence of Sanskrit. There are some words of new Indo-Aryan languages, *e.g.* Hindī, Punjabi, etc. in the dialect, called Pariyā, current in some areas. The influence of Sanskrit also can be noticed.

MONGOLIA

We have referred to the presence of some Sanskrit words in the Mongolian language, in the chapter on nature of India's contact with different countries (in the section, India and Mongolia). Here we note some Mongolian words derived from Sanskrit.

Sanskrit	*Mongolian*
Makara	Matara-Madara
Graha	Garaga-Graka
Śloka	Siluga
Abhiṣeka	Avisiga
Padmarāga	Badmarāga
Śirīṣa	Sirisa
Agaru	Agaru
Candana	Cindana

CEYLON

Mahākassapa of Udumbaragiri monastery was very much conversant with Sanskrit grammar. He wrote a grammar, entitled *Bālāvabodhana.* In the grammar, called *Sidat Samgara,* written by Anomadiassi, the influence of Sanskrit grammar is beyond doubt. This work reveals some imitation of the *Sārasvata, Kātantra* and *Siddhāntakaumudī.* It is said that the author of this work was a contemporary of king Parākrambāhu II (twelfth century). The contribution of Sanskrit, in the evolution of the language of Ceylon, was not negligible.

Sāriputta, a pupil of the above writer, wrote an exposition, called *Pañcikālaṃkāra,* on the *Cāndravyākaraṇa.* This exposition appears to have been lost. The *Līnārthadīpa* or *Pattrīkaraṇa* of Buddhanāga, the Elder, is an exposition belonging to the Cāndra school. It is unpublished, and is stated to have been written by Guṇākara.

On the Ceylonese language the influence of Sanskrit is there. In the inscriptions of this country, there are many Sanskrit words.

MALDIVES

In the vocabulary of the Daveli language of this country, there is considerable influence of Sanskrit. In later times, the mode of writing from the right to the left, like Arabic, came into vogue. The end-portion of the name of the country indicates the influence of Sanskrit.

PHILIPPINES

Sanskrit	*Filippino*
Kathā	Kathā
Duḥkha	Dukha
Guru	Guro
Śīghra	Sigga
Sūtra	Sutla

The role of Sanskrit is very important in moudling the national language of Indonesia.[184] The language of this country is called Bahasa[185]; this word is derived from Sanskrit *bhāṣā.* In the formation of some words of this language, the influence of Sanskrit is noticeable. Some Indonesian words and their Sanskrit originals are noted below:

Sanskrit	*Indonesian*
Āgama	Agama
Kusuma	Kesuma
Deva	Déoya
Putra	Putera
Viṣa	Visa
Bhūmi	Bumi

Sanskrit	*Old Javanese*
Bhakṣaṇa	Baksana
Bherī	Bahiri
Bhāṣaṇa	Bāsana
Bhikṣu	Biku
Bhīma	Bima
Bhūta	Buta

The renowned Indologist, Gonda, has pointed out that, in Juynboll's *Old Javanese-Dutch Dictionary,* there are 6,790 Sanskrit words, but old Javanese words are not more than 6925. In the Mālay Dictionary, the number of Sanskrit words is not less than 750. The above scholar further points out that there are some Sanskrit words in Pigafetta's *Mālay Dictionary* (1521). A good many Sanskrit words are found in the *Malaccan Dictionary,* compiled by a Chinese sometime between 1403 and 1511 A.D. Any *Balinese Dictionary* will reveal that there are many Sanskrit words relating to the literature and religion of this country. In the *Cam-French Dictionary* (1906) by Aynonier and Cabaton, there are 700 Sanskrit words out of a total of

9350 words. There are 1362 Sanskrit and Pāli words in Mefarland's *Siamese-English Dictionary.*

Sanskrit	*Turkish*
Ṛṣi	Irzi
Viṣṇu	Bisanu

LANGUAGE OF CHINESE

Sanskrit	*Turkestan*
Mahārāja	Maharaya
Uṣṭra	Uṭa
Bhojana	Bhoyangna

JAPAN

The pervasive influence of Sanskrit in Japan is perceived when we read that, in the medieval age, Japanese soldiers used to start battle after wearing helmets in which the word *Maṅgala* was written in Sanskrit characters. In wooden boards in the cemetry, we find writings in Devanāgarī script. At the bottom of some images of the Buddha and Bodhisattva, Sanskrit *Bījamantras*[186] are written in Devanāgarī script. The syntax of Japanese language is like that in Sanskrit—there are *Kartā* (nominative), *Karma* (object), *Kriyā* (action). There are many Sanskrit words in the Japanese vocabulary. Before climbing a holy mountain, the prospective climbers write, on their garments, the old *siddham* letter. Sometimes *Om* is also written.

ENGLAND

The language of the underworld in England is considerably influenced by Romany or the language of the Gypsies. The English word 'Slang' was first current among them. Such English words as Jockey, Bloke, etc. had also their origin in the Romany language. Shakespeare has delineated an evil character named Caliban. This word, in the language of the Gypsies, means dark, evil.

Since the times of the East India Company, many Indian words have infiltrated into English vocabulary. Most of these words came to India from foreign countries, but these were widely used in India, and the English people took them from India. Some such words are *guru*, *darbār*,[187] *bāzār*,[188] *puccā*, *paṇḍit*, *fakir*,[189] *purdā*,[190] *nabob*[191] (nawab), *veranda*,[192] *jānālā*,[193] *chutney*, *svarāj*, *sikār*,[194] etc. As an outcome of familiarity with Sanskrit and Bengali literatures, many English savants carried on research in Indology, and wrote learned treatises. Of them, the celebrated William Jones (1746-1794) founded (1784) the Calcutta Asiatic Society, and authored many treatises. The five Englishmen, named Hare (1775-1842), Collin, Palmer, William Carey(1761-1834) and Marshman (1794-1877) deserve to be saluted like the renowned *Pañcakanyās* (five holy women, viz Ahalyā, Draupadī, Kuntī, Tārā, Mandodarī).

FRANCE

The origin of the words bege (ear), surin (*churi*, knife), etc. is found in the Romany language. The word Bohemian, denoting a capricious fellow, is derived from a French word denoting gypsy.

ITALY

Sassetti, a merchant from Florence, lived at Goa for five years (1583-1588), and discussed many things relating to this country. It was, perhaps, he that, for the first time, discovered the affinity of Sanskrit with the principal languages of Europe.

AMERICA

There are some similarities between the Indian and old American languages. As an instance, we may cite the Tāmil word Catamaran denoting boat. Mexicans used the word in the same sense. Perhaps, some Aryan words and some Aryan people went to America through Polynesia. Poindexter has given a fairly long list of the words common to the Quechuya[195] languages and Sanskrit.[196]

AFRICA

There are some Indian loan-words in the vocabulary of Ethiopia.

GRAMMAR

GERMANY, AMERICA, ENGLAND

That Sanskrit grammar attracted the eye of admiration of foreign scholars is proved by the work of H. Roth (1610-1688), who wrote a Sanskrit grammar in Latin. He was the first scholar to discuss this matter in Europe. Whitney's (1827-1894) Sanskrit Grammar, Macdonell's Vedic Grammar (1910), etc. are like landmarks in the history of Indology in the West.

PORTUGAL

The Portuguese took a keen interest in Bengali grammar. Manoel-Da-Assumpsao's *Vocabulario em Indioma Bengalla E Portuguez* (1743) contains Bengali grammar and vocabulary written in Roman characters and printed in Lisbon.

SOUTH-EAST ASIA

Indian grammar exerted influence in Cambodia. From an inscription of Yaśovarman (reign 889-908), we learn that he wrote an exposition of the *Mahābhāṣya.* Vidyāpuṣpa, an employee of King Bhavavarman, was versed in Sanskrit grammar. Vidyāviśesa, an employee under Īśānavarman (617-635), grandson of Bhavavarman (6th cent.), was also conversant with the same grammar. In the reign of Jayavarman (657-681), a Brāhmaṇa, named Dharmasvāmī, was versed not only in Sanskrit grammar, but also in other Vedāṅgas (viz. *Śikṣā*-phonetics, *Kalpa*-ritualistic works, *Nirukta*—etymology,

Chandas-prosody, *Jyotiṣa*—astronomy). Śrīsvāmī, a protégé of Jayavarman II (802-850) acquired great proficiency in Sanskrit grammar. The *Aṣṭādhyāyī* has been mentioned in an inscription of Rājendravarman (middle of 10th cent.). Grammar was one of the subjects in the curriculum meant for princes. Cambodian inscriptions contain chronograms like those mentioned in the Sanskrit works and inscriptions of India.

From the inscriptions we learn that Indravarman III of Campā, was highly proficient in the *Aṣṭādhyāyī* and its commentary, *Kāśikā*. Indravarman VII is known to have been versed in Indian grammar. In Jāvā, some grammatical works have been found. Of these, the most prominent is the *Svaravyañjana*. The influence of Sanskrit on the language of Laos is clear. In Trans-Baiklaian Siberia, the *Aṣṭādhyāyī* is acknowledged as ideal for the evolution of language. In the work, *Kārakasaṃgraha*, of Bali, indebtedness to the *Kātantra* Vyākaraṇa and Kavīndra (greatest of poets) Pāṇini[197] has been acknowledged.

In the Khmer language, the influence of Sanskrit can be noticed in geographical names, terms relating to almanac, names of kings and administrative terms. Some place-names end in *pura, sthāna, paṭṭana, deśa*, etc. Till the fourteenth century, the names of the kings were Sanskrit, *e.g.* Rājendravarman, Indravarman, etc. The administrative vocabulary contains Sanskrit words like *Kulapati, Guṇadoṣadarśin, Grāmapāla, Dharmādhikaraṇa*, etc.

There were historical reasons for the influence of ancient Indian language on some of the languages of South-East Asia. There was maritime trade between India and that region. Besides, Indian colonies and empires were established there in very early times. This subject has been dealt with in the chapter on the nature of India's contact with foreign countries.

There are many Sanskrit vocables in the language of Sumātrā. In the vocabulary of Campā (Vietnam), there are

700 Sanskrit words.[198] About the fourth century A.D., Sanskrit was the official language in some of the countries of South-East Asia.

We state below some Sanskrit words and words derived from Sanskrit in the vocabularies of some countries of this region.

Sanskrit	*Mālay*
Svarga	Surga
Rasa	Rasa
Adhipati	Dipati
Sākṣī	Sākṣī
Agni	Geni
Sanskrit	*Balinese*
Māṃsa	Mangsa
Abhiṣeka	Biseka
Sanskrit	*Thai*
Ākaśa	Ākāśa
Icchā	Icchā (jealous)
Carācara	Carācara (Traffic police)
Nagara	Nakhon
Prajñā	Prajñā (philosophy)
Moha	Moho (angry)
Ratha	Ratha
Rājā	Racha
Vidyut	Vidyu (Radio)
Saṃgha	Saṃkha
Sthāna	Sathani
Sukhī bhavatu	Sukhī hotu

In connection with cultural contact between India and different countries, we have discussed the use of some Sanskrit words in Thailand.[199]

G. CULTURAL INFLUENCE

Similarities of Indian culture and the way of life are found in the customs and manners of some foreign countries. May be that the coincidence is, in certain cases, accidental. But, in other cases, Indian influence is not improbable.

INDUS VALLEY CIVILISATION AND FOREIGN CULTURE

Many seals, resembling those of the Indus Valley, have been found in the stretch of land washed by the Tigris and the Euphrates. A comparison of the Mesopotamian seals with those, discovered in West Asia, leads to the conclusion that either those seals were made in India or those were imitations of their Indian counterparts. The pictorial script of Indus Valley is much akin to those of Sumeria and Egypt. There is similarity between the script of the Indus Valley seals and that found in the plates of Easter Island. According to the renowned historian, Wooley, the Sumerians brought with them the arts from the East. Among other things, earthen vessels and cotton were exported from India to western countries even in the prehistoric age. In Akkadian language, Indian cotton was called vegetable cloth. King Assurabanipal (668-626 B.C.) planted wool-producing trees (i.e. cotton tree) among other trees. The Greek Herodotus (484-425 B.C.), Father of history, mentioned Indian cotton.

The following articles, produced in India, have been found in Mesopotamia: precious stones from Gujarāṭ, food-stuff and metal from Rājasthān or Baluchistān, pearl-oyster from South India.

In South Turkomania, under Soviet Central Asia, relics of Indus Valley Civilisation have been found. Thanks to the archaeological excavations by Soviet scientists in different areas of Soviet Central Asia, the proofs of India's contact with and influence in that region have been revealed.[200]

As a result of explorations by Archaeological Department of Denmark, various archaeological materials, resembling those of ancient India, have been discoverd in the island of Bahrein in the Persian Gulf. This has led some scholars to think that ancient Indian civilisation spread by sea-routes, through the above island, to West Asia and East Europe.

GERMANY

It was customary among the Nazis to use the sign of *Svastika.* Long before this custom, the gypsies of Norway used to have the *Svastika* sign tattood on their right shoulders.

MITANI, HITTITE, BABYLON

In the fifteenth or sixteenth century B.C., on the bank of the Euphrates, the Mitani kings had Aryan names. They used to worship the Vedic deities, Mitra, Varuṇa, Indra, etc. Winckler has noticed the mention of a few Indian deities in a treaty of peace executed between the Mitani King and the King of the Hittites in 1360 B.C. In the palace of Nebuchadnezzar (604-562 B.C.), the renowned king of Babylon, fragments of Indian Teak wood have been found. In the *Baberujātaka,* there is mention of the contact between Babylon and India by sea -route.

PĀKISTĀN AND AFGHĀNISTĀN

The stretch of land, lying between modern Iran and India and included in Pākistān and Afghānistān, was culturally a part of India.

TIBET

In connexion with Indo-Tibet relations, discussed in the chapter on the nature of contact between India and other countries, we have seen that Bengali scholars like Atīśa Dīpaṃkara went to Tibet, lived there and wrote many treatises. Even after that, for two hundred years or so many Indian scholars visited this land. The joint efforts of the scholars of the two countries produced Tibetan translations of many Sanskrit works. The Tibetan scholars were versed in Tantra and Yoga. They were adepts in secret Tāntric and Yogic rites.

In the wake of the spread of Buddhism, the Tibetans became curious about not only the religion of India, but also about all Indian arts and sciences. We have referred to the influence of Indian scriptures, literature, script, architecture and sculpture in Tibet in the regime of Srong-tsan Gampo (7th cent.). At the time of the next king, Khri-sron Ide-btsan (755 780), the Indian scholar, Śāntarakṣita, was invited to Tibet for propagating Buddhism.[201] But, due to vehement opposition by a group of people, he did not succeed in this work. At his advice, the Indian scholar, Padmasambhava,[202] was invited. He was a Tāntric Yogin versed in mystic rites. Having defeated the opponents in debates, he paved the way for the propagation of Buddhism. He also set up, at Lhāsā, a monastery like the Odantapurī monastery at Magadha in India. Under his training, the king and twenty-six others practised *Yoga,* and acquired some power. The king sent some Tibetans to Kashmir, Nepāl, etc., particularly to Nālandā for the study of Buddhist scriptures and Sanskrit. He also engaged Indian and Tibetan scholars to translate original Indian works into Tibetan.[203] The Tibetan scholars continued this work even after the death of the above king. Incidentally, it should be mentioned that the power-loving Chinese Buddhist monks challenged the Indian scholars. To a religious council, convened at Lhāsā in 794

A.D., the Indian scholar Kamalaśīla, with his associates, was invited to establish the superiority of his doctrine. The respectable Tibetan Buddhist scholars participated in it. The main point at issue was—is it possible gradually to attain Buddhahood by secret mystic rites or can it be accidentally acquired by absolute actionlessness ? The Indian scholars subscribed to the former view, while the Chinese advocated the latter. After a protracted debate, the Chinese were defeated. The king accepted the Indian opinion. As a result, the Chinese left Tibet.[204] Tradition goes that the supporters of the Chinese slew Kamalaśīla, and the king renounced the throne.

During the reign (814-836) of King Ral-pa-can, perhaps the largest number of Indians, including Kashmiris, visited Tibet with the object of developing and spreading Buddhism. Like the earlier king, he, too, invited scholars from Nepāl and India for improving the Tibetan language and for the refinement of translation in it. The death or assassination of this king was followed by a setback in Indo-Tibetan contact. After about two centuries, with the advent (1042) of the aforesaid Atīśa, this contact was revived, and, due to reforms in Buddhism and Tāntric practices, this religion was firmly established. This resulted in a spurt of translation, into Tibetan, of various Indian literary works and scriptures, particularly Buddhist Sanskrit works. The Tibetan translations can be divided into two main classes : Religious and Secular.

The scriptural works, preserved in the Tibetan *Tanjur* and *Kanjur*, are generally designated as *Tripiṭaka*. The message of the Buddha, as revealed in *Kanjur*, may be divided as *Vinaya, Sūtra, Tantra.* The *Tanjur* contains exposition, the philosophical works of Nāgārjuna (*c.* 2nd cent. A.D.), Asaṅga (*c.* 4th or 5th cent. A.D.), Vasubandhu (*c.* 4th or 5th cent. A.D.), etc. and some other secular works including the Tibetan translation of Sanskrit *Nīti* works.

In Tibet, administrative records used to be written in Sanskrit till 1642 A.D.

PERSIA

In the reign of Xerxes (468-465), there were, in the army, Indian soldiers dressed in garments made of cotton and holding bows made of cane. A band of Indian soldiers, in the army of Darius (*c.* 522-486 B.C.), fought against Alexander.

Besides Indian literary influence in Persia, Indian philosophy (e.g. Tarkaśāstra-logic) also had an impact on the Iranian lovers of learning.

EGYPT

Though there is no evidence of Indo-Egypt contact in the prehistoric age, some similarities are noticed in the culture and civilisation of the two countries. The attention of scholars has been drawn by similarities between the folk-art, language and culture of rural Bengal and rural Egypt. Some place-names in Bengal and Egypt are similar.[205] In the society of both India and Egypt, the worship of cow, sun and serpent was in vogue. Indigo, muslin and tamarind, produced in India, were found in Egypt.

The Greek Chrysostom (98-117) informs us that many Indians, who went to Alexendria for commercial purposes, settled there permanently.[206] His impression, about Indian Brāhmaṇas, was that their self-restraint, sense of justice and love of God were far more than those of other people. Pausenius has stated that Indian merchants came with strange creatures including parrots.[207]

CHINA AND JAPAN

Some kinds of resin, which were popular in these countries, were supplied by India. In the Japanese Museum, Sho-Sho-in, ancient Indian resin is preserved as a national asset. Japanese funeral and obsequial rites have similarity with those of India. Buddhist influence is noticeable in the administration of Japan. The Buddhist *Saṃgha* (monastic order) played a significant role in the practical administration. The impact of Buddhism is there on the educational system as well as on social service. A certain Indian was at the root of the introduction of the cultivation of cotton in Japan. It is learnt that, after shipwreck, he swam ashore in 799 A.D. in the Aichi Prefecture coast. To commemorate this event, that place was called Tenjiku meaning India (lit. heaven). A memorial temple was built in his honour, and his statue set up inside it. The art of making various articles from pieces of wood developed, to a surprising extent, in Japan. This craft is connected with Buddhism. Such wood was, at first, used to engrave Buddhist *Sūtra* and pictures. Buddhism and Buddhist manners and customs are the warp and woof of the cultural life of Japan. Flowers, used in the worship of the Buddha, were at the root of the Japanese love of flowers.[208] Their Tea-festival owes its origin to Buddhism; a certain Buddhist monk introduced the process of preparing tea-liquor. Due to the inspiration, derived from Zen Buddhism, serving of tea was with reverence, sanctity and calm. The cultivation of Indian philosophy, scriptures and literature, particularly of Buddhist philosophy, went on in Japan, and is still going on with avidity.

SOUTH-EAST ASIA

Before discussing the influence of Indian culture in this region, it should be stated that, in very early times, Indian kingdoms were established here. Since the second century A.D., the kings, who ruled over this far-off land, bore Indian names. The religion, social customs, language, script, etc. of the people of this region were Indian. So, these kingdoms may be called Indian colonial kingdoms. Such kingdoms were established between the second century A.D. and the fifth in Mālay Peninsula, Cambodia (Kampuchea), Annam, Sumātrā, Jāvā, Bali and Borneo. The local people naturally adopted the civilisation and culture of the rulers. As a result, their own life-style, mingled with the Indian, gave rise to a composite culture. Elsewhere we have referred to the vast Śailendra empire and the Śrīvijaya kingdom in South-East Asia. Due to the influence of these Indian states, the predominance of Indian ideas in the local culture lasted for about a thousand years.

Both Hinduism and Buddhism were in vogue in this region. The Śailendra kings were followers of the Buddhist Vajrayāna religion which arose out of Mahāyāna. Despite the wide prevalence of Mahāyāna, at some places, *e.g.* Central Jāvā, some scholars cultivated Hīnayāna.[209] It is learnt[210] from the account of I-tsing (seventh century) that almost all the Buddhists of Jāvā, Sumātrā and several neighbouring islands used to follow *Mūla-sarvāstivāda-nikāya.* It had four divisions viz. (1) Mūla-sarvāstivāda sect, (2) Dharmagupta sect, (3) Mahīśāsaka sect, (4) Kāśyapīya sect. It is further learnt from the above account that, at that time, Buddhism of the area concerned was imported from North or East India. I-tsing's account reveals that most of the Buddhist sects were followers of Hīnayāna approved by Buddhist Sanskrit scriptures.

In Bali, the caste-system, in accordance with Hindu custom, indicates Indian influence. In this country, Brāhmaṇa priests were very respected persons. In the villages of Bali, there are small temples in Hindu houses, built in honour of Hindu deities. In the sanctum sanctorum of the Balinese temple, the soul, supposed to reside in the mountain, is built to be united with the Hindu Trinity (Brahmā, Viṣṇu and Śiva); in it the role of Giriśa (living on a mountain) Śiva is the most important. On the highest mountain of this country, there are shrines of Viṣṇu, Maheśvara and Sun-God. Hindu custom has been mixed up with the local custom relating to the rite before the burning of the corpse.

In Thailand, two bells, with inscriptions in Chinese and Sanskrit languages engraved, have been found. In the folk-literature of this country, there is mention of Brāhmaṇas as advisers to the State. In some kingdoms of this country, the kings are called Mahārāja. The Indian names Gandhāra, Videha and Mithilā, etc. are found in some places. There are also some names which are Buddhist; *e.g.*, Bodhivṛkṣa, Pippalguhā. The people of this country are descendants of those who are believed to have come from India and China. Although according to Pāli and Chinese works, the people of this country have ethnic connection with the Chinese, yet Indian culture was adopted in a greater measure than the Chinese. There are many signs of Indian culture in South Thailand. Of these places, very ancient and important are the cities of Nakhon and Sritthammarata. Among other signs, there is the bronze-image of the Buddha (made in the second century A.D. in the Amarāvatī style), in the style of Bodhgayā, etc. There is a Sanskrit inscription in a Buddha-image. There are some Sanskrit writings in some Hindu images at the place, called Śrīdeva. The king, named Kamaheng, was familiar with the *Tripiṭaka,* Hindu rituals and astronomy. He established a school for the Hindu and Buddhist priests. In this country, the Hindu rites, relating to *Abhiseka* (coronation), *Cūḍākaraṇa* (tonsure), burning of corpse, agriculture, etc. were adopted. The Brāhmaṇas used to live in royal courts. It was their business to prepare horoscopes, examine good and evil omens, and to worship Hindu and Buddhist deities. The object of the Hindu festivals, called *Ālokāmāvasyā* (to be performed on the fourteenth day of the dark fortnight of the month of Bhādra) and *Dīpānvitā* (to be performed on a similar day in the month of Kārtika) was to illuminate the path of the souls of the departed forefathers. Similar festivals were in vogue in Thailand at least towards the end of the thirteenth century.

Like the Indians, the people of this country also believe in the deities Viṣṇu, Śiva etc., but hate the demons who are supposed to be hostile to gods. There are images of some Hindu deities too.

From the inscriptions, found in the kingdom of Funan (Indo-China), it seems that Indian religion, philosophy, politics and statecraft, etc, were widely studied in this country. This kingdom was originally Indian. According to scholars, the light of civilization dawned here with the advent of the Indian traders. The fact that this kingdom is located in half the way to China and that it contained abundant attractive articles induced the Indian traders to come here. Tradition has it that a certain Indian Brāhmaṇa married a princess, and established this kingdom in the first century A.D. He has been identified, in an inscription (seventh century) of Campā, as a scion of Soma race, named Kauṇḍinya. The spirit, whose worship was in vogue in this country, was ultimately transformed into Śiva Maheśvara.[211]

Indian culture was widespread in Cambodia. Many Brāhmaṇas lived here as respectable people. The inscriptions testify to the fact that Indian Brāhmaṇas came to this country, married in the royal families and settled permanently. A mixed caste, resulting from the union of Brāhmaṇas and Kṣatriyas, sprang up in this country under the name Brahmakṣatra. Despite the predominance of Hinduism, Buddhism was not altogether absent. The princes used to study Indian philosophy and literature. Even at present the Brāhmaṇas, living in royal courts and designated as Bakus, perform rites in the palace. The influence of Sanskrit is noticeable in some geographical names, names of kings, words relating to administration and to the almanac. Many place-names end in *pura, sthāna, paṭṭana, deśa,* etc. Till the fourteenth century, the kings had Indian names; *e.g.*, Rājendravarman, Indravarman, etc. In connection with administration, we find words like *Kulapati* (a temple-chief), *Guṇadoṣadarśī, Grāmapāla, Dharmādhikaraṇa,* etc. The inscriptions mention the Śaka-era. The oldest of such inscriptions is dated Śaka 533 (= 611 A.D.). There are, in these inscriptions, chronograms like those found in Sanskrit inscriptions and manuscripts in India.

A strange story is current about king Devānīka (Chinese Fan Chen-Ching). Having conquered Cambodia, he acted as the king in the fifth century A.D. He gave the name Kurukṣetra to a place containing a tank.[212] Certain places of South-East Asia were conceived as Vārāṇasī, Ayodhyā, etc. H.B. Sarkar believes that, in the consecration of these places, Ganges water, brought from India, was used.[213] The two Sanskrit words 'Viṣaya' and 'Pradeśaka' occur in some Cambodian inscriptions.[214] *Rājakulamahāmantrī*, *Pratyaya* (a particular class of royal employees), *Sāmanta*, *Gajapālā*—these words also were current. Besides, the use of some more Indian words is said to have been in vogue.

King Bhavavarman (sixth century A.D.) and his successors made many *Śivagiriśaliṅgas* (phallus) and Nandī and of Nandinī. During the reign (617-635) of Īśānavarman a princess married an Indian Brāhmaṇa, named Durgasvāmin.[215] The practice of a princess marrying a Brāhmaṇa from India continued in later times also, and was in vogue for a long time.[216]

Among the visitors to the hermitages of this country, the order of entrance was clearly fixed. The king had the precedence over all others. Next came the turn of Brāhmaṇas. In case there were many Brāhmaṇas, the order was determined in accordance with merit and learning. Brāhmaṇas were followed by Śaiva and Pāśupata Ācāryas. Of them again, those versed in grammar had the first preference. Of them, one, who was most versed in Śaiva Pāśupata doctrine and grammar, deserved the greatest honour.[217]

In Mālay, particularly in the Kedah region, Indian culture was pervasive. Most of the archaeological materials, unearthed in this country, relate to Hindu culture; some, however, pertain to Buddhists. The Pallavas of South India established colonies in Kedah. Some people from other parts of India too settled in this land. A stone inscription of Kedah contains the name of the Gupta emperor, Buddhagupta (*c.* 476-95). He is stated as living at Raktamṛttikā which is generally known as Rāṅgāmāṭi to the south of Mursidābād. In the Tāmil epic poem, *Cilapattikaram* (or *Silappadikaram*), dating back to the second century A.D., it is stated that many ships, loaded with various kinds of merchandise, used to come to South India from the port, Tondi, in Mālay. The Tāmil poetical work, *Paṭṭimapālai* (2nd or 3rd cent. A.D.) refers to the commercial contact between the two countries. Of the rosaries, discovered here, nearly eighty came from India. In Mālay, there are still some festivals in which Hindu customs are followed. The rite, relating to childbirth, bears witness to Hindu practice. Similarities between India and Mālay can be noticed in the education system, law, family life, inheritance, social matters, rites and customs relating to marriage, etc. and the attitudes of the people. In Mālay, people's conception of the king and monarchy, royal titles like Seri Pādukā, festival relating to coronation, royal prerogative, etc. are clearly of Indian inspiration. In ancient India, very good ships used to be made at a time when the neighbouring countries had no such arrangements. So, in the third century A.D., horses were shipped to Mālay and Indo-China.

In the funeral rites of Mālay, there are some Indian elements. Over a thousand Brāhmaṇas used to live in the kingdom of Ch'ih-tu. About the end of the sixth century A.D., corpses used to be burnt in accordance with the Indian practice.[218] Even in the coronation of Muslim kings, Indian elements are noticeable. When Perak Sultān ascended the throne, a Brāhmaṇa recited a *mantra* in corrupt Sanskrit, which praised the king's victory over enemies, his fortune and sense of justice. After this, he took an oath to the effect that he would rule justly like a Hindu monarch.[219] There was imitation of Indian law-courts in the courts of this country. In courts, the Brāhmaṇas had an important role.[220] From Chinese works we learn that, in some kingdoms of Mālay, the Brāhmaṇas became a part and parcel of the local societies.

In recent times, in some government announcements, the influence of Sanskrit has been noticed. In 1966, the brief form of an urgent political-cum-economic programme was given the name *Dwidharma* (Sanskrit *dvidharma*) and *Tjaturkārya* (Sanskrit *Catuṣkārya*).

In the upper echelons of the society in Java, respectable people had sometimes Sanskrit names; this is proved by some inscriptions written in old Javanese and Sanskrit. It is, however, not possible to say whether such people were Hindus from India or Javanese converted to Hinduism. As regards the name Pūrṇānanda, occurring in a Sanskrit inscription of West Jāvā, Vogel has remarked that the person concerned may have been born in India or to an Indian or a local man who embraced Hinduism. In inscriptions, the names of the common people are generally Javanese. There are, however, also such Indian names as Nārada, Pāṇḍava, Rāvaṇa, etc.

In worship in this country, the following articles, used in Hindu worship, figured among the local materials:

> *argha* (special offering), *gandha* (sandal paste), *dhūpa* (resin), and *akṣata* (rice dried in the sun).

An admixture of Hindu and local rites is found also in rites relating to the consecration of temples, etc. In both India and Jāvā, there is the custom of attributing divinity to the souls of the departed forefathers. A Javanese inscription (907 A.D.) refers to prayer to the departed soul.[221] The ritual of *Śrāddha*, performed in this country, though taken from the Hindus, reveals some local changes.

In Indian scriptures, the king has been regarded as God; e.g. *Manusaṃhitā*, VII.8. This attitude is found in certain places of South-East Asia. As an instance, we can mention the fact that the footprints of King Pūrṇavarman have been compared with those of Viṣṇu (*c.* 450 A.D.).[222] The image of Vajradhara of the deified king Indra (eighth century), considered to be the founder of the Śailendra dynasty, has been installed.[223] King Varmadeva (1135-57) has been characterised as *Madhusūdanāvatāra* (incarnation of Madhusūdana or Viṣṇu).[224]

In some charters of Central Jāvā, the Sanskrit words *rājādhirāja, rājaputra, rājaputrī, mahārāja,* etc. have been used. Also used are *sāmanta, mantrī, pati, likhitapatra, nāyaka, pratyaya,* etc. It is stated, in the seventh verse of the Keluraka inscription (782 A.D.) of Central Jāvā, that the spiritual preceptor of a Śailendra king came from Gauḍīdvipa (Gauḍ in West Bengal). It is stated, in verse 93 of the work, Nāgarkṛtāgama[225] (1365), that Indian Buddhists and Brāhmaṇas used to visit the royal court, and eulogized the kings by means of verses. The Vajrayāna of this time was syncretic. In verse 15 of the above inscription, the Buddhist Mañjuśrī has been, on the one hand, mentioned as Vajradhārī, and, on the other, characterised as Brahmā, Viṣṇu and Maheśvara. He represents all gods.

The bodices in the images of some women, found in East Jāvā, are in keeping with the fashion current in East India. Even in recent times, the ear-ornaments, used by the Serimpi dancers of Jāvā, are like the bronze ear-ornaments that were in vogue in Nālandā.

In Thailand, the following Sanskrit words were current:

Rājā, Yuvarāja, Uparāja, Dharmādhipa, Senāpati, Nagarapāla, Mantrī, Gajapāla, Koṣādhipati, etc.

The position of the Brāhmaṇas, in the functions of the royal court and in matters relating to judicial proceedings, was very high.[226] From archaeological materials and inscriptions we learn that the kings of the places, called Dvāravatī, Haripuñjaya, etc. The India-influenced Javanese art and architecture bear witness to indebtedness to India.

There are many examples of Indian culture in Thailand. Like Hindus, the people of this country also say *namaskāra* to those whom they meet. In Thai language, there are the words *praṇamya* and *vanda* (*vandya*). The week days bear Sanskrit names with some variations.

Sanskrit	*Thai*
Āditya (Ravivāra)	Aditaya
Candra (Somavāra)	Candra
Aṅgāra (Mangalavāra)	Aṅgāra
Budha	Budh
Bṛhaspati	Barahasabodhi
Śukra	Śukra
Śaura (Śanivāra)	Saura

Some personal names of this country have been taken from Sanskrit. The king was called Indrāditaya (Sanskrit Indra and Āditya). In the names of universities, hospitals etc. we find the use of Sanskrit words:

Sanskrit	*Indonesian Language*
Śilpakara	Silpakorna (Viśvavidyālaya)
Cūḍālaṃkaraṇa	Culalankorna (-Do-)
Vajra	Bajira (hospital)
Rāmādhipati	Ramadhibordi (-Do-)

Indian language is at the root of some popular proverbs and wise sayings current in this country. These are mostly related to the *Rāmāyaṇa, Mahābhārata* and Garuḍa. These reveal some influence of the *Pañcatantra* and *Hitopodeśa.*

Indian thought is noticeable in the script, literature and folk-literature of Thailand.

The kings of Campā assumed the title *Dharmamahārāja*; their names ended in-*varman.* In this country, years were counted according to the Śaka era. It is learnt from the account of Mātuān-lin[227] that the social life of Campā in the second half of the fourth century A.D., was considerably influenced by India. The royal garment and ornaments, customs relating to the funeral rites, etc. were like those in India. Many widows refrained from marrying a second time;

there were even cases where the widowed wife immolated herself in the funeral pyre of her husband. The Chinese sources also testify to the vogue of this practice. It is reported that, after the demise of king Harivarman in 1080 A.D., his fourteen wives courted death. From the sculpture of Campā and other South-East Asian countries as well as of India, it is clear that the women of ancient times used to keep the upper part of the body bare.

MAURITIUS

Besides the spread of Hinduism in Mauritius, some other cultural influences are also noticeable. Like the Indians, the Mauritians also observe some festivals like *Holi, Śivarātri, Rāmanavamī* and *Diwāli.* (See the daily newspaper, *Telegraph,* 11.4.90, p. 10).

BURMA

The kings of the Piu dynasty assumed the two Indian titles, *Varman* and *Vikrama*; *e.g.* Jayacandravarman, Sūryavikrama (d. 688). In some inscriptions of these kings, there are Sanskrit verses and their translation. In Ārākān, the Hindu kings of the Dharmarājānuja dynasty ruled from 600 to 1000 A.D. In the politics of this country, the role of Buddhism was important. In Burma, the Sanskrit terms *Rājā, Mantrī,* etc. were used. The local word 'Sming' is used, mainly at Pegu, to denote a king. It is derived from Sanskrit 'Svāmī'. Under the influence of Buddhism, there was development of art, education, literature and social life of this country. The bodiless spirit used to be worshipped. In some cases, male and female spirits were considered to be fused together perhaps under the influence of the Indian Ardhanārīśvara (half woman and half Śiva). The inhabitants of this country, belonging to the Mon or Talaing race, are considered to have been migrants from the Kṛṣṇā-Godāvarī region of India.

PHILIPPINES

Indian culture pervades these islands. Buddhism spread in this region. Hindu influence, however, is clear in the religious faith, names of deities and traditional accounts of heroism. Through Sumātrā, almanac, Buddhist folk-literature, alphabet, etc. reached Philippines. India, through Jāvā, exercised influence on the art of making metallic goods, jewellery and weaving. Items of dress like turban, ornaments, ancient name (e.g. Varuṇa) of coin, etc. appear to betray the impact of India. The lotus-emblem, on the sword of this country, was Indian in origin.

KOREA

There is Indian tonal influence on the strains of folk-songs of this land in general, Dance reveals the impact of India. India exerted influence on architecture also.

BORNEO

As a result of contact with the Indianised kingdom of Funan, and of maritime trade with India, this country became familiar with Indian culture.

CHINESE TURKESTAN

In this region, over 700 documents in Kharoṣṭhī script have been found. Written in Niyā Prākrit, these serve as evidence of Indian impact. Some coins of this country contain legends in this script. The Indians set up colonies here in the first few centuries A.D. The information, gathered from written documents, is briefly as follows.

Government was monarchical. The king was called Maharaya (Mahārāja) and the queen Devī. Dūta (envoy) is mentioned. Slave-trade was in vogue. There is mention of female slaves too. In the society, there were *Pṛṣṭhabhāris* (=*Pṛṣṭhabhārika*), i.e., those who used to carry loads on their backs. In long-distance journey, animals were employed for such work. Among the beasts of burden, the most useful was the camel. Cows and horses were very popular. The keepers of these animals used to get food and dress. The writing material was hide. The people's dress consisted of turban, upper garment and bodice. Garments were made of wool and animal-skin. The family was patriarchal. The birth of a son was an occasion for joy. There was traffic in girls. Stress was laid on the noble and pure conduct of life. People used to pray for victory in war and prosperity, but, did not lose sight of the transitoriness of wealth. They were eager for knowledge of grammar, music and dance, astronomy, poetry and painting.

Lands were of two kinds, belonging to Government and to individuals. Those of the latter kind were freely transferred. Kings used to grant lands to their proteges and slaves. People used to believe that bumper harvest could be expected from agriculture started on an auspicious day. Well-organised irrigation system appears to have been known. There were clear rules about the realisation of revenue. Among the craftsmen were sculptors, carpenters, potters, makers of bows and arrows, goldsmiths, etc. There is mention of Chinese traders.

Among the foodstuffs are mentiond *Ahata* (= *bhakta*, cooked rice), *taṇḍula* (raw rice) *dāḍima* (pomegranate), *marica* (pepper), aridaga (ādraka, ginger), *sakarā* (*śarkarā*, sugar), *ghṛda* (*ghṛta*, ghee), *gama* (wheat), *yava* (barley), etc. Meat-eating was a common practice, especially among the soldiers.

Among the coins, there are at least two Indian names, viz. *Māṣaka* and *Suvarṇa*. Cloths were measured by cubits. Lands were measured, rather specified, in accordance with the quality of seeds used in agriculture.

Thus, the over-all picture of the society has an Indian look.

SOVIET CENTRAL ASIA

There is evidence of the influence of the culture of prehistoric India on Soviet Central Asia. Some archaeological materials made of stone, bone, earth, and metals, etc. tend to indicate the impact of the culture of prehistoric and proto-historic India in this region. Indian culture of both the palaeolithic and neolithic ages spread in that country. The Indus Valley Civilisation had its impact on the region concerned in the Bronze Age through commerce and industry. The earthware, articles made of copper and bronze, ivory goods, terracotta seal, etc., found in that region, remind one of the Harappan civilisation. So, it appears that, centuries before the rise of Buddhism, Indian culture spread in Soviet Central Asia.

ARABIA

The Arabs used to import the following from India: spices, tigers, elephants, rubies, white sandalwood, ebony, and coconuts. Cotton was at first imported from India. Caliph Al Mamun encouraged cultural exchanges with India. With Arabia the cultural and commercial contact of South India was most intimate towards the end of the fifteenth century till the advent of the Portuguese. The Saif-I-Hindi (Indian sword) was a favourite weapon of the Arabians. Al Andalusi, in his work, entitled *Tabakat Al-Ulam,* has characterised India in the following words: a mine of wisdom and a source of law and politics. He has further remarked that in numbers, geometry and astronomy the mastery of Indian scientists is recognised, and, in their knowledge of medicines, they have surpassed all other nations. Yakubi also highly praised Indian scientists, and said that they were invincible in science, particularly in Āyurveda. Caliphs Al Mansur, Hārun Al Rashid, etc. engaged Indian ministers. Under the able administration of these ministers, Baghdad became an emporium of Indian culture. The Arabian Al Kindi wrote a treatise on Indian religion. Sulaiman and Al Māsudi wrote about various Indian matters. Al Nadim, Al Asari, Al Beruni, etc. deeply studied Indian religion and philosophy. In popular literature, science and religion, Indian life-style influenced the Muslim world. Some Indian wandering mendicants went to Baghdad in the regime of the Abbasid Caliphs. Zahir (*c.* 866) has described them.

Indian mysticism influenced the Jewish mystic ideas perhaps through the medium of the Sufis. It is called *Kabbala* by the Jews. It reached Egypt and West Asia. Miraculous power of letters, use of incantation and talisman, form of the deity, similarity between the body and universe-these ideas of the *Kabbala* have an astonishing similarity with the Indian *Tantra.* The impact of Hinduism is certain on pantheism and the transmigration of soul. The conception that God is infinite and incomprehensible is like the Upaniṣadic doctrine. In the seventeenth century, Aurangzeb expressed his liberal devotion to Islam. As a result, Sufism suffered a temporary setback, and the Sufis became attracted towards Vedānta.

EUROPE

On Europe the impact of India had been multifaceted since very remote times. The ancient Romans used to purchase many luxury goods made in India. Among such things were pearls, jewels, muslin, medicine, spices, resin, ghee, ivory, colour, cosmetics, oil, perfumes, etc.

The idea of the Greeks about the universe was, perhaps, moulded by India. There is remarkable similarity between Vedic society and that reflected in Homer's (*c.* 9th cent. B.C.) *Iliad* and the *Odyssey* both of which assumed the final shape in *c.* sixth century B.C.

Indian mysticism reached Europe in about 900 B.C.

An examination of the social condition of England reveals that a good many Indian ideas got into that country. These are belief in the other world, doctrine of transmigration, theory of incarnation, etc. These ideas may have been imbibed by the people of that country in various ways viz., study of Indian philosophy and religion, association with Indian labourers, Gypsies, etc. In the early years of Indo-European contact, the Europeans enthusiastically greeted Indian thoughts. In the wake of the firm establishment of British supremacy in India, the ruling nation developed a superiority complex and an imperialistic attitude towards whatever good there was in India. Thus, they looked down upon the Indians. As the scholarly Europeans came to know of India's glorious heritage, their attitude to India changed. The eulogy of ancient India, particularly of the Veda, by no less a person than Max Müller (1823-1900), the foundation of the Calcutta Asiatic Society (1784), the dedication of scholars like Jacobi, Winternitz, Wilson, etc. to the resusciation of ancient Indian literary and cultural heritage brought about a complete metamorphosis in the Europeans outlook on India. Justice Woodroffe became interested in Tantra; so much so that he not only brought out editions of Tāntric texts but also wrote extensively on them. The depth of his dedication is proved by the fact that he took to the Tāntric way of life. Some European poets and litterateurs were influenced by such Indian doctrines as desireless action (*niṣkāma karma*). America also came to look upon India with regard.

Among the British professional boxers, the role of the Gypsies was noteworthy at the time when boxing was done with uncovered fingers. Though the famous boxer Driskal is generally regarded as belonging to Wales, yet he was, in reality, a Gypsy. Tom Smith, Price, Hooper, etc. were noted Gypsy boxers. The gypsies migrated to the west from the East, particularly India.

The people, known as Goths, liked some Indian articles, particularly pepper and silk. Perhaps, they came to India, and went back home with the religion, culture, arts, pepper, spices and silk from this country.

Most of the bull-fighters of Spain belonged to the Gypsy community originally belonging to India.

Despite reaching the apogee of machine-culture, Russia sought the solace of the soul in the East. As the Russian frontier advanced towards Asia, the door of eastern culture began to open. Even before that, in 1840, Chadaien said that the Russians were the dear children of the East; they have adopted from the East the faith, law and religion. Gorky (1868-1936) told Romain Rolland that Russia was more imbued with eastern thoughts than China. Tolstoy (1828-1910) was very much conscious of the East, particularly India towards which he was respectful. He has reverentially referred to the Buddha in his work, entitled *Confession*. He exchanged letters with such great Indians as Mahātmā Gandhi, C.R. Dās, etc. He has quoted passages from the *Bhagavadgītā*, *Upaniṣad*, Tāmil *Kural*, etc.

AMERICA

In the realm of culture, there is similarity between the Indian and the Maya civilisations. It is noteworthy that India had the golden age of the Gupta rule (fourth to sixth century) when the Maya culture was at its zenith. Due to the similarity between the culture of Mayas and the Indians in respect of ancient legends, sculptures, architecture, religious faith and religious customs etc., some scholars think that the Maya civilisation was the result of the contact of the people concerned with the Asians, particularly Indians. The almanac of the Aztecs is like the basis of the Indian culture in America. The place of its origin is India. The Maya almanac is, to some extent, like that of the Hindu Age of India. The social condition in the South, Central and East Asia was favourable for the spread of Indian culture. May be that these regions had contact with the Maya America.

Scholars like Mackenzie are certain that the people of Peru and Mexico were aware of the Indian myths about gods. Among the Incas of Peru, there is a sort of caste-division as in India. Their society also was divided into four strata. The people of Peru used to worship the omnipotent and invisible Supreme Being (Paramātman). As some Indians (particularly in Bihar) chew tobacco leaves, smeared with lime-paste, so also the people of Peru used to chew dry cocaine leaves mixed with lime. Some scholars have noticed the similarity of the Indian kings and the kings of Mexico and Peru in royal insignia, dress and etiquette. The lion-seat and the lotus-seat of Mexico are like the Indian throne and lotus-seat. The umbrella, as a symbol of royalty, among the Mayas and the Incas is probably an imitation of the royal parasol of India and of the Asian countries influenced by India. The ideal divine man, Quetzalcoat, of the Mexican culture used to teach people that violence towards any creature is wrong. If a live creature was to be offered to a deity, then a bird or an animal might be given, but not a man. This is an echo of the age-old Indian principle of non-violence (*ahiṃsā*). The Mexican festival of Voledor is like the *Caḍakapūjā* of Bengal and that South Indian festival in which a man's body, pierced with a hook, is revolved. Macleod noticed this similarity.

The Brāmanical Trinity (Brahmā, Viṣnu, Maheśvara) has similarity with that of Mexico. There is similarity in the food of the Indians and Mexicans. Mexican tortilla has the shape and size of Indian bread or *Cāpāṭi.* Both these are made more or less in the same way. Like the members of the upper-class Hindus, particularly Brāhmaṇas, they offer particles of food to God before starting to eat meals. The Mexicans believe that there were four successive destructions of the Universe. This is something like the four Ages (*Satya or Kṛtayuga, Tretā, Dvāpara and Kali*) recognised in Indian Sāstras. The first Age, in both the countries, is believed to have been of a duration of 4,800 divine years. In royal emblems, etc. there is similarity in both countries. After the assassination, by the enemy, of her husband, a queen of that country immolated herself, like an Indian *satī,* in fire.

After the advent of the Spaniards, the old inhabitants of Inca kingdom, Cuzco, used to observe practices like those of the Indians, and to wear turbans on their heads. The man, from whom descended the Incas of Peru, was an Indian Brāhmaṇa of the title of Āiyār (found in Madras, present Tāmil Nādu). The Incas of this region used to wear sacred threads (*Yajñopavīta*). In boyhood, they used to undergo the ritual of *Karṇabedha* (piercing the ears). Some other Indian customs were also observed by them. They followed caste-system.

The sun-worshipping Aryans of North India introduced metallurgy, cultivation with irrigation, novelty of monarchy and the pure religion in Egypt, Mediterranean region and, beyond the Atlantic, in America.

There is marked affinity in the life-style of the Asiomericans and the Indians. In both the lands, we find the practice of chewing betel-leaves with lime, chewing cocoa leaves (like betel-leaves), smoking tobacco, use of a pouch of lime.

Of the various articles of export from India, cotton was very important. This article reached far-off America. In the coastal areas of Peru has been found cotton which was a hybrid of Indian cultivated cotton and the wild cotton of America. This commodity used to be exported to other countries too. Some think that coconuts, grown in this littoral region of India, used to be shipped to America. The word 'cocoa' is Portuguese. It seems it is they who, for the first time, carried coconuts to South America. E.B. Tylor[228] states that, a story like that of the proverbial tortoise (and hare), known in India, was current in old America. Maize, growing in ancient Peru and Chile, was like that grown in Assam by the Nāgās. There is no definite evidence of the export of Indian maize to America. This does not seem to have been improbable in view of the fact that maize of the above kind used to be cultivated in India even before Columbus (*c.* 1446/51-1506), the discoverer of America.

India has deeply influenced American thought. The renowned American philosopher, Emerson (1803-1882), believed that an immanent soul underlies everything in the world. The publicity of his main thesis and its propagation were through his *Journals.* At first, he came under the influence of Buddhism. But, the Hindu doctrine of the transmigration of soul convinced him that nothing in this world is destructible. Everything temporarily passes out of sight, but comes back. Fed up with the materialistic civilisation of the west, he turned to the east, and from Hinduism and Buddhism he learnt that all religions are basically the same. Another American savant,

Thoreau (1817-1862), was inspired by Indian ideals. His *Journal* contains many of his remarks on several treatises of the Hindus. Whitman, a stalwart among the supporters of intellectual freedom of America, was considerably swayed by Indian ideas and Sanskrit literature. The American Christian Movement was probably influenced by India. Its literature reveals Vedāntic doctrines. Its lady-founder, Eddy, used to think that material things and sorrow are false, and this realisation is the means of getting rid of all sorrows. This echoes Vedāntic ideas.

Some scholars have discussed Buddhist influence on Central America.[229] Some have shown that successive hordes of Asians visited that country. Architecture and language of special kinds were prevalent among them. Some archaeologists have tried to prove that the migrants carried Indian and South-east Asian culture across the Pacific to Old America. A few specialists have sought to establish, on various grounds, that, ten or twenty millenaries ago, men from Asia, particularly East Asia, went to America where they formed the first human settlement. This view is, however, controversial.

Thoreau, the naturalist and philosopher, writes in his *Walden* as follows:

"In the morning I bathe my intellect in the stupendous and cosmogonal philosophy of the *Bhagavadgītā*...... I lay down the book and go to my well for water and lo ! there I meet the servant of the Brahmin, priest of Brahmā and Viṣṇu and Indra, who still sits in his temple on the Ganges reading the Vedas, or dwells at the root of the tree with his crust and water jūg."

Thoreau, Emerson and some other contemporary intellectuals of America received English translations of sacred and secular Indian epics from Calcutta printers.

The participation of Vivekānanda (1863-1902) in the World Religious Congress in Chicago (1893) created, among the Americans, a new awareness of India, its culture, particularly the Vedānta philosophy.

Susan Bean, Curator of the Peabody Museum[230] in Salem, writes that, before Vivekānanda's arrival, "there were several New England merchants who were dracon to the intellectual stimulation India offered. Some of them spent many months in India." One such American was Charles Dall. He came to Calcutta in 1855, and met Rājā Rādhākānta Dev, President of the *Dharmasabhā*, and the renowened poet, Tagore.[231]

In recent times, the music of Ravi Sankar, the films of Mrinal Sen and Satyajit Roy, the presentation of Vedāntic philosophy by Svāmi Prabhupāda, the skill of such Indian-American professionals as the ophthalmologist, Prasānta Basu, the excellence of the writer, Bhārati Mukherjee, etc. have attracted the attention of quite a number of Americans.[232]

H. MUSIC AND DANCE

Arabia, Persia

In very remote times, Arbaia, Persia and the countries under Greece and Rome came into contact with India. It seems, long before the infiltration of the gypsies into these countries, Indian thought spread to some extent. An Arabian author, living in Spain, referred to an Indian treatise on music, particularly *Rāgas* (melodies). In some technical terms of Arabian music, some similarity with the terms of Indian music is noticeable. The influence of India in that country is probable in view of the fact that the Arabian writer Jahiz Abbas has mentioned love for Indian music in the courts of the kings. He has also referred to an Indian musical instrument called *Kaṅkal* which seems to have been the *Kingar* made of two bottlegourds. The Arabian *Makam Ich* is, perhaps, a Persian version of the Indian system of *Rāga, Tāla* and *Laya.* Yehudi Menuhin (1916-) is certain about the impact of India on Arabian music.

Those who entertain the common people with music in Persia, are mostly gypsies. The same remark applies also to Syria, Mesopotamia and Egypt. Firdausi (*c.* 935-1026) and the Arabian historian Hamza (d. 625) have characterised the gypsies as expert lute-players.

MAURITIUS

Indian immigrants to Mauritius took with them the folk music and dance of India. The Mauritians sing Bhojpuri and Mehendi songs. *Holi* songs about Rāma, Kṛṣṇa, *Cautāl, Dhāmār,* and *Jhumur* songs. (See the daily paper, *Telegraph,* Calcutta, 11.4.90, p. 10).

JAPAN

In Japan the oldest song-dance, *Gigaku,* is a kind of mask-drama. It was imported from Korea in 612 A.D. A man, named Mimshi, having learnt this in China, introduced it in Japan. As a matter of fact, it originated in India; the masks bear Indian characteristics. The dancers used to represent the lion and the eagle. In this also Indian influence can be gauged, because there is no lion in China and Japan. The eagle is called Rarur; this word can be taken as a corrupt form of Garuḍa. Japanese dance-song is divided into eight or more parts; e.g. *Bosatsu, Sariyobin, Konju, Bairo, Bato, Biyoo, Am Ni Nomai* and *Bamsurku.* Some of these terms appear to be rooted in Sanskrit. Thus *Bosatsu* is *Bodhisattva, Bairo* is *Bhairava* etc. According to a scholar Biyoo is a part of the Indian dance-drama *Nāgānanda* attributed to Harṣa. Perhaps the Chinese traveller I-tsing (675 A.D.) introduced it in China.

GREECE AND OTHER WESTERN COUNTRIES

There is no definite evidence of the mutual influence of Indian and Greek music. But, the description of lute, given by Aristotle (384-322 B.C.), applies to the Indian lute. Greece appears to have adopted the seven notes of the Indian song. The fact that Indian music originated as early in the Vedic age renders it probable that it exercised influence on Greece. The system of oldest Greek notes, called Mixolydic and Doric, have similarity with the ancient Indian heptatonic system. In a mural of Pompeii, there is a picture of the Indian lute. According to Strabo, music and musical instruments of Greece were imported from Thrace and Asia. Alexander's biographer,

Arrian, has written that music and dance were very popular in India ever since ancient times.

Indian music was well known in the west in the eighteenth-nineteenth century. Some western composers composed songs with Indian themes. Holst, Russel, Smith, etc., who composed songs, had curiosity about Indian music. Wagner (1813-1883) was indebted to Indian music.[233] Many European scholars wrote works dealing with Indian vocal and instrumental music; *e.g.* Danielou, Fox Strangways, Popley, etc. The French composer, Russel (1869-1937), came to India. His profound love for the *Rāga, Tāla* and *Laya* of Indian music has been reflected in his opera-ballet, Padmāvatī. In the Quarte Poems Hindous and Raga Mallika of Dilage there is the influence of Indian music. Indian music is the main thing in the annual Edinburgh festival. The Sarasvati-hymn of William Jones (1746-1794) reflects his knowledge about the heptatonic system of the Indian music, the permutation and combination of the seven notes and *Rāgas.*

The aforesaid Holst,[234] whose full name was Gustav Holst (1874-1939), was one of the prominent melodists of England. Among the works written by him on ancient Indian literature, the following may be noted:

- Song-dance *Sītā* (1899-1906), Symphonic poetical work *Indra* (1903), nine prayer-songs, in imitation of the *Ṛgveda* and fit for a solo singer (1907-1908), a sort of chamber-opera called *Sāvitrī* (1908), 14 *Karala* (*Kaṇṭha*), *Saṅgīta,* the *Meghadūta* (1910) composed for being sung in chorus and orchestra. He was a believer in the ideals advocated in the *Bhagavadgītā* till the end of his days. In a letter to his daughter, he wrote: Sanskrit literature has attracted me. It was, perhaps, due to the inspiration derived from Tagore's line—*maraṇre tunhu mor śyāmasamān,* that he wrote: lovely and soothing death, serenely arriving. His love for Indian aṣtronomy was at the root of his best song "*The Planets*". In it he has looked at each star with the Indian outlook.

The Gypsies were fond of music and dance. They loved

musical instruments, particularly the violin. Hungary, Romania, Bulgaria, Turkey and the entire Balkan Peninsula have been influenced by Gypsy-music. Gypsy songs are very popular and form an important part of the cultural life in Serbia, Russia and in some other countries. The Gypsies started living in Europe in the fifteenth-sixteenth century. The Hungarian dance, called Csardas, is like the dance of the Gypsies. Gypsy dance is very popular in Spain. According to some, it was the gypsies who introduced Bag-Pipe in Europe. Some think that the Gypsies themselves introduced the gypsies in Europe.

Some believe that the Guitar, very popular in western countries, is only another form of the Indian *sitar.* Some believe that the Romanian instrument, called Tsimbal, which is supposed to be the precursor of instruments like piano fitted with key-board, actually originated in India. The western scholars themselves admit[235] that the western violin and flute were made in imitation of the Indian lute and flute respectively.

I. LAW, POLITICS AND STATECRAFT

It is surprising that ancient India influenced some foreign countries even in the practical life of the people. There is an impression that, in ancient times, the Indians were engrossed with philosophy, eschatology, spiritual matters, etc. People under this impression dub ancient India as the brooding east. This is, however, erroneous. In those times also there were astute politicians in India and men with highly practical sense, who thought of material welfare. Ancient Indians formulated detailed rules for the conduct of the society; both civil and criminal law were highly developed. The account that follows will make it clear that ancient Indian law had a powerful impact on that of many countries. It should be noted that the monarchical form of government prevailed in India since remote antiquity so that political principles and statecraft arose long before the *Arthaśāstra* in which we find a systematic treatment of the subject for the first time.

The influence of Manu was profound in many foreign lands, and, curiously enough, an effective medium of this influence was the gypsies. Of them, those, who settled in the Western countries, adopted the avocation indicated by Manu for the people outside the fold of the caste-system.

CEYLON

There is considerable similarity between Kandy in Ceylon and India in the laws relating to property, marriage, adoption, etc.[236] We learn from the Buddhist work, *Mahāvaṃśa,* that Parākrambāhu, king of Ceylon, was conversant with the *Arthaśāstra* and other Indian works on politics. We are further informed that Parākramabāhu II was experienced in the rules laid down by Manu.

SOUTH-EAST ASIA

On the laws and politics of this region the influence of India, particularly of the *Manusmṛti* and *Arthaśāstra* is widespread. The laws of the countries concerned were formulated within the framework of Sanskrit Śāstras, particularly the *Manusmṛti* after a consideration of the local customs and usages and the judgements of the earlier judges. These laws were influenced also by Buddhism. For instance, though Hindu law allowed very limited rights to women, Buddhism was far more liberal in this respect.

Let us start with Cambodia. The earliest reference to Manu occurs in an inscription (Majumdar, *Inscriptioṇs of Kambuja,* no. 61). It is stated that the king got the direction about his duty towards the subjects from Yogīśvara, *i.e.* Yājñavalkya, and as the princes bowed before him, he seemed to be another Manu. There are two quotations from the *Manusmṛti* in an inscription of king Yaśovarman (889-900).[237] Manu is mentioned also in some other inscriptions.[238] One inscription (*Bulletin* ...d' *Extreme-Orient,* XLIII, 91) refers to a king versed in *Dharmaśāstra.* The local judicial procedure was based on its Indian counterpart. In an inscription,[239] dating back to about the eleventh century A.D., it is stated that a certain Brāhmaṇa, named Śrīkaṇṭhapaṇḍita was versed in Dharma and Śāstra. It is understood that, when a plaint was filed, an exponent of Dharmaśāstra recited Sanskrit verses about the subject to be decided, and the technical terms of Sanskrit Śāstra were used.[240]

In ancient Indonesia, the eighth and ninth chapters of the *Manusmṛti* were the source of the main law-books relating to civil and criminal law. Two law-books of this country are entitled *Devāgama* and *Svarajambu.* The first entirely and the second mostly follows Manu. Lecl'ere has remarked[241] that the modern Cambodian law is based on the aforesaid two chapters. Who introduced Manu's laws in this country and when, it is difficult to determine. If Liang Shu[242] is to be believed, then a Brāhmaṇa, named Kauṇḍinya II, reformed the laws in the light of the Indian system.

Indian Śāstra, particularly Manu exercised influence in Campā too. An inscription[243] states that king (fourth ?) Harivarmadeva (1074-1080) was versed in four *Upāyas*[244] and eighteen titles or subjects of dispute[245] according to *Dharmaśāstra.* In another inscription,[246] it is stated that king Jaya Indravarman IV (twelfth century) was conversant with all *Dharmaśāstras.*

In the laws of Thailand also there is the influence of ancient Indian Dharmaśāstra, especially of Manu. The eighteen titles of dispute, according to Manu, referred to earlier, division of slaves into seven classes, the principle that interest cannot exceed the principal, persons unworthy of being witnesses, etc. are found in the law of this country, which is called Dhammasattha in Pāli (Sanskrit Dharmaśāstra). Manu stands at the head of this country's law.

Manu figures very prominently in the laws of Indonesia. In the legal treatises, *Śivaśāsana* or *Pūrvādigama* (*c.* 13th or 14th cent.), it is stated that rules, prescribed by Manu, are laid down in it. It is stated, in the *Ṛṣiśāsana,* that Manu was the first monarch who introduced the *Śivaśāsana.* The Javanese treatises, *Kuṭāramānava, Svarajambu, Ādigama,* etc. have been composed on the basis of the *Manusmṛti.* Chapters eight and nine of Manu have been specially utilised in both civil and criminal law laid down in the *Kuṭāramānava.* It is, in accordance with Manu, that the following matters have been discussed:

eight kinds of thieves, six kinds of *ātatāyins,*[247] homicide, abuse, injury etc.

Besides, there are the rules, based on ancient Indian Law, relating to interest, slave, mortgage and inheritance of land, etc. The *Svarajambu* (*c.* 14th cent.) also draws mainly upon the above two chapters of the *Manusmṛti*; occasionally, the author's own views have also been stated. A few Sanskrit verses are scattered in the *Ādigama.* In this work also, various types of Dharmaśāstra have been discussed.

Among other works, written in Old Javanese, are the *Kramaning Sākṣi, Aṣṭādaśa vyavahāra, Devadaṇḍa,* etc. The first work contains some verses in corrupt Sanskrit; a few such verses occur in the *Manusmṛti.* The *Aṣṭādaśa-Vyavahāra* commences with the words *avighnamastu.* Though written in Javanese, it contains some writings in Sanskrit. 1292 A.D. is, perhaps, the upper limit of its date of composition. The *Devadaṇḍa* is also called *Dharmavicāra.* Portions of the Javanese treatise, *Nītipraya,*[248] remind one of the *Arthaśāstra.* There is an admixture of popular and political principles in the *Nītiśāstrakakawin,* written in Old Javanese. This work, dating back to about the second half of the tenth century, contains 125 stanzas in different metres. There is some similarity between the *Kāmandakarājanīti,* composed in the above language, and the Sanskrit *Kāmandakīya-nītisāra.* In the Javanese work, sage Kāmandaka gives instructions, *inter alia,* about royal duties which include the taking care of the priest, Brāhmaṇas and those who are versed in the Vedas. There is evidence that the *Arthaśāstra* was not only studied in this country, but its principles also were actually followed in the administration.

Manu's influence is quite considerable on the laws of Mālay. According to Winstedt,[249] most of the patriarchal law, *Adat Temenggong*, of this country was of Indian inspiration. About this composite law, intended for the various denizens of the port, information is available mainly in the following treatises :

Malacca Digest (*c.* 1450), *Pehang Digest* with Supplement (1596), *Kedah Digest* (1650). The following matters, in the laws of Mālay, are influenced by Indian Dharmaśāstra : most of the ten crimes, for which death-penalty is prescribed, are like those in Hindu law, heavier punishment for a person offending against a person of superior caste, modes of punishment like the cutting of the tongue, shaving the head, etc., marrying a forcibly abducted girl (*Rākṣasa* and *Paiśāca* forms of Indian marriage), fine for sexual offence, impaling the offender to death for certain crimes, etc.

Winstedt observes (*The Malayas*, p. 108) that, in comparison with Civil Law, the Criminal and constitutional Laws have been influenced by India to a greater extent. He further says (*Ibid.*, p. 113) that Hindu Law has been followed in the case of offences in which slaves are involved. He has also pointed out the influence of Hindu law relating to the mortgage of properties (*Ibid.*).

The installation of Manu's statue, in early times, in the Philippines is an index to the reverence to this great law-giver. It is preserved in the Art Gallery of the Senate Chamber of the Philippine Republic.

BURMA

On the laws of this country Manu's influence is not negligible. The Pāli *Dhammasattha* was written (*c.* 1174) by a Burmese named Dhammavilāsa (real name Sāriputta). Among the Pāli works on law, it is the most prominent. The king of Martaban, Wagaru or Wareru (1280) got a *Dhammasattha* compiled, and gave it the name Wagaru *Dhammathat.* By and large, the eighteen titles of dispute have been adopted in it;

there are, however, some changes. A comparison of this work with those of Manu, Yājñavalkya and Nārada, relating to Vyavahāra, reveals that the author of the former has dealt with those matters in which there is difference between the laws of the Hindus and the Buddhists. As an instance, we can mention *Prāyaścitta.* In Sanskrit *Dharmaśāstra,* there are elaborate descriptions of and rules about *Prāyaścitta.* But, the Buddhists considered it to be unnecessary. According to them, morally speaking, no punishment can be awarded. The Buddhists believe that the good and bad results of good and bad deeds are inevitable. The Wagaru *Dhammasattha* was rendered into Pāli by Buddhaghosa (sixteenth century); the name of the translation is *Manusāra.* The very titles of some later works on law indicate the influence of Manu; e.g. *Manu-Yin* (1756), *Manu-Kyay* (1758-60), *Manusara-Shwe-Myin, Manuvannana.*

In this connection, it should be noted that some law-books of this country reveal the influence of Pāli literature. For instance, the aforesaid *Manu-Kyay* betrays the influence of the following Pāli treatises :

Jātaka (Mahosadha, Vidhura and parts of the *Suttapiṭaka*), *Milindapañha, Samantapāsādikā, Kaṃkhāvitaraṇī* (commentary on the *Pātimokkha*), *Visuddhimagga, Sāratthadīpani-ṭīkā* (commentary on *Vinayapiṭaka*).

JAPAN

Japan was, perhaps, not influenced by the Indian legal system. But, it seems that the *Manusmṛti* was introduced in this country long before the birth of the Buddha. There is Japanese translation of the *Arthaśāstra.*

The works on politics in Laos are based on Sanskrit works. Of these works, the most well-known is the *Rajasavani.* This treatise contains commentaries on verses culled from Sanskrit works. It discusses the political expedients of four *Upāyas*[250] and six *Guṇas.*[251]

CHINA

Budge of British Museum, London, has informed us that, he has noticed direct mention of Manu's rule in a manuscript discovered in China.

PERSIA

It is understood that, for the administration of the empire of the Persian king, Darius (sixth-fifth cent. B. C.), laws were framed in accordance with the *Manusmṛti.*

Through the followers of Zoroaster the worship of Manu and the study of the *Manusmṛti* were introduced in West Asia and in some countries of the West.

EUROPE

Greece

In certain matters, relating to statecraft, there are striking similarities[252] between the work of Aristotle (fourth century B.C.) and the *Arthaśāstra* attributed to Kauṭilya. Both think that the State will be based on justice. The State shall be self-reliant in food and armed forces. According to both, the State will follow religion. Both think that the peoples' happiness and prosperity will be related to the State. These ideas may have arisen in India and Greece independently. It should, however, be noted that, as a result of the invasion by Alexander, a pupil of Aristotle, and because Greek principalities were established in North-West India, the exchange of ideas between the two countries was facilitated. So, Aristotle might have been influenced by the *Arthaśāstra.* The general impression is that the *Arthaśāstra* originated in the fourth century B.C. If that be so, then its influence on Aristotle cannot be ruled out. It should, however, be mentioned that, according to a recent theory, the *Arthaśāstra* came into being in the second century A.D.[253]

We have discussed the influence of the political subjects of India in foreign countries since early times. It is interesting to note that, even after Indian independence, India continued to have its impact abroad. Sometime after the declaration of independence, at the instance of Jawaharlal Nehru, the then Prime Minister of India, the First Asian Relations Conference was held in Delhi. Many Asian countries participated in it. Marshal Tito of Yugoslavia and President Nasser of Egypt supported the policy of non-alignment proposed by Nehru. Under the Presidentship of Soekarno of Indonesia, the First Non-Alignment Conference was held at Bandung. He and Nkruma of Ghānā (Africa) were powerful exponents of the above policy. So also was Chou-en-lai of China. Such conferences were held subsequently in Cairo, Belgrade and Colombo.

The Third World is constituted by over one hundred countries. They were against joining any of the power blocs of America and Russia; and played an important role in the UNO for keeping international peace. All Asian countries, excepting Japan, all African countries, excluding the region ruled over by the Whites, the Latin American countries and Yugoslavia in Europe are parties to the Non-Alignment Movement. The Executive Body is called Co-ordinating Bureau of Non-aligned countries. Its meetings are held annually.

In pursuance of Buddhist principles, Nehru introduced *Pāñcaśīl* (five rules of political conduct), in international politics. Most of the Asian countries, including China and a few western countries, accepted it in principle; occasional breaches are, however, noticed here and there. The five principles are :

1. Not to use force in solving international problems.
2. Not to interfere in the internal affairs of another country.
3. Not to interfere with the sovereignty of the participating countries.
4. Ironing out of differences of opinions by negotiation and removing mutual animosity.
5. To maintain international peace, amity and discipline.

In the world-politics, Mahātmā Gāndhi's policy of non-violence plays a significant part. This policy deeply influenced the Civil Rights Movement of the Blacks in America. Martin Luther King (1929-1968), their leader, openly acknowledged his indebtedness to Gāndhi. His movement was crowned with success.

Very recently, I.R.A. prisoners in Belfast, though not expressing in so many words, adopted Gāndhi's principle of fasting for the protection of their rights.

After the establishment of England's political relation with India, the latter indirectly influenced the politics of the former. The need for the administration of India moulded some skilled administrators. What is called utilitarian thought was influenced by the experience and expertise acquired by the British in India. J. S. Mill criticised the doctrine of Liberty, Equality and Fraternity. About his work he said that it was nothing but turning the Indian lamp to the European problems. British India was at the root of these two, Imperialism and the reform of Civil Service.

OTHER WESTERN COUNTRIES

The jurists, appointed (600 A.D.) by Emperor Justinian, were influenced by the *Manusmṛti.*[254]

The poets of England, Shelley (1792-1822), Byron (1692-1763), Keats (1795-1821), Southey (1774-1843), etc. were familiar with Manu's principles.[255]

Voltaire (1694-1778) thought that, of all the works got from the east, the *Manusmṛti* was of the greatest quality. It is understood that those, who formulated laws for Napoleon, consulted this work. In course of describing the impact of Manu on various countries, especially in the western world, L. Jaeolliot writes in his work (entitled *The Bible in India,* preface, XII): Manu inspired Egyptian, Hebrew, Greek and Roman legislation, and his spirit still permeates the whole of our European Laws.

AFRICA

Egypt

Some scholars have shown that, in the regime of Ptolemy (285-247 B.C.) the financial and economic structure was like that of India. In both the countries, the state had monopoly right over oil, salt and mines.[256] There was similarity in the administrative systems of the two countries. In view of close commercial intercourse, the influence of the *Arthaśāstra* in Egypt is not unlikely.

J. GEOGRAPHICAL NAMES

An index to the depth of Indian influence abroad is the Indian names of various places in foreign countries. The name of the principal city of Delaware in New York (America) is Delhi. The name of a region in Hungary is Behar. These similarities cannot be explained away as accidental. In some cases, certain areas in the foreign countries were deliberately given Indian names. In south-east Asia, Indian civilization spread widely. The Campā and Kambuja are Indian names. In Burma, Śrīkṣetra (Prome) and Haṃsāvatī (Pegu) indicate Indian influence. In that country, the following names also are Indian :

Aparānta, Avanti, Vārāṇasī, Dvāravatī, Gandhāra, Kamboja, Kaliāsa, Kusumapura, Mithilā, Rājagṛha, Utkala, Vaiśālī, etc.

The name of the river Irāvatī in Burma, is similar to that of the Irāvatī, a tributary of the river Sindhu in India. The names Golnagar, Kalaspur, Rāmpur, etc. bear witness to Indian influence. The names Arimaddanapura, Vssuṅomiyo, etc. are clearly Sanskritic, the former is Arimardana in Sanskrit, and the latter means Viṣṇu's city.

The name Kambuja, as stated above, is found in Indian literature. Certain cities of the south-eastern countries have Sanskrit names; *e.g.*, Tāmrapura, Ayodhyāpura, Vikramapura, etc. Amarāvatī and Campāpura in Campā are Indian names. Some rivers in Bali have Sanskrit names; *e.g.* Gaṅgā, Sindhu,

Yamunā, Kāverī, Sarayū, Narmadā. The name Borneo is regarded as derived from Porubei which again is believed to have been derived from Pūrvadvīpa as mentioned in the *Arthaśāttra.* A place in Borneo is called Vaprakeśvara. In Jāvā, there are canals named Candrabhāgā, and Gomatī. The name Jāvā owes its origin to the Sanskrit Yavadvīpa. It is said that the name Sumātrā is derived from Samudra. In Sumātrā, the names Śrīvijaya and Indragiri are Indian names. In the name of Mālay Peninsula, the similarity with the Indian Malaya mountain is clear. The name Tāmraliṅga is Indian. A capital of the Śailendra Empire was Kataha, a word perhaps derived from Sanskrit Katahadvīpa. The residential area of the Thais at Unnan, in Indo-China, is called Gandhāra; a part of it is called Videha whose capital is Mithilā.

In South-east Asia, the names Pippalaguhā, Bodhivṛkṣa, Gṛdhrakūṭa, etc. are connected with Buddhism. The combined name of certain kingdoms of the Thais was Kausāmbi. Certain places in between the border of Unnan and the frontier of Cambodia and Thailand are called Suvarṇagrāma, Unmārgaśilā, Yonakarāṣṭra, Haripunjaya, etc.; all these are Indian names. The Thai capitals Jayaprakara, Sukhodaya and Sajjanālaya are typically Indians names. Lobpuri (Lavapurī), Dvāravatī, Ayudhyā and Śrīkṣetra remind one of India.

The main geographical names in Ceylon are Indian :

Abhayagiri, Anurādhapura, Guptaśālā, Puṅkhagrāma, Jarjaranadī, Dīrghavāpī, Gaṅgāsrīpura, Giritala, Jambudroṇī, Jayagaṅgā, Jayavardhanapura, Kalyāṇī, Laṅkā, Suvarṇabhūmi, Tāmraparṇī. The names Nālandā and Ujjayinī are also there. In the Ceylonese chronicle, the mountainous area in Ramanya or Burma has been called Malaya.

K. GAMES AND AMUSEMENTS[257]

Different countries from Egypt to Wales were formerly regarded as the homelands of chess. The Arabians introduced this game in Europe before a thousand years. As a result of the discovery of the manuscripts of certain Sanskrit works by European scholars, it has been definitely established that this game originated and prevailed in India under the name Caturaṅga.

Chess made its way into Persia in the regime of Anushirwan (531-579). In Persia and Arabia, it was given the name *Chatrang* and *Satranj* respectively. These names appear to have been derived from Sanskrit *Caturaṅga.*[258] From Persia the Arabs carried Chess to Spain. From there chess appeared in the court of king Charlemagne (742-814; reign 768-814) Emperor of the Franks.

Al Yakubi (9th cent.), an Arabian writer, and some other ancient writers have stated that this game is Indian; it shows people's dependence on fate. The chess-board represents the year.

There is an opinion that the Japanese game *Sunorok* or *Sugoroko* was obtained from India. It is played in Japan under the name *Nard.* It is generally supposed to have originated in Persia. But, the aforesaid Yakubi thinks that it was Indian. In whatever country it may have originated, it came to Japan from India through Central Asia and China. The Japanese dice resemble those discovered in the ruins of the Indus Valley Civilisation. These have three facets and six faces, and contain the numbers from one to six. It is noteworthy that such dice is very much similar to those used in different countries of the world since ancient times.

In about 700 A.D., chess went to China from Kashmir through the ancient trade-route. The earliest reference to it in China is found in the work, entitled *Niu Seng jus* it *Kuai lu* (end of 8th cent.). The title means 'Book of Wonders'. It seems, it travelled along with Buddhism. In the first millenary A.D., Indian racing game was introduced in China. The Chinese game, *T'shu-p'u* appears to be another form of the Indian *Catuṣpada* which, according to Himley, specialist in Chinese games and sports, originated in West India, and was adopted in China in the regime of the Wei Dynasty (220-265).

Catuṣpada has the modern name *Caupar,* Chinese boxing, known as *Shaolin,* originated in India. It is said that a certain monk, named Bodhidharma, taught this to the monks for the maintenance of their health and self-preservation.

The aforesaid game of *Sunoroku* is known as *Shawn-liu* in China. It was introduced in China from India in the seventh century or earlier. According to Wei-shu, it was imported from the region known as Hu which stood for some place contiguous to India. Karl Himley has shown that, according to the work, *Hum jun shi (*sometime between 960 and 1279 A.D.), the game of *T'shu-pu* originated in West India. Its original name was *Catuṣpada.* It got into China in the period between 220 and 265 A. D.

Most of the South-East Asian countries learnt chess from India. Some countries, however, like Siam (Thailand) learnt it through China.

The Indian game, known as *pacisi,* spread to different foreign countries. It was a favourite game in the Mughal court. A form of it was not only current, but also very popular in Mexico even before the time of Columbus (*c.* 1446/51-1506). The Mexican game of *Patolli* was very much akin to *Pacisi.*[259] It is called *Pasit* in Burma, *Bakkis* in Somaliland, *Pacis* in Persia, *Barjis* in Arabia, *Parcis* in Spain.

The game of *Ludo* in England is another form of *Pacisi.*

L. INSCRIPTIONS AND COINS

One of the main evidences of India's influence in foreign countries is the Indian inscriptions found in them. In some countries, the influence of Sanskrit is noticeable in the inscriptions written in the local languages.

Many Sanskrit inscriptions came to be written in Nepāl before 650 A.D. As examples, we can mention the early Licchavi epigraphs like the Changunarayan Pillar Inscription (464 A.D.) of Mānudeva. The earliest epigraphs in Nepāl are the Rummindei and Nigali Sagar Pillar Inscription of Aśoka (3rd cent. B.C.) written in Prākrit.

A Sanskrit inscription of Hamawa proves that Hinduism made its way into Burma long before the fifth century A.D. An inscription of Pagan, dated 1442 A.D., refers to the gift of 295 works to a monastery. Of these works, some bear Sanskrit names. Some Mon inscriptions of Burma contain many Sanskrit words. In the beginning of an inscription, found at Minpagan, there is a Sanskrit verse from the *Mukundamālā*, composed by Kulaśekhara. Both Sanskrit and Pāli were used in the inscriptions of Burma.

The inscriptions of Ceylon contain many Sanskrit words. Sanskrit verses have been quoted in Eḍu inscriptions written in the old Sinhalese language. Some inscriptions are written in Sanskrit. In this country, Pāli and Prākrit inscriptions are more numerous.

In Cambodia, hundreds of Sanskrit inscriptions were written.[260] Most of them belonged to the period from eighth century A.D. to the tenth; some, however, are older. These inscriptions unmistakably point to the fact that Sanskrit was widely and deeply cultivated in this country. Their poetical style is commendable. The 58 inscriptions, studied by H.B. Sarkar,[261] reveal that the following Sanskrit metres have been mainly used in them :

Śloka or Anuṣṭup, Upajāti, Indravajrā, Upendravajrā, Śārdūlavikrīḍita, Vasantatilaka, Sragdharā, Mālinī, Vaṃśasthavila, Pṛthvī, Mandākrāntā, Vaitālīya, Aupachandasika, Svāgatā, Triṣṭubh.

There are also skilful uses of the figures of speech, Upamā, Śleṣa, Ullekha, Yathāsaṃkhya, Vyatireka, Dṛṣṭānta, Utprekṣā, etc. The ideas and descriptions, etc. contained in the inscriptions, testify to the imaginative power and originality of the composers. An inscription quotes Manu's verses. In an inscription of Rājendravarman (middle of tenth century) contains four verses which appear to have been modelled on the *Raghuvaṃśa*. Some inscriptions of Yaśovarman (889-900) reveal the author's familiarity with the *Bṛhatkathā*, *Setubandha*, *Rāmāyaṇa* and *Mahābhārata*. One inscription mentions the

Sūryaśataka. From an inscription of the aforesaid Yaśovarman, we learn that he wrote an exposition of the *Mahābhāṣya.* Some inscriptions refer to *Horāśāstra, Kāmasūtra,* etc. Vedāntic influence is clear on an inscription (seventh century) of Mahendravarman. In some inscriptions, we find the name of Suśruta (perhaps later than 2nd cent. A.D.) and names of some medicines. Some inscriptions reveal Śaivite influence; they occasionally refer to Parameśvara which seems to stand for *Parameśvarāgama.* This *Āgama* (*c.* eighth century) is regarded by the people of the Liṅgāyata sect as one of the original treatises. Different inscriptions refer to the familiarity or proficiency of the kings and other persons in the following Śāstras :

Caturveda, Six Vedāṅgas, six systems of philosophy, Grammar, Dharmaśāstra, Arthaśāstra, Jyotiṣa (Horāśāstra), Dhanurveda, Gāndharvaveda (Saṅgīta), Buddhist religious texts, the doctrines of the Śaivas, Pāśupatas and Pañcarātras, Tantra.

Śivasoma's inscription states that he learnt scriptures from Lord Śaṃkara who is believed to be identical with Śaṃkarācārya, the renowned exponent of non-dualistic Vedānta. According to the veteran historian, R.C. Majumdar, this inscription alone is the most authentic evidence about the date of Śaṃkarācārya. The above king, perhaps, flourished in the middle of the ninth century A.D.

It is learnt that, in the reign of Jayavarman (657-681), a certain Brāhmaṇa, Dharmasvāmin by name, was versed in the Veda and Vedāṅgas. During the reign of Jayavarman II (802-850), a scholar, named Śrīsvāmin, acquired deep proficiency in the Vedas and Indian philosophy, particularly Nyāya. Vidyāpuṣpa, an employee under Bhavavarman (sixth century), was well conversant with Nyāya-vaiśeṣika. Vidyāviśeṣa, an employee under Īśānavarman, grandson of the above king, was a good scholar in Nyāyavaiśeṣika.

Over 100 inscriptions of Campā bear testimony to the cultivation of Sanskrit language and literature. The earliest

Sanskrit inscription, composed in high-flown poetical style, dates back to the third or fourth century A.D.

In the kingdom of Funan, in Indo-China, four Sanskrit inscriptions have been discovered.

In Mālay, two Sanskrit inscriptions, written in a south Indian script, have been found at Ṗenang. This appears to have been written in the fourth century A.D. and contains some Sanskrit words. The Ligor inscription (Śaka 697-775 A.D.) of this country indicates the prevalence of the Brāhmī script. A Sanskrit inscription, found in the kingdom of Tāmbraliṅga, dates back to the sixth century A.D. or earlier. Four inscriptions (682-686), in the Sanskritised Mālay language, of one Śrivijayarāja have been found in coastal areas of North Sumātrā and Philippines.

Seven Sanskrit inscriptions (fourth century A.D.), found in Borneo, indicate the one-time existence of a Hindu kingdom there and of Sanskrit works on religion and other matters. Some inscriptions contain such Sanskrit words as *Bahudāna, Jīvadāna, Bhūmidāna,* etc. In an inscription of Mūlavarman, found at Kulei in Borneo, there is similarity with the Pallava script of South India.

A stone inscription of Thailand indicates the cultivation of Sanskrit learning. Some inscriptions of different dates are written in Sanskrit; *e.g.* those written in Dāravatī (Dvāravatī) and Śrīvicala (Śrīvijaya) periods. A rock-inscription (1492), in honour of King Sukhotai (Sukhodaya), is the earliest specimen of Thai language. It contains many Sanskrit words. Most of the inscriptions of this country are written in verse. Of the several Sanskrit metres, used in them, *Anuṣṭup* appears to have been the commonest. Among other metres, *Upajāti* has been widely used. *Vasantatilaka* also is a favourite metre of the writers. The figures of both word and sense have been used. Of the latter, the most frequent is *Utpreksa.* Two examples:

Somavaṃsyo' pyari-dhvānta-pradhvaṃsana-divākaraḥ /

(Phnom Phra Vihar Inscription of Bhavavarman, Verses)

[About a king - though born in the lunar race, he is like the sun]

Yaṭ kāminī-nikara-niscala-mānasasthe' /
'pi sthātumarhati hṛdi sa mahākavīnām //

(New Panom Rung Inscription, Verse 2)

[About a certain king -

Who, though residing in the firm minds of ladies, was worthy of getting a place in the hearts of great poets.] *Upamā* is also found at many places. The poet remarks about a certain king -

Kulaṃ dyotayan-nāsīd, gaganaṃ candramā iva

[Written at the foot of the Buddha's image, Wat Mahathat, Lopburi, verse4]

[As the moon illuminates the sky, so also that king glorified his race.]

Among other figures of sense, noteworthy are *Virodha, Yathāsaṃkhya, Samāsokti* and *Saṃkara.* Among the figures of word, *Anuprāsa* has been widely used. Various kinds of *Anuprāsa,* viz. *Cheka, Vṛtti, Śruti, Antya* and *Lāṭa,* have been used.

Though classical Sanskrit has been used in the inscriptions, yet, occasionally, we meet with unfamiliar, even un-Pāṇiniyan words; *e.g.* Unmanā for Umā (Suan Phak Kard Palace Inscription). Awkward seems to be the word *Smara* used by *Umā* to denote Śiva (Dop Siem Prasad, Aranyaprathet, Lines 8-9).

An inscription (304 A.D.) of East Jāvā is written in Sanskritised Javanese language. Some Old Javanese epigraphs refer to Pāṇini, *Kātantra* and *Cāndra-vyākaraṇa.*

A Kharoṣṭhī inscription has been discovered near Khoṭān in Central Asia. Also found are some Indian coins.

The Greek king, Menander (reign in Punjab - *c.* 160 to 140 B.C.), referred to in connexion with Religion, introduced, out of deference to Buddhism, coins in imitation of Buddhist coins. A coin, issued by another Greek king of India, Diodoros, contains Indian features.

The Kushāna conquerors appear to have imitated Greek coins. They, however, substituted the figure of Herakles for that of Zeus. The figure of Herakles may have been intended to represent Śiva; Megasthenes seems to have indicated that these two deities were popularly identified with each other[262] in India. It may be noted that the Kushāna king Vima Kadphises (Kadphises II), whom Kanishka I (*c.* 78. 120 A.D.) is believed to have succeeded, was a follower of Śiva and issued a large number of coins.

M. MISCELLANEOUS

Some say that Ikebana, which is a popular art in Japan, originated in India. It is also believed that, through those travellers who went to Japan via China, the Indian idea of *Maṅgala-kalaśa*, along with various kinds of Buddhist art, reached Japan.[263]

In South-East Asia, the system of book-keeping, coinage and methods of weighing, etc. are, to a great extent, like those in India. Time was when, before the introduction of metallic coins, the medium of exchange was cowries in different parts of India, *e.g.* Bengal, Bihar, Orissa, etc. This method prevailed also in Siam (Thailand), Jāvā, Philippines, etc. In determining weight, *Raktikā* (indicated by *Guñjā*)[264] and *Mañjarī* (the seed of a kind of tree) were used in India, the former in the northern parts and the latter in the south. This method was current in South-Asia too. Coins like the Indian *Taṅkā* (silver coin) were used in Siam and Burma. In some inscriptions of Jāvā, some Sanskrit terms have been used to denote coins of different denominations; e.g. *Kārṣāpaṇa, Suvarṇa, Māṣa,* etc. In the 17th-century Jāvā, the length of cloth was indicated, as in India, by cubits.[265]

In very recent times, the current thought and efforts in America regarding easy methods of learning Sanskrit are as follows.[266] V. Houston, assisted by D. Lavitre, has been exploring the possibilities of learning this language within a very short time, Houston, depending on handwriting and recitation, has devised what is called immersion method. He claims that, by this process, one can be familiar with phonetics, can learn how to read and pronounce Sanskrit correctly. He further claims that he has been able, by this method, to teach *more students in a year* than the number of students taught, in the University method, *within fifteen years.* Four years ago, Richard Briggs, a great lover of Sanskrit, declared that many things of Pāṇini's grammar could be easily taught with the computer. Houston observes that, in the world, Sanskrit is the only language by which mathematical subjects can be expressed with absolute accuracy. Houston is now round about 40. Twenty years ago, he practised *Haṭha-yoga* which involves certain postures, *e.g.* standing on one leg, holding the arms upwards, inhaling smoke with the head inverted, etc. and has since been practising *yoga* (abstract meditation) designed to effect concentration of mind. He has said that, as a result, he progressed in his studies admirably. After receiving the first college degree, he lived a solitary life in a New England forest. Under the influence of Yogin Rāmānanda Miśra (better known as Brahmānanda), he studied Sanskrit for ten hours a day. Then he tried, by writing a dissertation on Pātañjala Yoga, to obtain the M.A. degree of Columbia University. His initial effort was to draw up a curriculum for M.A. in Yoga, in which the Sanskrit Yoga aphorisms have to be mastered.

According to some scholars, the western writers, Carpenter, Havelock Ellis, Lawrence, etc. got inspiration from the *Kāmasūtra,* and influenced the elite of Europe. In their protest against the taboo about sex-life in earlier times, they got moral support from the *Kāmasūtra.*

There is considerable similarity between the alchemy (*Rasasiddhi*) of India and Arabia; the latter may be indebted to the former. The renowned alchemist of Madras (Tāmil Nādu), Rāmdebar, informs us that, having gone to Arabia, he assumed the name Yakub and taught this subject. Arabian toxicology was influenced by Indian thought, particularly by that of Caraka (*c.* 1st or 2nd cent. A.D.)

From certain rock edicts of Aśoka (e.g. Nos. II, XIII) we came to learn that he established hospitals for humans as well as animals, and planted medicinal herbs in the kingdom (Syria and West Asia) of Antiochus II (261-246 B.C.)

There are some minor matters in which India did some service to the outside world. For instance, Indian soldiers fought on the side of Artanerxes, the last Achaemenian emperor in his losing fight in the Battle of Arbela. In his expedition against Italy, the Greek king Pyrrhus of Epirus had, in his army, Indian soldiers with elephants. Hannibal, the Carthagenian General, had Indian soldiers in his army when he led his army against Rome. It was through the path of communication between the East and the West, opened up by Iran, that, for centuries, literature, art, philosophy and science had an unfettered movement from one nation to another. Iran extended full cooperation in this matter.

There is evidence that Indian silk and other textiles used to be exported from India to Iran in very remote times.

Great interest in Indology led some foreign scholars, notably Aurel Stein of Hungary, to undertake explorations at various places in India and Central Asia. As a result, he collected many images of the Buddha, Sanskrit manuscripts and ancient paintings. Of the several works, in which he laid down the result of his explorations, the most outstanding was the *Serindia* (1921) in five volumes.

The Hungarian, E. Baktay (1890-1963), came to India, and lived here from 1926 to 1929. He travelled widely, and acquired a first-hand knowledge of the culture and heritage of India. He published a collection of speeches of Gāndhiji in 1926. On his return to Hungary, he wrote several books on different aspects of Indian life, art and religion. His most extensive work was *India, her past, present, religions, peoples, towns, land and art monuments*, Budapest, 1931 (Expanded form, 1941; abridged form, 1928). A scholar of varied interest, he published (1921) a book on Rabindranāth, followed by a separate volume of short stories of Indian writers. His adaptation of the *Mahābhārata* (1923) was zealously acclaimed. In a later edition, he included an adaptation of the *Rāmāyaṇa*.

Mahātmā Gāndhi's personality and freedom movement had a powerful impact on the Hungarians. The Press of that country published sympathetic reports about him and his activities. Several editions of the translation of Romain Rolland's famous book on Gāndhi were published (1922, 1924, 1925, 1930). A book on this great man, written by Miklos Moriez (b. 1886) a Hungarian, was published (Torda, 1927). Baktay published (Budapest, 1926) a selection of Gāndhi's writings and speeches. Germanees also wrote a biography of Gāndhi. In Gāndhi's non-cooperation movement the Hungarians saw a parallel to their 'passive Resistance' against the Austrians after the suppression of the Hungarian War of Independence (1848-1849).

The Hungarians' admiration for Subhās Bose was attested by a book, containing his speeches, published (1944) in that country.

FOOTNOTES

1. Vide lecture delivered, at the Ramkrishna Mission Institute of Culture, Calcutta on the occasion of its 46th foundation day by Professor Trevor Ling of Manchester University (see *Statesman*, Calcutta Edition, 30/1/84).
2. Lecture delivered, on the occasion of the bicentenary celebrations of Asiatic Society, Calcutta, by the noted British historian and a former Director of School of Oriental and African Studies, London, C.H. Philips (vide *Statesman*, Calcutta edition, 16/1/84).
3. Marshall, Indian Epics have no Historical Basis, *Statesman*, Calcutta, 15/1/84. It may be noted that the main initiative for the foundation of the society came from distinguished persons of Great Britain and Scotland.
4. See M. Yoshimasha, On the resemblance of Indian, Chinese and Japanese Mathematics, *Arhat Vacana*, March, 1990, Vol. 2, No. 2, Indore.
5. Conflicting opinions about the relation between the mathematicians of Greece, particularly Pythogoras, and to India have been discussed by G.N. Banerji in *Hellenism in Ancient India*, p. 180 ff.

6. History of Mathematics.
7. About him, see E.S. Kennedy, *Dictionary of Scientific Biography*, Vol. II; E.C. Sachau, *Indo-Conversant Arabische* etc.; S.K. Chatterjee, *Al Beruni Comm. Vol.*; J. Gonda, *Remarks*. Al Beruni's quotations from Sanskrit texts, ibid.
8. See Calcutta daily (Bengali), *Ānandabājār Patrikā*, 18.7.79.
9. R.N. Rai, Brahmagupta's works and Their Influence in and outside India, *Proc. of First International Sanskrit Conference*, Vol. II, pt. 2.
10. D.E. Smith, *History of Mathematics*, 1912, vol. I, p. 145.
11. Yavaneśvara and Utpala, *JBBRAS*, 30, pts. 1-2 pp. 1-8.
12. W.W. Tarn, *Greeks in Bactria and India*, pp. 313-14, 380-81, 390-91.
13. Bennet's English Translation of Odes, 2/17/ Lines 17-24.
14. See D.M. Bose and others *op.cit.*, p. 261, for a list of medical topics found in common in *Āyurveda* and the Tibetan medical system.
15. D.M. Bose and others, *op.cit.*, p. 262.
16. See Liyanaratne, J. : Indian Medicine in Śrī Laṅkā, *Bulletin de l' Ecole Francaise de Extreme Orient*, 1987, Vol. Lxxvi, Paris.
17. Bose, D.M. & others, *A Concise History of Science in India*, p. 260.
18. J. Filliozat, Les Gajaśāstras et les auteurs Grees, *Journal Asiatique*, 222, 164-75, Paris, 1933.
19. D.M. Bose and others, *op. cit.*, p. 273.
20. A.B. Keith, *History of Sanskrit Literature*, 1920, p. 509.
21. D.M. Bose and others., *op. cit.*, p. 261.
22. J. Filliozat, Les Gajaśāstra, etc. *Jour. Asiatique*, 222, 164-74, Paris, 1933, pp. 194-95.
23. *The Wonder that was India*, 1971, p. 502.
24. *American Historical Review*, April, 1960, p. 516.
25. Needham, *Science and Civilization in China*, IV. 282.
26. Clebert, *The Gypsies*, p. 195.
27. H. Kuhn, *Germanische Kunst der Völkerwanderving.*
28. Vide *Vimāna in Ancient India*, Calcutta.
29. See N.C. Sinha, Sanskrit Across the Himalayas, *Proceedings of First International Sanskrit Conference*, vol. II, pt. 1; K.K. Roy, Sanskrit and the Indo-Tibetan Languages, *Ibid.*; F.W. Thomas, *Indian Studies in Honour of C. Lanman*; J.K. Balvir, *L'Histoire de Rāma en Tibetana*, etc.

30. The influence of the *Manusaṃhitā* in this country has been discussed in connection with Law.
31. L. Sternbach, General Appeal of Subhāṣita Literature in Sanskrit, *Proceedings of First International Sanskrit Conference,* II, pt. 1.
32. The influence of the *Manusaṃhitā* in this country has been discussed in the Section on Law.
33. Edited, with translation and Notes, by S. Levi, Delhi, 1957.
34. *Ibid.*, 1958.
35. Edited S. Rani, with notes, Delhi, 1961.
36. See *Sanskrit Texts From Bali,* ed. S. Levi, Fragments of the Sanskrit *Gāyatrī* incantation have also been found: The Kidung literature of Jāvā (partly chronology and partly historical romance) bears witness to Sanskrit influence.
37. Highly polished Javanese language. In it, as in Sanskrit dictionaries, Sanskrit synonyms of selected words are written.
38. It stands for a poetical composition in Javanese.
39. Ed., with Dutch translation, by A. Teeuw, The Hague, 1950.
40. K. Motwani, *Manu Dharmaśāstra,* p. 313.
41. *Ibid.*, p. 322.
42. Tjok Rai Sudharta, Sanskrit in Bali, *Proceedings of the First International Sanskrit Conference,* Vol. I, pt. 1; J. Filliozat, Sanskrit as a link language, *Proceedings of the First International Sanskrit Conference,* II, pt. 1.
43. C. Sarapadnuke, Sanskrit and Thailand, *Proceedings of First International Sanskrit Conference,* II, pt. 1.
44. P. Lajanich, Some observations about the Thāi translations of *Kathāsaritsāgara* and narrative Literature of Ancient India, *Summaries of Papers, Fifth World Sanskrit Conference,* Vārānasi, 1981, p. 212.
45. L. Sternbach, General Appeal of *Subhāṣitas* in Sanskrit Literature, *Proceedings of First International Sanskrit Conference,* II, pt. 1; E. Lorgeou, Suphasit Siamois, *Bulletin de 1' Athenee Oriental,* 1881, 1882.
46. R.C. Majumdar, Study of Sanskrit in South-East Asia, *Proceedings of First International Sanskrit Conference,* I. pt. 1; L. Sternbach, General Appeal of Subhāṣitas in Sanskrit Literature, *Ibid.*, II, pt. 1; H.B. Sarkar, *Cultural Relations Between India and South-East Asian Countries.*
47. A kind of sacrifice in which all the possessions of the sacrificer have to be given away as sacrificial fee.

48. R.C. Majumdar, Study of Sanskrit in S.E. Asia, *Proceedings of First International Sanskrit Conference,* I, pt. 1.
49. Murshidābād in West Bengal.
50. R.C. Majumdar, Study of Sanskrit in South -East Asia, *Proceedings of the First International Sanskrit Conference,* I, Pt. 1; L. Sternbach, General Appeal of *Subhāṣitas* in Sanskrit Literature, *Ibid.*; L. Finot, Recherches de la literature Laotienne, *BEFEO,* 22.6.
51. J.R. Fransisco, The Philippines and India, Indian Influence in the Philippines, Sanskrit in Philippines Language and Literature, *Proceedings of First International Sanskrit Conference,* II, Pt. 1.
52. O.H. De, A. Wijesekera, Sanskrit and Sinhalese Literature, *Proceedings of First International Sanskrit Conference,* II, Pt. 1; Paññāsāra, Sanskrit Literature extant among the Sinhalese: *Epigraphia Zeylonica* vol. II, p. 168; Vol. III, p. 154; History of Ceylon (University of Ceylon), Vol. I, Pt. 1, pp. 42 f.
53. K. Motwani, *Manu Dharmaśāstra,* p. 232.
54. See Suzuki, *Essays in Zen Buddhism,* 2nd Series, 1933, p. 187.
55. *Pi-yen* means "Green Rock". *Chi* means 'collection', and *Lu* record. Green Rock was the name of Yüan-wu's study.
56. *Ibid.*
57. For influence of Sanskrit in Japan, vide H. Kimura, Sanskrit Studies in Japan, *Journal of Oriental Research,* Madras, 1956-57.
58. J.W. De, Jong, An old Tibetan Version of the *Rāmāyaṇa, Proceedings of First International Sanskrit Conference,* II, *Ibid.*; L. Sternbach, General Appeal of Subhāṣitas in Sanskrit Literature, *Proceedings of First International Sanskrit Conference,* II, pt. 1.
59. See, H.W. Bailey, *Khotanese Buddhist Texts,* Cambridge, 1981 (2nd ed.).
60. M. Moghegh, *Pañcatantra* in Persian and Arabic Literature, *Proceedings of First International Sanskrit Conference,* II, pt. 2; S. H. R. J. Naini, Influence of Sanskrit on Persian Literature and Thinking, *Ibid.*; H.L. Chopra, Sanskrit Classics in Persian, *Ibid.*; M. Majoub's Detailed Discussion About *Kalila* and *Dimna* has been published in Teheran, 1349, Hizri era; S.M. Fazullah, Persian translation of Sanskrit Works etc., *Proceedings of First International Sanskrit Conference,* II, pt. 2; B.D. Verma, Persian Translation of *Gītāsāra,* Ibid.

61. M . Moghegh's aforesaid article.
62. P. Aalto, Sanskrit and Mongol Language and Literature; *Proceedings of First International Sanskrit Conference*, II, Pt. 1; R.R. Mongolia, Śāntideva's *Bodhicaryāvatāra* and Mongolian Everlasting Songs, *Ibid.*
63. The other name is *Gulshān-I-Ibrāhimi*, Its English translation by Briggs is entitled *The History of the Rise of the Muhammadan power in India.*
64. S.M. Fazullāh, Persian translation of Sanskrit Works, *Proceedings of First International Sanskrit Conference*, II, pt. 2.
65. Ibn Al Nadim has given, in his work *Fihrist* (988 A.D.), a list of the Arabic translations of different Indian works.
66. P. Aalto, Sanskrit and Mongol Language and Literature, *Proceedings of First International Sanskrit Conference*, II, pt. 1; R. Mongolia, Śāntideva's *Bodhicaryāvatāra* and Mongolian Everlasting Songs, *Ibid.*
67. For the study of Sanskrit literature in England and other European countries, see Gaurānga Sengupta, *Videśīya, Bhārat-Vidyā-Pathik*; S.C. Banerjee, *A Companion To Sanskrit Literature*, 1989, Appendix II.
68. K. Motwani, Manu and the Modern World, *Proceedings of First International Sanskrit Conference*, II, pt. 2.
69. K. Motwani, Manu and the Modern World, *Proceedings of First International Sanskrit Conference*, II, pt. 2.
70. In this philosophy, only objects of sense are recognised and all kinds of supersensuous things are denied. According to this doctrine, the universal man is the sole deity to be worshipped.
71. Eitel, *Three Lectures on Buddhism*, 1884, p. 3.
72. Rādhākrishnān, *Eastern Religions and Western Thought*, p.138, fn. 1.
73. *Legacy of India*, 1937, p. 5.
74. *Greek Thinkers*, Vol. I, p. 127.
75. See Bethlenfalvy, *India in Hungarian Learning and Literature*, p. 5.
76. His biography was written by the Hungarian scholar, Theodore Duka (1825-1908), and published both in English (*Life and Works of Alexander Csoma de Koros*, London, 1885) and Hungarian, 1884).
77. Quotations taken from *India in Hungarian Learning and Literature* by Bethlenfalvy, p. 11.

78. See Bethlenfalvy, *India in Hungarian Learning and Literature*, p. 13.
79. Vide Oesterley's notes in his German version of *Baitāl Pachisi*, Garsin de Tassy in *Jour. des Savans*, 1836, p. 415; Dr. Köhler, *Orient und Occident*, II.
80. See Banerji, *Hellenism in Ancient India.*
81. For details, see Bongard Levin and Vigasin, The Image of India.
82. To be distinguished from the artist, N. Roerich.
83. On Rabindranāth and Russia, see A.P.G. Danilchuk, *Bhārat, Rabindranāth O Soviet Union* (in Bengali), Calcutta, 1395 Bengali era; Rabindranāth, *Rāśiyār Ciṭhi* (in Bengali).
84. Vide A.P.G. Danilchuk's article on this Indologist, published in the Bengali weekly *Desh*, Calcutta, 5.5.90.
85. For a list of some types of Indo-European folk-tales which probably migrated from India westward, see G.N. Banerjee, *Hellenism in Ancient India.* Mulk Rāj Ānand writes (The *Talegraph*, daily newspaper, Calcutta, 14/9/90 as follows: No honest critic will deny that India gave the tale, the short story, the parable and proverb to the world.
86. Exists in four versions, one attributed to each of the following persons : Śivadāsa, Jambhaladatta and Vallabhadasa and an unknown author. According to Hertel, Śivadāsa's version did not originate long before 1487 A.D. Vide Oesterley, *Baitāl Pacisi*, pp. 185-187.
87. I-Ken, Touti Nameh, Eine......Märchen von Nchschebi, 1882, pp. 17, 89.
88. Rosen.
89. For the spread of the story in different parts of Europe, see Chauvin, viii. 194-196; Dawkins and Halliday, *Modern..... in Asia Minor*, pp. 253, 254, 523; Coxwell, *Siberian and other Folktales*, pp. 768, 775, 880; A.H. Krappe, The Legend of Amicus and Anelius, *Modern Language Review*, xv, 923, pp. 152-161.
90. About this, see G. Mallery, *Introduction to the Study of Sign Language*, Washington, 1880. Also see Kauṭilīya *Arthaśāstra*, I, xi, 21, xii, xiii, II, xxvii, 43.
91. Vide Penzer, p. 21.
92. Vide Penzer, p. 122.
93. Vide Burton, vol. vi, p. 127. Similar idea occurs in two more stories, viz. Tale of Kumār, al-Zaman and History of Gharib and his brother Ajib.

94. Vide Gibb, *History of Forty Vezirs,* 1886 (in Turkey it is known a Quira Vezir Tārikhi). The title of the English version of the Story is the story of the Forty Morns and Eves.
95. *Irañianism,* p. 34.
96. This is the common rendering of *Śūnyavāda.* Nihilism means denial of all existence. But, *Śūnyavāda* actually denies only the phenomenal world and not all realities. Behind the phenomenal world, there is a reality which canot be described.
97. *The Message of Plato,* pp. 13-14.
98. Ranade's Writings - see *History of Philosophy : Eastern and Western,* I, 37.
99. T. Gompez, *Greek Thinkers,* I. 206-207.
100. E.J. Urwick, *The Message of Plato,* p. 14.
101. *Ibid.* pp. 27-28.
102. Plato, *Republic,* III, IV, 412-27.
103. Filliozat, *Revue de l' Histoire des Religions,* 1945, 59-91; *Les Relations Exterieures de l' inde,* 1956, pp. 31-60.
104. Goodwin, *The Great Mystics,* p. 27.
105. Rādhākrishnan, *Eastern Religions* etc., p. 200.
106. Epiphanius, *Life of Manas.*
107. More persons than one of this name are known. The Nāgārjuna, who was exponent of Mādhyamika philosophy, is believed to have flourished about the 2nd cent. A.D.
108. In this connection, also see the section entitled Cultural Contact.
109. *Eastern Religions and Western Thought,* p. 116.
110. For the significance of this *mantra,* see Exploration in Tibet (CU) by Prajñānānanda; *Blue Annals,* G. Roerich, Calcutta, 1954, pp. 40 ff.
111. *History of Buddhism in India and Tibet* (Obermiller), p. 170; *Blue Annals,* (pp. 187 f.) tells us that as many as twelve monastic schools were established in the province of Khams.
112. The districts of Peshawar and Rāwālpindi, in Pakistan.
113. Designation of several lands in the Far East.
114. A particular mode of sitting in religious meditation.
115. Built by Sūryavarman II in the city of Angkorthom in Kambuja Kingdom.
116. S. Levi, *Sanskrit Texts from Bali.*
117. Rādhākrishnan, *Eastern Religions and Western Thought,* 1940, p. 158 and f.n. 3.

118. C. Lal, *India and Japan*, p. 48.
119. See Amitābha Chakraborty's article, entitled Koriyā upadvīpe bhāratasabhyatā, published in *Ānandabājār Patrikā*, 14/10/84 A.D.
120. *Numismatic Chronicles*, 1893, pp. 126-127, p. 1. x, fig. 2.
121. Vidiśā (Bhilsā).
122. R.C. Majumdar, *Advanced History of India*, 1982, p. 136.
123. Harnack, *History of Dogma*, i, 1894, p. 229.
124. Apollonius of Tyana, trs. Phillimore, 1912, Book iii, chs. 10 and 50.
125. W. King, *The Gnostics and their Remains*, Ancient and Medieval, 2 nd. ed., 1887, p. xiv.
126. Rādhākrishnan, *Eastern Religions and Western Thought*, 1940, p. 207, f.n.
127. *Ibid.*, p. 208.
128. *Ibid.*
129. C.H. Gordon, *Before the Bible*, p. 238.
130. *The Platonic Tradition in English Religious Thought*, 1926, pp. 7, 9.
131. *Humanism and Technic in Greek Studies*, 1936, p. 11.
132. *Political Thought*, 1939, p. 7.
133. In it the *Anāmikā* (ring finger) and *Kaniṣthā* (little finger) are turned upwards, curved and apart from each other. Vide *Saṅgītaratnākara* (of Śārṅgadeva), Nartanādhyāya, verse 134.
134. D.A. Mackenzie, *Myths of Pre-Columbian America*, p. 58.
135. P. Kirchoff, *Sibretiro del, XXXV Congress International de Americanistas*, p. 88.
136. *History of Christianity*, 1867, Vol. II, p. 41.
137. The doctrine of the followers of this view are called Gnostic; they may be called the advocates of the doctrine of knowledge. Scott, in his *Hermetica* (1924, I, p. 14) says that the fundamental doctrine of this school is this - blessed are those whose mind is pure; because they alone shall see God.
138. *Egypt and Israel*, 1923, p. 113.
139. In the second century from the rise of Islam (in the sixth century), a class of saints or peoples, fond of solitude, was called Sufi. 'Suf' means wool. Most of these people generally used to wear woollen garments. Hence, they were called Sufi.
140. R.C. Zachner, *Hindu and Muslim Mysticism*, pp. 93-94.

141. Regulation of breath as an accessory of *Yoga*. It is threefold: *Pūraka* (inhalution), *Kumbhaka* (holding or restraint of breath) and *Recaka* (exhalation).
142. D.M. Long, *The Wisdom of Balahvar*, pp. 24-29.
143. N. Notovitch, *Jesus Christ*.
144. Rādhākrishnan, *Eastern Religions and Western Thought*, 1940, p. 152.
145. Assignment of the different parts of the body, to different deities, which is usually accompanied by prayers and corresponding gesticulations including the touching of some parts of the body.
146. Rādhākrishnan, *Eastern Religions and Western Thought*, p. 158, f.n. 2. As evidences, he has mentioned the two works. E.A.W. Budge, *Barlam and Yewasef ... Buddha and Bodhisattva*, 1923; Takakusu, *I-tsing*, 1896, p. 224.
147. Rādhākrishnan, *Eastern Religions and Western Thought*, 1940, pp. 203-204.
148. Kennedy, The Gospels of the Infancy, *J.R.A.S.*, 1917, pp. 210, 212.
149. For a comparative estimate of Buddhism and Christianity, see Chaishin Yu, *Early Buddhism and Christianity*, Delhi, 1896.
150. *Journal of Pāli Text Society*, 1923, pp. 43-44.
151. Obligations of the New Testament to Buddhism, *Nineteenth Century*, 1880, p. 975; A.J. Edmunds, *Buddhists and Christian Gospels*, 1908.
152. For detaits, see Chaishin Yu, *Early Buddhism and Christianity*.
153. *History of Buddhism in India and Tibet*, Obermiller, 1932, II, pp. 183-184.
154. *Blue Annals*, Roerich, 1954, p. 40.
155. Obermiller, *History of Buddhism in India and Tibet*, 1932, II, pp. 183-184.
156. Archal doorway, portals.
157. Angkor Vat temple is in the city of Angkor Thom which was the capital of Cambodia.
158. *Etudes d'Orientalisme* : *L'Art Pāla* etc., p. 282
159. *Ibid.*, p. 284
160. *Vide MLBD News-letter*, a monthly Indological Bibliography published by Motilal Banarsidass, Delhi, January, 1990.
161. Vide Amitābha Chakraborty's article, Koriyā Upadvīpe Bhāratsabhyatā (Bengali), *Ānanda Bājār Patrikā*, 14/10/84 A.D.

162. Name of a particular style of architecture and arts. This style prevailed in Roman Europe in the period between 1050-1200 A.D. with massive vaulting and round arches.
163. J. Bowle, *A. New Outline of World History.*
164. See *Mystic India*, Tokyo, 1937; J. Appasamy, *A Vision of India*, Delhi, 1979; Bethlenfalvy, A *Painter's Pilgrimage*, Delhi, 1979.
165. *Charles Fabri, his Life and Works* by Bethlenfalvy, reported to have been in press.
166. Vide his paper, Mathurā of the Gods, *Marg*, 1954.
167. *Marg*, 1955.
168. Published in Year Books, 1964, 1966, 1967, 1969, 1971.
169. See S.K. Chatterji, *India and Ethiopia*, p. 20.
170. *History of Architecture*, I, 142-3
171. *India and Ethiopia*, p. 28.
172. Vide his paper, Indian und abessinen, *op. cit.*, p. 407.
173. *India and Ethiopia*, p. 49.
174. Also written as Axum The Centre of Ethiopian State and its culture. Ethiopia of to-day.
175. It is interesting to note that, according to the *Lalitavistara*, there were 64 forms of writing in India.
176. *Indian Epigraphy*, pp. 202-204.
177. Vide *JASB* (Letters) Vol. I, 1935, No. 1.
178. For details, see H.B. Sarkar, *Cultural Relations between India and S.E. Asian Countries*, pp. 168 f.f.
179. From Chinese sources we learn that it was founded by a Brāhmaṇa, named Kauṇḍinya, in the first century A.D.
180. Perhaps written by one of the Indian Brāhmaṇas who lived in this region since the first century A.D.
181. Vide Banerji, *Hellenism in Ancient India*, p. 214.
182. Zoroastrian scriptures.
183. See the Section on India and Tibet.
184. H. Spitzbardt, The Lexical and Morphological Impact of Sanskrit on Modern Indonesian, *Proc. of First Int. Skt.. Conf.*, II, pt. 1.
185. H. Spitzbardt, Sanskrit Loan-words in Bahasa Indonesia, *Journal of Oriental Research*, Madras, XXXVI, 1970.
186. Literally seed. Technically it indicates certain cryptic and monosyllabic sounds like *hūm*, *hrīm*, etc.
187. Originally Persian.
188. Persian.

189. Arabic.
190. Originally Persian.
191. Originally Arabic.
192. Originally Persian.
193. Portuguese Janella.
194. Persian.
195. The language of the Incas of Peru.
196. M. Poindexter, *The Aryan-Incas*, II, p. 118. For the influence of Sanskrit and Tāmil on the Quechuya language, see *Journal of Asiatic Society*, Vol XXIX, No. 3, p. 20.
197. It is interesting to note that to a poet Pāṇini some verses are attributed in the anthologies (e.g. *Saduktikarnamrta.)*
198. R.C. Majumdar, Study of Sanskrit in S.E. Asia, *Pro. of First International Sanskrit Conf.*, I, pt. 1.
199. C. Navawonga, Sanskrit words in the Thai Language, *Proc. of First Int. Skt. Conf.*, II, pt. 1.
200. For details, see Bongard-Levin and Vigasin, *The Image of India*, Ch. VI (Anc. Indian Civilisation in the light of new archaeological excavations in Soviet Central Asia).
201. *Blue Annals*, pp. 34-39, 142; *History of Buddhism in India and Tibet*, p. 187.
202. For his life and activities, see *Journal of Asiatic Soc. of Bengal*, 1881, p. 8; *The Book of Great Liberation* (Evans Wanz), pp. 182 ff.
203. For a list of the various works, translated into Tibetan, see *The Indian Nītiśāstra in Tibet* (S.K. Pathak), pp. 98 ff.
204. *History of Buddhism in India and Tibet*, II, pp. 191 ff.; Petech *Study of the Chronicles of Ladakh*, p. 7.
205. S.K. Ray, *Pre-historic India and Ancient Egypt*; S.M. El. Mansouri, *Art-culture of India and Egypt.*
206. *Orations*, XXXII, 373.
207. *Hellados periegists*, III. 12, IV. 34, VII. 29.
208. *Ikebana* (Japanese flower-arrangement) is well-known throughout the world.
209. The account of the Buddha's *Mahānirvāṇa* and the burning of his corpse which the Chinese pilgrim, Huining prepared at the place, called Ho-ling, with the assistance of Juavadra, is different from that according to Mahāyāna. See H.B. Sarkar, *Cultural Relations between India and South-East Countries*, p. 224.
210. I-tsing, *A Record etc.* (Trs. Takakusu), p. XXIV.

211. Pelliot, *Le Fou-Nan*, pp. 261-262.
212. R.C. Majumdar, Holy Kurukshetra in Laos, *Journal of Asiatic Society*, vols. 34-35, Bombay, 22-25.
213. *Cultural Relations between India and South-East Asian Countries*, p. 119.
214. *South-East Asian Review*, II, 1977, p. 36; Barth and Bergaigne, *Inscriptions Sanscrits ... Cambodge*, no. XVIII, DOST. XIV-XV, p. 156.
215. Coedes, *Inscriptions du Cambodge*, IV, p. 27.
216. *Ibid.*, p. 58.
217. Barth and Bergaigne, *Inscriptions Sanscrites de Champa et du Cambodge* (complete ed.), p. 421.
218. Text and trs. in Wheatley, *The Golden Khersonese*, pp. 26 ff.
219. R. Winstedt, *Malaya and its History*. pp. 26-7.
220. Wheatley , *The Golden Khersonese*, pp. 26-30, 48, 51; Coedes, *Indianized States*, p. 294, notes 112-117.
221. H.B. Sarkar, *Corpus of the Inscriptions of Java*, II, No. LXX, p. B. 6-7.
222. *Ibid.*, l, No. 1
223. H.B. Sarkar, *Journal of Indian History*, 1973 (identification of the image etc.).
224. Brandes-Krom, Old Javansche Workonden.... Vol. 60 (1913).
225. Th. Pigeaud's translation, entitled Java in the fourteenth century, Vol. III.
226. Wales, Siamese State Ceremonies.
227. Marquis d' Hervey de Saint-Denis, *Ethnographic* (trs.), pp. 422, 425. This account was penned nearly eight hundred years after the destruction (3rd cent. A.D.) of Tunsun, a city-state of Mālay.
228. Report of the British Association, 1894, p. 774—On the diffusion of Mythical Beliefs.
229. Arnold and Frost, *The American Egypt*.
230. This museum plans to participate in the Calcutta Tercentenary celebrations by bringing the exhibition of Yankee Traders and Indian Merchants to India later in 1990.
231. Vide article, entitled The American connections, published in the daily newspaper, *Telegraph*, dated 17.3.90.
232. *Ibid.*
233. Abhedānanda, *India and Her People*, pp. 216-221.

234. About him, see Dipaṃkar Sen's article, Iuropīya Saṃgīte bhāratcarcā, *Ānandabājār Patrikā*, Agrahāyaṇa 18, 1390 B.S.
235. Garratt, *The Legacy of India.*
236. Derrett, The origin of the Laws of Kandyans, *University of Ceylon Review*, October, 1956.
237. Majumdar, *Inscriptions of Kamboja*, no. 66.
238. E. G., *Inscriptions du Cambodge*, ed. Coedes, IV. 127, VI. 289A.
239. *Inscriptions du Cambodge* (Coedes), II. 130.
240. Coedes, *The Making of South-East Asia*, p. 223.
241. *Recherches... Cambodiennes.*
242. Account of the Liang Dynasty (502-557) by Yao Ssu-Lien (d. 637 A.D.).
243. Mi-Son Stele Inscription (1081 A.D.), R.C. Majumdar, *Champa*, II, no. 62.
244. *Sāma* (conciliation), *Dāna* (gift), *Bheda* (dissension), *Daṇḍa* (war). Vide *Manusmṛti*, VII. 109.
245. According to Manu (VIII. 4-7) *Ṛṇādāna* (non-repayment of debt), *Nikṣepa* (deposit), *Asvāmivikraya* (sale by one not being the owner), *Sambhūya-samutthāna* (partnership business), *Dattasyānapākarma* (non-delivery of a promised thing) *Vetanādāna* (non-payment of wages), *Saṃvid Vyatikrama* (violation of contract); *Kraya-vikrayānūśaya* (repentance after purchase or sale), *Svāmipālavivāda* (quarrel between the master and keeper of animals), *Sīmā-vivāda* (boundary dispute), *Daṇḍa pāruṣya* (too severe punishment), *Vākpārūṣya* (abuse), *Steya* (theft), *Sāhasa* (violenee), *Strī-saṃgrohaṇa* (adultery with women), *Strīpuṃ-dharma* (reciprocal Duties of women and men), *Vibhāga* (partition of inheritance), *Dyūta* (gambling), *Samāhvaya* (animal-betting).
246. Majumdar, *op. cit.*, no. 81.
247. *Agnida* (incendiary), *garada* (poisoner), *śastrapāṇi* (one approaching with a lethal weapon in hand), *dhanāpaha* (stealer of an amount of money which, being stolen, leads to the starvation of the owner), *kṣetrāpahāri* (stealer of one's productive land), *dārāpahārī* (one who abducts another's wife).
248. Hooykaas, *Journal of Greater India Society*, IXV. 34 f.f.
249. *The Malayas : A Cultural History*, p. 91.
250. *Sāma* (conciliation), *Dāna* (gift), *Bheda* (dissension), *Daṇḍa* (punishment, war). See Manu VII. 159 and comm. thereon.

251. *Sandhi* (treaty of peace), *Vigraha* (war), *Yāna* (march, expedition), *Āsana* (indifference, wait and see policy), *Dvaidhībhāva* (splitting the army into two; according to some, duplicity), *Saṃśraya* (alliance with a powerful king). Manu VII 160.
252. Saletore, *Ancient Indian Political Thought and Institution,* pp. 191-290.
253. About this, see our observations under chronology.
254. K. Motwani, Manu and the Modern World, *Proc. of First International Sanskrit Conference,* II, pt. 2.
255. *Ibid.*
256. Rostovtzeff, *Cambridge History of India,* VII, 154.
257. S.C. Banerji, *A Companion to Sanskrit Literature,* 2nd ed., pp. 768 f.f.
258. It means a thing having four limbs. Chess has been so called after the army in ancient India, consisting of four wings, i.e. *Hastin* (elephant), *Aśva* (horse), *Ratha* (chariot) and *Padāti* (infantry). In the game, as current in India, the *Ratha* is called *Naukā.* In English, these are called Bishop, Knight, Rook and pawn respectively. These four are accessories to the king who is called *Rājā* in India. He has a Minister called *Mantri* in India and Queen in English.
259. According to Norman Brown, one John Hamilton introduced it in America in the 1860s. Vide *India and Indology,* ed. R.Rocher, 1978, p. 302.
260. R.C. Majumdar, *Inscriptions of Kambuja.*
261. H.B. Sarkar, *Cultural Relations between India and South-East Asian Countries,* p. 273.
262. See *Ind. Ant.* VI, p. 122.
263. English Newspaper *Statesman,* Calcutta, 6.2.82, p. 3.
264. A red and black berry of the shrub of the name.
265. S. Purchas, *Purchas his Pilgrims,* III, pp. 508-9.
266. Sanskrit meets the Computer, article published in the newspaper, *Telegraph,* Calcutta, 29.7.89.

CHAPTER V

Foreign Influence in India

In a previous chapter, we have seen that, from the very dawn of civilisation, India had been connected, in various ways, with the outside world. Ever since the pre-historic times, she had contact with various countries of Asia, Europe and Africa. The connection with America also may be inferred. The media, through which this contact was established, have been separately dealt with in one chapter. In various aspects of culture, India exercised influence in foreign countries throughout the ages. This influence was, however, not a one-way traffic. India, too, was influenced by foreign thoughts in various ways. In some cases, this influence was directly perceived and, in others, inferential. In many matters, striking similarity between India and other countries is noticed. But, in all cases, the relation of lender and borrower cannot be determined. In this chapter, we shall deal with the impact of foreign countries on India under the following heads :

1. World of ideas, literature, language, religion,
2. Science and Technology,
3. Music,
4. Sculpture,
5. Architecture,
6. Painting,
7. Coins and inscriptions,
8. Politics and Statecraft,
9. Miscellaneous.

WORLD OF IDEAS ETC.

In the domain of ideas, the debt of India to the foreign countries is uncommon, and is not repayable. The thought-currents, which flowed from Persia, China, Greece, Rome, etc., were merged in the ocean of the ideas of India.

The influence of Islam in India is not negligible. This religion recognises the unity of God, and decries idolatry and caste-distinction. This engendered among the Indians a mental attitude which was favourable for the propagation of Sufism, and love alone has been recognised as of the greatest importance. People of many low classes, who suffered from repression in the Hindu society, got an escape in Islam to which they were converted. The ferment, created by the contempt, with which the Muslims looked upon caste-distinction and idolatry, went some way in strengthening the *Bhakti* cult among the Hindus. Consequently, earnest devotion of *Bhakti* came to be admitted as the way to the happiness of life. *Bhakti* cult, of course, arose in South India centuries before Islam. Under the influence of Islam, this doctrine perhaps got a fillip and spread in North India. Islam may have had some role behind the preachings of Caitanya (1485-1533) about the glory of love and devotion. He had disciples both among the Hindus and the Muslims. He laid greater stress on *Bhakti* than on caste-distinction; in other words, in his philosophy, devotion transcended the difference between castes. *Caṇḍālo' pi dvijaśreṣṭhaḥ hari-bhakti-parāyaṇaḥ* (even a Caṇḍāla, devoted to Hari, is superior to one of *dvija* class (Brāhmaṇa, Kṣatriya and Vaiśya; generally Brāhmaṇa) — this declaration of Caitanya, perhaps, dissuaded some people of the so-called low classes from embracing Islam. An attitude of syncretism of Hinduism and Islam is clear in the teachings of Kabīr (*c.* 1440-1518), Dādū, Nānak, etc. Kabīr was opposed to idol-worship and ritualistic practices. At present, several lacs of Indians are followers of Kabīr. To this school belong the sect called *Satnāmī* and the followers of Dādū. Nānak (1469-1539) tried to effect a fusion of Hinduism and Islam in the one religion called Sikhism. In doing so, he looked upon religious attitude as more important than religious practices. His religion was free from idolatry, difference of castes, communalism, etc. He used to believe in one God, Rāmānanda used to exhort his disciples of all castes; among his disciples were cultivators, tanners, barbers and Muslim weavers. All of them used to dine together.

Some scholars, notably S.K. Chatterji, think that there was Sufi[1] influence on the medieval religious life of India. This influence was felt also in the organisation of the monastic life of certain Indian Vaiṣṇava sects.[2] S.K. Chatterji observes, "Iranian Sufism brought some new literary and mystical atmosphere and ideology in some of the Vaiṣṇava *Bhakti* scholars of India, and these were assimilated within Indian religion".[3]

Sufism became so popular in India that many Sufis permanently settled in this country. Mansur Al Hallaj (858-911) was one of the early Sufis who came to India. Al Hujuri (d. 1072) was the oldest of the Sufis who settled in India. Adherents of different religions held him in high esteem. Mainuddin Chisti came from Central Asia in *c.* 1192 A.D., and founded the Chisti sect or school. Many people assemble at his graveyard in Ājmer every year to pay their heartfelt respects to his departed soul.

The currency of Persian, Hindi and Urdu in India is an evidence of the co-existence of Hindus and Muslims is this country. Urdu began to be written in Arabic. The Muslims, Āmir Khusro, Jāysi, etc. wrote Hindi poems. Enlightened Muslims like Ālāol produced Bengali literature in literary Bengali. The Hindu and Muslim rulers provided the impetus for the development of Indo-Islam culture and literature. The evidence of the patronage, extended by the Muslims to scholars irrespective of community, is furnished by the Bengali version of the *Mahābhārata,* written at the instance of Nāsir Shāh (1285-1325) of Gauḍ, and the Bengali rendering of the *Bhagavadgītā* by Mālādhar Vasu at the direction of Husain Shāh (1493-1519). In South India, the Kutubshāhi and Ādilshāhi rulers actively helped in the development of the local language and literature.

Iran influenced Indian theology also in some respects. The Middle Iranian form *Mihr* (denoting Sun) was imported into India by the Iranian Magas (Magi) or priests. The name was Indianised, and became Mihira in Sanskrit. The Iranian Mihr appeared in India as accompanied by his son Raevant who was adopted in Hindu theology as Revanta, God of the Chase. It is interesting to note that the deities, in Indian iconography, are represented as barefooted. But Sūrya, in a composite Indo-Iranian iconography, in the period following the advent of Mihr (Mihira), was dressed as an Indian prince with short waist-cloth and jewels on his body; he put on top-boots, particularly in the North Indian images. This is due to Iranian influence. Iranian Mihr was depicted as a Persian horseman with top-boots.

In the wake of the Muslim domination in Persia, Islam became widespread; so much so that, under its powerful impact, the local religion, Zoroastrianism, suffered to a great extent. In fact, it was all but effaced there. At this juncture, a large number of Parsis migrated to India in about 936 A.D. They brought with them the sacred fire of ancient Iran. They built a temple for it in India. After passing through many adverse circumstances, they succeeded in establishing the fire at Udwada, a small town about eight miles north of Bombay. Gradually, the Parsi community grew in size. The reason of the survival of this small community in an alien soil is that the Parsis remained true to the teachings of Zoroaster, and did not give up their distinct identity as a religious group.

According to Hopkins (*Religion in India*), Śaivite phallic worship began in India due to late Greek influence. Christians claim that, in the regime of Indo-Parthian king, Gondophernes or Gondophares (reign sometime between 20 and 48 A.D.), this religion reached the frontiers of this country. Kāndāhār, Kābul and Takṣasilā were included in the kingdom of this ruler. A Christian tradition has it that, having come to visit this kingdom, St. Thomas, an exponent of Christianity, died a martyr.

Though the precise time of the advent of the Jews in India is not known, still it may be said that, in the beginning of the Christian era, the Jews got an asylum in Cochin. They were followed by the unknown Christian missionaries who were either merchant adventures or migrants from the region of the Red Sea and Persian Gulf. In the history of the Christian influx into South India, three seaports played a great role. These are Canganore and Goa on the west coast and Tranquebar on the east. Maritime trade connected these ports with west Asia and beyond. Christianity ramified in all directions from the above ports. The three streams, viz. Syrian, Roman Catholic Church and the Protestant contributed to the spread of this religion.

The aforesaid St. Thomas (Mar Thoma), a Syrian Christian, is said to have established several Churches on the Mālābār coast, and converted many Indians. It appears that, unable to stand persecution that started in Persia, Christians from Persia and Mesopotamia migrated to Mālābār in 345 A.D. Gradually, they built up a Christian colony. Definite historical evidence is available about the existence of a Church in South India in the sixth century A.D.

In the closing years of the sixteenth century, the Syrian church had to promise allegiance to the Roman Church. In courses of time, in the nineteenth century, the Syrian Christians came to be divided into the following groups:

1. Romo-Syrians - owing allegiance to the Pope of Rome.
2. Jacobite Orthodox Syrians - owing allegiance to the Jacobite Patriarch of Antioch.
3. Mar Thoma Syrians - Organised into a Church absolutely independent of foreign control.
4. Chaldean Syrians - under the jurisdiction of Nestorian 'Catholics of the East'.
5. Members of the Church of South India until recently closely connected with western churches.

Western missions like the Carmelites, London Missionary Society, Church Missionary Society, Basel Mission rendered invaluable service to the people of Mālābār by promoting literacy, raising the status of women and encouraging cottage industries irrespective of caste and creed. The Church of Mālābār contributed a lot to the growth of Mālāyālam literature, promotion of school and college education, the adaptation of Christianity to Indian conditions. Thanks to these Christians, some sort of cohesion took place among the different communities in the realms of politics and philanthropy.

India's cultural contact with the west got a fillip after the arrival of Vasco da Gama in Calicut in 1498. The Roman Catholic Church also played a significant part in ameliorating the social and cultural lite of South India.

Protestant Christianity in South India originated at a place near Trichinopoly. Besides preaching and converting people, the Christian missionaries served the society as teachers, agricultural specialists, sanitary engineers, etc. Rural uplift was a part of the missionary activities. Another contribution of the missionaries was the development of the South Indian vernaculars. Their service towards alleviating the distress of the underprivileged or backward classes of people is memorable.

This having been the state of things, it was no wonder that Christianity and Hinduism exercised mutual influence. For example, the Syrian Christians of Mālābār adopted some customs of the Nairs of Mālābār. The *Tirukkural*, an ancient Tāmil poetical work, appears to have drawn, *inter alia*, upon Christian scriptures.[4] Some parallelisms between the *Bhagavadgītā* and the Gospel of St. John are believed, by a few scholars, to be due to the influence of Christian ideas. Grierson is of the opinion that the Brāhmanical *Bhakti* movement got an impetus from Christian beliefs through the medieval *Bhāgavata* reformers of the South.[5] Garbe, R.G. Bhandārkar and Macnicol substantially endorse Grierson's views. According to Macnicol, the influence of Christian teaching on later Vaiṣṇavite and Śaivite theism was quite considerable and increased from about the thirteenth century.[6] Rāmānuja, the outstanding exponent of *Bhakti* cult, had "some acquaintance with the Christian truth."[7] Bhandārkar suggests that "Some of the finer points on the theory of *prapatti* may be traced to the influence of Christianity."[8]

Thus, Christianity has found a real abode in South India, and has a place in the family of Indian Religions.

When Christianity made its way into north India is a matter of speculation. According to Latourette,[9] this religion probably arrived in India before the end of the third century A.D. It is, however, almost certain that, in the seventh century, Christianity was fairly widespread in north and north-west India. Patna in Bihar was the seat of a metropolitan in 1222 A.D. According to Marco Polo[10] (Indian visit—end of 13th century), of the six great kings of Middle (i.e. Central) India, three were Christian.

The regimes of Muhammad bin Tughlak (1325-1351), Timur (invasion of India, 1398) and some Muslim rulers dealt a death-blow to Christianity. As a result, the churches disappeared by the end of the 15th cent.

The arrival of Vasco da Gama in Calicut in 1498 gave a new turn to Christianity in India. The Church in north India grew up in the wake of the establishment (1510) of the Portuguese power in Goa. Different orders of Christians, Franciscans, Dominicans and Jesuits appeared as missionaries of the gospel. They preached the message of Christianity in different parts. Akbar cordially received (1580) a Jesuit Mission. The arrival (1793) of William Carey opened a new chapter in the annals of Christianity in India. With the spread of the religion, different missions entered India, and zealously propagated it in various ways among the common people suffering repression, as well as the tribals, living in the dismal darkness of ignorance. This resulted in the awakening of the sense of community among them, provided them with the minimum necessaries of life. The missionaries also provided facilities for modern education by setting up educational institutions in towns and rural areas. In these matters, the Serampore missionaries played the most important role. Serampore Mission was established in 1800 A.D. Of the missionaries, very renowned were Carey, Marshman, Ward, etc.

India was benefited in various other ways by this contact with the west, and from the British administration. It was the British Govt. that introduced (1853) Railway and the Postal system (1854). These facilitated inter-provincial cultural and commercial contacts.

Under the British rule, a sea-change took place in politics and statecraft. Novel arrangements were made for framing laws at the centre and the provinces. Though the personal laws of the Hindus and Muslims were not changed, yet the British systems of Civil and Criminal laws were introduced. These applied to the entire country. The new police administration also is the gift of the British.

Scientific outlook, rationality, humanism, freedom from superstitions and social dynamism — these resulted from the British systems of education and administration. A great ensuant was the awakening of national consciousness. In pre-British times, barring the reign of Aśoka and Mughal rule, especially the reign of Akbar, India was parcelled out into many petty kingdoms or principalities often engaged in conflicts. This lack of political cohesion stood in the way of a sense of national unity. It is true that the alien rule was responsible for our repression and for the bitter animoisity between the Hindus and Muslims. Nevertheless, in fairness, it must be admitted that they indirectly contributed to our national movement. Western education engendered in us a national feeling and whetted our desire for freedom. The French Revolution (1789) and The Russian Revolution (1917) opened our eyes, and generated in us an independent spirit which spurred us to throw off the shackles of foreign domination. Under the British, the whole of India came under one banner. This awakened our national feeling. The result of all this was the formation (1885) of Indian National Congress, and the campaign for independence proceeded apace. Most of those, who were in the vanguard of this movement, were highly educated in the western system, *e.g.*, Tilak (1857-1920), Gokhale (1866-1915), Bipin Pal (1858-1932), Lālā Lājpat Rāi (1856-1928), Aurobindo (1872-1950), Surendranath Banerji (1848-1925), M.K. Gandhi (1869-1948), etc. Aurobindo's philosophy was influenced by the western doctrine of evolution, and the western positivism relating to the material world. Gāndhi was considerably influenced, in his protest against the foreigners' aggressive attitude and activities, by Tolstoy's writings. He was probably inspired by the American author Thoreau's (1817-1862) *On Civil Disobedience* (1849) to defy British law. On the eve of the launching of Quit India Movement in 1942, he referred to Thoreau as his teacher or guide in a letter to the Americans.

The life and outlook of Subhās Bose, who left an indelible impress on the history of Indian National Movement, were, to a great extent, moulded by his western education and upbringing. According to R.K. Murti and Girijā Mukherji, having intimate knowledge of Subhas, Cambridge played a very significant role in the full development of Subhas' life and personality. In a letter to Hemanta, he highly praised the British for their energy, sense of discipline, punctuality, precise thinking about the minute details and doing things correctly, robust optimism, keen commonsense, patriotism, egalitarian outlook, love of liberty, etc. Bose's classmate, Sukthankar, said that, during his stay at Cambridge, he became rational, and Hegel's thesis—antithesis—synthesis had a powerful impact on his outlook. The American writer. Lebra, noticed British military ideas in Bose's Āzād Hind Fauz. Besides theoretical educations in the western style, he got practical training, in his sojourn in Europe (1933-1936), in Germany, Italy, Austria and other countries. The kind of political and economic condition of India, envisaged by him, was a synthesis of communism and national socialism in the Indian background. Inspired by Western secularism, he thought that religion was a personal affair, and had no place in the national life.

The establishment, at Adyar in Madras, of a branch of Theosophical Society was a landmark in the religious and political life of India. The eloquence of Annie Besant (1847-1933), who came to live in India in 1893, and her analysis of Hinduism in the western method restored faith in this religion in the minds of those who, under the impact of western education and culture, looked down upon Hinduism as a bundle of superstitions and outmoded having lost all relevance in the contemporary world. They became conscious of the glorious past, and were fired with the desire of reconstituting the nation.

The reorientation of the people's outlook led to the foundation of the Brāhma Samāj (1828), Tattvabodhinī Sabhā (1839), etc. in Bengal, Prārthanā Samāj in Mahārāṣtra. These organisations aimed at social reform by opposing idolatry, child marriage, narrow casteism, etc.

The appearance of Dayānanda (1824-83) was an important event in the social scenario of the country. Though lacking formal western education, he was a living symbol of the renaissance which followed the introduction of western learning. He denounced child-marriage and caste-system, and aimed at the eradication of superstitions. He encouraged widow-marriage. His Ārya Samāj (1875) converted all willing persons of any caste or creed by the newly conceived process of *Śuddhi*. He played a commendable role also in the National Movement. Thanks to the efforts of his followers, Dayānanda Anglo-Vedic College was established at Lahore for the propagation of English learning. The new awakening, resulting from western education, appears to have also influenced Rāmkrishna (1834-1886). Though lacking formal western education, he had a great awareness of the spirit of the times. He symbolised a synthesis of all religions.

Though at first opposed to western education, the Muslims afterwards became ardent admirers of it. Western thought infiltrated into Islamic culture in Delhi in the second quarter of the nineteenth century. Western books were being written in Urdu. On the initiative of the Muhammedan Literary Society (1863) in Calcutta, the Muslims became aware of western education and culture. Jinnah (1876-1948), the chief architect of Pākistān, was highly educated in the western system.

The activities of the British people were of crucial importance in introducing English education, social reforms, women's education, development of Bengali language and literature, etc. The western system of education was firmly established by the Despatch (19th July, 1854) of Charles Wood. This resulted in the cultural renaissance of Bengal, and, for that matter, of India. A great product of renaissance was Derozio (teaching 1826-31), Professor of Calcutta Hindu College. With some students he started the Young Bengal Group whose aim was to live for truth, to die for truth, leading a life of morality, eradication of all superstitions, etc.

Among the social reforms were the abolition of Satī (1829) mainly through the initiative of Rāmmoha (1772-1833), abolition of slavery (1843), legalisation of widow-remarriage (1856) chiefly at the instance of Vidyāsāgar (1820-91). In this connection, we should also mention efforts to put a stop to the custom of human sacrifice and infanticide.

In this period, another living symbol of freedom from blind customs, rationalism and consciousness of human rights was Vivekānanda (1863-1902). By his inspiring writings and speeches he instilled into the minds of the people the necessity of abjuring untouchability, service of man regarded as Śiva, reforms of Hinduism, etc.

The British administrators and missionaries made memorable contributions towards easy prose writing after rendering the Bengali language free from the fetters of

Sanskrit. In this connection, the Fort William College of Calcutta deserves special mention. The English scholar, Halhed (1751-1830), composed a Bengali Grammar, entitled *A Grammar of the Bengali Language.* Though the book is written in English, the illustrations and quotations are in Bengali. The credit of introducing printing press in India belongs to the Englishmen. Wilkins, an employee of East India Company, was the first man to introduce Bengali characters for printing with a press in Hooghly. The above grammar was the first printed treatise to contain Bengali characters partly.

Even in the post-independence period, India has learnt a lot of politics and statecraft from England, America, Ireland, etc. But, India's political values and institutions are mainly based on British experience. The two basic principles of democracy, viz., human rights and equality of human beings, are the gifts of the West. The present Indian administrative service is only a modern version of the British Civil Service.

The two stalwarts of the freedom struggle, Gāndhi and Nehru, were highly educated according to the western system. Marxism exercised considerable influence on their socialistic outlook, and Nehru's conception of democratic socialism.

India has learnt developed forms of agriculture and various industries from the Western countries. In the realm of science, India is infinitely indebted to the west.

We have already seen the contribution of the west to our education. The freedom of the press and its role in forming public opinion and curbing the autocratic activities of the government are the gifts of the British.

The western influence was not an unmixed blessing for India. For example, the British system of Permanent Settlement (1973) led to the rise of the Zamindāri system. It facilitated the collection of revenue on the part of the government. But, it was abused by many Zamindārs who enjoyed huge unearned money, became absentee landlords indulging in vicious habits and utterly neglecting the interest of the tenants. The most disastrous policy of the British government was that of divide and rule. This fostered communal animosity between the Hindus and the Muslims resulting in communal disturbances and the slaughter of people. The greatest harm that this policy did to India was her vivisection represented by the division of the country into two states, India and Pākistān.

In conclusion, we should note that however harmful as administrators the British might be, as a nation they were highly developed, and helped in many ways in opening our eye of knowledge. According to Gāndhi, the English, though contemptuous as rulers, were, nevertheless respectable as men. The Indians have cast off the shackles of dependence, but has embraced western learning and thoughts.

We have already referred to the simplification of the Bengali language and the introduction of prose writings by the British. The history of Bengali literature, right from the *Caryāpada* (tenth century) to the end of the eighteenth century, is one of poetical works. Up to this period, the Bengali literature dealt with only gods and goddesses and the activities of ideal men. Thanks to the influx of western thought and education in the nineteenth century, a new era dawned in Bengali literature. On the one hand, Bengali prose writing began to develop, and, on the other, problems of human life, its joys and sorrows, hopes and frustrations etc. came to be subjects of the literature. The epoch-making activities of Rāmmohan, who mastered the English language, and came into close contact with the British, introduced a prose style and human values in Bengali literature. In this connection, respectful mention should also be made of Vidyāsāgar and Bankimcandra (1838-1894).[11] Madhusudan (1824-1873) made uncommon contribution by introducing new ideas in Bengali literature; both of them drank deep at the fountain of English literature; In language, India has borrowed many foreign words. There is a historical reason for this. India came into very close contact with Arabia, Persia,

England, France, Portugal, etc. Some of these countries came as traders while others appeared as rulers. In the case of both, the necessity of learning foreign language arose. As a result, foreign words crept into the vocabularies of the provincial languages of India. We give below some foreign loan-words in the Bengali vocabulary.

Persian	*Arabic*	*Turkish*	*Portuguese*	*Dutch*	*English*	*French*
Āndāj	Āin	Ālkhāllā	Ātā	Iskāpan	Āphis	Olandaj
Ostāgar	Ākkel	Ujbuk	Ānāras	Iscrup	Iṣṭisan	Kartus
Kheyāl	Ātar	Urdu (Camp)	Ālkātrā	Turup	Uḍpencil	Kupan
Jāhāj	Kabālā	Kāñcī	Ālpin	Ruitan	Kutlet	
Darbār	Kecchā	Kābu	Ālmāri	Hartan	Koṭ	
Dastābej	Ketāb	Kuli	Kabar		Kort	
Durbin	Khāsi	Cakmaki	Kāmrā		Gelās	
Peyālā	Jilā	Cāku	Kerāṇi		Kup	
Pestā	Tahabil	Bibi	Gāmlā		Ceyār	
Bāzār	Tājjab	Bonckà	Girjā		Ṭikiṭ	
Verandāh	Dalil		Gudām		Thiyētār	
Sahar	Doyāt		Jānālā		Ḍepuṭi	
Sikār	Nabāb		Tāmāk		Puliś	
Sinduk	Fakir		Toyāle		Baykaṭ	
Supāris	Māmlā		Nilām		Bāksa	

Certain English words are used like prefixes to Bengali words; e.g. *hāph-hātā, phul-hātā, hed-paṇḍit.* From French some affixes and prefixes have been adopted by the Bengali language, e.g.—*giri* (*kerānigiri*), - *dār* (-*jotdār*), - *bāj* (*māmlābāj*), - *sai* (*mānānsai*), *phi* - (*phi-haptā*), *be* - (*be-hāt*).

Some Persian or Iranian words have crept into Sanskrit vocabulary. For example,

Old Persian *Karsha* is used in Skt. *Kārṣāpaṇa* (a coin, a measure of metal).

Old Persian *Khshatrapavan* has given Skt. *Kṣatrapa* (governor, Satrap).

Old Persian *Asabāri* has become *Aśvabhāra* in Skt.

From old Persian *Frāmaṇa* has come Skt. *Pramāna.* Middle Iranian *post* (skin or parchment to write on) gives *pusta* (book) in Skt.

At least three languages of India have their vocabularies enriched by Persian vocables. These are Urdu, Sindhi and Kashmiri.

Some foreign words have become a part and parcel of the vocabularies of some Indian languages. For example, the Bengali word *Suraṅg* or *Suruṅg* is derived from Greek syrinx. The Kashmiri word *Kampana* has the English original Camp. The word *Kalama* is derived from Greek *Kalamos.* To the Greeks we owe the terms *dramma* and *dīnāra* (Latin *denarius*) denoting particular coins. According to some, *pustaka* also has a Greek source; in Aristophanes — pyzion, tablet to write upon. Indian *phalaka* is perhaps, derived from Greek *plakos,* plaque. *Piṭka* is perhaps, Greek *pittakion,* tablet.[12] In connection with astronomy, we have seen that some Greek terms have been incorporated into Indian astronomy.

During Muslim regime in Delhi, Persian was the court-language. In practice, all regional Muslim rulers used this language for official purposes. The most powerful influence of Iranian is found in the growth of Urdu the vocabulary of which contains a number of Arabic words also.

On Sanskrit literature foreign influence is quite considerable. According to some scholars, *e.g.* Weber, Windisch, etc. the ancient Indian drama owes its origin to Greek drama. The fact that, in wake of Alexander's invasion, some Greek principalities were established in north-west India, and that a theatre, resembling Greek theatre, has been discovered in Sītābeṅgā cave (Madhya Pradesh) tend to justify the above conjecture.[13] There are, however, counter-arguments in support of the theory of indigenous origin of ancient Indian drama. The opponents also point out fundamental differences in the dramatic technique between Indian and Greek dramas; *e.g.* the absence of the three unities (viz. of time, place and action) of Greek drama in its Indian counter-part.

Some other foreign literature also provided materials for some Sanskrit works. For example, the *Kathākautuka* (1505—NSP, ed., Bombay, 1901) of the Kashmirian Śrīvara is based on the well-known story of Yusuf and Zulekhā[14] narrated by Mullā Jāmi. This poetical work contains an admixture of Śaivism and the above Persian story which again has been derived from an ancient Hebrew story. Another Kashmirian, Bhaṭṭa Āhlādaka (15th cent.), draws upon the Persian literature for the theme of his work, entitled *Delarāmākathāsāra*[15] (Kāvyamālā ed., Bombay, 1902).

Peterson, in his introduction to the edition of the *Kādambarī*, compares some important points between Kādambarī Leucippe and Clitephon, and holds, with M.G. d'Alviella, that Indian romance was directly borrowed from the Greek. This view is refuted by S. Levi in *Quid de Graecis veterum Indorum monumenta tradiderint*, p. 60.

Other scholars, however, think otherwise. The romances of the two peoples are totally different in plan and spirit. In Sanskrit romance, the thread of the story or the adventures of the characters play an insignificant part. The manner is more important than matter. All stress is laid on rhetorical embellishment, minute descriptions of nature, detailed account of exploits and of mental, moral and physical qualities. In Greek romance, the story is everything. The reader is hurried from one adventure to another, the wilder and more improbable the better. Fine composition is virtually disregarded, description and appreciation of nature are practically avoided. Another factor is to be considered in this connexion. Indian romance was written for the cultured readers. But, Greek romance was meant for uncultured masses.[16]

It has been held by some, that the *Rāmāyaṇa* and the *Mahābhārata* were influenced by the Homeric epic *Iliad*.[17] Dion Chrysostom (117 A.D.), followed by some other Orientalists, thought that the authors or compilers of these epics were inspired by Homeric poems recited in North-West

India by Greek rhapsodists. Some over zealous protagonists of this theory would go so far as to regard the above Indian epics as translations or adaptations of the Homeric epics. As regards *Rāmāyaṇa,* they are of the opinion that the Homeric episode of Helen has similarity with that of Sītā in *Rāmāyaṇa.* In both the cases, a foreign sovereign abducts the wife of a prince who, with allies, recovers her after many adventures and combats. It is also pointed out that the *Rāmāyaṇa* twice refers to the Yavanas denoting Ionians, Greeks. According to Lassen (*Indische Alterthumskunde,* II, 505), the account of Arjuna's defeating the rival suitors for the hand of Draupadī, through his superior skill in archery, might be ascribed to Homeric influence. Some scholars find resemblance between certain personages in Indian and Homeric epics; *e.g.* Nestor and Jāmbuvat, Ulysses and Hanumat, Agamemnon and Sugrīva, Patrocles and Lakṣmaṇa. Those, who reject the above theory, assert that there is not even a remote similarity between the stealing of Sītā and the rape of Helen, between the advance on Laṅkā and that on Troy. Moreover, in the Indian epic, the abduction of Sītā is an important part of the story. But, in the Homeric songs, the rape of Helen is introduced as the motive of the war, and is not narrated in extenso. It is further pointed out that there is only a very remote similarity of motive between the bending of the bow by Rāma and that by Ulysses.[18] The two references to *Yavana* have been proved to be spurious.[19] Moreover, as Weber points out, the word Yavana denotes not only Greek, but many of the alien races that made inroads into North-West India from time to time. The theory of translation of the Homeric epics does not stand on any ground.

Those, who advocate the theory that the *Rāmāyaṇa* was influenced by Homer, put forward the convenient argument that the Indians got the idea from the recitation of Homeric poems in Greek-occupied areas of North-Western India. As a matter of fact, however, it appears that the original *Rāmāyaṇa* antedated Alexander's invasion (327/326 B.C.), and, perhaps, belonged to the pre-Buddhistic age (6th-5th cent. B.C.). The city of Pāṭaliputra (Palibothra of the Greeks) was built about 400 B.C. and, in about 350 B.C., became the capital of an empire. The *Rāmāyaṇa*, though referring to the cities of Eastern Hindustān, is silent about this important city. Thus, it seems that the epic originated before the foundation of the city. The epic mentions Ayodhyā as the capital of the kingdom of Kosala. But, the name Sāketa is given to it by the Buddhists and Jains. It is said that Lava made Śrāvasti his seat of Government. The *Rāmāyaṇa* can, therefore, be supposed to come into being when the old capital of Ayodhyā was not yet deserted; by the Buddha's time, the Kosala capital was under King Prasenajit of Śrāvasti. The *Rāmāyaṇa* mentions Mithilā and Viśālā as two independent principalities; by the time of the Buddha, they were united into the single city of Vaiśāli under an oligarchical government.

Added to the above arguments against the Greek origin of the *Rāmāyaṇa* is that based on astronomical grounds. Some scholars (*e.g.* Krishnamachariar in his *History of Classical Skt. Lit.*, pp. 16-17) believe that the Indians derived their knowledge of the zodiacal signs from the Chaldeans, and not from the Greeks. So, the astronomical data in the *Rāmāyaṇa* cannot be taken as a proof of Greek influence. Lassen's aforesaid view is nothing but a conjecture. Even if similarity is conceded, it might be a sheer coincidence; masterminds may have thought alike.

Tarn's analysis of relation of Greece and Asia (and, for that matter, India) deserves attention. According to him, broadly speaking, what Asia received from Greece is mostly the externals of culture, but not its core. Barring some urban institutions, the Orient has not received much of substance from Greece. The reason was that Asia firmly believed that culturally she would be more viable than

Greece. Actually that is what happened.[20] Excepting some Greek influence on Indian sculpture, the existence of Greece was not of much consequence to the history of Indian culture.[21]

SCIENCE AND TECHNOLOGY

Astronomy and Astrology[22]

Astronomy, both pure and applied, was highly developed in ancient India. We shall briefly discuss India's indebtedness to foreign countries in this respect. Let us start with Greece. Some of the main arguments in favour of Greek influence on Indian astronomy are as follows :

(i) Greek astronomers have been highly praised by Indian authors. For example, there is the following verse in the *Bṛhatsaṃhitā* (2/15):

> *Mlecchā hi yavanās-teṣu samyak śāstramidaṃ sthitam /*
> *Ṛṣivatte'pi pūjyante kiṃ punar-daivavid dvijaḥ //*

(ii) The very title of the Sanskrit work, *Pauliśasiddhānta* indicates Greek influence. This title has been given after the name of the Greek *Paulus* (fourth century A.D.) living in Alexandria.

(iii) Weber and Kern think (Kane's *History of Dharmaśāstra,* V. 1, p. 584) that some Greek technical terms have infiltrated into Sanskrit astronomy. According to Burgess, all the technical terms, used by Varāhamihira, are found in the same sense in the astrological work, *Episagoge,* of Paulus Alexandrinus (*c.* 378 A.D.). The terms concerned are as follows :

Anapha, Āpoklima (inclination), Ākokera (Makara), Ara, Asphujit, Dreṣkāṇa or Dṛkkāṇa (decan), Duruddhara Duscikya, Dyuna, Harija, Heli, Hivuka, Horā, Hṛdroga (Kumbha). Ittha (Mīna), Jituma (Mithuna), Jīva, Jūka (Julā), Jyāmitra (Chord), Kriya (Meṣa), Kulīra (Karkaṭa) Kaurpya (Vṛcika), Kendra (anomaly), Kona, Kumadrtuma, Leya (Siṃha), Liptā (minute as a measure of time),

Mimna, Mesurana, Pakhena, Panafara, Pāthona (Kanyā), Rihpha, Sunapha, Taukṣika (Dhanu), Tāvuri (Vṛṣa), Trikoṇa, Vesi.

(iv) Sphujidhvaja's *Yavana*[23]*-Jātaka* is the Sanskrit version[24] of a Greek treatise (269 A.D.) on planets.

(v) The *Vṛddhayavana-Jātaka* may be the translation of a Greek work. It is attributed to Mīnarāja Yavanācārya who is supposed to be identical with Greek Minos.

(vi) Neugabauer is certain[25] that the basic inspiration of Indian astronomy came from Greece. According to him, the very fact that the model of Greek Eccentric-epicyclic is a sufficient evidence of Greek influence.

(vii) In the *Bṛhajjātaka* (ch. 27, verses 2, 19, 21), Varāha has stated that he has written only what the Yavanas had said the above chapter is named *Dreṣkāṇādhyāya.*

(viii) About *Viṃśottarī, Aṣṭottarī* in connection with *Daśā* and *Antardaśā,* Utpala's commentary on the eighth chapter of the *Bṛhajjātaka* quotes many verses attributed to Yavaneśvara. Utpala has mentioned Yavanendra in his commentary on verse VI/2 of this work. On verse VII/1, there is mention of both *Manittha*[26] and *Yavana.*

(ix) According to E.J. Webb, it was the Greek scientist who threw light, for the first time, on the zodiacal system with which we are familiar. He says that, according to Pliny,[27] the discoverer of this was Cleostratus (*c.* 520 B.C.).[28]

Greek influence is likely from the fact that the fragments of the *Vṛddha-garga-saṃhitā* or *Gārgī-saṃhitā* contain, in a pseudo-prophetic form, some allusions to Greek rule in India.[29]

To the above arguments some would add that, among the Indian astronomers, Āryabhaṭa was the first to hold that the earth was spherical and that it rotated on its axis, and in this respect he was influenced by Greece. This is, however, merely conjectural.

Some of the main arguments against Greek influence are as follows :

(i) According to Thibaut, it is not proper to associate the *Pauliśasiddhānta* with the Greek Paulus; because Paulus wrote on applied astronomy, whereas this work deals mainly with pure astronomy. A certain scholar is of the opinion that Pauliśa was the name of an Indian sage after whose name the above treatise has been entitled.

(ii) About the Greek words, supposed to have been incorporated into Indian astronomy, Kane's arguments are as follows :

Of the words, *Kulīra* and *Trikoṇa* are purely Sanskrit and need not be supposed to have come from Greece. Greek source of the word *Jīva* is doubtful. Generally, this word is supposed to have been derived from Greek Zeus which is supposed to have similarity with Sanskrit *Dyaus*, not with *Jīva*. The word Zeus is Indo-European, and denotes heaven or sky.

In ancient Indian astronomy, the term 'horā' has been used in three senses; but, it has not been used to denote hour. May be that this word, having this meaning, was accepted in Greek from Egypt or Babylon; because, it has been used in this sense after the lapse of a long time. It is doubtful whether Hipparchus (140 B.C.) used it in this sense in very early times. *Hivuka, Jāmitra, Dyūna, Kendra*—these words have several Sanskrit synonyms. So, their Greek origin is not free from doubt. The reason for their mention in the *Bṛhajjātaka* is, perhaps, that as these were used by ancient Greek authors of Sanskrit works, Varāha has recognised them for the sake of completeness. The word *Kendra*, too, indicating the first, fourth, seventh and tenth conditions, has two Sanskrit synonyms, viz., *Kaṇṭaka* and *Catuṣṭaya*. Besides, this term has been used in different senses in the works of India and Greece. Thus, it appears that only a few Greek words like *Anaphā, Sunaphā*, etc. have been used in Indian astronomy in which these have no great significance.

(iii) As regards Neugabauer's opinion, Kane holds[30] that,

though the *Sūryasiddhānta* is based on the Greek Eccentric and Epicyclic device, yet, the Indian scholars have introduced many changes in it by dint of their independent thought, They were not blind imitators.

(iv) The Indian astronomer, Garga, flourished about 50 B.C., Ptolemy at least 200 years later, and Firmicus was born four centuries after him. So, India learnt about zodiacs from the Greeks—this statement is not proved. The *Bṛhajjātaka* and Firmicus differ about *Dreskāṇa* and *Bhāva.*[31]

(v) India and Greece, perhaps, derived knowledge about Zodiacs from Babylon independently, and almost in the same period.

(vi) The view of Weber and some other scholars that India learnt about zodiacs in the fourth century A.D. through Greek Firmicus and Paulus, is not tenable; because, the symbols of some zodiacs on the railing columns of Bodhgayā date from the first century B.C.

(vii) There is no definite evidence of Indian Nāgā ascetics or gymnosophists having lived in Greece, and coming back to India and introducing Greek elements or terms into Indian astronomy.

(viii) In the *Bṛhajjātaka*, the classification of zodiacs and certain other matters reveal difference from the views of Ptolemy. So, it cannot be held that no Sanskrit work on astronomy has been composed on the lines of Ptolemy's works. There is no direct evidence of the influence of Hipparchus or any other Greek astronomer on Indian astronomy.

There is mention of Maya's views in Varāhamihira's *Bṛhajjātaka* (7/1) and *Bṛhatsaṃhitā* (24/2/50, 29/56/8). In the commentary on the *Bṛhajjātaka* (7/13), Utpala has quoted a verse in Āryā metre, attributed to Maya. It is stated, in a verse quoted in the last chapter of the extant *Sūryasiddhānta* and in Utpala's commentary on the *Bṛhatsaṃhitā* (2/14), that Sun-god imparted knowledge of astronomy to the Dānava (demon) king, Maya. This has led some scholars to infer the influence of the Maya civilisation of Mexico in America. In this connection, it may be noted that, in the chapter on Indian influence in foreign countries, we have shown cultural affinity between America (Incas, Mayas etc.) and India. Ancient Indian astronomers were conscious of the fact that the earth is spherical and that there is America (called Pātāladeśa) in the other hemisphere—this is proved by the twelfth chapter, called *Bhūgolādhyāya*, of the *Sūryasiddhānta*.

Now let us come nearer to India, to Mesopotamia and Babylon. With Mesopotamia India had links since very remote times. These links were strengthened in the wake of Alexander's invasion (326 B.C.). Neugabauer seems to think that the major portion of Greek astronomy was known in Mesopotamia in about the middle of the second millenary B.C., and thence this science spread towards the east.[32] In the third century B.C., the Indians, having seen figures of zodiacs on the columns and boundary-stones in Babylon, incorporated them into their astronomy. Since the revelation of the history of astronomy by the Assyrian scientists in the valley of the river Euphrates, Babylon had been regarded as the homeland of the knowledge of zodiacs.[33] According to Meissner,[34] the conception of various figures of zodiacs had been in vogue in Babylon since the sixth century B.C. Sarton thinks[35] that, in this respect, perhaps Babylon influenced the oriental countries of Iran, India, China, etc. Neugabauer also shares this view.[36]

In the *Jyotiṣa* Vedāṅga there is mention of the longest and the shortest days and of their difference. Some western scholars; *e.g.*, Neugabauer (*Exact Sciences in Antiquity*, p. 178) finds Mesopotamian influence in it. Kane has dismissed this view (*History of Dharmaśāstra*, V, pt. 1, p. 542).

A remarkable fact about Mesopotamia is that the oldest horoscope has been discovered in this country, not in Greece nor in Egypt.

There is no semblance of Roman influence[37] on Indian astronomy excepting the word *Romaka* in the title of the work,

Romakasiddhānta. According to some, *Romaka* stands for Alexandria. S.B. Dikshit[38] thinks that the treatise, called *Romaka,* attributed to *Śrīṣeṇa,* is different from the *Romakasiddhānta* summarised in the *Pañcasiddhāntikā.* In his opinion, the latter work was composed earlier than 150 A.D. In the beginning of the *Sūryasiddhānta,* it is stated that Sun god taught this science to Asura (demon) Maya in the city of Romaka. Weber (1820-1901) thinks that there is a covert reference to Ptolemy in the name Asura Maya. This is, however, controversial.

The contribution of Babylon to Indian astronomy is undoubted, and the influence of Greece also must be admitted. But, it cannot be asserted that, in astrology, India is wholly indebted to Greece. Scholars like William Jones (1746-1794) think that this science had been in vogue in India ever since the Vedic age; it should not be supposed to have been borrowed from any particular country.

It seems, the zodiacal system was known in India as early as in the *Ṛgveda.* The purport of *Ṛgveda,* I. 24.8 and I. 164.11 is as follows. Lord Varuṇa paved a wide way through which the sun could traverse. In the cosmic wheel, there are twelve spokes; it revolves round the vault of the sky again and again; but never wears out.

Greek influence was spread in Indian astronomy even before Manilius, Ptolemy and Firmicus. What has been stated in the *Bṛhajjātaka* (27/2, 19, 21) is, according to his own admission, based on the *Yavana-śāstra.* According to Kane, the reference here is to some Yavana writer preceding Ptolemy and Manilius.[39] Before forming any conclusion about western influence on Indian astronomy, we should bear in mind that many Sanskrit works on this science have been lost, a fact which can be ascertained from the works of Varāhamihira and the quotations made by Utpala. In the circumstances, a full objective assessment of Greek influence on India is not possible.[40]

The Iranian priests (Magas) brought with them Chaldeo-Greek astronomy from the Hellenistic world, and taught it to the Indians.[41]

There has been considerable development of astronomy and astrology in England, and India has been benefited thereby. Compared with India and Greece, the civilisation and culture of England are much later.

It should be noted that the Muslims also appear to have influenced Indian astrology to some extent. For example, the astrological work, *Jyotirvidābharaṇa*, wrongly attributed to Kālidāsā,[42] betrays Arabic influence. Under the Muslim regime, Arabic and Persian influences became marked. It was in this period that *Tājikas* appeared. The word *Tājika* is derived from Persian Taiji, 'Arabic'. Judging from the numerous manuscripts and editions, Nīlakaṇṭha's *Tājika* (1587), in two parts called *Saṃjñā*- and *Varṣa-tantra*, was a very popular work.

OTHER BRANCHES OF SCIENCE

According to some specialists, the method of application of metallurgy in Indus Valley Civilisation developed under the influence of the ancient Sumerian Civilisation of the Middle East. In later times, the Iranian art of metal-work was introduced into India. This art developed to a high degree in Iran from the period of the Luristan bronzes, pretty long before the establishment of the Achaemenian empire. It acquired further excellence in Sassanian metal-craft (*e.g.* ornaments, utensils, especially engraved plate and repousse work, etc.) in gold, silver and bronze. An index to the popularity of this art in India is that two Modern Indian words, denoting metal-workers of certain types, were derived from Iranian language. These are *Sekrā* in Bengali and *Thaṭherā* in Hindi.

The Western sciences of physics and chemistry have been, and are still widely studied in our colleges and universities. In physics, J.C. Bose (1858-1937), the Nobel

Laureate C.V. Raman (1888-1917), S.N. Bose (1894-1974), M.N. Sāhā (1893-1956), - all trained in the western method, achieved outstanding position in the history of global science. In chemistry, P.C. Roy (1861-1944), by his researches, placed India on a pedestal of glory. H. G. Khurana (1922—), by his researches in genetics, earned the Nobel prize. Although he is an American citizen, yet there is no denying the fact that he originally belonged to India, and was trained in the western method. Engineering and technology, which are now very popular in India, are the gifts of the West. The Kushāna king, Kaniska (reign *c.* 120-144 A.D.) appears to have engaged Greek engineers in his kingdom.[43]

In connection with foreign influence in India with respect to medical science, we should add a note on the Unāni or Iunāni method of treatment. The word *Unāni* or *Iunāni* is Persian in origin. It is derived from Yavana (Greek) or Ionia (Greece). This method of treatment actually originated in Greece. European historians and medical men called it Arabian. The reason is that they became familiar with it through Arabian medical writers. The Arabic writers learnt it from the Greeks, developed it with their experience gathered from Persian medical tradition and Indian medical system as well as in the light of their own observation and experiments. The Indians called it *Unāni* as they knew it to be based on the system of Yavanas or Greeks. The Greek system was founded by Hippocrates (*c.* 460-377 B.C.), and developed by Aristotle, Galen and other Greek writers. This system, mastered by the Arabic medical writers, was introduced by the Muslims in India in the eleventh century. Thenceforward it has been avidly cultivated in this country. It thrived side by side with the indigenous Āyurvedic system. The physicians, who practised it, were called Hākims.

MEDICAL SCIENCE

Some remarkable similarities are noticed in the medical science of Greece and India. These are too close to be passed over as accidental. The mandatory and prohibitory rules prescribed in the *Carakasaṃhitā* (1st-2nd cent. A.D.) about the physicians have similarity with the oath of the physicians contained in the work of the Greek Hippocrates. The points of similarities are as follows :

(*i*) Three stages of fever—initial, middling and advanced.

(*ii*) Classification of remedies - cold, hot, dry, oily.

(*iii*) Remedies in contrast to each other.

(*iv*) Emphasis on prognosis.,

(*v*) Effect of the seasons on diet.

(*vi*) Use of intoxicants for curing certain diseases. In this connection, it may be added that, as a rule, the Smṛtiśāstra prohibits alcoholic drink for the Brāhmaṇas, Kṣatriyas, Vaiśyas, particularly for the Brāhmaṇas.

(*vii*) Eating earth in particular diseases.

(*viii*) Birth of a twin as a result of the division of the semen virile into two parts.

(*ix*) Vitality of the foetus in the seventh month.

In these respects, who the borrower was cannot be definitely determined. Chronologically, however, it seems that India was the borrower. If however, Caraka drew upon a traditional source, then the case might have been otherwise. If Pythagoras was indebted to Indian geometry, then Indian influence on Greek medicine is likely. He and Plato believed in the transmigration of souls. This also lends countenance to the theory of Greek borrowing from Indian medical science.[44]

The Muslims introduced in India the method of treatment generally known as Unāni or Hākimi. In royal courts, the hākims enjoyed an honoured position, and treated the sick at a comparatively less expense.

The system of homoeopathic treatment has been very popular in India, especially among the common people. This science originated in Germany where it was invented by Hahnemann (1755-1843). In India, the court of Ranjit Singh of Punjab tried to introduce it in 1835. Bengal, attempted unsuccessfully to introduce this system of treatment in 1851. Later on, Vidyāsāgar (1820-1891), Rājā Rājendralāl Mitra (1822-1891), Bhudeb Mukhopādhyāy (1827-1897) and Mahendralāl Sarkār (1833-1904), among others, made earnest endeavours to propagate homoeopathy in Bengal. Sarkār adopted it as the means of his livelihood. In Vārāṇasī, Loknāth Misra tried his best to propagate it. In the Deccan, Father Müller, with a view to providing the poor with an easy and cheap system of medical treatment, set up homoeopathic dispensaries and hospitals, and was rewarded by the then Government of India.

The West Bengal Government recognised, by an Act of 1963, the homoeopathic system of medical treatment, and accorded to the homoeopaths the same status as that of the allopaths. The Government also took over the Colleges teaching homoeopathy. In 1972, India Government recognised the homoeopathic system of treatment (Vide Government of India's *Minutes of Health*, Memo. No. 29 -16/ 71 - M.A., dt. 14.9.72).

MATHEMATICS

Both the countries have considerable similarities in mathematics. According to some, the numerals of India have been derived from the first nine letters of the Greek alphabet. In geometry, there is astonishing similarity between the Vedic *Śulvasūtra* and the Greek works. The Pythagoras theorem[45] is a uniqne example.

MUSIC AND DANCE

There is historical evidence that western singers were accorded welcome in the royal court of Broach (Majumdar, *Advanced History of India*, 1978, p. 135). The Arabian Muslims invaded Sind in the beginning of the eighth century A.D. occupied portions of it, and gradually extended their territory. Islamic music at first spread in the region of Sind, and gradually merged into Indian music. The Sufi devotees were lovers of music. In prayer, they used to sing Kāwāli songs about divine love. This type of song is very popular even to-day. A Muslim ruler of Jaunpur was the father of Kheyāl songs which are highly popular now-a-days. North Indian songs present a mixed form of Indo-Iranian songs. Āmir Khusru (d. 1324 or 1325 A.D.) was the pioneer of songs of a new style. Certain *Tālas* like *Khāmāj* are Iranian. Some musical instruments, used in India, have been obtained from the Muslims. Among these are Tablā,[46] Sarod,[47] Nākārā,[48] Rabāb,[49] etc. These were imported from Arabia or Persia.

At the instance of Delhi Sultanate, a synthesis of Hindu and Muslim music had been effected to a great extent. In their courts assembled many musicians from various countries. For instance, there were Hindus, Iranians, Turkish. This synthesis developed to a great extent under Akbar (1556-1605). The Darbāri music was the creation of his time. The renowned Tānsen adorned his court. The descendants of Tānsen and his disciples built up different *Gharāṇās* (distinct styles) of songs.

From the west we have got harmonium, piano, organ, guitar, violin, etc. Of these, the violin has come from Portugal; its Portuguese name is viola. The other instruments are English. The harmonium was made, for the first time, in 1840 A.D., and introduced into India towards the middle of the nineteenth century. There is western influence on tune and *tāla* of the songs of Rabindranāth. Some Indian composers like Sorābji (b. 1892 or 1894) composed songs in accordance with the western style. Ustād Āli Ākbar Khān (1920-) adopted some harmonies from western melody.

There are indications that Indian music absorbed foreign elements. For instance, the terms *Turuṣka-toḍi, Turṣka gauḍa* hint at Turkish origin. The term *Śakarāga* indicates Scythian influence. *Kāmbojī, Khāmbāja* or *Khāmācī* was probably imported from Kambuja (Cambodia, modern

Kampuchea). The name *Boṭṭa,* as applied to a *Rāga,* is taken by some to have been derived from *Bhoṭṭa* or *Bhoṭa* which refers to Tibet. *Bhammāna,* according to some, hints at its Armenian origin.

That musicologists were aware of the foreign elements in some *rāgas* is proved by the fact that Mataṅga (sometime between the fifth and the seventh cent. A.D.), in his *Bṛhaddeśī,* observes - *saṃkīrṇā ca matā nityaṃ jñeyā vaideśa-sambhavā;* it is mixed, and originated in a foreign land.

Some have noticed Greek influence on the types of dance, called *Hallīsaka*[50] and *Rāsa,*[51] related to Kṛṣṇa. In this connexion, it is noteworthy that Kṛṣṇa appeared as the Supreme Lord among the Greeks. Such a Greek was Heliodoros (*c.* 2nd cent. B.C.) of the Besnagar inscription. It is also thought that the dramatic style *Ārabhaṭī*[52] originated in the west of the Indus and south of Baluchistan; it was called *Ārviṭi* by the Greeks. In it has been noticed a combined form of Indian *Rāsa* and Greek *Hallīsaka.* The dance-style, called *Ārabhaṭī,* is also considered to have been influenced by the Greeks.

SCULPTURE

Greek influence on Indian sculpture[53] is undoubted. In this connection, the characteristics of Gandhāra art have to be discussed. Some historians and specialists think that the art of this region was learnt from Greece or from Asia Minor and the Roman empire influenced by Greece. It is for this reason that the Gandhāra art is called Indo-Greek or Graeco-Roman. This art was introduced in India by the Greek kings of Bactria and North-West India. The idea of representing the founder of Buddhism as a human being perhaps originated in Greece. It should be noted that though the style was influenced by Greece, the subject was absolutely Indian. In it have been reflected the faith and conduct of the Buddhists. In rare cases, a Greek subject has been adopted. R.C. Majumdar aptly says that the sculptors had Greek hands, but Indian mind. In the evolution of a Buddha-image, there is imitation of the Greek God Apollo. This image is the chief specimen of Gandhāra art. The Indian sculptors were considerably influenced in the conception of the Buddha, Bodhisattva and various scenes connected with the Buddha stories. From a drinking scene it seems that it arose in the Gandhāra region after the Greek model. The bearded face was made in imitation of the Greek Satyr. In the Mathurā school of art, the garments of women are not Indian; perhaps it was influenced by the Greeks. In Mathurā, there is also the influence of Gandhāra art. In it indirect Greek influence is noticeable. It was, at one time, thought that the Buddha image of Gandhāra was the model of the Buddha images at Mathurā and other places. It was subsequently admitted that sculptures in both the regions were in dependent of each other. The notable difference between the two is that, in the Gandhāra image, greater stress was laid on physical grace and beauty. In the sculpture of the other place, the sculptor tried to evoke a spiritual attitude. Buddhist sculptures, excavated by Leitner in Peshawar Valley, preserved in Oriental Institute at Woking, are, according to him, specimens of Graeco-Buddhist sculpture. Best specimens of Graeco-Buddhist art are preserved in the Museums at Calcutta, Lahore, Peshawar, British Museum and Museum für Volker-Kunde at Berlin. Besides a few specimens found in the Punjab, Graeco-Buddhist specimens were discovered in the region between the Indus and the Jhelum.

Foucher discerns, in Sānchi sculptures, subtle indications of Hellenic influence in some examples of bold foreshortening, in the presentation of three-quarters of the face-figure, etc.

In Egypt and Babylon, some deities were conceived as having the heads of animals and birds. In India, too, some such deities appeared in post-Christian times, *e.g.* the elephant-faced Gaṇeśa, horse-necked Viṣṇu. *En passant*, we can mention also the Kinnaras supposed to haunt the Himalayan region. They were conceived as demigods with horse-faces.

In Section 1 (supra), we have added a note on the image of the sun-god influenced by Iran.

ARCHITECTURE

As a result of Persian domination (*c.* middle of 6th cent. B.C. to 331 B.C.), Persepolitan capital was introduced in Indian architecture. There is a theory that the best pillars of Aśoka were constructed by foreign architects engaged by him. Those, who believe in this theory, are of the opinion that foreign influence on Indian architecture continued long after Aśoka. Before Aśoka (3rd cent. B.C.), columns to commemorate victory, etc. were not perhaps built. For educating the public, he got pillars constructed with edicts inscribed. According to some, Alexander (4th cent. B.C.) introduced this system.

It is noteworthy that, before Iranian contact, houses, palaces, walls and ramparts used to be built with timber. There were, however, some Cyclopian structures of huge ill-dressed stones here and there; *e.g.* at Rājagṛha in Magadha. These were, according to some, pre-Aryan. Scholars believe that Indian learnt from Iran the art of building in well-dressed stone on a large scale in classical times from Iran from the fifth or fourth cent. B.C. onwards. The massive Maurya Palace at Pāṭaliputra (Patna) is believed to have been a copy of the Iranian palace of Persepolis. Columns with bull and lion capitals and certain decorative features also were borrowed from Iran.[54]

The symbol of the sun, found in certain specimens of Buddhist architectures, is supposed by some to have been first conceived in Assyria. The trident in the winged sun's orb is also supposed to have originated in that country.

It is said that, for the construction of mosques and mansions, Bābur (1526-1530) invited the disciples of the famous Albanian architect, Sinan, from Constantinople. In the regime of Humāyun (1530-1540), the huge mosque (*c.* 1540), built at Fatyābād in the Hissar district of Haryana, contained, in accordance with the Persian style, decorations with enamelled tiles. Persian and Mongol types of architecture were followed in the Bāhmani Kingdom of South India in the second half of the fifteenth century. During Akbar's reign (1556-1605), many palaces and mansions were built in Delhi and Āgrā; these are memorable specimens of contemporary architectures. On the Mausoleum (1605-1613) of Akbar at Sikandrā, the influence of the Khmer architecture of Cochin China has been inferred. V. Smith noticed a synthesis of Asian and European types in the construction (1632-1653) of Tāj Mahal, one of the wonders of the world. The hands of Italian and French builders in its construction have been presumed. But, on reasonable grounds, Moinuddin has shown that the above impression is erroneous. In view, however, of the contact of Mughal India with the western world, particularly the Mediterranean region, western influence on the Indian architecture of the 16th century was nothing impossible.

The contribution of Muslims to the architecture of India was unrivalled. The mansions of Fatehpur Sikri, the Red Fort of Delhi, Āgrā Fort, etc. are mute witnesses to architectural skill. Furthermore, numerous mosques, mausoleums, specimens of architecture built in the geometrical method, pillars, palaces, etc. testify to the refined taste of the Muslim builders. These specimens were the result of a fusion of the architectural deftness of the people of Arabia, Persia, Turkey, Central Asia and other countries.

The rulers of the Bāhmani kingdom of Deccan invited foreign engineers and technicians. Their military and civil architecture, to a considerable extent, was influenced respectively by Europe and Iran. They were not very much swayed by the local style. Their buildings betray imitation of the royal palaces of Delhi and the columns of Iran. Indian Muslims are, in many respects, indebted to the Sassanians of

Persia and the Byzantine school. In course of time, the architectural patterns of Muslims got inextricably mixed up with the Indian style. As illustration, we can point out that the Muslim conquerors imitated the brickbuilt mansions current in Bengal, and followed, in their own structures, the characteristics of Hindu architecutue. They adopted the skill involved in the construction of the wooden houses of Kashmir, and the Gujarati pattern in West India.

Architecture considerably developed during the regime of Sher Shāh (1539-45). His mausoleum at Sāsārām in Bihar is a magnificent example of Indo-Iranian architecture. Built at the centre of a huge artificial lake, 1,400 ft. long on one side, its width is 250 ft. Humāyun's mausoleum is another monument to architectural excellence. Containing some Iranian features, it has been characterised as the Indian interpretation of Iranian architectural thought. There is a blend of Hindu-Muslim architectures not only in the mansions of the Mughal period (1526-1858), but also in Hindu temples. Such a temple (1590) is associated with the name of Govinda Deo. Some royal palaces of Rājasthān and other buildings have Mughal characteristics.

Some special features appeared in the Turko-Afghan architecture. Scholars like Fergusson have characterised the architecture of this period as Indo-Saracenic or Pāṭhān. Scholars like Havel, however, think that the body and soul of the architecture of this period were Indian. As a matter of fact, it combined Indian and Muslim patterns. Marshal aptly says that this pattern is not merely a local transformation of the Islamic style nor only a special form of the Hindu style. It combined both the styles in a manner that made it difficult to determine exactly how much was Islamic and how much Indian. In India, architecture of the Brāhmaṇic, Jaina, and Bauddha patterns existed. With those Islamic elements began to be mixed up in the wake of Muslim advent, *i.e.* from the middle of the seventh century A.D. Islamic pattern does not mean a particular pattern of any particular country. It is composite, because it contains Arabian, Persian and Turkish elements. The people of this country carried with them the architectural styles of western and central Asia, North Africa and South-West Europe. This composite architecture, depending on local religious ideas and personal predilection, assumed different forms in different regions. This is the reason why diverse architectural patterns are found in Jaunpur, Vaṅga, Bijāpur, Gujarāṭ, etc. Due to the presence of Muslim majority at Delhi, there was the preponderance of the Islamic influence in the mansions there. The predominance of the local style is found in Jaunpur and Deccan. The Muslim conquerors of Bengal adopted the local patterns of brick-built mansions, and followed Hindu ideals. In Gujarāṭ, the Muslim victors followed the beautiful local architectural style. In Kashmir, they adopted the pattern of wooden architecture. In certain cases, the necessary changes in the temples were made in accordance with the needs of the conquerors.

The reason behind the fusion of Indian and Islamic architectural styles was their twofold similarity. One of them was that rooms or columns surrounded the open courtyard. As a result, such temples would be easily turned into mosques. Another point of similarity lies in variously decorated *maṇḍapas* etc.

The best specimen of the Delhi style is the Kutb Minār. It contains high bastions, inscriptions written in beautiful handwriting and beneath the balcony stalactite[55] and corbeling.[56] Besides the aforesaid Minār, there are several beautiful specimens of Islamic-Indian architecture, *e.g.* the mosque in the Dargāh of Nijāmuddin Āuliya, the Alāi Darwāzā of the aforesaid Minār, the mausoleum of Feruz Shāh, son of Rajab of Delhi, the Atāl Devi mosque of Jaunpur, Barāsonā and Choṭāsonā mosques at Gauḍ (West Bengal), Ādinā mosque of Pāṇḍuā, the mausoleum of Feruz Shāh Bāhmani of Gulbārgā, the mausoleum of Muhammad Ādil Shāh of Bijāpur, etc.

In the Mughal period, chiefly the earlier style was followed and developed. Some innovations, however, can be noticed. Bābur (1526-1530) has, in his memoir, criticised the style of buildings in Hindustān. As stated earlier, he engaged foreign architects.

The Muslim architecture of India can be divided into certain distinct types :

Periods are approximate

1. Pāṭhān style - 1193-1554.

It was in vogue in Delhi and the neighbouring Provinces up to the second battle of Pānipat (1556).

2. Jaunpur style - 1390-1475.
3. Gaḍmāndā type - 1203-1575.
4. Gujarāṭ-Āhmedabad type - 1390-1577.
5. South Indian Muslim style - 1590-1660.
6. Mughal type - 1525-1750.

The tradition of the Muslim architectural style is still found in the construction of mosques with their domes and roofs. Pointed arch and geometrical decoration are some of the noteworthy exterior features of the mosques. The architectural style that evolved in places like Gauḍa (present Murshidābād district and southernmost part of Māldā) and Pāṇḍuā (a small village in Māldā district) in Bengal towards the end of the fourteenth century, was in vogue up to the end of the Pāṭhān regime. In it, terracotta and chisel-cut bricks were in use.

The great impact of the ancient Maya civilisation of America on Indian architecture can be easily gauged. The titles of the two Sanskrit treatises on *Vāstuvidyā* (house-building), entitled *Mayamata* and *Mayaśāstra,* appear to indicate Mayan influence. The similarity of Mayan temples, particularly of their *Śikhara* and *Gopura,* with those of Indian temples, is clear. Incidentally, it may be mentioned that the *Mahābhārata* contains description of the construction of palaces for Pāṇḍavas by the Mayan architects at Indraprastha.[57] The Sabhāparvan (50/25) contains a reference to the assembly-hall of Yudhiṣṭhira having been constructed by the architect Maya. Verses 1/13, 3/28 of this Parvan state that Maya built '*Vimānapratimā sabhā*', we learn that it could be shifted from one place to another at will.

There is no specimen of any structure in an entirely Greek pattern. But, the Indo-Greek architects adopted some Greek models; this is noticeable in columns and in the decoration of capitals.[58] There are Ionic pillars in the temples of Taxila (Takṣaśilā). The *Kapota* (Sanskrit *Viṭaṅka*-pinnacle), is, to a great extent, like the Greek *Corona* (part of cornice) with broad vertical face, usually of considerable projection. The lotus is made, in many respects, according to the Corinthian model. The base of a column, of sandstone, preserved in Lahore Museum, is, according to Cunningham (*Arch. Sur. of India*, II, p. 129) is the "first specimen of pure Greek architecture that has been discovered in the Punjab." A building, which is, perhaps, a monastery, has been found at Shāh-Dehri in Peshāwar Valley, with pillars the capitals of which appear to have been derived from the Ionic. In all topes, where any fragment of capital remained, they were quasi-Corinthian. In Kāshmir and Salt Range in the Punjab, there are a few temples with columns; these have been described as Doric. The most famous among these is the Temple of Mārtaṇḍa in Kāshmir. The column of Heliodoros (*c.* 140-130 B.C.), referred to elsewhere, clearly shows traces of Greek influence. The most remarkable similarity with Greek temple is noticeable in the temple of Jhandial (*Annual Rep. of Archaeological Sur. of India*, 1913-14) which is unlike any temple as yet known in India.

There are historical reasons behind Hellenic influence on Indian architecture. Greek architects came to Bactria when the Satraps, after Alexander, ruled at Balkh. These people worked in that region till the Greek style was established. Afterwards they came to India. So, Greek style got mixed up with the Indian.

After the introduction (1757) of British rule in India,

Indian architecture was considerably influenced by that of Europe. Many mansions were built in accordance with the European pattern in the capital city of Delhi. In some cases, we find a fusion of the Mughal, Victorian and Gothic architectures. In very recent times, high-rise mansions are being built in imitation of American architecture.

Jairāzbhoy holds that the town-planning in the *Arthaśāstra* has some similarity with the Greek pattern. From this, however, we cannot definitely ascertain the borrower; there is probability of borrowing on the part of India in the wake of Alexander's invasion. The style that prevailed from the end of the 17th cent. to about the middle of the nineteenth survives in the specimens at Lucknow, Mysore, etc. The special characteristics of the Mughal style, in its initial phase, were adopted from the Muslim architecture of Gujarāṭ. Some of the noteworthy features were the use of Hindu ornamentation, arch, use of white and red stones, entrance with half-dome, etc. The unique contribution of Muslim architecture was the laying out of gardens. Specimens of this are found at Sikāndrā, Tāj, Shālimār garden of Kāshmir, etc.

PAINTING

Foreign elements are noticed in this art too. The frescos of Ajantā (5th-7th cent. A.D.) reveal fascination for Persian life. We notice, among them, Persian men and women in small panels, Persian couples drinking in intimacy, and the grant scene of the Sassanian ambassadors visiting the court of a Deccan king. In the thirteenth century, the Mongol conquerors introduced Chinese art in Persia. It was a synthesis of the Buddhist, Iranian, Bactrian and Mongol styles of art. Some scholars think that successive hordes of nomadic tribes of Central Asia brought the art of painting from the north to India. The Indian-Chinese-Persian mix influenced the Indian schools of painting at the time of Akbar (1556-1605), and there was historical reason behind it. Bābur (1526-1530) hailed from Chinese Turkestan. Humāyun (1530-1540; 1555-

1556), as a refugee in Persia, devoted himself to the cultivation of Sino-Persian art of painting. While returning to India, he brought with him two famous painters, named Sayyid Ali and Khwājā Abdus Sāmād, disciples of Rihzad, the Raphael of the East. They came to Humāyun's court in 1550 A.D. Humāyun and Akbar learnt painting from them, and engaged them in illustrating the book, entitled *Dastan-i-Āmir Hāmzāh.* This heralded Mughal painting. Sino-Persian impact on the paintings of these two artists is clear. In the court of Akbar, there were also some painters from Persia and other countries. In the court of Jahāngir (1605-1627) also there were some foreign artists, e.g. Abul Hasan of Herat, Muhammad Nādir and Muhammad Murād of Samarkand, etc. The emperor used to purchase foreign paintings of excellent quality. Though Persian influence was dominant in the initial stage, afterwards Indian style surpassed it. At the time of this emperor, a new Mughal style originated. Though very much fond of architecture, Shāhjahān (reign 1628-1658) was not averse to painting. His son, Dārā (1614-1662), too, was fond of arts, though he was mainly interested in philosophy. The specialists hold that, even before the Mughal regime (1526-1858), Persian art of painting influenced the Indian art of painting. This art of the Mughal period is called Indo-Persian. It was in the regime of Jahāngir that the Mughal painters came into contact with the European art of painting. Since then, there developed the tendency of emphasising nature as a theme. In the Deccan, under the influence of Persian and Turkish painters, the South Indian art of painting originated, and gradually developed. The painters of Bengal cultivated the art of printing of silken cloth in Japanese form. In the last decade of the nineteenth century, the art of painting, introduced by Abanindranāth Tagore (1871-1951), was a wonderful synthesis of the indigenous, Japanese, Mughal and Persian styles.

In 1936, the Art Rebel Society was founded in Calcutta. Some artists, *e.g.* Bholā Chatterji, Abani Sen, etc., connected with it, tried to introduce the western style in a novel way by producing subjective paintings in the western form. The western style, in some form, had been present in the paintings produced in Calcutta, Bombay and Madras ever since the inception of this art in these places. Among the followers of the artist, Annadā Bāgchi, this art laid stress on the painting of portraits. Some artists of the first half of this century, *e.g.* Jāmini Gānguli, Atul Basu, Hemendra Majumdar, etc. of Bengal, achieved distinction in painting portraits and nature. Among the non-Bengali artists, Amritā Shergil was one of those who distinguished themselves by producing paintings in the western style. Shergil combined western Impressionism with the Indian attitude.

In 1943, in the wake of the Second World War, some artists, inspired by new values, developed an international outlook, founded an institution called Calcutta group. It was their aim to introduce contemporary ideas into the art of painting and to internationalise it. Later on, most of the artists of this group received training in western countries, and attempted to extend the bounds of the contemporary Indian painting. In the post-war period, internationalism with its influence on abstract paintings characterised Indian painting to a great extent.

In the domain of painting, Hungary exercised considerable influence on India. Amritā Sher-Gil,[59] one of the greatest painters of modern India, born to Hungarian mother, spent most of the formative years of her life in Hungary where she studied art, and even after return to India, maintained contact with that country. Her paintings are generally based on Indian themes no doubt, but European, especially Hungarian influence is discernible to the expert eye. Some of her paintings depict Hungarian scenes.

Charles Fabri, about whom we have written in connection with sculpture, was deeply impressed by Indian dance. He played a significant role in according recognition to the Odissi school of dance. He was one of the early admirers recognising the merit of the female dancers, Indrāni Rehmān and Yāmini Kṛṣṇamūrti.

His paper, Dance in India, published in *Indo-Asian Culture*, X. 1, New Delhi, 1961, is noteworthy.

COINS AND INSCRIPTIONS

From Pliny's account, we come to know that many luxury goods used to be exported from India to Rome. Many sesterses (Roman coins) have been unearthed at places having commercial links with Rome. According to scholars, the reason for the currency of golden coins in the Kushāna reign, starting with Kadphises II (*c.* 78-110 A.D.), was the influx of a good deal of gold from the Roman empire.

Greek influence on Indian coins has been proved; this influence started as early as the second century B.C. Greek and Prākrit legends were written on the coins issued by the Indo-Bactrian kings. Some specialists are sure of foreign influence on the gold coins of the Gupta period (*c.* 320-510). Some Gupta coins contain figures of deities in imitation of Greek deities. Attic coins are the models of several Indian coins. On their body is inscribed Greek language. Their beauty reminds us of the schools of Proxytalis or Lucippus. In an inscription on a seal at Besnagar (ancient Vidiśā), there is mention of Demetrios (3rd cent. B.C.), king of Bactria. Coins of Demetrios are, perhaps, the first to show the result of compromise between Greek and Indian methods of coinage. There is Greek legend on the obverse, and Indian translation in Kharoṣṭhī on the reverse. Some rare coins are those of Eukratides (*c.* 190-160 B.C.) who conquered parts of north-western India, found in the Punjab. Indian coins of the two Greek rulers, Pantaloon and Agathocles, who were contemporaries of Eukratides, are the only specimens of coins of Greek princes, with Brāhmī inscriptions. In the stone mould for making medals, there is similarity with the Indo-Bactrian drachma.[60] Indian artists were not blind imitators. They made a synthesis of the foreign and Indian ideas.

According to some, it is almost certain that India had taken, from the Greeks, the idea of inscriptions on stone and of the legends on money.[61]

Parthian characteristics are found on the Śaka coinage of India. The earliest of such coins are those of Maues.[62]

A result of the spread of Persian domination in north-west India was the introduction of the Kharoṣṭhī[63] script in that region.

Greek script also appears to have been in vogue in India at least in the fourth century B.C.[64]

POLITICS AND STATECRAFT

The long domination of parts of north-west India by Persia under the Achaeminians, Parthians and Sassanians, from the sixth century B.C. to several centuries after Christ, facilitated Iranian influence in India. This influence was not confined merely to culture and language. The Iranians taught the Indians a lot of politics and statecraft too.

The first great empire in India in the historic times was that of Magadha, founded by Mahāpadma Nanda (*c.* 412 B.C.) and usurped and extended by Candragupta Maurya (reign *c.* 322-298 B.C.). It was further extended by his grandson, Aśoka (*c.* 273-232 B.C.). The Maurya empire was organised on the lines of the Achaemenian empire. The Maurya Administrative Boards, State Departments and Officers were in imitation of those of the Achaemenian empire. Aśoka appears to have copied even the direct narrative style of Darius' inscriptions in old Persian, as will be evident from the following quotation :

Inscription of Darius
Qa (ha) ti Darayava (h) us xsayaQiya

Inscription of Aśoka
devānaṃ piya Piyadasī rājā āha

MISCELLANEOUS

Besides the matters discussed so far, some countries of the East and the West have influenced India in various ways in the different walks of life.

The influence of Greece was manifold. Indian philosophers mixed with the intelligentsia of Athens. Merchants from India used to go to the market of Alexandria for trade and commerce. It is said that the first Maurya king was eager to engage a professor of logic from Greece. Aśoka gave the responsibility of ruling over a prosperous province and an important irrigation project to an influential Yavana (Greek). Kanishka seems to have engaged some Greek engineers.

Dion Chrysostom, the noted Greek orator, informs us that the Indians used to sing the poem of Homer. It is stated that they made a version of this work in their own language. So, they were familiar with the pangs of Priam, the laments of Andromache and Hecuba as well as the heroic exploits of Achilles and Hector.

Buddhism forged firm links between India and Ceylon (Sri Lankā). We have got much reliable information about the rise and development of this religion.

It is an important fact of Indian sociology that the Iranian priests, who settled in India, came to be known as Maga Brāhmaṇas or *Śākadvīpīya* Brāhmaṇas; *Śākadvīpīya* from *Śakadvīpa* (island of Śakas) *i.e.* Sistan (Sakas-thāna). They crossed over to India through East Iran of which Sistan was a part. They were regarded as Brāhmaṇas (albeit inferior to the indigenous Vedic Brāhmaṇas) for two reasons. They taught to the Indian Chaldeo-Greek astronomy which they brought with them. Secondly, they were Sun-worshippers. They gradually became a part and parcel of the Hindu society, and a respectable community. The same did not happen to some later Iranian settlers, like the Zoroastrian Parsis, who started seeking refuge in India from after the advent of Muslims into Iran, particularly in the 12th-13th centuries.

Some kinds of textile were imported into India from Iran; *stabaraka* mentioned in the *Harṣacarita* of Bāṇabhaṭṭa (7th cent. A.D.). Levi suggests that Persian tapestry used to be brought to India by Greek ships and merchants.[65] Some scholars suggest that the drop curtain (*yavanikā*) in a dramatic performance in India used to be made of Persian tapestry. The Indian Muslims of the elite class have been deeply influenced by Persian culture, poetry and romance. The Hindu intellectuals of India have partaken of the varied fare, cultural and literary, presented by that country through centuries.

The Muslims were at first intruders from outside. In course of time, they spread over a wide area mainly in North India and some parts of the South. They also converted numerous people to Islam. In the domain of politics, their contribution is quite considerable. They introduced various kinds of reforms in the time-worn system of administration. They deserve special credit in military matters. In fact, they established military oligarchy. They introduced new weapons as well as military tactics and strategy. The new religion, *Din-i-Ilāhi,* introduced by Akbar, paved the way of peaceful co-existence of the different religious communities. The effect of this system was what is now-a-days called emotional integration. According to the Jesuit writer, Bartoli, it produced a synthesis of the *Qurān, Purāṇa* and *Bible.* Thanks to the patronage of the Mughal emperors, particularly Akbar, a distinct school of painting developed. We have already discussed Muslim influence on Indian architecture. Sher Shāh (1472-1545) introduced important innovations in the system of administration. He divided the entire empire into 47 divisions called *Sarkārs,* each of which was divided into several Parganās. Having surveyed all the lands, he arranged to realise revenue directly from the cultivators. The *Kabuliyats,* which he distributed among the tenants, contained statements of their rights and the kinds of revenue payable by them. His another exploit was the introduction of a new coin. Another laudable work done by him was laying out of wide and very long roads which facilitated commercial contact among the different regions. The main road was Grand Trunk Road. This road (1540-1545), 1500 *Krośas* (=3000 miles) long, connects Sonārgāon in Bāngladesh with the Indus in Punjab. This road still exists, and has connected Calcutta with Amritsar in Punjab.

The Muslim influence was responsible for the reorientation in the industry of linen and silk cloths. This influence also affected the making of woollen shawls and mats. Dacca, now in Banglādesh, was the centre for manufacturing very fine and costly luxury cloth; the manufacture was confined to the Muslim community; it was known as *muslin.*[66] Some kind of *muslin* used to be manufactured also in Calicut; but Dacca muslin was more well-known. The contribution of Muslims to the cultural life of India was immense. The influence was felt in dress and decoration in urban life, language, literature, etiquette, fine arts and crafts, food, luxury and refined taste, etc. Muslim influence is still working in parlours, harems and dining rooms. The Darbāri fashion of the Muslims has influenced Hindu dress. It is said that Nurjāhān invented the otto of rose.

India's contact with Irān was established at the time of the advent of the Aryans or even earlier. This contact was the most intimate during the Muslim regime. As a result, various fine arts and crafts of Irān were imported into India. These included the method of enamelling, the method of making earthen vessels which were painted and covered with a fine layer of glass, Kāshmiri gift, studding iron, steel, etc. with sheets of gold and silver etc. The contribution of Persia to Indian painting and architecture has been discussed. In aristocratic circles, Persian garments and etiquette have been widely accepted. The Iranian contribution to the Indian cuisine and sweets is noteworthy. The present-day sweets called *Barfi* and *Qālāquānd* are Irānian in origin. So also are *Jalebi, Mihindānā, Bālushāhi, Nānkhāṭāi,* different kinds of

Halwa. Irān gave us also various kinds of *Polāo, Biriyāni* in place of the ancient *Māṃsaudana* (rice mixed with meat). In place of ancient Indian *Śūlyamāṃsa* (roast-meat) we got from Irān *Kābābs* and *Kawurmās* of different kinds. It is learnt that fruits and vegetables of various kinds had been used since the Sassanian times.[67]

It should be noted that, in dress also, Irān influenced India to some extent.[68] In many parts of India, men used to wear three pieces of unsewn cloth; *dhoti, aṅgavastra* (cover of the upper limbs) and *uṣṇīṣa* (wrapped round the head). The three-piece garment for a woman consists in a *Sāri* reaching down the heels, a scarf for the upper body and head and underwear. To these were added, due to Irānian influence, the trousers, coat and tunic for men and skirts and blouses for women; these styles mostly prevailed in North India.

Strange as it may seem, it is nevertheless true that the Japanese were anxious to get Buddhism to be established in India in all its glory. The influence of Japan and some other Asian countries is felt in Buddhist philosophy and literature. The Japanese industries and politics have had a powerful impact on India.

There have been cultural ties between India and the West since early times. It is learnt that the Maurya king, Bindusāra (4th-3rd cent. B.C.) requested the Greek king of Syria, Antiochus I Soter, to send sweet wine, dry figs and a Greek professor of Logic. Antiochus agreed to send the first two, but informed him that the sale of a professor was illegal. Before the introduction of British rule, the Indians were almost ignorant of modern science and its progress. As a result of the introduction, in the nineteeth century (1834-1845), of English education, they gradually became familiar with it. The western world, especially England, not only gave us scientific education, but also opened the gate of research. Many Indian scientists went to the western countries, and were trained in the methods of modern research. The foundation (15th January, 1784), in Calcutta, of the Asiatic Society, by William Jones paved the way for investigations about the various branches of Indian learning. Thanks to the efforts of the British Government, several departments were set up for investigations in different branches of science; *e.g.* Botanical Survey of India (1890), Zoological Survey of India, Archaeological Survey of India. Voluminous treatises on the respective subjects were published from these departments. For the promotion of study and research in Indology, the Government initiated the work of collecting manuscripts, relating to various branches of ancient Indian learning, in Sanskrit, Prākrit and Pāli, from different parts, rural and urban, of India. Voluminous catalogues were published recording all details of the manuscripts collected, and also details of the manuscripts which could not be collected. Intellectual stalwarts like Max Müller (1823-1900), William Jones (1746-1790), Wilson (1786-1860), etc. engaged, nay dedicated themselves for the study of Indology. The German savant, T. Aufrecht (1822-1907) published (1891, 1896, 1903) his monumental *Catalogus Catalogorum* containing details about manuscripts, published and unpublished, preserved in the libraries and collections of manuscripts throughout the world. The unremitting zeal and untiring efforts of the western scholars resulted in the publication of the Vedas and other valuable scriptures and literary works. Some of them were also translated into European languages, particularly English.

The contribution of the British rulers to the introduction and promotion of women's education (1846-1853) was memorable. Bethune, President of the Education Council and a member of the Executive Council of the Governor General, took a bold step by establishing (1849) the Bethune School. In this work, he was assisted by the progressive Bengalis like Vidyāsāgar (1820-1891) and Madanmohan Tarkālamkār (1817-1885). An American, named Charles Dall, drawn to the intellectual stimulation India offered, arrived in Calcutta in 1855. He urged the intellectuals of

Calcutta not to be satisfied with the small liberties being given by the British, and exhorted them to work for full freedom.[69] Another European stalwart and great scholar of Russia, Minayev, deserves mention in this connection. He came to Bengal in 1886, when there was strong anti-British sentiment and feeling of national independence was fast growing. Minayev supported India's aspirations for independence.

The communism, that has become so popular in India, is also a gift of the west. Another innovation of far-reaching consequence, introduced by the British, was the newspaper. In 1780, for the first time, the newspaper called *Hickey's Gazette*, was published. It was followed by *Bengal Journal.* In both these papers, vulgar language was used. For preventing this, Governor General Wellesley (1769-1852) introduced the system of censorship prior to the publication of the newspapers. This law was made more rigid in 1813. In 1818, it was relaxed by Hastings. As a result, newer papers began to be published. Hastings realised that, for the facility of administering a country of the dimension of India, freedom of the press was necessary. This idea was translated into action by Metcalfe (1785-1846) with the help of Macaulay (1800-1859), by enacting a law which ushered in a new era in Bengal. Ever new news-papers began to be published. The members of the Young Bengal Group, who were pupils of Professor Derozio (b. 1809), devoted themselves to various social reforms; *e.g.* introduction of jury to help judicial administration, prevention of torture of the coolies engaged in the island of Mauritius, permission to lawyers of Mufassil courts to use English in lieu of French, etc.

In the world of sports, the very popular game of cricket originated in England nearly three hundred years ago. It was imported to India after the introduction of British rule. The history of Indian football is also similar. Tennis originated in Egypt or, according to some, in Persia. In 1874, an Englishman, named Wingfield, introduced it in England. It is rather curious that a lady, named Otterbridge, introduced this game in the USA.

In the world of amusement, Cinema has now become a part and parcel of the social life of India. Thousands of people, men, women and children, from all walks of life enjoy seeing talkies on the screen. Directors, producers, technicians, etc. are earning their livelihood by it. The filmstars, both men and women, are amassing immense fortune by providing entertainment to the people. Such a thing is also the gift of the west. At first (1877), there were silent pictures. Talkies were introduced a few years after World War I, when the machine, called Oscilloscope, was invented. In India, Cinema show started (7th July, 1896) in Watson's Hotel in Bombay.

At present, radio, TV, video, etc. are found in every nook and corner of this country. All these we have got from the West.

FOOTNOTES

1. Derived from *Sūf* (wool), it means one who wears a garment of wool. Sind became a Stronghold of Sufism.
2. S.K. Chatterji, *Iranianism*, p. 29; Islamic Mysticism; Iran and India, Vol. I, No. 3 of *Indo. Iranica*, Calcutta, 1946.
3. *Ibid.*, No. 2, 1946.
4. See G.U. Pope, *The Sacred Kurral of Tiruvaḷḷuva-Nāyanār*, London, 1886, Intro, p. iv.
5. Vide *Ency. of Religion and Ethics*, First ed., II, p. 550.
6. See N. Macnicol, *Indian Theism*, 1915, p. 277, and *Cultural Heritage of India*, R.K. Mission, Calcutta, 1983, p. 558.
7. *CHI*, noted above, p. 558, fn. 10.
8. *Ibid.*
9. *A History of the Expansion of Christianity*, 1940, III, p. 283.
10. Codiers, *Marco Polo*, II, p. 437.
11. Mulk Rāj Ānand writes (*The Telegraph*, a daily paper of Calcutta, dated 14.9.90) as follows :
    We have taken the novel from the West as it developed there from Chaucer's *Canterbury Tales* downwards to James Joyce.
12. Vide D' Alvielle - Ce que l' inde doit a la Grece.
13. The protagonists of this hypothesis add another argument based on the use of the word *Yavanikā* in Sanskrit drama.

The word is derived from *Yavana*, which, according to them, denotes Greek. It should be noted that *Yavana* may mean any foreigner, and, in this case, perhaps stands for Persian; because *Yavanikā* or the curtain used to be made of Persian tapestry.

14. See S.C. Banerji, *Cultural Heritage of Kashmir*, pp. 93-94.
15. For subject-matter, see *Ibid.*, pp. 95-96.
16. Vide Banerji, *Hellenism in Ancient India*, pp. 222, 223.
17. See the paper, entitled Has Rāmāyaṇa copied Homer ? *Indian Antiquary*, II. 219; III. 124, 267; XIII. 336, 480.
18. See Jacobi, *Das Rāmāyaṇa*, pp. 94 ff.; Winternitz, *HIL*, I, pp. 514-515.
19. See Winternitz, *Ibid.*, p. 515.
20. *The Greeks in Bactria and India*, 1938, p. 67.
21. *Ibid.*, p. 376.
22. On the relation between India on the one hand and Greece and Egypt on the other, see Keith, *JRAS*, 1910; Kaye, *JRAS*, 1910; Thibaut, *Astronomie, Astrologie and Mathematik*, 1899; D.M. Bose and others, *A Concise History of Science in India*, 1971, chap. 2.
23. This word is derived from Ionia which was originally a hilly area in the coastal region of Asia Minor. In Pāṇini's time (*c.* fourth century B.C.), the word *Yavanānī* denoted wife of *Yavana*. At the time of Kātyāyana, author of the supplementary rules of Pāṇini, this word came to mean the script of the Yavanas. In course of time, any and every Greek used to be designated as Ionian. See W. Durant, *Life of Greek*, 1939, p. 134; Sarton, *A History of Science*, p. 162; Kane, *History of Dharmaśāstra*, V, pt. 1, p. 516, f.n. 743.
24. G.N. Banerji, *Hellenism in Ancient India*, p. 144.
25. *Archives Internationales D'Histoire Des Sciences*, April-June, 1955 (p. 171 and Note 22).
26. Two persons of this name are known; one was a contemporary of Berossus (*c.* 280-261 B.C.), author of *History of Egypt*. The other was author of the metrical work, *Apotelasmata* dealing with applied astronomy. Both were Greek.
27. *Natural History* (77 A.D.).
28. *Names of Stars* (Webb), pp. 163-175, 189.
29. A.B. Keith, *A History of Skt. Lit.*, 1928, p. 528.
30. *History of Dharmaśāstra*, V. pt. 1, pp. 601-02.

31. *Ibid.*, p. 582, f.n. 869.
32. *Archives Internationales d' Histoire des Sciences*, April-June, 1955, p. 170.
33. B. Leclercq, *L'Astrologie*, p. 53; Heath, *Greek Astronomy*, Intro., p. XVI.
34. *Babylonian and Assyrian*, Vol. II.
35. *A History of Science*, p. 78.
36. *Journal of Cuneiform Studies*, Vol. 7, No. 3, pp. 100-102.
37. S.C. Vidyābhusan, Romaka or city of Rome as mentioned in Ancient Pāli and Sanskrit Works, *JASB*, 2, 1906, pp. 1, f.f.
38. *Indian Antiquary*, Vol. 19, pp. 133-142.
39. *History of Dharmaśāstra*, p. 583.
40. E. Burgess, *JAOS*, VI, p. 480.
41. S.K. Chatterji, *Iranianism*, p. 24.
42. See S.C. Banerji, *Kālidāsa Apocrypha*, pp. 205-206.
43. R.C. Majumdar, *Advanced History of India*, 1978, p. 135.
44. See W. Hamilton, *History of Medicine*, I, 43.
45. On this, see our observations in connection with Mathematics in Chap. IV.
46. Arabic word.
47. Persian.
48. Arabic Nakkārah.
49. Persian.
50. "A circular dance performed by women under the direction of man" (Monier Williams).
51. "Name of a particular dance practised by cowherds, especially the dance practised by Kṛṣṇa and the *gopīs*." Monier Williams.
52. "The violent manner which accords with the sentiments of fury, horror and terror. It employs magic, conjuration, conflict, rage, fury and underhand devices." Keith, *Sanskrit Drama.*
53. For details, see G.N. Banerji, *Hellenism in Ancient India.*
54. S.K. Chatterji, *Iranianism*, p. 27.
55. A kind of powdered substance hanging like particles of ice from the roof of the cave.
56. Bunch of stone etc. engraved in the wall.
57. Name of a city which appears to have been connected with Yoginīpura, another name of present Delhi.
58. For Greek influence on Indian architecture, see G.N. Banerji, *Hellenism in Ancient India.*
59. See *Amritā Sher-Gil*, Bombay.

60. Ancient Greek Silver Coin.
61. Vide D'Alvielle-*Ce que l' inde doin a la Grece.*
62. Either a Śaka or an Indo-Parthian king who ruled over Arachosia and the Punjab in *c.* 90 B.C. His name is known only from coins.
63. See our observations on Script in the introduction.
64. *Ibid.*
65. See A.B. Keith, *Sanskrit Drama*, p. 61.
66. Made by hand with indigenous cotton grown at Dacca. Muslin-trade reached a high degree of development under the Mughals. It used to be manufactured up-to the beginning of the 19th century. The price of a piece of *muslin*, made for Aurangzeb, was 1250 rupees in contemporary currency.
67. S.K. Chatterji, *Iranianism*, p. 30.
68. *Ibid.*
69. See the article, The American Connection, published in the daily newspaper, *Telegraph*, Calcutta, dated 17.3.90.

APPENDICES

I

NOTES ON IMPORTANT PERSONS MENTIONED IN THE WORK

Ābdur Rāzzāk

Hailing from Herat, he was sent in 1443 as an envoy, and wrote an interesting account of Vijayanagar.

(Khwaja) Ābdus Sāmād

One of the two painters who were brought by Humāyun (reign 1530-1540, 1555-1556) from Persia.

Ābul Hāsān

A painter from Herat, who lived in the court of Jahāngir (reign 1605-1627).

Ābu Mashār

Arabian astronomer.

Ābu Nāsr (d. 1280)

To him is attributed the Mongolian version of the Arabic translation of the *Pañcatantra.*

Ābu Nasr : Al-Farabi

Greatest philosopher of Islam before Avicenna. Died in 950 A.D. Belonged to Transoxiana. Famous for his commentaries on Aristotle. He is commonly called "second teacher" after Aristotle.

al Asari

Ābul Hāsān Asari. Born 874, he died at Baghdād in 935. Renowned theologian said to have authored 300 works.

al Battani (877-918)

Arabian mathematician influenced by Indian mathematics.

al Beruni (970-1045)

Arabian traveller and a great scholar. He visited India and wrote an account of this country, entitled Tahkik-i-*Hind.* It is a valuable source of information about contemporary Indian learning and society.

albuquerque, A. de

Governor of Portuguese possessions in India from 1509-1515.

al Huzure (d. 1072)

Oldest among the Sufis living in India.

al-Idrisi (1100-1165)

A noted geographer of Arab Spain. Born at Centa (Spain). Studied at Cordova. Was patronised by the Sicilian monarch, Roger II. His principal work is entitled *Nuzhat al-Mushtaq,* etc. (The Stroll of one desirous of crossing the horizons of the Globe).

Al Khwarijmi

Muhammad Musa al Khwarijmi. Belonged to Baghdād, and lived during the reign of the Ābbāsid Caliph at Mamun early 9th cent. A.D. Died about 844. Noted for his contribution to mathematics, geography, astronomy and history.

al Mansur

Ābbāside ruler of Arabia.

al Māsudi (d. 956 A.D.)

Born in Baghdād, he was a renowned Arabian historian and geographer. He visited India. He wrote a 30-volume history.

See Nicholson : Literary *History of Arabs.*

al Fazari (d. 796 or 806)

Arabian astronomer who translated into Arabic the Indian astronomical works *Brāhmasphuṭa-siddhānta* and *Khaṇḍakhādyaka.*

Amoghavarṣa

Name of three Rāṣṭrakūṭa kings of Deccan. Amoghavarsa I (814-77), Amoghavarsa II (917-18), Amoghavarsa III (934-939).

Antiochus Theos (261-246 B.C.)

Greek king of Syria and West Asia.

Antiochus I Soter

Son of Seleucos and king of Syria. Contemporary of Maurya-king Bindusāra (*c.* 300-273 B.C.).

Anushirwan or Nushirwan

It is the name of the famous Sassanian monarch who lived in the 6th century A.D.

Aristoxenus - 4th cent. B.C.

Greek philosopher.

Ashurbanipal

King of Babylonia from 668 - *c.* 627 B.C.

Assumpsão, Manoel-da-

His work, *Vocabulario em idioma Bengalla E Portuguez* (a Bengali grammar and glossary) was printed, in Roman characters, in Lisbon (1743). It was the first grammar of the Bengali language.

Athenaeus (*c.* 200 A.D.)

Greek grammarian.

Atīśa Dīpaṃkara (980-1053)

Bengali Buddhist scholar who, at the invitation of the Tibetan king, went to Tibet, reformed Buddhism there, and wrote several works on Buddhism, particularly on Tantra. He lived there up to his death.

[See A. Chattopādhyāy : *Atīśa and Tibet*]

Aufrecht, T. (1822-1907)

German scholar who edited the entire *Ṛgveda.* His *Catalogus Catalogorum* is a Catalogue of Catalogues of Sanskrit MSS., preserved in different collections in India and abroad.

Augustus

Roman Emperor. The Indian Pāṇḍya king sent an envoy to him in 26 B.C.

Bārbosā

Jesuit traveller who came to India in 1516 A.D. He wrote an account of India, particularly of Vijaynagar.

Bardesanes (155-233)

A Babylonian who is known to have written on the religious thought of the Hindus and Buddhists. He never came to India.

Barmaki Family

Of Iran and a resident of Afghanistān. Writer and Vizier under ancient Ābbāsid Caliphs (8th cent.). Renowned as a patron of culture and as tolerant of others' religious and philosophical views.

The family was interested in works of public utility. Their ancestor was Chief priest of a Buddhist shrine. After going to Basrā (*c.* 66) the members were converted to Islam. Their influence lasted for 17 years. Yahya, son of Khalid in Barmak, died in 805 A.D.

Bārthemā

European traveller who lived in India from 1503 to1508 A.D. He wrote an account of India.

Bartoli

Jesuit writer and clergyman. He visited India at the time of Akbar (1556-1605), and left an account of this country.

Basham, A.L.

World-famous Indologist. His *The Wonder that was India* is a well-known treatise. During the last days of his life, (eighth decade of the present cent.) he served as a Professor in Asiatic Society, Calcutta.

Basilides

Flourished sometime in the third decade of the second century A.D. The incorporation of Hindu and Buddhist thoughts in Christianity was the result of his endeavour. Information about him is found in the *Philosophumena* of Hippolytus and in *Miscellanies* of Clement of Alexandria.

Bernier, F.

Renowned French physician. Lived in India from 1656 to 1668. He left an account of India as he found it in the closing years of Shāhjahān's rule and the beginning of the reign of Aurangzeb.

Bethune, J.E.D. (1806-1862)

Law Member of Supreme Council of India and President (1848) of Bethune Council of Education. A great patron of Bengali literature. At his instance, Michael Madhusudan devoted himself to the cultivation of Bengali literature instead of English. Bethune's most memorable deed was the foundation (1849) of Native Female School, the precursor of the present Bethune School.

Bhandarkar, R.G. (1837-1920)

A Mahārāṣṭra Brahmin, a great scholar and social reformer.

Bhānubhakta

Renowned as the author of the Nepāli Rāmāyaṇa.

Blavatsky (1831-1891)

Madame Blavatsky initiated (1875) the Theosophy Movement in New York.

Bodhidharma (6th cent. A.D.)

Indian scholar who went to China, and helped in the Chinese translation of Buddhist texts.

Bodhisena

An Indian with whose name the Japanese alphabet is associated.

Bonhoyefer

Strong protester of Hitler's despotism in Germany. Believed in Gāndhi's Non-violent Revolution and Passive Resistance.

Bose, Satyendranāth (1894-1974)

Great mathematician and physicist. He advanced Einstein's proposed theory about the characteristics of the gas of electro-magnetic radiation.

Braid, James, (1795-1860) England

Surgeon and pioneer investigator of hypnosis. His findings provided a major impetus to development of French school of new psychiatry.

Burgess, A. (b. 1917) England

Novelist, critic.

Burgess, H. 1825-1892 England

Made wood pulp for paper.

Charlemagne (*c.* 742-814)

King of the France (768-814). He conquered the major portion of west Europe, inhabited by Christians.

Cyrus (*c.* 558-530 B.C.)

Persian emperor who ruled over the region between the rivers Kābul and Indus.

Demetrios

King of Bactria. He conquered a portion of north India in about 190 B.C.

de Ville, E.G. 1849-1924 America

Perfected first practical method of philogrammetry.

Eddy, M.R. (1821-1910) America

Discoverer and founder of religious faith known as Christian Science.

Elliotson, J. (1791-1868) London

Physician. Advocated use of hypnosis in therapy.

Eukratites

A Bactrian Greek who defeated Demetrios (V.V.) in prolonged conflict (160-156 B.C.), and occupied some portions of western India.

Ferista, M.K. (*c.* 1570-1612)

Born in Persia, he was an employee under Sultān Ibrāhim Ādil Shāh II of Bijāpur. He composed, in Persian, the celebrated historical work, entitled *Tārik-i-feristā* or *Gulsān-i-Ibrāhimi.*

Fichte, J.G. (1762-1814)

Philosopher. First of the great transcendental Idealists.

Galen (129-199) Italy

Great physician. One of the most distinguished physicians of antiquity.

Gampo

See Srong-tsan Gampo.

Hadrian (117-138)

Roman emperor.

Halhed, N.B.

An employee of the East India Company, he composed, for the English employees of the Company, *A Grammar of the Bengali Language* (1778). It is written in English with illustrations and quotations in Bengali. It was the first Bengali printed work.

Hāmzā Ibn Āli (985- sometime after 1021)

One of those who introduced the religious system called Draj or Druj. Nothing is known about his life prior to his entry (1017) into Egypt. He was an exponent of the religious faith of the Fatimiyan Caliph, al Hekim. He was connected with an independent religion which became more acceptable than the conventional Islam.

Hargovind Khurānā (1922 -)

Born at Rāypur in India, he carried on research in America, and won Nobel Prize (1968) in Physiology. The subject of his research was Genetic Code. As a result of his research, he declared (1970) the synthesis of entirely artificial gene.

Hartmann, Evon (1842-1906) Germany

Metaphysical philosopher.

Hartmann, J.F. (1865-1936)

German astronomer.

Hartmann, N. (1882-1950) Germany.

Philosopher.

Hartmann, S. (1869-1944)

Art critic, novelist, poet.

Hārun Al Rashid (786-803)

A Caliph of Baghdād.

Hecateus (549-486 B.C.)

A contemporary of Scylax (q.v.), he was a historian and the father of geography in Greece. From the account he left, the Greeks learnt some facts about India.

Hector

Son of Priam and Hecuba in the Homeric poem Iliad (*c.* 9th cent. B.C.).

Hecuba

See Hector.

Hegel, G.W.F. (1770-1831) Germany

Idealist philosopher. One of the great creators of a philosophical system that influenced development of Existentialism, Marxism, Positivism, Analytic philosophy.

Heliodoros

Greek envoy sent, by Antialkidas, Bactrian king of Taxila (Takṣaśilā) (*c.* 140-130 B.C.), to the Śuṅga king Kāsiputra Bhagabhadra. Heliodoros was a Vaiṣṇava, and established a monolithic column (*Garuḍadhvaja*) at Besnagar in Madhya Pradesh. All this is written on the body of the column. It is also written that he was versed in the *Mahābhārata.*

Heraclitus (*c.* 540-480 B.C.)

Greek philosopher famous for his views on cosmology. According to him, in the well-ordered universe, fire was the basic thing. Nothing is known about his life. The book, he appears to have written, is lost. His views are known from references to or quotations from his writings by later writers.

Herodotus (*c.* 484-425 B.C.)

Greek historian. Known as father of history. He wrote an account of India.

Hicky, J. A.

Editor of *Bengal Gazeite*, the first newspaper of India. It first appeared in 1780.

Hipparchus (also Hipparchos)

Flourished between 146 and 127 B.C. Born at Nica Bithynia, now Iznik, Turkey. The greatest astronomical observer of antiquity.

Hippocrates (*c.* 460-377 B.C.)

Greek physician traditionally regarded as the father of medicine.

Hippolytus (*c.* 170-235)

Italian martyr. He was the first to defy the Pope. First among the Roman monks to write on theology and philosophy. He was accused of the faith in dual divinity. The *Philosophumena* is regarded as his *magnum opus.* Fragments of his works are available.

Hitler (1889-1945)

Leader of National Socialist German Workers' party since 1921. Dictator of Germany (1933-1945). He was the man who caused World War II.

Hiuen-ta

Chinese traveller. He came by sea-route to Tāmralipta (modern Tamluk in Midnapore district of W. Bengal), and wrote a travelogue.

Hua

Famous surgeon of China. In his earliest biography (233-297), it is stated that his skill in medical treatment was only an imitation of the great Indian physician, Jīvaka.

Hussain Shāh (1493-1519)

A ruler of Bengal.

Holmes

American monk. He said that Gāndhi was the incarnation of Jesus.

Humboldt (Karl) Wilhelm, F. von 1767-1835 German

Language scholar, philosopher, diplomat and educational reformer. His contribution to the development of language science became highly valued in the 20th century.

Ibn Khurdadbih

Iranian in origin. First half of 9th cent. A.D. He was a postmaster. His work, *Kitābul Masalik,* etc. (Book of Roads and Countries) is an official guide-book, and is the oldest extant geographical work in Arabic.

Justin (Marcus Junianus Justinus)

Flourished in 3rd cent. A.D. Roman historian who was author of *Epitome,* an abridgment of the *Historiae Philippicae* etc. by Pompeius Trogus whose work is lost. It is chiefly a history of Macedonian and the Hellenistic monarchies, with Parthia. It preserves material that is valuable to students of the Hellenic World.

Kant, I. (1724-1804)

German philosopher, Formost thinker of the Englighten-ment. One of the greatest philosophers of all times.

Kipling, R. (1865-1936)

Instructor of morality, short story writer and poet. Strong supporter of British monarchy. His narratives and poems about the British soldiers in India and Burma are well-known.

He is also famous for juvenile stories. His works like *Junglebook*, *Kim*, etc. testify to his prose style. He was awarded Nobel Prize in 1907.

Leucippus

Greek philosopher of the fifth cent. B.C. Referred to by Aristotle, Greek philosopher (d. 322 B.C.) as Father of atomic theory. It is difficult to distinguish his contribution from that of his famous pupil, Democritus. Fragments only of his writings on this subject exist. His basic theory is that matter is homogeneous.

Macaulay, T.B. (1800-1859)

Baron. Famous English poet, essayist, historian and politician. First Law Member of Governor's Executive Council. He symbolized progress in various spheres, Indian administration, spread of English education, framing of Indian Penal Code, etc.

Macdonell, A.A.

A great European Indologist. His *Vedic Grammar* (1910) and *History of Sanskrit Literature* are well known.

Madanmohan Tarkālaṃkār (1817-1858)

Poet and educationist. A classmate of Vidyāsāgar. A professor of Sanskrit literature in Sanskrit College, Calcutta. Court Pundit and Deputy Magistrate. He helped Bethune (q.v.) in the spread of women's education. Edition of various Sanskrit texts and compilation of anthology of Sanskrit verses, with translation, are some of his achievements.

Mahuan (15th cent.)

Chinese writer who left an account of India.

Manaka

Indian physician, a protege of Hārun Al Rashid, Caliph of Baghdād. He translated some Sanskrit works into Persian and Arabic.

Mānik

Perhaps another name of Manaka (q.v.).

Maṇithhācārya

Mentioned in Varāhamihira's *Bṛhajjātaka* (7/1, 11/9). In

the commentary on this work (7/9), Bhaṭṭa Utpala has quoted Sanskrit verses attributed to Maṇittha. A work, entitled *Horāśāstra,* is associated with the name of Maṇittha.

Mansur Al Hallāj (858-911)

An ancient Sufi who came to India.

Manucci, N.

Italian traveller who came to India in the 17th cent., and lived almost throughout Aurangzeb's reign (1658-1707). He wrote an account of contemporary India.

Marco Polo (1254-1324)

A Venetian who came to India in 1288 and 1293, and wrote an account of this country.

Matthew Arnold (1822-1888)

European poet and writer. Renowned as an essayist and critic. He has written also on dharma. His aim was to analyse the Victorian Age, to write about the woes of this period.

Ma-twan Lin

Chinese writer who wrote about India.

Maugham, S. (1874-1965)

British novelist, playwright and short story writer. The main characteristics of his writings are - simplicity, absence of embellishments, keen sensitiveness to human nature, universal background.

Mauhan

Traveller who came to Bengal in 1406. He wrote an account of Bengal.

Mayo

Author of *Mother India.* In it she has depicted the seamy side of Indian society.

Meghavarṇa (*c.* 352-379)

King of Ceylon.

Meghnād Sāhā (1893-1956)

Renowned Astrophysicist. Famous for Thermal ionisation equation (1920).

Meisner, W.

Famous German physicist.

Melissus (5th cent. B.C.)

Greek philosopher and the last significant representative of the Eleatic School.

Menander

Indo-Bactrian king who ruled over Punjab in *c.* 160-140 B.C. In Pāli, he was called Milinda. His dialogue with the Buddhist ascetic, Nāgasena, is written in the Pāli work, *Milindapañha.*

There was also a Greek dramatist of this name.

Mihiragula

Son of the Huna leader, Toramāna. He established capital at Sialkot (Punjab).

Mill, J. S. (1806-1873)

British philosopher, politician, economist and exponent of Utilitarianism. In his works, there is discussion of the main topics of the philosophical and economic thoughts of the 19th cent.

Mīnarāja

A Yavana teacher who, according to some, was identical with the Greek Minos.

Ming-ti (58-75)

Chinese Emperor.

Mīrā Ben

Real name Madelin Slade. Born to affluent European parents, she became a disciple of Gāndhi, and lived in his hermitage.

Moinuddin Chisti

Having immigrated from Central Asia to India in *c.* 1192, he founded the Chisti sect. His tomb at Ajmer (Rājasthān) is a holy place for Muslims.

Monserrate, Fr. Antonio

Highly educated Jesuit monk. Sent (1580) by the Portuguese ruler of Goa to Akbar who appointed him to teach Portuguese to his son. He wrote a valuable account of the Mission to which he belonged. It contains reliable information about Akbar's reign.

Mpu Seda

Author of the Javanese poetical work, *Bhārata-yuddha.*

Muhammad Nādir

This painter from Samarkand adorned the court of Jahāngir (reign 1605-1627).

Muhammad Murād

A painter in the court of Jahāngir (reign 1605-1627).

Muqāfā

Arabian scholar. He translated (*c.* 750) into Arabic the Pahlavi version (6th cent.) of the *Pañcatantra.*

Nietzsche, F. (1844-1900) German.

Classical scholar, philosopher and critic of culture. He had great influence on continental philosophy and literature.

Numenius of Apamea

Flourished in late second century A.D. Greek philosopher. Mainly responsible for the transition from Platonist Idealism to a Neoplatonic synthesis of Hellenistic, Persian and Jewish intellectual systems, with particular attention to the idea of ultimate being or deity and its relation to the material world.

Philostratus

Name of at least three members of a family of ancient Greek writers.

Philostratus, F. (*c.* 170-245 A.D .)

Philostratus (b. *c.* 190 A.D.)

Philostratus called the 'Younger'.

Plotinus (205-270)

Philosopher and religious genius. He transformed a revival of Platonism in the Roman Empire into Neoplatonism. He had great influence on the thought of the Islamic world and on European thought till the late 17th century.

Plutarch (d. 431/432 A.D.)

Greek philosopher. At one time, head of the Platonic school of Athens.

Porphyry (*c.* 234-305) Syrian.

Neoplatonist philosopher. Famous biographer of Plotinus and commentator of Aristotle's Categories, which set the stage for medieval development of logic and the problem of universals.

Pythagoras (6th cent. B.C.)

Philosopher of Samos in Greece. Said to have believed in transmigrations of sought and explanation of the Universe in terms of numbers. Pythagoras' theorem is well known in geometry.

Rabindranath

Renowned poet, novelist, composer of songs, short story writer of Bengal. Born in 1861 he died in 1941. He was awarded Nobel Prize for literature for the English version of his work, entitled *Gītāñjali.*

Rāmacandra Kavibhāratī

A scholar of Gauḍa, who went (*c.* 1245) to Ceylon, and was converted to Buddhism.

Ranade, M.G. (1852-1904)

A Mahārāṣṭra Brāhmin. Dedicated to the welfare of people, he was a scholar and social reformer.

Rihzad

Persian painter, known as the Raphael of the East.

Roe, Sir Thomas

Came (1615) as envoy from James I, king of England, to Jahāngir for negotiating about the security of English merchants.

Romain Rolland (1866-1944)

French writer and a devotee of Rāmkrishna (see under Chronology). Renowned as a biographer of this saint.

Roth, H. (1610-1688)

He wrote in Latin a Sanskrit grammar. He was the first European to deal with this subject.

Rudradāman

Two kings of this name. Rudradāman I was Śaka Satrap of Saurāṣṭra, and ruled from *c.* 128 to 150 A.D. Rudradāman II ruled from *c.* 301-305 A.D.

Ruskin (1819-1900)

Famous English prose writer, critic and artist. Supporter of the revival of Gothic architecture. In this respect, he exercised great influence on the English people of the Victorian Age. Leader of those who opposed Govt.'s policy of Laissez faire.

Sarat Dās (1849-1917)

A Bengali who had the courage of going to Tibet, where the entry of non-Tibetans was prohibited, twice in 1879 and 1881. He, for the first time, translated into English the Tibetan work, *Pag-sam-zon-zang.* He also wrote two books, entitled *Indian Pandits in the land of snow* and *Tibetan-English Dictionary.*

Schopenhauer (1788-1860)

German philosopher who paid eloquent tributes to the Upaniṣad.

Shāhrukh

Sultān of Persia, who sent (1443) Abdur Razzāk as an envoy to India.

Sheng Ching

A Chinese writer. In his travelogue, there is information about India.

Śikṣānanda (652-710)

Khoṭānese scholar who went to China, and translated Buddhist texts.

Sāhā Meghnad

See Meghnad Sāhā.

(Mir) Saiyad Ali

One of the two painters brought by Humāyun (reign 1530-40, 1555-56) from Persia.

Sambhoṭa

A Tibetan, sent by Tibetan king Srong-tsan Gampo (q.v.), to India for studying Sanskrit scriptures.

Sarton, G.A. (1884-1956)

Scholar and writer. Famous among contemporaries. Versed in the history of science.

Satyr

Forest-god of the Greeks. Supposed to have a human form, but ears and the tail like those of a horse.

Schlegel, A.W. Von (1767-1845)

German scholar and critic, who played an important role in the German Romantic Movement. Besides translating Shakespeare's works, he contributed a lot to Sanskrit literature. The first scientific edition and Latin translation of the *Bhagavadgītā* are some of his noteworthy achievements.

His brother, F. Von Schlegel (1772-1829) also was a writer and critic. The greatest achievement of this lover of Sanskrit language and literature was the initiation of the study of Indian linguistics in Germany. The translation of parts of the *Śakuntalā, Mahābhārata,* etc. testifies to his scholarship.

Scylax

Perhaps the earliest Greek writer of an account of India. He was appointed (*c.* 510 B.C.) by Persian emperor, Darius (q.v.), to discover the course of the Indus.

Vide Herodotus, 4/44.

Serapion (middle of fourth cent. B.C.)

A theologian and Bishop of Egypt. Believed in the divinity of Jesus Christ. On this subject he wrote a learned treatise.

Sorābji, K.S. (b. 1892 or 1894).

Famous composer. In the songs, composed by him, he has brought about a synthesis of the eastern melody and western harmony.

Sphūjidhvaja

Mentioned by Bhaṭṭotpala, in his commentary on the *Bṛhatsaṃhitā,* as Yavaneśvara (Greek king).

Steinbech, J.E. (1902-1968)

Became famous in the thirties by writing excellent novel about cultivators. Awarded (1962) Nobel prize in Literature.

Strabo

Greek historian. He wrote an account of India at the time of Alexander's invasion (326 B.C.). In it, many portions of Megasthenes' *Indika* were quoted.

Srong-tsan Gampo (reign 629-650)

Tibetan king who founded the capital at Lhāsā. He maintained cultural contact with India.

Sulaimān

Arabian merchant and traveller. Perhaps the first Arabian to write an account (851 A.D.) of India.

Sumpā

Author of the Tibetan chronicle, entitled *Pag.*

Sūryavikram (d. 688)

A king of Burma.

Syce (1845-1945)

Famous linguist. He was proficient in many languages including Sanskrit. He wrote about 20 ancient and modern languages.

Tylor, E.B. (1832-1917)

Englishman. Anthropologist regarded as the founder of cultural anthropology.

Vasco da Gama

Portuguese navigator. He reached Calcutta, an Indian port, in 1498. He was the first European to set foot on India. He discovered the direct sea-route between Europe and India.

Vasubandhu (4th or 5th cent. A.D.)

Famous Buddhist philosopher, brother of Asaṅga. Author of many works. Commented on *Mahāyānasūtra, Saddharmapuṇḍarīka* and *Mahāparinirvāṇa-sūtra.*

Victor Hugo (1802-1885)

Poet, dramatist, novelist. Most prominent French Romantic writer.

Vijaysiṃha

Mentioned, in the two chronicles of Ceylon, viz. *Dīpavaṃsa* and *Mahāvaṃsa,* as the founder of the first royal dynasty of that country.

Vīrakorca

Probably a king of this name ruled in India. Vide Copper Plate inscription of Nandivarman III, Pallava king of South India.

Vītapāla

Dhīmān and Vītapāla were renowned artists under the *Palas.*

Voltaire (1694-1778)

French writer of satire; known as Father of French prose literature. A strong protagonist of independence and progressive ideas. He had tremendous influence in contemporary Europe, especially in French society. His writings fuelled the French Revolution.

Whitman (1819-1892)

American writer influenced by Indian thought and Sanskrit literature.

Whitney, W.D. (1827-1894)

He became famous by writing a book, entitled *Sanskrit Grammar* (Leipzig, 1879).

Yākubi, Ahmed

Famous Arab historian and geographer (d. 897 A.D.).

He wrote a history of the world which he brought down to the year 872.

Yaśovarman (reign 889-908)

Cambodian king. There are many Sanskrit inscriptions of his regime.

II

NOTES ON IMPORTANT WORKS MENTIONED IN THE WORK

Āmir Hamza

See Dāstān-i-Amir-hamzah

Avestā

Holy book of the Persians. The Sassanian priests used this word to indicate the language of Zarathustra and the works of him and of the religious teachers preceding him.

Bakhsāli Manuscript

Discovered in 1881 at village Bakshāli near Peshāwār. Preserved in Bodleian library at Oxford. It dates back to a period between the third cent. and the fourth, according to some, to the 12th cent. according to others. It deals with arithmetic, algebra, geometry, mensuration and various other matters.

Bower Manuscript

Discovered by one, named Bower, in 1890, at Kāshgar in Central Asia. It comprises seven treatises dealing with

(1-3) medical science ;

(4-5) Cubomancy ;

(6-7) *Mahāmāyūrī Vidyā*, a charm for counteracting the poison caused by snake-bite.

Cilappatikaram (2nd cent. A.D.)

Renowned Tāmil epic poem. It refers to Indo-Mālayan trade relations.

Dāstān-i-Āmir-hamzah

Persian work dealing with the imaginary heroic exploits of Āmir Hamzah, an uncle of the Prophet of Islam. A 17th cent. Bengali poet, Ābdur Nabi, translated the poem into Bengali; the translation took the form of an epic.

Elenchos

Its subject-matter is the refutation of long-established doctrine of the Christian religious community. In it, the Upaniṣad-based doctrines of the Brāhmaṇas of Tagavena (Tungavena or Tuṅgabhadrā in the Decean) have been briefly stated. Its another name is *Philosophumena.*

Enoch

First book of Enoch, also called Ethiopic Book of Enoch, a pseudoepigraphical work resembling authentic biblical literature, but non-canonical. Only complete extant version is an Ethiopic translation of a previous Greek translation made in Palestine from original Hebrew or Aramaic.

Hicky's Gazette

The first newspaper (1780) published in India. Suppressed by Hastings in 1782 for its persistent attacks on the Government and its personnel.

Hippocratic Collection

The works, known by this title, were not all actually written by Hippocrates. They probably constituted the library of the medical school at Cos, where he taught. It deals with anatomy, clinical subjects, diseases of women and children, prognosis, treatment by diet and drugs, surgery, etc.

Hudud-al-alam

(Regions of the world)

A geography written in Persia in 982 A.D.

Iliad

An epic poem by the Greek poet Homer (*c.* 9th cent. B.C.) At the end of the narrative there is mention of the siege of the city of Troy for the rescue of the heroine, Helen.

Kata Pason Aireseon Elenchos

See Elenchos.

Kural

Renowned Tamil poem composed by Tiru Bālluvar after 500 A.D. It deserves a high position among the literary works on Indian metaphysics. It has been translated into several provincial languages of India and some of the European languages.

Les Races Aryans de Peru

Written by Lopez, it mentions, *inter alia*, that there is the influence of the *Rāmāyaṇa* and the *Mahābhārata* on the poetical literature of Peru (America).

Manuṣya Jātaka

An astrological work in Arabic with a Sanskrit commentary in Devanāgarī script.

Milindapañha

A Pāli treatise dealing with the dialogue between the Greek king, Milinda, and the Buddhist monk, Nāgasena. Milinda is the Pāli name of the Indo-Greek king who ruled over the Punjab from about 160 B.C. to 140 B.C.

Odyssey

An epic poem by the Greek poet, Homer (*c.* 9th cent. B.C.). Its main theme is the description of the heroic exploits of Odeysseus (Ulysses) returning to Ithaca after the siege of Troy.

Open Door to Hidden Heathendom (1651)

Dutch translation of the Sanskrit works, *Nītiśataka* and *Vairāgyaśataka*, done by the Dutch priest, Abraham Roger. It was the first Sanskrit work to be translated into an European language.

Oxyrhynchus Papyri

Many pieces of papyrus (a kind of paper made from a kind of grass) discovered in the village, called Oxyrhynchus, in Egypt. These date back to the period from 250 B.C. to 700 A.D. Most of these are written in Greek and Latin. Some are written also in Egyptian language, Hebrew, Arabic, etc. Among these are religious writings (e.g. *New Testament*) and best portions of classical Greek literature.

Pag Sam Jon Jang

A Tibetan chronicle, composed by Sumpā, and translated into English by Sarat Dās.

Periplus of the Erythrean Sea

Composed, in the second half of the first century A.D., by a sailor living in Egypt. It contains a good deal of information about India.

Philosophumena

See Elenehos.

Seven Hedin Collection

Preserved in Stockholm (Sweden), it contains portions of the Indian *Āgamaśāstra.*

Suppliant Woman

A drama by the Greek scholar, Eschylus. It briefly depicts Indian lifestyle.

Suprematic

A poetical work by Victor Hugo. It appears to have incorporated Upaniṣadic ideas.

Timaeus

A work of Plato (428-348 B.C), it discusses pathology of the medical science.

Tutināmā

Persian version of a Sanskrit original containing seventy stories purported to have been related by a parrot. It was first translated by one Maulana Ziauddin Bakshi during the middle of the 14th century A.D. The Persian version was translated into Urdu by Haidar Baksh Haidari of Fort William College, Calcutta, and published by John Gilchrist in 1801.

Weber Manuscript

It contains the translation of some prescriptions relating to medical treatment, written in Sanskrit, into Kuchi language of Central Asia.

III
IMPORTANT PLACES MENTIONED IN THE WORK

Agnideśa

Name of a region on the way from Kuchi to Tun Hwang in Central Asia.

Ākhun Dheri

A place in Gandhāra (q.v.). Here an image of three divinities together (*c.* 3rd cent.) has been discovered. In the middle, there is the image of Śiva.

Akkad

Ancient name for the modern part of middle Iraq, home of ancient Babylonian civilisation. People and their language are called Akkadian.

Alexandria

A city founded by Alexander (4th cent. B.C.) in Egypt. It was a renowned centre of Hellenic culture and a great port through which trade and commerce were carried on between India and the western world.

Amarāvatī

Name of a city in the district of Guntur in Madras (Tamil Nādu). During the rule of the Sātavāhanas, (*c.* 60 B.C. - 4th cent. A.D.)

It was the main centre of Hindu culture. An independent school of painting, sculpture and architecture developed here. This school was earlier than those of Mathurā and Gandhāra, and is absolutely free from Greek influence.

Angkor Thom

A city in Cambodia (Kampuchea), containing the magnificent temple, called Angkor Vat.

Angkor Vat

A wonderful Śaivite temple (10-4-9-1066) in the city of Angkor Thom in Cambodia (Kampuchea)

Ārākān

A strip of land on the east coast of Bay of Bengal. It had been a Hindu colony since ancient times, perhaps from even before Christian era. In the beginning of the 15th cent., when the king of Burma occupied Ārākān, the Ārākān king regained it with the help of the Sultāns of Bengal, and continued to rule as a vassal of the reigning Sultān.

In the Mughal regime, the king of Ārākān invaded Bengal several times. Two outposts of Ārākān were established in Chittāgong and Sandip in East Bengal (now Banglādesh), and oppression continued from these places. Shāyestā Khān (governor of Bengal, 1663-93) occupied these two outposts, and curbed the Ārākānese oppression to a considerable extent. In 1784, Burma occupied Ārākān. As a result of war from 1824 to 1826, Ārākān was annexed by the British.

Under Muslim rule, in the 17th cent. two Bengali poets adorned the court of Ārākān. One of them was Daulat Kāji, author of *Satī Mayanā O Lorcandrāṇī,* and the other was Ālāol, author of the *Padmāvatī* and of a few other poetical works.

Attic

Name of Athens in Greece.

Babylon

A very ancient land on the back of a tributary of the river Euphrates in South Iraq.

Bactria

The land between the Hindukush and river Oxus. It was included in the Syrian empire of Seleucus (General of Alexander).

In about 202 B.C. it became an independent Hellenic Kingdom. King Demetrios conquered (*c.* 190 B.C.) parts of Punjab and Afghānistān. Thus the people of north western India came into close contact with the Hellenic people of Bactria.

Bagdo Khānaulā

Name of a holy mountain in Mongolia.

Besnagar

The ancient city of Vidiśā, in Madhya Pradesh, was known by this name in later times. Here stands Heliodoros' Column built, in honour of Vāsudeva, by the Greek, called Heliodoros who was sent as an envoy by Antialkidas (*c.* 140-130 B.C.), the Bactrian King of Taxilā.

Boghāz Kyoi (or Keui)

In Asia Minor. At this place has been discovered inscription of about 14th cent. B.C. It contains the names of Kings, Daśaratha, etc. and of Vedic deities, Indra, Varuṇa, etc. This throws some light on the age of the Vedas.

Bolivia

Name of a country in South America.

Byzantium, Byzantine culture and civilisation

Byzantium or Constantinople (modern Istānbul) was made the capital of the Roman empire in 330 A.D. In 395, emperor Theodosius divided the Roman empire into eastern and western parts. In the eastern or Byzantine empire was included Macedonia, Thrace, Greece, Crete, Asia Minor, Syria and Egypt. Byzantium fell in 1453.

The period from 330, especially from 375 to 1453, was the period of the Byzantine empire. In this period, arts, literature, especially architecture developed to a great extent.

Campā

A colonial kingdom founded by Indian Hindus in the 2nd cent. A.D. It is Annam (Vietnam) in Indo-China; its capital also is called Campā. Many temples of Hindu deities and Sanskrit inscriptions indicate widespread Hindu influence in this country. In the 16th cent., the Mongolian people, living in Annam, brought about the end of this kingdom.

Candraketugarh

Name of a place in the district of 24-Parganās (North), about 25 miles north-east of Calcutta. According to some, it is the Gānge of the Periplus (1st cent. A.D.) and the Gangaridai of Ptolemy (2nd cent. A.D.). Terracotta images of Yakṣiṇīs, various seals, cast copper coins, etc. have been discovered here. These date back to the Śuṅga (*c.* 185-73 B.C.) and post-Śuṅga ages. Brick-built temples and dwelling houses began to be constructed here since Gupta Age (*c.* 320-510 A.D.) Pieces of black painted grey earthwares have also been found.

Chaldea

In modern Irāq. Formerly it was included in South Babylon. It has been repeatedly referred to in the *Old Testament*. Sometimes, the name was used to refer to entire Babylon. As a matter of fact, it was generally used to indicate the region between the Arabian desert and the delta of the river Euphrates, above the Persian Gulf. Its earliest mention occurs in the story of an Assyrian King (884-859 B.C.)

Chaṇgnan

In China. Indian astronomy used to be cultivated in the astronomical institution established here.

Chichen

A place in Mexico, having traces of Indian culture.

Coatzumalhuapa

Guatemala in America. There are traces of Indian culture at this place.

Constantinople

See Byzantium.

Dakota

A place in USA.

Dandan Ulik

In East Turkestan. Certain articles, discovered here, indicate, the influence of Śaivism.

Dilwara Temple

Renowned Jaina temple at Mount Ābu in Rājasthān.

Ethiopia

A country in Africa.

Euphrates

River of S.W. Asia. Rising in Turkey, it crosses Syria and enters Irāq.

Far East

China, Japan, Mongolia and South-East Asian countries, Java, Sumatra, etc.

Fort William

Built in 1696-1715 for the defence of Calcutta. Sirāj-ud-daulāh, Nawab of Bengal, occupied it. The British regained it in 1757. Later on, the fort was shifted. In the old site are located the General Post Office, Customs House, etc.

In 1800, Fort William College was established by Lord Wellesley. The object was to educate the new civil servants of East India Company. Education in various subjects, *e.g.* science, arts, law, etc. was imparted in this college. The Bengali Department was opened in 1801. Among the works, published by this institution, were the earliest works in Bengali prose, *Rāmāyaṇa* of Kṛttivās and *Mahābhārata* (part) from Serampore Baptist Mission Press.

Fu-nan

Ancient Chinese name of Kambuja (Cambodia, modern Kampuchea).

Gandhāra

Ancient name of the region comprising the districts of Peshāwar and Rāwalpindi in Pakistan.

Gauḍa

Ancient name of the region comprising the districts of Māldā and Mursidābād in West Bengal. Some say that it was so named as large quantities of *guḍa* (molasses) were produced in this area.

Gordez

A place in Afghānistān. Archaeological materials, relating to Śaivism, dating back to 7th-8th cent. have been unearthed here.

Hāmāwā

Name of a place in Burma.

Ionia

Originally a country in Asia Minor.

Itza

There are traces of Indian culture at this place, situated in Mexico.

Kambuja

See Fu-nan.

Kampache

A place in Mexico, having a dancing image (5th or 6th cent. A.D.) of Śiva.

Karṇasuvarṇa

Name of the capital of the ancient Gauḍa (q.v.) kingdom. Same as modern Mursidābād.

Kāshgar

Included in Central Turkestan. The Kushān King, Kaniska, wrested (sometime between *c.* 120-44 A.D.) this place from the Chinese. In the seventh century, Buddhist influence was widespread here. Hiuen Tsang has written about it.

Keda

Ruins of Śiva-temple are found at this place in Mālay.

Khorā

Name of a place in Central Asia. It was a centre of Indian culture, especially of Buddhism.

Khoṭān

A region in Central Asia. Time was when many Indians used to live here. Some Sanskrit treatises have been found here. Many Buddhist topes and monasteries have been discovered in this region.

Kotohi

A place in Japan.

Kuchi or Kuchā

A city in Turkestan. A centre of Indian culture, particularly of Buddhism, towards the beginning of the Christian era. It was from here that a Buddhist monk, named Kumārajīva, was taken by the Chinese as a captive. Since then he preached Buddhism in that country.

La Venta

In Mexico, having signs of Indian culture.

Levant

A general term used to indicate the countries in the east of the Mediterranean and neighbouring areas.

Mahāsthāngarh

A place in Bagurā district of Banglādesh. Ruins of the ancient Puṇḍra city have been found here. Excavations here have yielded many archaeological materials, *e.g.* terracotta dolls and idols, ruins of temples of Gupta Age (*c.* 320-510 A.D.).

It has been proved that it was an important place as early as at least the first century A.D.

Māldives

A country constituted of a group of islands situated about a 1000 kilometres south west of Trivandrum and about 400 miles by sea from the western coast of Srilankā.

Maynāmatī

The Maynāmatī-Lālmāi range of hills is situated not very far from the town of Comilla in Banglādesh. Excavations here have yielded copper-plates, gold and silver coins, Buddha-images and ruins of Buddhist monasteries and topes. These have helped in the reconstruction of the forgotten history of Samataṭa (q.v.). In this area evidences have been found about the spread of Sahajayāna doctrine, prosperity of the kingdom of Paṭṭikera (q.v.), cordial relation between the rulers of Samataṭa (q.v.) and Ārākān (q.v.)

Mesopotamia

Site of a very ancient civilisation in Irāq.

Middle East

Combined name of Turkey, Irān, Afghānistān and Central Asian democratic countries.

Minpagan

A place in Burma.

Mitanni

Name of an ancient state in north-western Mesopotamia. It was founded by the Hurrians.

Moche

A place in Mexico, having traces of Indian culture.

Nazca

In Mexico. There are traces of Indian culture in this region

Near East

Not much used now-a-days. Formerly it was used as the combined name of the region comprising present Egypt, Lebanon, Syria, Palestine, Saudi Arabia, Yemen, Aden, Oman, Iraq, Quait.

Novalishe

In the Philippines. Many archaeological materials, some of which relate to India, have been unearthed.

Pagan

In Burma, having a Vaiṣṇava temple.

Pāhārpur

A place in Bangladesh, about three miles west of Jāmālganj Railway station. Called Somapura under the Pāla rulers. A copperplate, found here, dating back to 479 A.D., is the earliest archaeological find. In the post-Gupta Age, there was a rich Brāhmaṇical temple here. The style of sculpture in the images of Śiva, Kṛṣṇa and Annapūrṇā, found at Pāhārpur, is of high order. The Buddhist Saṅghārāma, built here by king Dharmapāla (*c.* 770-810), is famous under the name Sompura Mahāvihāra in Tibetan works and is the largest in India. This institution, deprived of royal patronage under the Sena rulers of Brāhmaṇical pursuasion, disappeared in the Muslim regime. Excavations here have yielded many archaeological materials.

Palanque

In Mexico. There is the renowned Cross here.

Pantaran

In East Jāvā. Here *Rāmāyaṇa* scenes were painted in the 14th cent.

Pegu

A place in Burma.

Penang

A place in Mālay. Sanskrit inscriptions have been found here.

Peru

A country in South America.

Prambanan

In west Jāvā. *Rāmāyaṇa* pictures, dating back to the 9th century, have been found here.

Puṇḍravardhana

Modern Pāṇḍuā. In later times, located six miles north of Firuzābād, Māldā and 20 miles north-east of Gauḍa (q.v.).

Śailendra Empire

The Śailendra dynasty was established in the eighth century, and continued to rule till the 13th century. This empire comprised Mālay Peninsula and almost the whole of Mālay Archipelago, Sumātrā, Jāvā, Bāli and Borneo.

Samataṭa

Mentioned in Samudragupta's Allāhābād Inscription as a tributary kingdom. It was in modern Banglādesh. In the *Bṛhatsaṃhitā* (6th cent.), Samataṭa and Vaṅga have been mentioned as two separate kingdoms. According to Hiuen Tsang (7th cent.), this kingdom was on the seacoast, on the south of Kāmrup and Assam. It lasted till the 13th cent.

Shikoko

Name of an island in Japan.

Shosho-in

The main store in the principal provincial temple, known as Todaiji, established at Nara in 745 A.D.

Sitābengā

A cave in Sargujā, Madhya Pradesh. In it, a theatre, like Greek theatre, has been discovered.

South-East Asia

It comprises Thāiland, Mālaysia, Singāpore, Philippines, Burma, Vietnam, Laos, Kampuchea, Indonesia, Transbaikalian Siberia; (Asiatic Russia), etc.

Sravana Velgolā

A place at Mysore (Karnāṭaka). According to a Jaina tradition, Candragupta Maurya, having renounced his kingdom, came here and starved himself to death. On a hill at this place is a monolithic image of Jaina Gomata more than 56 ft. high. It is, perhaps, unique in the world.

Śrīśaila

Kambuja Kingdom.

Srivijay Kingdom

A city and a kingdom of this name existed in Mālay Archipelago. The city has been identified as modern Palembing in Sumātrā. The above kingdom was established by Indian colonists towards the close of the 13th cent.

Sumeria or Sumer

The stretch of land lying between the rivers Tigris and Euphrates on the western extremity of Asia. Southern part of ancient Babylon (modern South Irāq). The Sumerians were the earliest civilised nation of Asia. There were quite a few prehistoric places in Sumer in the first half of the third milennium B.C.

Saurāṣṭra

Name of some parts of Kāthiāwad and Gujarāṭ. According to some, older name of Surāṭ.

Suvarṇadvīpa, Suvarṇabhūmi

Ancient name of Indo-China and Indonesia in South-East Asia. Sometimes the islands are separately called Suvarṇadvīpa. Perhaps people used to believe that much gold was available in this region.

Tagao

A place in Afghānistān, where archaeological materials, relating to Śaivism and dating back to 7th-8th cent., have been discovered.

Tāmraparṇī

Name of Ceylon in Pāli works and in inscriptions of Ceylon.

Tarikistan

In Soviet Central Asia. The name of Nārāyaṇa occurs in a fragmentary inscription (2nd cent. B.C.) of this place.

Thaton

Name of a place in Burma.

Tīrabhukti

Tirhut in Bihār.

Tun Huang

In Central Asia. Figures of Hindu deities are found in paintings of this place.

Turfān

In Central Asia. It was a centre of Indian culture, especially of Buddhism.

Uxmal

A place in Mexico, having traces of Indian culture.

Vikramaśila

A renowned Buddhist monastery founded, at Pātharghāṭā in Bhāgalpur district of Bihār, by the Pāla king, Devapāla. In course of time, it was turned into a well-known centre of learning. It was from here that the great Atīśa Dīpaṃkara went to Tibet (1038).

Viṣṇukrānta

A regional name occurring in Śaktimaṅgala Tantra; The area from the Vindhyas to Java.

IV
RACES AND DYNASTIES

Andean

Andean civilisation comprises the aboriginal Indian cultures centred in the highland and coastal areas of western and north-western South America, that flourished from 3500 B.C. to 16th cent. A.D. (Spanish conquest).

Austro-Asiatic

People of this race lived in India in the prehistoric age.

Aztec

A race living in Aztlan or White land. They had a vast empire covering the present Central and South Mexico in the 15th cent. A.D. and the early part of the 16th cent. The place of their origin was, perhaps, North Mexico. In the 14th cent. and sometime in the 15th, these people lived on agriculture and were feudal subjects.

Candella

A Rājput race. The people of this race claimed to be Kṣatriyas. According to some, originally they were a tribe named Gond or Bhar, and were raised to the status of Kṣatriyas after acquiring the kingdom.

They ruled over Bundelkhand (Vindhya Pradesh) between the south of the Yamunā and north of the Vindhyas. Beautiful specimens of their architecture exist in Khajurāho and other places. After the decline of the Pratihāras towards the end of the 10th cent., they extended their sway over north India.

Inca

Indians of South America. They ruled over a vast empire till the Spanish victory (1532). This empire spread, along the Pacific coast and in the Andean highland, from the northern extremity of Ecuador to Central Chile. Having established their capital at Cuzco in the 12th cent. they began their victorious march in the beginning of the 15th cent., and established their sway over the Andeans. Their technology and architecture were of high order. The ruins of their culture still exist in the region of Andes.

Kalacuri

A royal dynasty that lived in Mālwā and north Mahārāṣṭra. Also known as Haihaya. The name of their kingdom was Cedi which was included in the present Madhya Pradesh. The king of this dynasty ruled from the 11th cent. to the eighth decade of the 12th.

Karkoṭa

Name of a royal dynasty of Kāshmir. The kings of this dynasty ruled from the seventh century to 855 A.D.

Khmer

People of Cambodia (Kampuchea) belonged to this race.

Magi

Plural from Magus, a member of ancient Persian priestly caste. The three Magi, the wise men from the East, who brought offerings to the infant Christ. (Matthew, 2.1).

Sassanian Dynasty

Of Iran, founded in 224 A.D. The Arabians destroyed it between 637 and 651 A.D. It was named after Sasan. There was great progress in arts and learning during this period.

V
LANGUAGES
MENTIONED IN THE WORK

Languages of special types are indicated below

Hittite

Language of a race of people who lived in Anabolia (Asia Minor) in West Asia in the period between 2000 and 1200 B.C. The Hitti empire had its capital near Boghazkeui, a village about 150 miles east of Ānkārā, capital of Turkey. This language has been determined as a very ancient branch of Indo-European family.

Kavi (or wi)

Name of a highly polished Javanese language.

Khmer

Language of Cambodia (present Kampuchea)

Romany

Included in north Indo-Aryaṇ family. In different continents, taken together, about 30 lac people of the gypsy class speak this language.

Tokharian

An extinct Indo-European language. It was current in Central Asia in the first millennium A.D.

VI

IMPORTANT DATES[1]

(In alphabetical Order)

Aihole Inscription of Pulakeśin	II 634 A.D.
Alberuni's visit to India	C. 1030 A.D.
Alexander's invasion of India	327-326 B.C.
Arthaśāstra	Generally assigned to 4th cent. B.C.
Aśoka	C. 269-232 B.C.
Aṣṭādhyāyī	See Pāṇini
Bharata	See *Nāṭyaśāstra*
Buddha	C. 563-483 B.C. Nirvāṇa 486 B.C., according to tradition.
Caitanya	1486-1538 A.D.
Fa-hien's visit to India	399 A.D.
Gupta Age	C. 300-647 A.D.
Hiuen-tsang's visit to India	630-645 A.D.
Indus Valley Civilisation	C. 2500-1500 B.C.
I-tsing's visit to India	671-695 A.D.
Kālidāsa	Controversial. Generally believed, by modern scholars, to have flourished around 400 A.D.

1. For further information see S.N. Pradhan, *Chronology of Ancient India*; R. Singh, *A Dictionary of World Chronology*; M. Dutt, *Chronology of India;* C.M. Doff, *Chronology of India*; Sitanathy, *Chronology of Ancient India.*

Kalhaṇa	See Rājataraṅgiṇi
Kāmasūtra	C. 3rd cent. A.D.
Kauṭilya	See *Arthaśāstra*
Kurukṣetra Battle (Nucleus of the *Mahābhārata*)	C. 1000-900 B.C.
Lakṣmaṇasena (King of Bengal)	Accession 1178 A.D.
Mahābhārata	Present form finalised C. 4th cent. A.D.
Mahābhāṣya	See Patañjali
Mahāvīra	d. 468 B.C. (According to others, 528 B.C.)
Manu-smṛti (or saṃhitā)	Extant text between 2nd cent. B.C. and 2nd cent. A.D.
Megasthenes	Visit to India 302 B.C.
Nāṭyaśāstra	Perhaps earlier than 4th cent. A.D.
Pāḷa rule in Bengal & Bihar	C. 760-1142 A.D.
Pāṇini	C. 4th cent. B.C.
Patañjali	C. 2nd cent. B.C.
Pulakeśin II	See Aihole Inscription
(Mahā-) Purāṇas	Earliest extant Purāṇa perhaps 3rd cent. A.D. and the latest 15th cent. A.D.
Rājataraṅgiṇi	Present form c. 2nd or 3rd cent. A.D.
Rāmāyaṇa	Present form finalised about 2nd or 3rd cent. A.D.
Ṛgveda	Highly controversial. Different dates from 12,000 B.C. to 1,000 B.C., suggested by scholars. According to Winternitz, C. 2,500-2,000 B.C.

Śaka Year (Śakābda)	Commencement 78 A.D.
Sena rule in Bengal	C. 1118-1199 A.D.
Tantra	Generally believed to have originated in literary form in or after 5th or 6th cent. A.D.
Vātsyāyana	See *Kāmasūtra*
Vikramāditya	Appellation of different kings. Of them the Gupta king Candragupta II ascended throne in c. 380 A.D.
Vikrama Saṃvat	Commencement 57 B.C.
Yājñavalkya-smṛti	C. 100-300 A.D.

VII
A NOTE ON GYPSIES

The following information has been gathered from an article, published, by Dipak Kumar Das, in the Bangali Calcutta daily, *Ānandabājār*, d/23.8.98.

Charles Leyland has been trying to discover the origin of Gypsies.

According to some, the term Gypsy has been derived from Egypt which was the original home of this community. Gypsies are known as Gitāni in France, Sinita in Italy, Jitāno in Spain, Gypsy in Britain and America, Luri in Iraq , Kāuli in Afghanistan, Cinghānls or Cingānes in Turkey and Syria, Beduin in Arabia.

Some historians think that more than 1,500 years ago, the ancestors of Gypsies used to live in the north-west of India and the banks of the river, Indus. From the third century B.C. onward they migrated to the north-west Asia and then to Egypt. Between the thirteenth century and the sixteenth, they fannedout in Europe and America.

It has been found that, of all the peoples of the world, the Gypsies have the greatest affinity with the Indians in language, customs and physical characteristics. Hence, in the opinion of the above-named scholar, Indians were the original ancestors of the Gypsies. Some instances of linguistic affinity between the Indians and the Gypsies:

Language of the Gypsies	*Language of India*
Aṅguṭha	Āṅgul
Dānta	Dānt
Deval	Devatā
Gāon	Grāma
Mā	Mā
Mānuṣa	Mānuṣa
Nāka	Nāka
Pāni	Jāl
Rāt	Rāt
Jib	Jibh
Śālo	Śālā

Select Bibliography

SANSKRIT WORKS

(Texts and Translations)

(In *Devanāgarī* Alphabetical order)

Aparājitapṛcchā (on architecture), ed. P.A. Mankad, 1950.

Arthaśāstra, ed. G. Sastri, Eng. trs. by Shamasastri, Bangalore, 1915 (2nd ed., 1923); by J.J. Meyer, Manover, 1925, R.P. Kangle, Bombay, 1963; Hindi ed. Bhārtīya Yoga, Bareilly, 1973.

Āryabhaṭīya, ed., with *Bhaṭṭadīpikā* comm. and general index, by H. Kern, Leiden, 1874; Entire work trs. by P.C. Sen Gupta in *Jour. of Deptt. of Letters*, Calcutta University, vol. 16, 1927; W.E. Clark (with notes), Chicago, 1930.

Karaṇatilaka Kāmasūtra, ed. D. Sastri, with Skt. *Jayamaṅgalā* comm. and Hindi comm., Varanasi, 1964; Trs. into Eng. by K.R. Iyengar, Lahore, 1921; into German by R. Schmidt, W. Friedrich, Leipzig, 1897 (2nd ed., Berlin, 1900); into French by F. Lemairesse, G. Carre', Paris, 1891.

Kathāsaritsāgara of Somadeva, Tawney's Eng. trs., ed. by Penzer, 10 vols. (Ocean of Story)

Khaṇḍakhādyaka, ed. P.C. Sengupta, with comm. of Pṛthūdakasvāmin, Calcutta, 1941; B. Chatterji, with comm. of Bhaṭṭotpala, Eng. trs., Intro. and notes, Delhi, 1970. Trs. into Eng. by P.C. Sen Gupta, 1934.

Caturaṅgadīpikā (of Śūlapāṇi), ed. M. Ghosh, Calcutta, 1936.

Carakasaṃhitā, ed., with Eng., Hindi and Gujarāṭi trs., by Āyurvedic Society, Jamnagar, 1940.

Chāndogyopaniṣad

Nāṭyaśāstra, ed. M. Ghosh, Calcutta, vol. I, 1967, vol. II, 1961. Bengali trs. by Sures Bandyopadhyay, Calcutta, vols.

I-III; Trs. into Eng. by M. Ghosh, Calcutta, vols. I, II, 1951, 1961.

Pañcasiddhāntikā, ed. with comm. and Eng. trs. by G. Thibaut and S. Dvived, Benares, 1868.

Purāṇa - For titles and contents of the eighteen principal Purāṇas, see S.C. Banerji, *Studies in Mahāpurāṇas*, Calcutta, 1990.

Brāhmasphuṭa-siddhānta (Brahmagupta), ed. with *Siddhāntaprakāśikā* comm. by M. Ojha, Benares, 1961.

Bṛhatsaṃhitā (Varāhamihira), ed. S. Dvivedi, with Bhaṭṭotpala's comm., 1895, 1897, with trs. and notes, by M.R. Bhat, 1981.

Manu-saṃhitā, ed., with Kullūka's comm., by J.L. Sastri, and Intro. by S.C. Banerji, Delhi, 1975.

Yājñavalkya-smṛti, with *Mitākṣarā* comm., NSP ed., 1926 (3rd ed.).

Saṃgītaratnākara (of Śārṅgadeva), with comms. of Siṃhabhūpāla and Kallinātha), published from Adyar Library, Madras, 4 vols., 1951, 1953, 1959; Eng. trs. ch. I by C.K. Rājā, Adyar Lib. Ser. No. 51, 1945, ch. VII by KIK. Rājā, and R. Burnier, *Adyar Lib. Bulletin*, vol. XXII, pts. 3-4; Eng. trs . also by Shringy and Sharma; Bengali trs. by S. Bandyopādhyāy, Calcutta, 1379 B.S; Hindi trs. by S.C. Banerji, chs. I-IV, Calcutta.

Suśruta-saṃhitā, ed. with '*Nibandha-saṃgraha*' comm. of Ḍalhaṇa, by J.T. Acarya, NSP, 1915. Eng. trs. by K. Bhiṣagratna, Calcutta, 1907-1916. Index and Appendices by same author, Calcutta, 1918. Eng. trs. by U.C. Dutt and A.C. Chattopādhyāy (3 fasc.), Asiatic Society, Calcutta.

Sūryasiddhānta, ed. with *Gūḍhārtha-prakāśikā* comm., by F.E. Hall and B. Sastri, Calcutta, 1959, Eng. trs. by E. Burgess (A Textbook of Hindu Astronomy, with notes and appendix), 1860.

Tantra - Works on Tantra are numerous. For titles and contents of some important Tantras, see S.C. Banerji, *A Brief History of Tantra Literature*, Calcutta, 1988.

BENGALI
(In Bengali alphabetical order)

Koriyā O Jāpāner Prācīn Sāhitya evaṃ Bhāratīya Saṃskṛti - H.B. Sarkar, Calcutta, 1985.

Deśvideśer Saṃskṛti - P. Bagchi.

Prācīn Bhārate Udbhid-vidyā - G.P. Majumdār, Calcutta.

Prācīn Bhārate Vijñān-carcā - R.C. Majumdār, Calcutta.

Prācīn Bhārater Jñān Vijñān - S. Bandyopādhyāy, Calcutta, 1366 B.S.

Prācīn Bhārater Aparādh-tattva

O Yauna-vijñān - S. Bandyopādhyāy, Calcutta.

Prācīn Bhārater Saṃgīt-cintā - A. Sanyal, Calcutta.

Bhārat Rabīndranāth O Soviyet Iunion - Danilchuk, 1395 B.S.

Bhārat O Madhya Eśiyā,

Bhārater Jāti Paricay - B.C. Guha, Calcutta, 1949.

Hindustān Ārabonki Najar men - ed. M. Ali.

Ravīndranāth O Tār Viśvavīkṣā - Tubyansky.

Videśīya Bharat Vidyāpathik - G. Sengupta, Calcutta, 1977.

Saṃgīt O Saṃskṛti - Prajñānānanda, Calcutta.

WORKS IN ENGLISH AND OTHER LANGUAGES

Abhedānanda : *India and Her People.*

Āchārya, P.K. : *Hindu Architecture in India and Abroad.*

Agoncills, T.A. : *The Oriental Heritage of the Philippines,* Asian History Congress, New Delhi, 1961.

Ahmed, N. : *Islamic Culture,* XVIII, 1944 (April) - *Muslim Contribution,* etc.

Alberuni : *India,* Trs. Sachau.

Allen, D.C. : *Star-crossed Renaissance.*

Alphonso : *Disciplina Clericalis.*

Al Razi : *Kitāb Al Habi.*

Ambrose, K. : *Classical Dances and Costumes of India,* New Delhi, 1980.

Andron : *Dravidian Languages*, 1965.

Anikeyev : *On Materialist Traditions in Indian Philosophy*, 1965.

Archer, W.G. : *Central Indian painting.*

———— : *Kangra Painting.*

Arfert : *Das Motiv vonder..... Erzahlung-Litterateur*, 1897.

Arnold and Frost : *The American Egypt.*

Aufrecht, T. : *Catalogus Catalogorum.*

———— : *A Short and General Explanation and Discourse on the Manners, Habits, Language, Faith and Philosophy of the Indians.*

———— : *Avicenna and Indian Science*, International Con. on the Millenary Celebration of Avicenna, 1981.

Assumpsao, M. da : *Vocabulario em Indioma Bengalla E Porluguez.*

Bagchi, P. C. : *India and China*, Bombay, 1950.

Bailey, H. W. : *Khotanese Buddhist Texts*, London, 1981 (2nd ed.).

Balvir : *L' Histoire de Rāma en Tibetana.*

Banerji, G. N. : *Hellenism in Ancient India*, New Delhi, 1981.

Banerji, J. N. : *Development of Hindu Iconography*, Calcutta, 1956.

Banerji, S. C. : *Sanskrit Beyond India*, Calcutta, 1976.

———— : *Kālidāsa Apocrybha*, Varanasi, 1989.

———— : A *Companion to Sanskrit Literature*, 2nd ed., Delhi, 1989.

———— : *Cultural Heritage of Kashmir.*

———— : A *Brief History of Tantra Literature*, Calcutta, 1988.

———— : A *Companion to Middle Indo-Aryan Literature*, Calcutta, 1977.

Bapat, P.V. : *Evidence of Indian Culture in S.E. Asia*, Nagpur, 1964.

Barlaam and Josaphat.

Barth and Bergaigne : *Inscriptions Sanscrites de Champa et du Cambodge.*

Basham, A.L. : *The Wonder That was India*, 1967,

———— : *A Cultural History of India*, Delhi, 1975.

Beal : *Life of Hiuen-tsang.*

Bell, C. : *Tibet Past and Present.*

———— : *Religion of Tibet.*

Bentley, J. : *South Indian Paintings.*

Bethlenfalvy, G. : *India in Hungarian Learning and Literature*, Delhi, 1980.

Bevan, E. : *House of Seleucos.*

Bhattacharya, T.P. : *A Study on Vāstuvidyā.*

Bielski, M. : *Polish Chronicle of the whole world.*

Bloomfield : *Life and Stories of Pārśvanātha.*

Bolte and Polivka : *Anmerkungea ... Hansmarchan der Bruder Grimm.* Leipzig, 1913.

Bongard-Levin, G. and Vigasin, A. L: *The Image of India*, Moscow, 1984.

Bongard-Levin and Ilyin : *Ancient India: A Historical Survey*, 1969.

Bose, A. : The Wind From the East, pub. in *Image of India in Western Creative Writing*, Karnatak University.

Bose, P.N. : *Indian Teachers in Buddhist Universities*, Madras, 1923.

Bose, D.M. and Others : *A Concise History of Science in India*, New Delhi, 1971.

Bose, M. : *Classical Indian Dancing*, Calcutta, 1970.

Botero, G. : *Cosmographia.*

Bouche-Leclereq : *L' Astrologie Grecque*, 1899.

Boulanger : *The Life and Teachings of Siddhārtha Gautama*, 1911.

Bowle : *A New Outline of World History.*

Briggs : *The History of the Rise of the Muhammedan Power in India.*

Brown, Norman (ed. R. Rocher) : *India and Indology*, 1978.

Bouquet, A.C. : *The Christian Faith and Non-Christian Religions*, London, 1958.

Buddhaprakāsh : *India and the world.*

Budge, E.A.W. : *Barlaam and Yewasef....*Bodhisattva, 1923.

Bülcke, C. : *Rāmakathā* (in Hindi), Allāhābād, 1950.

Bunkyo, A. : *Study on the Early Tibetan Chronicles.*

Burnouf, E. : *Introduction..... .... Buddhisme Indien*, 1844.

Burrow, T. : *Sanskrit Language.*
Burton : *Nights.*
Busk : *Sagas from the Far East.*
Cajori : *A History of Mathematics,* New York, 1958 (2nd ed.).
Cambode : *American History.*
Cambridge History of India
Chai-shin Yu : *Early Buddhism and Christianity,* Delhi, 1986.
Chhabra, B. : *Expansion of Indo-Aryan Culture,* Delhi, 1965.
Chaman, L. : *Hindu America,* Bombay, 1960.
Chapekar, N. M. : *Ancient India and Iran,* a study of their cultural contacts,
Charlesworth : *Trade-routes and Commerce of the Roman Empire.*
Chatterjee, S. K. : *Some Aspects of Indo-Iranian Literary and Cultural Traditions.*
———— : *Kirātajankṛti,* Calcutta.
———— : *India and Ethiopia,* Calcutta, 1963.
———— : *The Rāmāyaṇa,* Calcutta, 1978.
———— : *Iranianism,* Calcutta, 1974.
Chattopadhyay, A. : *Atīśa and Tibet.*
Chaudhuri, J.B. : *Muslim Patronage to Sanskrit Learning,* Calcutta 1945.
Chaudhuri, R. : *Sufism and Vedānta.*
Chien : *Buddhism in China.*
Childe : *New Light on the Most Ancient East,* 1934.
(Russian) *Chronicles of Times Past.*
Choudhary, P. : *Indian Origin of the Chinese Nation,* Pts. I, II.
Chrysostom : *Orations.*
Chulkov, M. : *A Historical Description of Russian Commerce.*
Clebert : *The Gypsies.*
Coedes : *Inscriptions du Cambodge.*
———— : *Indianised States.*
Colebrooke, H.T. : *Miscellaneous Essays,* 1937, vol. II.
———— : *The Painter in Ancient India.*
Coomaraswamy, A.K. : *Masterpieces of Indian Sculpture.*
Coxwell : *Siberian Folktales.*
Cosquin : *Contes Indiens et l' Occident,* 1922.

Cunningham : *Coins in Ancient India.*
Curtius : *Die Griechische Kunst in Indien.*
Decameron
Dani, A.H. : *Indian Palaeography,* Oxford, 1963.
Das, S. C. : *Indian Pandits in the Land of Snow.*
———— : *Tibetan-English Dictionary.*
Dasgupta and De : *History of Sanskrit Literature,* Calcutta, 1947.
Datta and Singh : *History of Hindu Mathematics.*
Datta, B. N. : *Mystic Tales of Lāmā Tāranātha,* Calcutta, 1944.
Desai, S. N. : *Hinduism in Thāi Life,* Bombay, 1980.
Devanandan, P.D. : *The Gospel and Renascent Hinduism,* London, 1959.
———— : *Christian Concern in Hinduism,* Bangalore, 1961.
Dhruva Comm. Vol. III.
Dikshit, S. B. : *History of Indian Astronomy* (in Mārāṭhī).
Diringer, D. : *The Alphabet,* London, 1953.
Dodds, E. R. : *Humanism and Technique in Greek Studies,* 1936.
Dodwell : *India,* 1936.
Doff, C. M. : *Chronology of India.*
Durant, W. : *Life in Greece.*
———— : *The Story of Civilisation : Our Oriental Heritage,* 1935.
———— : *Caesar and Christ.*
Dutta, M. : *Chronology of India.*
Dutta, N. : *Early History of the spread of Buddhism and the Buddhist Schools.*
Edmunds, A.J. : *Buddhist and Christian Gospels,* 1908.
Effinger, N. : *The Heartland of Asia,* London, 1971.
Eggeling : *India Office Catalogue ...,* V.
Eitel : *Three Lectures on Buddhism.*
Eliade, M. : *Shamanism,* London, 1964.
Encyclopaedia of Indo-Aryan Research (Thibaut on Indian Astronomy, etc.).
Epiphanius : *Life of Manes.*
Evans, W. : *Great Liberation of Tibet,* Oxford.
Exact Sciences in Antiquity (Neugabuer's writings).
Farrington : *Science and Politics in the Ancient World.*

Ferishta : *Tārikh-I-Ferishtā* (trs. by Briggs, q.v.)
Fernando, P.E.E. : *Ceylon To-day*, January, 1962.
Filliozat, J. : *The Classical Doctrine of Indian Medicine*, Delhi, 1964.
———— : *Les Relations Exterieures de l' inde*, 1956.
———— : *A General History of Sciences*, London, 1957.
———— : *Revue de 1' Histoire des Religions*, 1945.
Fisher, J.F. : *Trans-Himalyan Traders* - economy, society and culture in North-West Nepal.
Foucher, A. : *L' Art Graeco-Bouddhique du Gandhāra.*
Francis and Neil : *Eng. Trs. of Jātaka.*
Francisco, J. R. : *Indian Influence in the Philippines*, Quezon, 1964.
———— : *The Philippines and India*, etc., Manila, 1971.
Franke, A.H.A. : *Antiquities of the Indian Tibet*, 2 vols., Calcutta, 1914.
———— : *History of Western Tibet*, London, 1907.
Frere : *Old Deccan Days.*
Garbe, R. : *India and Christendom*, La Salle, 1959.
Gardner, P. : *A History of Ancient Coinage*, Oxford, 1918.
Garrat, G. T. : *The Legacy of India*, Oxford, 1938.
Garrison, F. H. : *An Intro. to History of Medicine.*
Gaster : *Example of the Rabbis.*
Gedney, W.J. : *Indic Loan Words in Spoken Thāi* (Ph. D. Thesis, Yale University), See Satyavrat Sastri's book, *Studies in ... Thāiland*, p. 7, f. n. 1.
Gesta Romanorum
Gibb : *History of the Forty Vezirs.*
Glanville, S.R.K. (ed.) : *Legacy of Egypt*, Oxford, 1942.
Godakaikura, C. E. : *Sinhalese Literature*, Colombo, 1955.
Gokak, V.K. : *India and World Culture*, Delhi, 1972.
Golombek, H. : *The Game of Chess*, London, 1956.
Gompez, T. : *Greek Thinkers.*
Gonda, J. : *Sanskrit in Indonesia*, Nagpur, 1952.
Gonzenfach : *Sicilianische Märchen*
Goodrich : *History of the people of China.*

Goodwin : *The Great Mystics.*

Gordon, C.H. : *Before the Bible.*

Gupta, S.P. : *Archaeology of Soviet Central Asia and the Indian Borderlands,* Vols. I-II, Delhi, 1978.

Guseva : *Hinduism,* 1977.

———— : *Jainism,* 1968.

Griffiths, B. : *Christ in India,* Essays towards a Hindu-Christian Dialogue, New York, 1967.

Grimm : *Kinderund Hausmärchen*

Grousset : *L'Art Pāla and Sena.*

Halbfars, W. : *India and Europe, an essay in Philosophical understanding,* Delhi, 1990.

Hall : *Ant. Hist. of the Near East.*

Hamilton, W. : *History of Medicine.*

Harnack : *History of Dogma,* 1894.

Heath : *Greek Astronomy.*

Hegel : *Philosophy of World History.*

Heine-Gordon and Ekholm : *The Civilisation of Ancient American History and Culture of the Indian people, Vols.* I, II, Bharatiya Vidya Bhavan.

Hippocratic Collection

Hippolytus : *Philosophumena* (Also called *Kata Pason .... Elenchos*)

Hitti, P. K. : *History of the Arabs,* London, 1960.

———— : *History of Mexico,* pub. from Foreign Affairs Deptt. of Mexico.

———— : *History of Skt. Outside India,* pub. by Institute for Oriental Study, Thane.

Hiuen-tsang : *Travels or Records of Western Lands.*

Hoernle : *The Bower Manuscript,* 1914.

Horace : *Ode to Maecenas,* Eng. trs. by Bennet.

———— : *Manuscript Remains of Buddhist Lit. found in F. Turkestan,* Oxford, 1916.

Hoffman, H. : *Religions of Tibet.*

———— : *India's Contribution to World Thought and Culture,* Madras, 1970.

Indicopleustes : *Christian Topography.*
Inge : *The Platonic Tradition in English Religious Thought,* 1926.
Isherwood, C. : *Vedānta for Modern Man*
———— : *Vedānta for Western World.*
I-tsing : A *Record of the Buddhist Religion as practised in India and the Mālay Archipelago,* Eng. trs. by Takakusu.
Jacobi, H. : *De Astrologiae Indicae,* Bonnae, 1872.
Jacolliot, L. : *The Bible in India,* New York, 1868.
Jaiswal, S. : Commercial Contacts Between Kashmir and Rome, *ABORI,* LXXV, 1994.
Jamsai, M. : *Thāi Rāmāyaṇa,* Bangkok, 1967 (2nd ed.).
Jervis, J. B. : *Indian Metrology.*
Kane, P. V. : *History of Dharmaśāstra,* V.
Kanjilal, D.K. : *Vimāna in Ancient India,* Calcutta.
Karaka : *History of the Parsis,* 1884.
Kaye, G.R. : *Memoir No. 18 of Archaeological Survey of India.*
———— : *The Bakḥshāli Manuscript,* 1927-32.
Kennedy, E.S. : *Dictionary of Scientific Biography.*
Keith, A.B. : *Sanskrit Drama.*
———— : *Buddhist Philosophy in India and Ceylon,* India, 1962.
Kern, H. : *A Manual of Indian Buddhism.*
Khandalavala, K. : *Pāhāri Miniature Painting.*
Khwarizmi : *Jiz.*
King, W. : *The Gnostics and Their Remains, Ancient and Medieval,* 2nd. ed., 1887.
———— : *Buddhism and Christianity,* Philadelphia, 1962.
Kramrisch, S. : *Indian Sculpture,* Calcutta, 1933.
Kühn, H. : *Germanische Kunst der Volkerswanderung.*
Lal, C. (ed.) : *India and Japan,* Hoshiarpur, 1959.
Lancaster, L.R. Yu, C.S. (Eds.) : *Introduction of Buddhism to Korea,* New Cultural Patherns, Berkeley, 1989.
Lebedev : *An Impartial Review of the Systems of East Indian Brahmins, their sacred rites and national customs,* 1805.
Leclereq, B. : *L Astrologie Grecque.*
Leeb Classical Library Series, vol. VII.
Legge : *Travels.*

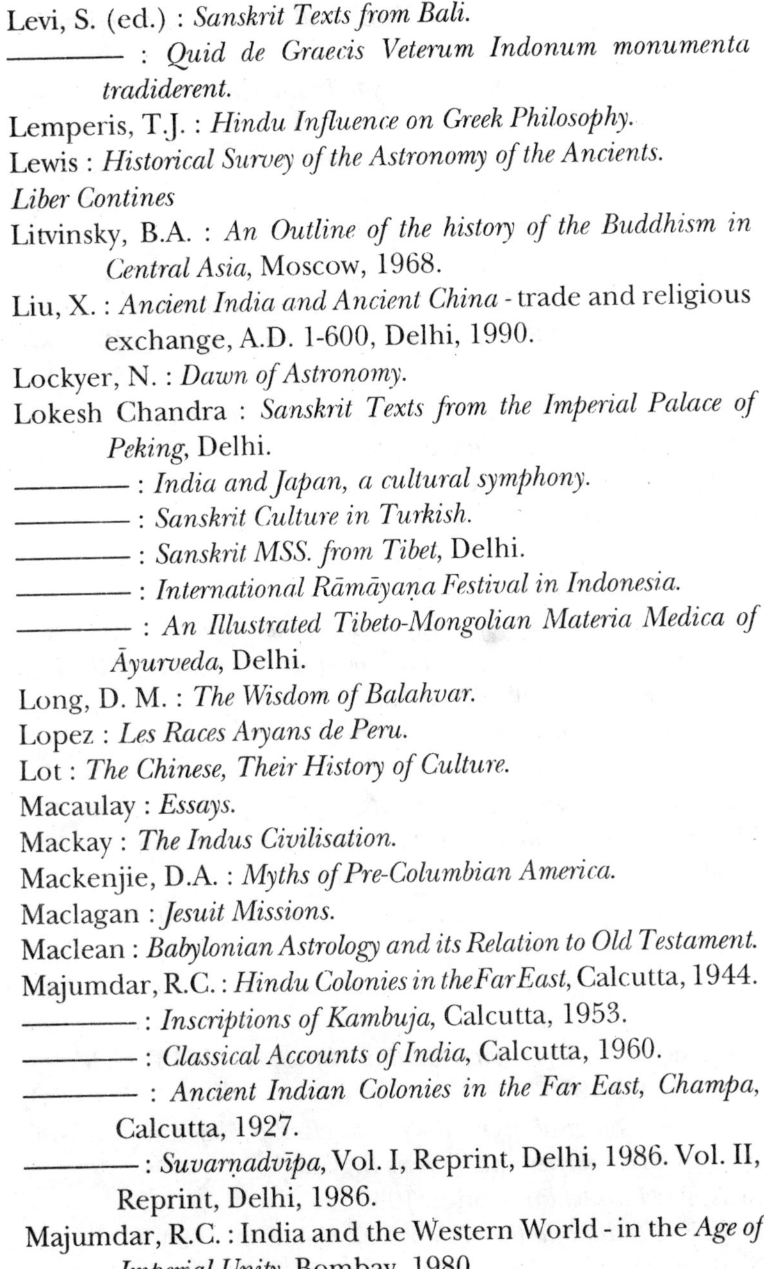

Levi, S. (ed.) : *Sanskrit Texts from Bali.*

——— : *Quid de Graecis Veterum Indonum monumenta tradiderent.*

Lemperis, T.J. : *Hindu Influence on Greek Philosophy.*

Lewis : *Historical Survey of the Astronomy of the Ancients.*

Liber Contines

Litvinsky, B.A. : *An Outline of the history of the Buddhism in Central Asia,* Moscow, 1968.

Liu, X. : *Ancient India and Ancient China* - trade and religious exchange, A.D. 1-600, Delhi, 1990.

Lockyer, N. : *Dawn of Astronomy.*

Lokesh Chandra : *Sanskrit Texts from the Imperial Palace of Peking,* Delhi.

——— : *India and Japan, a cultural symphony.*

——— : *Sanskrit Culture in Turkish.*

——— : *Sanskrit MSS. from Tibet,* Delhi.

——— : *International Rāmāyaṇa Festival in Indonesia.*

——— : *An Illustrated Tibeto-Mongolian Materia Medica of Āyurveda,* Delhi.

Long, D. M. : *The Wisdom of Balahvar.*

Lopez : *Les Races Aryans de Peru.*

Lot : *The Chinese, Their History of Culture.*

Macaulay : *Essays.*

Mackay : *The Indus Civilisation.*

Mackenjie, D.A. : *Myths of Pre-Columbian America.*

Maclagan : *Jesuit Missions.*

Maclean : *Babylonian Astrology and its Relation to Old Testament.*

Majumdar, R.C. : *Hindu Colonies in theFar East,* Calcutta, 1944.

——— : *Inscriptions of Kambuja,* Calcutta, 1953.

——— : *Classical Accounts of India,* Calcutta, 1960.

——— : *Ancient Indian Colonies in the Far East, Champa,* Calcutta, 1927.

——— : *Suvarṇadvīpa,* Vol. I, Reprint, Delhi, 1986. Vol. II, Reprint, Delhi, 1986.

Majumdar, R.C. : India and the Western World - in the *Age of Imperial Unity,* Bombay, 1980.

Majumdar R.C., Ray Chaudhuri and Datta (ed) : *History of Bengal,* Dacca, 1943.

———— : *An Advanced History of India,* Calcutta, 1978. (4th ed.).

———— : India's Influence on the Thought and Culture of the World, *Svāmī Vivekānanda Centenary Memorial Volume,* 1963.

Maltovic : *Serbian Folklore.*

Mallery : *Intro. to the Study of Sign Language,* Washington, 1880.

Mansel, D. : *The Gnostic Heresies of the First and Second Centuries,* 1875.

Mansouri, S.M.El : *Art-culture of India and Egypt.*

Marshal, J. : *Mohenjo-daro and the Indus Civilisation,* 1931.

Maugham, S. : *Razor's Edge.*

———— : *Writers' Notebook.*

Mayer : *Political Thought,* 1939.

Mayo : *Mother India.*

M'Crindle : *Invasion of India by Alexander the Great,* 1993.

Meester, M.E. (ed.) : *Oriental Influences in Eng. Lit. of the 19th cent.,* Heidelberg, 1915.

Meissner : *Babylonian and Assyrian.*

Mercator, G. : *Cosmographia.*

Milman, D. : *History of Christinity,* 1867.

Miner, E. : *An Intro. to Japanese Court-Poetry,* Stanford, 1968.

Mode, H. : *The Harappā Culture and the West,* Calcutta.

Motichandra : *Trade and Trade-routes in Ancient India.*

Motwani, K. : *Manu Dharmaśāstra.*

Mukherjee, P.K. : *Indian Literature in China and the Far East.* Calcutta, 1938.

Mukherjee, G.N. : *History of Indian Medicine,* Vols. I-II, Calcutta, 1923-1929.

———— : *Surgical Instruments of the Hindus,* Calcutta, 1913-14.

Murray : *Discoveries and Travels in Asia.*

Mus, P. : *Barabudur,* Hanoi, 1935.

Nag, K. : *India and the Middle East,* Calcutta, 1954.

Naik, M.K. : *The Image of India in Western Creative Writing.* Dharwar, 1970.

Nainar, S.M.H. : *Arab Geographers' Knowledge of Southern India.*
Nakamura, H. : *Japan and Indian Asia,* Calcutta, 1961.
———— : *Ways of Thinking of Eastern Peoples,* Honolulu, 1964.
Nath, R. (ed.) : *India as seen by William Finch* (1608-11), Jaipur, 1990.
Needham : *Science and Civilisation in China.*
Nehru, J. : *Discovery of India,* 1955.
Neill, S. : *Christian Faith and Other Faiths,* London, 1961.
Neugabauer : *Exact Sciences in Antiquity,* Princeton, 1952.
Nicholson : *Literary History of Arabs.*
Notovitch : *Jesus Christ.*
Numismatic Chronicles, 1893.
Obermiller : *History of Buddhism in Tibet.*
Oesterley : *Baitāl Pachisī.*
Okakura : *The Ideals of the East.*
Oldenberg : *Buddha, his life, doctrine and order.*
Oldenburg : *Buddhist Legends,* 1894.
———— : A *Collection of Sinhalese Tales,* 1931.
———— : *Material on Buddhist Iconography,* 1901.
———— : *An Album of Buddhist Representations from Kazan Ecclesiastical Academy,* 1903.
———— : *Modern Organisation of the Study of the Fine Arts and their Technique in India,* 1931.
———— : *Bibliotheca Buddhica.*
Old Testament - Isaiah, 47, 1, 5, 13.
Osipov : *Short Study in India's History upto 10th cent.,* 1948.
Pallas, P. : *Comparative Dictionary of World Languages.*
Pandey, R.B. : *Indian Palaeography,* pt. I, Benares, 1952.
Parrinder, G. : *Gītā and Bible,* London, 1962.
Pathak, S. K. : *The Indian Nītiśāstras in Tibet,* Delhi, 1974.
Pelliot : *Le Fou-nan.*
Periplus of the Erythrean Sea.
Petech : *A Study of the Chronicles of Ladakh.*
Peterson : (ed.) *Kādambarī,* Introduction.
Petrie, F. : *Egypt and Israel,* 1923.
Phillimore (trs.) : *Apollonius of Tyana,* 1912.

Physiologus

Plato : *Republic*, III, IV.

Pliny : *Natural History.*

Pocoke : *India in Greece.*

Poindexter, M. : *The Aryan-Incas.*

Pradhān, S.N. : *Chronology of Ancient India.*

———— : *Praeparatio Evangelica* (Eusarius), XI, 3. *Oxyrhynchus Papyri*

Prajñānānanda : *Historical Development of Indian Music*, Calcutta, 1973.

———— : *Music of the Nations*, Delhi, 1973.

Ptolemy : *Guide to Geography / Tetrabiblos.*

Puri, S. and S. Charoen : *The Rāmakīrti* (*Rāmakien*), Bangkok, 1949.

Rādhākrishnān, S. : *Indian Philosophy*, 2 vols.

———— : *India and China*, Bombay, 1954.

———— (ed.) : *History of Philosophy-Eastern and Western*. I (Ranade's writing).

———— : *Indian Philosophy*, 2 vols.

———— : *Eastern Religions and Western Thought*, 2nd ed., 1940.

Raghuvir : *Tibet - a Souvenir*, Delhi, 1960.

Raghuvir and Yamanoto : *Rāmāyaṇa and China.*

Ralston : *Russian Folktales.*

Rapson, E.J. and Others : *Kharoṣṭhī Inscriptions discovered by Sir Aurel Stein in Chinese Turkestan*, Vol. I, Oxford, 1920.

Rawlinson : *Intercourse between India and the Western World*, Cambridge, 1916.

———— : *Legacy of India.*

Raghavan, V. : *The Rāmāyaṇa in Greater India*, Surat, 1975.

———— : *India in Ceylonese History, Society and Culture.*

———— : *Sanskrit and Indian Studies in USA.*

———— : *Sanskrit Studies in Russia.*

———— : *Sanskrit and Allied Indological Studies in Europe*, Madras, 1956.

———— : *Innermost Asia*, III, Oxford, 1921.

Ray, S.K. : *Pre-historic India and Ancient Egypt.*
Ray, N.R. : *Brāhmaṇical Gods in Burma,* Calcutta, 1932.
———— : *Theravāda Buddhism in Burma,* Calcutta, 1946.
———— : *Sanskrit Buddhism in Burma,* Calcutta, 1936.
Ray, P. : *History of Hindu Chemistry in Anc. and Med. India,* incorporating History of Hindu Chemistry by P.C. Ray, Calcutta, 1956.
Roy Chowdhury : *Man, Malady and Medicine,* Calcutta, 1988.
Roychoudhury, H.C. : *Studies in Indian Antiquity.*
Roy, D.N. : *The Philiphines and India,* Manila, 1929.
Regmi, D.R. : *Ancient Nepal,* Calcutta, 1960.
———— : *Medieval Nepal,* Pt. I, Calcuta, 1965.
Reisner : *Ideologies of the East. Studies in Eastern Theocracy,* 1927.
Rhys Davids, T.W. : *Buddhism, its history and literature.*
Rinchen, B. : *Four Mongolian Historical Records,* 1959.
———— : *Report of the British Association,* 1894, p. 774 - on the diffusion of Mystical Beliefs.
Roerich, G. : *Blue Annals,* Calcutta, 1954.
Rogers, B. : *Science,* V.P. 131.
Rogerius, A. : *De open - Deure tot heh verboregen Heydendom* (Open Door to Hidden Heathendom), 1651.
Rolland, R. : *Life of Rāmakrishna.*
Rosenberg : *Intro. to the study of Buddhism Through Chinese and Japanese Sources, 2* vols., 1918.
———— : *Literature of the East,* 1919.
Rostovtzeff : *Cambridge History of India,* VII.
Ruskin : *Lectures in Art.*
———— : *Unto the Last.*
Sachau : *Alberuni's India.*
———— : *Indo-Conversant Arabische.*
Saha, K. : *Buddhism in Central Asia,* Calcutta, 1970.
Saimtyves : *Les contes de Perraudt,* 1923.
Salatore : *Ancient Indian Political Thought and Institutions.*
Sankrityayan, R. : *Tibbat Men Bauddhadharma,* (Hindi) Allahabad, 1940.
Sarkar, J.N. : *Fall of the Mughal Empire.*

Sarkar, H.B. : *Indian Influence in the Literature of Java and Bali*, Calcutta, 1984.

———— : *Some Contributions of India to the ancient civilisation of Indonesia and Malaysia*, Calcutta, 1970.

———— : *Literary Heritage of S.E. Asia*, Calcutta, 1980.

———— : *Cultural Relations betwen India and South Asian Countries.*

———— : *Corpus of the Inscriptions of Java.*

Sarton : *A History of Science.*

Sāhitya Akademi (Delhi) : *The Rāmāyaṇa Tradition in Asia*, New Delhi, 1980.

Sander, L. : *Palographischeszu dem Sanskrit Handschriften der Berliner Turfansammlung*, Wiesbaden, 1968. *Preliminary Report on a Journey etc.*, London, 1901.

Saraswati, S.K. : *A Survey of Indian Sculpture.*

Saunders, K.S. : *The Study of Buddhism.*

Scherbatskoy : *Theory of Knowledge and Logic all to later Buddhists*, Vol. I, 1903, II 1909.

———— : *Logic in Ancient India*, 1902.

———— : *The Central Conception of Buddhism and the making of World Dharma.*

———— : *Buddhism Logic*, 2 vols, 1930-32.

Schleicher : *Lithuanian Legends.*

Schmidt : *Griechicehe Märchen.*

Schroeder : *Pythagoras und die Inder*, Leipzig, 1984.

Schultz, S. : *Comparative Literature*, Oregon, Vol. II, 1962 (On Thomas Mann).

Scott : *Hermetica*, 1924.

Seal, B.N. : *The Positive Sciences of the Ancient Hindus*, Varanasi, 1950.

Secretum Secretorum

Sewell : *Forgotten Empire.*

Shastri, S. : *Studies in Sanskrit and Indian Culture in Thailand*, Delhi, Ahmedabad, 1982.

Shastri, K.N. : *Foreign Notices of South India.*

Shushtery, M. : *Outline of Islamic Culture*, Bangalore, 1954.

Silappadikaram (Tāmil)
Singhal, D.P. : *India and World Civilisation*, Vols. I, II, Calcutta, 1972.
Sircar, D.C. : *Indian Palaeography*, Delhi.
Sitanath : *Chronology of Ancient India.*
Sivaramamurti, C. : *Indian Sculpture.*
Smith, D.E. : *History of Mathematics*, 1912.
Smith, V.A. (ed.) : *Travels of Bernier.*
Srivastava, K.M. : *Angkor Wat and Cultural ties with India.*
Sternbach, L. : *Literature of Burma* (Pandit D. Shastri Fel. vol., Delhi, 1974).
St. George, P.P. : Vedāntic Analogies in Shelley's poetry, Unpublished Thesis, Tufts University, 1964.
Stacy, R.H. : *India in Russian Literature.*
Stein, M.A. : *Ancient Khotan*, I, Oxford, 1967.
Sternbach, L. : *The Spreading of Cāṇakya's Aphorisms over Greater India*, Calcutta, 1969.
Stutfield : *Mysticism and Catholicism*, 1925.
Stutterheim, W. : *Rāma Legend and Rāma-reliefs in Indonesia*, 2 vols., Munchen, 1924.
———— : *Studies in Indonesian Archaeology*, The Hague, 1956 (Appendix - Ancient Javanese Bhima Cult).
Suzuki, D.T. : *Essays in Zen Buddhism*, 2 nd Series, Kyoto, 1933.
Takakusu : *I-tsing*, 1896.
Taraporewala, I. J. S. : *Elements of the Science of Language.*
Tarn, W.W. : *Greeks in Bactria and India.*
———— : *Hellenistic Civilisation*, 2nd ed., 1930.
Tataniya (Trs. by S.S. Gitman) : *The Gypsy Language*, Moscow.
Tavera, T.H. Pardo de : *El Sanskrito en la langua Tagaloq*, Paris, 1887.
Tawney : *Oriental Translation Fund.*
Tennyson : *Defence of Lucknow.*
Thakur, S.C . : *Christian and Hindu Ethics*, London, 1969.
Thibaut : *Astronomie, Astrologie and Mathematik*, 1899.

Thomas, F.W. : *The Mutual Influence of Mohamedans and Hindus,* 1892.

———— : *Tibetan Literary Texts,* etc. I, London, 1935.

Thomas, W. : *Hinduism Invades America.*

Thompson, R.C. : *The Reports of the Magicians and Astrologers of Nineveh and Babylon,* London, 1900.

Thoreau : *Walden*

Tilak, B.G. : *Arctic Home in the Vedas.*

———— : *Orion.*

Tolstoy : *The Kingdom is within you.*

Toynbee, A.J. : *One World and India.*

Tsengty, T. : *Historical Study of Tibet, Tibet To-day and Yesterday.*

Tsybikov : *A Buddhist Pilgrim in the places of Tibet,* 1919.

Tutināmā.

Urwick, E.J. : *The Message of Plato.*

Van Gulik, R.H. : *Siddham,* Nagpur, 1956.

———— : *An Essay on the History of Sanskrit Studies in China and Japan,* Nagpur, 1956.

Waddell : *Lamaism.*

Wales : *Siamese State Ceremonies.*

Wanz, E. : *The Book of Great Liberation.*

Warmington, E.H. : *The Commerce Between Roman Empire and India,* 2nd ed., Delhi, 1974.

Webb : *Historical Relations of Hindu with Greek Medicine.*

Wheatley : *The Golden Khersonese.*

Wheeler, M. : *The Indus Valley Civilisation,* 1953.

Wilson : *Essays on Skt. Lit.*

Winstedt : *Some Records of the Gypsies in Germany.*

———— : *Malay and its History.*

Winternitz, M. : *History of Indian Literature,* vols. I-III.

Woodman, D. : *Himalayan Frontier.*

———— : *Yu, Chai-Shin - See Chai-Shin Yu.*

Yule and Cordier : *The Book of Ser Marco Polo,* II.

Zachner, R.C. : *Hindu and Muslim Mysticism.*

Zaliznyak : *Grammatical Study of Sanskrit.*

JOURNALS, PAPERS

English

Adyar Library Bulletin, Reno - Influence of Indian (Thought on French Literature).

Alberuni Comm. Vol. (articles of S.K. Chatterji and J. Gonda).

American Antiquity, XVIII, No. 3, pt. 2, 1953 (Paper by G.F. Ekholm).

Archives Internationales D' Historiee des Sciences, April-June, 1955.

Arhat Vacana, March, 1990, Vol. 2, No. 2, Indore (On the resemblance of Indian; Chinese and Japanese Mathematics)

B.S. G.W. 1882.

BEFEO, Particularly of 1948 and 1955 (Paper by Damais) and 1964. (Paper by K. Bhattacharya).

Brahmvidyā, 35 (Sternbach on Nīti Lit. of Ceylon).

BSOAS, 43 (Sternbach-Lokanīti and Burmese Nitikyan and their sources).

Bulletin of National Institute of Sciences in India, No. 21, 1962 (Transmission of Scientific Ideas).

Bulletin de l' Athence Oriental, 1881, 1882 (Lorgeou-Suphasit Siamois).

Bulletin de l' Ecole Francaise de Extreme Orient (Indian Medicine in Sri Lanka)

Det. Kal. Danske Videnskabernes Selskab, Histerisk-Filoogiske meddesler, XXXI, 6, 1969 (Asiatic Influence in American Folklore).

Deś (Calcutta Bengali weekly), 5.5.90 (Danilchuk on Tubyansky).

Epigraphia Indica, VIII, p. 36.

Glory of India (Qrly. Jour. of Indology) V, Nos. 3,4, 1981, pub. Motilal Banarasidass, Delhi (article by D. Frawley).

Historical Bulletin, VII, No. 2, 1963 (Francisco - Analogous customs etc. in India and the Philippines).

Indian Literature, Sāhitya Akademi, Delhi, 1967 (Article by R.K. Das Gupta, entitled Western response to Indian literature).

Indian Antiquary, vol. 19 (pp. 133-142), Vol. 23 (pp. 154-159).

Indian Historical Quarterly, IX, 1933 (S.C. Mukherjee, Architecture of the Taj and its architect).

Indian Culture, II (Pizzagalli, Discovery of Sanskrit and Italy in 16th cent.).

Indian Studies in Honour of C. Lanman (Paper by P.W. Thomas about Tibet).

Indo-Aryan Culture, XI, No. 4, 1963 (Architect of the Taj Mahal).

International Conference on Science and Religion (Souvenir) Delhi, 1988, article entitled Science in Purāṇas, by Sures Chandra Banerji.

Journal of Asiatic Society, Vol. 29, No. 3, p. 20.

Jour. of Royal Asiatic Society, 1910, p. 752.

Journal of Asiatic Society, Calcutta, 1989 Vols XXXI, Nos. 3-4 (V. Nair-India and China)

Journal of Asiatic Society of Bengal, 1894, pt. 1 (pp. 744-63). 1906 (pp. 1 f.f.) 1949 (pp. 41-89).

Journal of American Oriental Society, 6 (pp. 1-94), 75 (No. 3), p. 172. 91.3 (Sternbach's paper on Similar Thoughts in Mahābhārata, the literature of Greater India and in Christian Gospels).

Journal of Asiatic Society of Bengal, 1882 (S.C. Das, Contributions to the history of religion etc. in Tibet) 1894, pt. 1, pp. 744-63. 1906, pp. 1 f.f. 1949 pp. 41-89.

Journal Asiatique, 222, 164-75, Paris, 1933 (Paper by J. Filliozat)

Journal of Bombay Branch of Royal Asiatic Soc., 30, pts. 1-2, pp. 1-8.

Journal of Cuneiform Studies, vol. 7, No. 3.

Journal of Deptt. of Letters, Calcutta University, vol. 18 (pp. 1-56).

Journal of the Economic and Social History of Orient, Oct. 1988, XXXI, Pt. III, Warmond, The Netherlands (The Yavana Presence in Ancient India).

Journal of Greater Indian Society (U. N. Ghosal & others), 18 vols.

Journal of Gypsylore Society, New Series, IV, 1910-11 (pp. 160-940).

Journal of History of Science, New Delhi, XVI, No. 1, 1981. pp. 64-76 (S. Mahdihassan on Alchemy in Greek, Arabic, Sanskrit and Chinese).

Journal of Indological Studies, Haryana Sahitya Akademi, Vol. II, Nos . 1-2.

Spring, 1987 (Sanskrit in the Renaissance of European Languages.)

Journal of Near Eastern Studies, IV, p. 16.

Journal of Oriental Institute, Baroda, VIII, 1958 (Story of Nala-Damayantī, etc.).

Journal of Oriental Research, Madras, 1956-57 (H. Kimura on Sanskrit Studies in Japan and China).

Journal of Pāli Text Society, 1923. (Rhys Davids on similarity between Buddhism and Christianity).

Journal of South-East Asian Studies, March, 1989, Vol. XX, No. 1. (H. P. Ray - Early Maritime Contacts Between South and South-East Asia).

Modern Language Review, XV. 923 (Legend of Amicus and Anelius).

Mem., Soc. Amer. Arch., 9, 1953 (Paper by Ekholm - A possible focus of Asiatic influence in late classic culture of Mexico).

MLBD Newsletter (Motilal Banarsidass, Delhi), Jan., 1990.

Numismatic Chronicle, 1893, pp. 126-127.

Philippine Historical Review, I, no. 1, 1956 (On the date of coming of Indian influence in the Philippines).

Poona Orientalist, VIIII, pp. 68-80. VII, no. 1 (Sternbach's paper on similar social and legal institutions in Ancient India and Ancient Mexico.)

Prazdnoye Veremya Vpolzu upo treblennoye (Issue no. XVIII, 1759) Jour. of Religion, April, 1938 (article of J. Werner - Greeks and Jews).

Proc. of 1st International Skt. Con., Vol. II, pt. 2 (Brahmagupta's works and their influence in and ouside India by Rai); Vol. 2, pt. 1 (paper of N.C. Sinha-Skt. across the Himalayas and of K.K. Roy, Skt. and Indo-Tibetan Languages; of Sternbach about Subhāṣta literature).

Revue de l' Histoire des Religions, 1945 (Filliozat, La doctrino de brahmanes d' apres Saint Hippolyte).

Statesman (daily paper), Calcutta, 6.2.82, p. 3; 30.1.84 (Lecture by Trevor Ling). 16.1.84 (lecture by C.H. Philips); 15.1.84 (Observations of Marshal).

Summaries of Papers, Int. Skt. Conf. 1972 (Paper on Śālihotra saṃhita in Arabia).

Telegraph (a Calcutta daily) 17.3.90 (Article - The American Connection), 11.4.90 (Hindu culture in Mauritius), 29.7.89 (Skt. meets the computer).

The Hibbert Journal, L, X, pp. 178-181.

University of Ceylon Review, Oct., 1956, (Article by Derrett).

Also see the following journals *BSOAS*, XXIV, p. 527; XII, pp. 47-48, 764 f.f.; XXVII, p. 609, VII, pp. 895, 909-12, II. pp. 47 f.f.; *Asia Major*, II. (Old Series), pp. 270-71; *Bulletin de l' Eiole francaise d' Extreme - Orient*, LXI, 1974, pp. 22, 58; *Indiyskiye Rukopisi V Turkmeni*, No. 1, 1966, p. 26; *Jour. of Asiatic Society*, XI, 1969, pp. 10-11, 63 f.f. *Indian Jour. of Linguistics*, II, No. 1, pp. 47 f.f.; *East and West*, IX, 1958; *Vishweswarananda Indological Jour.*, 1974, pp. 240 f.f., *Epigraphia Zeylonica*, I, p. 13; *Sino-Indian Jour.*, July, 1947; *Jour. of Indian History*, XL VII, pp. 43-64; *Indian Historical Quarterly*, XII, pp. 124 ff.

BENGALI

Ānandabājār Patrikā, Calcutta, 18.4.93 B.S. (Article, entitled Iṃgrejer Saṃskṛta Kavitā, by Gopikā Bhattacharya).

—— 14.3.93 B.S. 29.6.85 A.D. (Article, entitled Tibbatī Rāmāyaṇa, by Prasad Maiti).

—— 18.7.79 (report about *Manuṣyajātaka*).

—— 19.2.84 (Jābhār Viṣṇu Avatār by R. Ray).

—— 14.10.84 (Koriyā Upadvīpe Bhārat-sabhyatā by A. Chakravarti).

INDEX